THE
UNRAVELLING

EMMA SKY

THE UNRAVELLING

HIGH HOPES AND MISSED OPPORTUNITIES IN IRAQ

ATLANTIC BOOKS
London

First published in hardback in the United States in 2015 by PublicAffairs™, a Member of the Perseus Books Group.

First published in hardback in Great Britain in 2015 by Atlantic Books, an imprint of Atlantic Books Ltd.

1 2 3 4 5 6 7 8 9

A CIP catalogue record for this book is available from the British Library.

Hardback ISBN: 978-1-78239-257-6
E-book ISBN: 978-1-78239-259-0
Paperback ISBN: 978-1-78239-260-6

Printed and bound by CPI Group (UK) Ltd, Croydon, CR0 4YY
Book design by Jane Raese

Atlantic Books
An Imprint of Atlantic Books Ltd
Ormond House
26–27 Boswell Street
London
WC1N 3JZ

www.atlantic-books.co.uk

TO

GENERAL RAYMOND T. ODIERNO

AND ALL THOSE WHO SERVED IN IRAQ

DURING THE AMERICAN ERA

AND

TO MY IRAQI FRIENDS

CONTENTS

PART I
DIRECT RULE
JUNE 2003-JUNE 2004

PART II
SURGE
JANUARY-DECEMBER 2007

ABBREVIATIONS

AFN	American Forces Network
AQI	al-Qaeda in Iraq
BOC	Baghdad Operations Command
BUA	Battle Update Assessment
BUB	Battle Update Brief
CHOPS	Chief of Operations
CLC	Concerned Local Citizens
COIN	counter-insurgency
CPA	Coalition Provisional Authority
DFAC	dining facility
DFID	Department for International Development
EFP	explosively formed projectile
FCO	Foreign and Commonwealth Office
FOB	Forward Operating Base
FRAGO	fragmentary order
GOI	government of Iraq
IED	improvised explosive device
ISAF	International Security Assistance Forces
ISF	Iraqi security forces
JAM	Jaysh al-Mahdi
JOC	Joint Operations Command
KIA	killed in action
KDP	Kurdistan Democratic Party
KRG	Kurdistan Regional Government
MNF-I	Multi-National Force—Iraq
NGO	non-governmental organization
OCINC	Office of the Commander-in-Chief
POLAD	political adviser
PRT	Provisional Reconstruction Team
PUK	Patriotic Union of Kurdistan

RAF	Royal Air Force
RPG	rocket-propelled grenade
SOFA	Status of Forces Agreement
TAL	Transitional Administrative Law
TOC	Tactical Operations Center
UNAMI	United Nations Assistance Mission for Iraq
USAID	United States Agency for International Development
WIA	wounded in action
WMD	weapons of mass destruction

PREFACE

NOTHING THAT HAPPENED in Iraq after the overthrow of Saddam Hussein in 2003 was preordained. And there was nothing inevitable about the way the story unfolded.

This memoir recounts my experiences in Iraq over more than a decade. My story starts when I responded to the British government's request for volunteers to help rebuild the country after the fall of the regime and found myself responsible for Kirkuk, trying to diffuse tensions between the different Iraqis scrambling to control the province. It continues through the Surge when I served as the political adviser to General Ray Odierno; goes through the drawdown of US troops; and ends with the takeover of a third of Iraq by the Islamic State. It is a tale of unintended consequences, both of President Bush's efforts to impose democracy and of President Obama's detachment; of action as well as non-action.

The Unravelling describes the challenges of nation building and how the overthrow of an authoritarian regime can lead to state collapse and conflict. It reminds us of the limitations of external actors in foreign lands, but also where we can have influence. Those the US-led Coalition excluded from power sought to undermine the new order that was introduced. And those we empowered sought to use the country's resources for their own interests, to subvert the nascent democratic institutions, and to use the security forces we trained and equipped to intimidate their rivals. There was more the US could have done to help broker a deal among the elites and to ensure the peaceful transfer of power through elections. Instead, the US took the risky gamble of betting on Nuri al-Maliki, in the mistaken belief that he shared the same interests and goals as us, and that he would use the dramatic decline in violence brought about during the Surge to build up a "sovereign, self-reliant and democratic Iraq." The failure of this policy became only too apparent when the Islamic State (Da'ash) catapulted to prominence in June 2014, taking control of vast swathes of Iraqi territory and presenting itself as the defender of Sunnis against the Iranian-backed Shia-led regime in Baghdad; and when the Iraqi Security Forces deserted and dissolved.

PRESIDENT BARACK OBAMA became the fourth American president to order airstrikes on Iraq, following in the footsteps of George H. W. Bush, Bill Clinton and George W. Bush. The initial airstrikes were to stop Da'ash from exterminating Iraq's minorities and taking over Erbil. However, following the beheadings of two American hostages by Da'ash, the US quickly expanded its airstrikes into Syria. Americans were no longer war weary. They were scared again—and wanted retribution.

Never had Obama expected to find himself in such a position. He had campaigned for president pledging to end the Iraq war. In 2009, still in his first year in office, he was awarded the Nobel Peace Prize for his "extraordinary efforts to strengthen international diplomacy and cooperation between peoples."

Obama, who had presented himself as the president who would extract America from its foreign entanglements and focus on nation building at home, has reluctantly taken the country back to war in the Middle East—with no sense of how it will end.

Da'ash is the hideous product of a sacralised determinism born out of secular failure. The dramatic changes in the regional balance of power in Iran's favour (brought about not least by the Iraq war) and the deep social, economic and political problems in the Arab world (which sparked the "Arab Spring") have convinced some Sunnis that we live in an ungodly age of political injustice where suffering, terror and armed conflict are the true tests of righteousness—and will be rewarded. Others simply want revenge for what they see as Iranian triumphalism and Sunni humiliation. Regional actors—state and non-state—have sought to project their influence and mobilise the faithful by supporting sectarian actors in different countries. And many Arab governments remain incapable of responding to the demands of their increasingly young and interconnected populations. Da'ash feeds on a Sunni sense of disenfranchisement and grievance and claims to offer a better future in the form of an idealised past—an unmoored, postmodern Caliphate with globalised ambitions and a new territorial base. The rise of Da'ash (the successor to al-Qaeda in Iraq) and the sectarianisation of conflict in the region are symptoms of highly complex and intractable pathologies in the Middle East. They show that ideas matter. But if the very conditions that gave rise to Da'ash are not addressed, then its ideology will continue to attract adherents, and it will likely be succeeded some time in the future by son-of-Da'ash. And the cycle will continue.

The Unravelling is essentially the story of women and men, of Iraqis and Americans, of soldiers and civilians, ordinary and yet extraordinary, whose lives became so entwined in "the land between the two rivers." It is a story I have chosen to share to honour the efforts of those who strived, to remember the lives that were lost, and to pay tribute to a broken country that I came so much to love.

The Iraq war and its outcome affected few Americans. There is little willingness to really reflect on or take responsibility for what happened there. The legitimacy of the war was disputed right from the outset. Iraqis blame the US for destroying their country; and Americans blame Iraqis for not making use of the opportunity given to them. Politicians try to use the situation in Iraq for political advantage, without much consideration of Iraqis themselves: Democrats blame Republicans for invading Iraq in the first place and Republicans blame Democrats for not leaving troops there. The US military blames US government civilians for not doing enough; and the latter blames the former for trying to do too much. Brits blame Tony Blair.

But what happened in Iraq matters terribly to Iraqis who hoped so much for a better future, and to those of us who served there year after year. If we refuse to honestly examine what took place there, we will miss the opportunity to better understand when and how to respond to instability in the world.

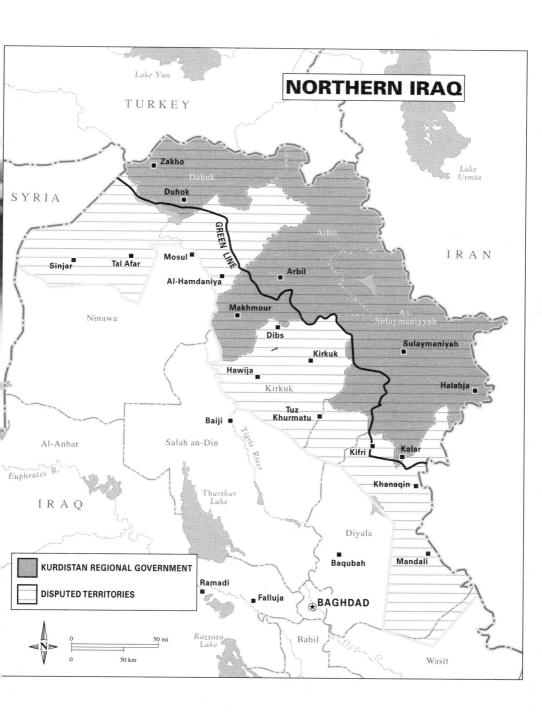

NORTHERN IRAQ

TURKEY

Lake Van

SYRIA

Lake Urmia

IRAN

■ Zakho

Dahuk

Duhok ■

Arbil

GREEN LINE

■ Sinjar   ■ Tal Afar   Mosul ■

Al-Hamdaniya ■

■ Arbil

Ninawa

Makhmour ■

As Sulaymaniyyah

Dibs ■

Sulaymaniyah ■

Kirkuk ■

Hawija ■

Kirkuk

Halabja ■

Tuz
Khurmatu ■

Baiji ■

Tigris River

Al-Anbar

Salah an-Din

Kifri ■   Kalar ■

Euphrates R.

IRAQ

*Thurthur
Lake*

Khanaqin ■

Diyala

Baqubah ■

Mandali ■

■ KURDISTAN REGIONAL GOVERNMENT

☐ DISPUTED TERRITORIES

Ramadi ■

Falluja ■

⊛ BAGHDAD

0   50 mi

N

0   50 km

*Razzaza
Lake*

Babil

Wasit

Iraq

by Adnan al-Sayegh
translated by Soheil Najm

Iraq that is going away
With every step its exiles take. . . .
Iraq that shivers
Whenever a shadow passes.

I see a gun's muzzle before me,

Or an abyss.
Iraq that we miss:
Half of its history, songs and perfume

And the other half is tyrants.

PROLOGUE

THE IRAQ INQUIRY

14 JANUARY 2011. It was a chilly morning. I got off the number 87 bus at the Houses of Parliament and walked past Westminster Abbey, turning left down Great Smith Street. I was dressed in a suit for the first time in years. I had an appointment to appear before the Iraq Inquiry (also known as the Chilcot Inquiry). It was not a war crimes tribunal. No official in the UK—or US—would ever be held accountable for the decision to go to war in 2003 or the way in which the post-war phase was implemented. But it was an investigation into what had happened, in order to draw lessons for the future. Hundreds of officials had already given their testimony since the Inquiry was established in mid-2009. Now it was my turn.

I entered a nondescript building. An official appeared, handed me a badge and showed me to the room. I was introduced to the commissioners: Sir John Chilcot, a career diplomat and senior civil servant who chaired the Inquiry; Baroness Usha Prashar, a member of the House of Lords; Sir Roderic Lyne, a former ambassador; and two historians, Sir Lawrence Freedman and Sir Martin Gilbert. I took my seat on one side of the table, facing my interrogators. I felt slightly apprehensive, but I kept telling myself that nothing could faze me after my Iraq experience. No one was going to die.

BARONESS PRASHAR: Can we start with some background information first? Can you describe how you were recruited to work for the CPA [Coalition Provisional Authority]?

EMMA SKY: There was an e-mail that was sent around the Civil Service asking for people to volunteer to go and work for the CPA. It was going to be Brits and Americans administering the country. I wasn't in the Civil Service. I was in the British Council. The e-mail was forwarded to me. I expressed interest and became a secondee to the FCO [Foreign and Commonwealth Office] and then on to the CPA.

BARONESS PRASHAR: And what briefing were you given before you went to Iraq?

EMMA SKY: I was not given a briefing. There was a phone call. It basically said, you know, you've spent a lot of time in the Middle East. You will be fine. Turn up at RAF Brize Norton. As soon as you get to Basra, there will be somebody to meet you . . . They will be standing there with a sign with your name on it and they will take you to the nearest hotel . . .

BARONESS PRASHAR: But apart from a phone call were you given any information about the Security Council Resolution 1483 and its implications for serving in the CPA?

EMMA SKY: I don't recall receiving any.

BARONESS PRASHAR: It would be helpful if you can just describe what your role and responsibilities were during your period at the CPA.

EMMA SKY: The CPA looked at the country as . . . fifteen provinces plus Kurdistan. So in each of the fifteen provinces they had a senior civilian, who was known as the governorate coordinator, and assumed the role a governor would play . . . responsible for the administration of the province, working with the US military, working with Iraqis, finding local leaders, working out who could take what responsibilities, building up their capacity to govern the province themselves.

BARONESS PRASHAR: And what were your specific responsibilities? What were you tasked to do?

EMMA SKY: There was no job description. We weren't given outlines of what our jobs were . . . I don't recall receiving an outline of what my job was until maybe September. So up until then it was really how I interpreted what my role should be . . .

SIR RODERIC LYNE: I just wonder if I can come back to the beginning of this conversation just to make sure I've really understood it. When you went out there, you say you had no written briefing, no terms of reference, no instructions and you did not have any oral briefing from anybody other than to turn up at Brize Norton and fly out to Basra?

EMMA SKY: No.

SIR RODERIC LYNE: Nothing at all?

EMMA SKY: No, not before I left the UK. I don't recall any at all except the one phone call. When I got to Basra, obviously there was no one there with a sign with my name on it—nor a hotel. So I went on to Baghdad. I made my way to the Palace and there I met the British team . . . I spent a week going round the Palace seeing how things worked, getting as many briefings as I could. They said: we have enough people here. We don't have enough people in the north. Go north. So I went to Mosul. They said: we've got someone here. I went to Erbil. They said: we've got someone here but we haven't got anyone in Kirkuk. So I went to Kirkuk. I didn't know I was going to Kirkuk when I left the UK.

SIR RODERIC LYNE: So when you left the UK, you didn't know where you were going. You presumably didn't even know what kind of clothes to put in your suitcase?

EMMA SKY: Well, no. I was only going for three months.

THREE HOURS AFTER it had begun, the interrogation wound to a close. I looked towards Sir John Chilcot, hoping for some words of reassurance, willing him to recognize that despite the impossible challenge, I had tried my hardest in very difficult circumstances.

Judging from Sir John's face, he was reeling from what I had told him. I had been opposed to the war and naturally suspicious of the military. Yet I had volunteered for three months to help get Iraq back on its feet— and within weeks of the fall of Saddam I had found myself governing a province. By the time I left Iraq many years later, I had served as the political adviser to American generals through the surge and the drawdown of US troops. A British woman, advising the top leadership of the US military . . . I suppose it must have seemed an unlikely story.

PART I

DIRECT RULE

JUNE 2003–JUNE 2004

1

TO THE LAND OF
TWO RIVERS

All we are saying is give peace a chance.
—JOHN LENNON

IT WAS MID-MORNING on Friday 20 June 2003. At the RAF base at Brize Norton, west of London, I stood waiting for the flight to Basra with two hundred or so British soldiers. I was struck by how young and innocent they looked. Some were still pimply teenagers in clean and starched uniforms. Huddled together in their groups, a few stared at me, but most blanked me as if I did not exist. I felt quite out of place. I had never flown on a military plane before and did not have a ticket. However, I was pleased to discover that my name was on some register and that was all that mattered. I gave my rank as "civilian," checked in my bag and boarded.

It was certainly a no-frills airline, with no seats assigned. During the flight, a soldier handed out packed lunches. I grabbed one, and quickly ate the stale sandwich and chocolate bar. I tried to sleep, but I was both excited and apprehensive. I was being seconded to the Foreign and Commonwealth Office to help administer Iraq for a couple of months while the country got back on its feet. I was confident that the FCO knew what it was doing. I had just not yet been informed. The invasion had occurred three months previously and the war was supposedly over. I was not unduly worried.

At Basra International Airport I wandered into the terminal and sat waiting for my bag. I looked around the airport, taking in the once grandiose and ornate interior, now damaged by war, looting and neglect.

Military Bergen rucksacks and guns wrapped up in canvas came round on the carousel. And then, a little incongruously, my bright-purple backpack. I lifted it onto my back and headed off in search of Customs. But there were none. No stamping of the passport. No entry visa. No Iraqis.

I had been told that someone would be waiting for me, placard in hand. But nobody was. It didn't take me long to realize that no one was expecting me. The place was swarming with British soldiers who seemed to know where they were going. I went upstairs to where "transit passengers" were accommodated. It was the corridor from hell: 120°F, no windows, no fans, no air conditioning and florescent lighting which stayed on all night thanks to a generator. All along the corridor male soldiers lay on cots and mats, stripped down to their underwear. I did not think that was an option for me. Nor did I have a sleeping mat. I stretched my towel out on the concrete and lay down on top of that. Some of the soldiers were already snoring away, but I got little sleep.

In the morning I lined up for the Porta-Johns, went to the communal shower (which had no water) and sat down to eat breakfast. My first meal in Iraq was a "Meal Ready to Eat," US military rations that British soldiers had "acquired" to break up the monotony of their own. I followed the instructions carefully: open packet; take out contents; fill bag with cold water up to the level mark; put back silver packet; fold bag at top and wait. Sure enough the bag began to heat up, cooking the contents of the silver packet. And within ten minutes I was tucking into tortellini. Not the first breakfast I expected to eat in Iraq, but I was starving.

I decided to head for Baghdad, in the hope that someone there was expecting me and had a job for me to do. I hitched a lift on an RAF C-130 Hercules. For a civilian, this was an experience in itself. Military flights were basic. There was no protection from the temperature or the noise. I strapped myself into one of the seats that ran alongside the frame of the plane and hung my arms through the red meshing behind me, keeping my limbs away from my body in an attempt to cope with the heat. I listened intently to the safety instructions barked out by one of the RAF crew, pointing at the different doors: "If we crash into the sea, you go out that exit. If we crash on land, you go out this exit." I really thought we *were* crashing when the plane descended rapidly in a spiral. The pull of gravity left my whole body feeling it was being violently compressed.

I was later told that this was a "corkscrew landing" to avoid being hit by missiles.

I arrived at Baghdad International Airport at around midday. Emerging from the plane, it felt as if a hair dryer on its hottest setting was being thrust in my face. Respite from the scorching heat was provided in a large air-conditioned tent where some US soldiers sat around watching television. The BBC was running a "Great Britons" series; featured that day was Princess Diana.

After hours of waiting, I got on a military bus that took me the half hour ride to the Republican Palace, now the headquarters of the CPA. After empty wasteland, the airport road passed houses set back from the road and hidden by palm trees. I did not see any Iraqis. But for the US military presence, I might have been arriving in Amman in the heat of the summer midday, when everyone was taking siesta. At the palace I reported to the British office, which was staffed by British diplomats. My name was on a list of "secondees" and they had been expecting my arrival. A British colonel welcomed me warmly. There was nothing to worry about, he said, except for trigger-happy Americans. That was the main threat to Brits.

I wandered around the huge palace, seeking to learn its mysteries. Originally built for King Faisal II, it was renamed the Republican Palace after the king's assassination in the 1958 coup. The palace had been spared in the "shock and awe" bombardment of Baghdad. What was dubbed the "Green Zone" was now developing around it.

In one of the great rooms the domed ceiling was covered with a painting of the al-Aqsa Mosque in Jerusalem and flying horses, while one wall had a massive mural of Scud missiles pointing to the sky. Saddam Hussein's name and initials were engraved on every wall. I stepped outside and looked up. Four huge bronze busts of Saddam's head adorned the palace roof. US engineers were considering how to decapitate them.

Life in the Republican Palace in those early days was extraordinary. It was a swarming mass of soldiers, with a smattering of civilians. Offices had been set up all over the palace, but their location constantly moved. Signs would appear on doors announcing the new incumbents, with directions to the former office now in some other part of the palace. There was no air conditioning, the electricity was erratic and the water system was frequently down. Stately rooms and corridors had become dormitories, reminiscent of wartime hospitals. The lucky ones found fans to blow the sweat across their bodies when the electricity came on. There were no toilets or showers in operation inside the palace. We traipsed to the facilities that had been set up outside the palace's back door.

The shower block had certain hours designated for women, and other hours for men. At times we showered with mineral water; and some days even the floors were washed with mineral water. The Porta-Johns were regularly full to bursting point, with the stench vomit-inducing. I found a bed upstairs in the palace in a room where two other women were sleeping. However, within days a sign on the door informed us that the room was now an office. I managed to get a room in the nearby al-Rashid Hotel, by persuading someone who was leaving not to check out and to give me their key. It was an eighteen-storey concrete building within the Green Zone. There were no longer any signs of the mosaic of President George H. W. Bush's face which had been installed in the floor of the lobby following the First Gulf War, so that every visitor would trample over it as they entered. It had been dug up a few weeks before by US soldiers.

"Life support" was provided by Kellogg Brown & Root (KBR), a subsidiary of Halliburton, the US multinational that specialized in oilfield services. KBR was responsible for feeding us, for sending our laundry to Kuwait for cleaning and for all the other tasks which are required to keep an army up and running. The former ballroom was now the canteen, or chow hall facility. Three times a day I would queue along the side of the room, pick up a tray, plastic plate and plastic cutlery, choose between chicken and hamburger with "freedom fries" (renamed in reaction to France's opposition to the war), which were served by Pakistanis, collect a soda or sweet iced tea and sit down at one of the tables to eat.

Over the next few days, I was briefed by a series of army officers and diplomats about the CPA, the progress to date and the challenges. I tried to get my head around the internal US rivalries. I was told that the US Department of Defense had set up the Office for Reconstruction and Humanitarian Assistance, under the leadership of a retired US general, Jay Garner. But within days of Garner arriving in Iraq, the White House had grown nervous of his plans to hand over to a transitional Iraqi government and to hold elections within ninety days. They decided that they needed someone with greater political acumen and, on 11 May, Paul Bremer was appointed to head up the new CPA, subsuming the Office for Reconstruction and Humanitarian Assistance.

Bremer did not believe there were credible Iraqi leaders who could assume power, and he decided that the CPA had to directly administer the country for an undefined period. America was going to rebuild Iraq, as it had rebuilt Germany and Japan after World War II. In order to over-haul the basis on which the state was run under Saddam, Bremer de-creed that the CPA was dissolving the Baath party and disbanding the Iraqi security forces. But in so doing, the US was removing the sinews of the state that had held the country together. There was now a power vacuum and a free-for-all.

While most Brits were based in Basra, a few were scattered in other provinces. I was told I was to be based in the north and that I should travel there in a few days. I had now been in Iraq about a week and had not spoken to a single Iraqi. I wanted to take a look at Baghdad before I headed north. The security situation had become a concern and we were only supposed to leave the palace with an armed escort. But an opportu-nity came when an American general agreed to take me along with him to the Sheraton Hotel. At the hotel he shook my hand, wished me luck and then turned a blind eye as I slipped through the security cordon, out past the concertina wire and into the street.

I found myself walking along the east bank of the river Tigris on Abu Nuwas Street, named after one of the greatest Arabic poets of the Islamic Golden Age and a reminder that for several centuries, until the Mongol conquest of Baghdad in 1258, the city had been the cultural capital of the Arab world. I had no idea what modern-day Baghdad was supposed to look like. None of the city's former glory, fabled in the tales of *The Thou-sand and One Nights*, was visible among the rubbish strewn everywhere, the feral cats and the wild dogs. At the beginning of the twentieth cen-tury, a third of the population of Baghdad had been Jewish. This land had once witnessed one of the world's most thriving Jewish communities. It was by the rivers of Babylon that Jews had once sat down and wept at the destruction of the Jewish temple. But the rise of Arab nationalism and the foundation of the State of Israel had led to the emigration of most of Iraq's Jews, and now fewer than a dozen remained.

Shot-up photo of Saddam. *Photo by Brandon Aird*

Spotting a sign for an art gallery, I went in. Iraqi art was renowned throughout the Middle East. *"Salaam aleikum,"* I said. *"Aleikum salaam,"* the man in the gallery responded. He was delighted to have a visitor. He introduced himself as the gallery owner and brought me *chai*, tea served in a small glass with plenty of sugar. "I hid all the artwork in my home during the war," he told me. The Coalition bombing had only targeted government installations. It was the *Hawasim* which had come afterwards that had concerned him. It took me a moment to understand that *Hawasim* referred to looters. Saddam had dubbed the US invasion *Harb al-Hawasim*, the final war, and had emptied the jails in the run-up to the war. The gallery owner had yet to put the paintings back on the walls, but he took me up some stairs to show me the piles of artwork that he had. "All Iraqis," he said, "are happy to see the end of Saddam." He went on, "But we are frustrated with the lawlessness—and the lack of electricity and water." I had heard that every time the Coalition repaired the infrastructure, saboteurs blew up installations and thieves pulled up the piping and stole the copper. "I want to reopen the gallery with an Internet cafe," he told me, "but the problem is electricity."

Continuing down the street, I came to a mosque and took my camera out. Seated behind a trolley in front of the mosque were two money-changers, with wads of Iraqi dinars set out in front of them. "Don't take a picture of the mosque," one of the men said. "Take a picture of this." He hitched up his *dishdasha*, so that I could see his leg, amputated below the knee. "This is what Saddam did." The horrors of the past were beginning to emerge: the mass murders, the ethnic cleansing, the torture, the fear that Iraqis had lived with for decades.

I walked on. I stopped in front of what once would have been an ornate house. The gate was hanging off its hinges. It was as if a fierce storm had raged through the city, removing everything in its wake. But it was human hands that had gutted the building from top to bottom, leaving only the structure. An Iraqi man saw me staring at it. "This is a Hobbesian world," he spat out in disgust, shaking his head. "Sorry?" I replied. "Hobbes, Hobbes . . ." he repeated, before walking off. His words reverberated in my head as I wandered back to my pick-up point at the Sheraton. Who was this Iraqi and how did he know about Hobbes?

AFTER MY "INDUCTION" in Baghdad, I boarded a US military C-130 and flew north up to Mosul and then on to Erbil, the seat of the Kurdistan Regional Government. At the Khanzad Hotel, headquarters of CPA North, I met up with Liane Saunders, a friend from Oxford, who was in the Foreign Office and now the deputy regional coordinator for CPA North. I was told that I would be based in Kirkuk, but first I was to join the delegation of Ambassador Bremer for a tour of the north.

I caught sight of Bremer on the helicopter pad. He appeared dashing and energetic, immaculately dressed in a suit with the combat boots which came to be his signature. I thought he was in his mid forties until someone told me he was in his sixties. He was surrounded by bodyguards from Blackwater, a private security company. Travelling in Bremer's entourage had all the glamour and excitement of a presidential campaign trail. We flew by helicopter from Erbil to the city of Sulaymaniyah. It was my first time on a helicopter and I was terrified I would throw up. Kurds turned out in great numbers to greet us with flowers and kisses, holding up placards thanking the US and the UK for liberating the Kurdish lands.

Sky on helicopter next to Ambassador Bremer, who is studying Arabic on flashcards. *Photo by Matthew Fuller*

The roads into town were lined with peshmerga, Kurdish fighters, who had fought alongside Coalition troops.

I accompanied Ambassador Bremer to his meeting with Jalal Talabani, the leader of the Patriotic Union of Kurdistan (PUK). Bremer spoke about the new Iraq with passion and optimism. He discussed the establishment of a Governing Council for Iraq, which would consist of twenty-five Iraqis, representing all communities and regions in the country. He said we were also looking to identify a group to draft the Constitution, which would then be discussed across the country in various forums and put to a national referendum. Once approved, the Constitution would pave the way for free and fair elections, giving the Iraqi people the opportunity to elect their own representatives.

We flew on to the town of Sari Rash, north of Erbil, where we had similar discussions with Masoud Barzani, the leader of the Kurdistan Democratic Party (KDP), the other main Kurdish political party. Bremer motioned for me, as the new arrival, to sit next to him at lunch, opposite Barzani. He asked me about myself and the work I had been doing before.

I spoke about Palestine and Israel; of poverty elimination; and of justice reform around the world. Conversation then turned to the Fourth of July, and Barzani and Bremer both looked at me—the Brit—for comment. I responded, "We wish all our former colonies the success of America." They beamed. And I thought to myself, how on earth had someone like me come to be part of this American-led occupation of Iraq?

We celebrated America's Independence Day with the Kurds by the shores of Lake Dukan. It was apparently the largest lake in Kurdistan, created by the construction of a dam on the Little Zab River in the 1950s. I sat watching the sun set over the mountains. "The Star-Spangled Banner" was played over the public address system. Barham Salih, the deputy leader of the PUK, made a rousing speech about America and democracy. "We Kurds," he said, "used to say that our only friends are the mountains. This is no longer the case." I had spent the afternoon at Barham's house leafing through one of his prize possessions: Saddam's family album. There were pictures of Saddam the husband; Saddam the father, with his two boys; Saddam the gardener, in his pyjamas tending the plants. It was so disconcerting, because he appeared so ordinary. Somehow during all the looting in Baghdad, the album had fallen into Barham's possession.

Later, the Kurds began to dance in a line around the swimming pool, joined by American soldiers, as well as a few civilians including myself.

At one stage in the evening, someone had pointed out to me an American officer and told me it was Colonel Mayville, who was in command of the brigade based in Kirkuk. He was sitting to the side, looking very serious, and deep in conversation with other soldiers. It was days later before I found out that he had been directing a raid that evening against a group he suspected of plotting to assassinate the man he had recently installed as the governor of Kirkuk. The group turned out to be Turkish Special Forces.

The next day we flew by helicopter to Kirkuk. As the doors of the helicopter had been closed on previous occasions, I decided not to wear the seat belt as last time it had left grime stains on my shirt. Suddenly, we lifted off with the doors wide open. I shouted out in panic. But no one could hear me. I was seated on the outside, with every chance of falling out as the helicopter flew acrobatically. I gripped the seat beneath me, hanging on for dear life, staring at my knees, too terrified to look at the stunning scenery. I was hugely relieved when we landed on the airfield in the capital of the province in which I was to be Ambassador Bremer's representative, with the grand title of Governorate Coordinator of Kirkuk.

FOUR MONTHS EARLIER, as the drums of war were beating, I had travelled to the US to visit Ground Zero in New York. Looking at the empty space where the Twin Towers had once stood, it was easy to understand why the attacks of 11 September 2001 had left Americans feeling angry and vulnerable—and wanting revenge. Yet many of the ordinary Americans I spoke to had no desire for war with Iraq, and did not see a connection with 9/11.

At the time, I was thirty-five years old and living in the UK, in Manchester, working for the British Council as an adviser on governance and justice. Through the Council, I worked on numerous initiatives, including prison reform in Brazil, access to justice in Nigeria, human rights in Bangladesh and violence against women in Jordan. I had gained experience of working in different countries and cultures, of designing projects, and of joining teams, leading teams. I happened to be in Cairo on 9/11, assessing how to strengthen Egyptian human rights organizations. In my hotel room, I watched live CNN coverage of the attacks on the Twin Towers. There was feverish excitement across Cairo: at last, America was getting a dose of its own medicine; the "Great Satan" was experiencing some of the pain it inflicted on others in the world; America was getting its comeuppance. That night, as I floated in a felucca out on the Nile, I had a sense that our world would never be the same.

At the British Council I was also involved in examining where the enmity towards the West was coming from, and I was asked to put together a scenario of how the world might look in ten years' time if the US and UK went to war with Iraq. I was opposed to the war, concerned about its legality and the rationale behind it. Saddam was one of the greatest villains in the world, but I didn't believe there was a connection between al-Qaeda and Saddam. I feared the effects on the Arab world of another humiliating military defeat and a foreign occupation, which could be exploited by Bin Laden and his ilk to attract more recruits to international terrorism. I called the war scenario the "Last Crusade," and described how the invasion would lead to the fragmentation of Iraq and regional war.

I had decided that if the invasion took place, I would find a way to work in Iraq, to apologize to Iraqis for the war, and to help them rebuild their country. It was not a surprise to anyone who knew me that I would go to Iraq. It was the sort of thing I would do.

I WAS BORN IN LONDON in 1968. My parents separated when I was a month old and I grew up not knowing my father, a Jewish man whose family had emigrated from Eastern Europe. My mother found work as a live-in housekeeper. She was determined that I receive a good education. When I was four, she took a job as a matron at Ashfold, a boys' prep school in a Jacobean mansion, set in thirty acres of beautiful grounds near Oxford. We lived in the school, on the top floor.

When I reached the age of seven, I was accepted into the school as a boarder—one of only five girls. It was a wonderful experience. I remember sitting on the floor with all the boys watching old war movies projected onto a big screen, with escapes from prisoner-of-war camps; traipsing through woods at night, camouflaged with leaves, to reclaim the flag of my team; and reading of great adventures—Thor Heyerdahl and his Kon Tiki expedition, or the journeys of Richard Burton and John Speke through Africa in search of the source of the Nile. I never felt limited by gender. I played for the school's junior soccer team, going by the name of Fred Blogs during matches so that the opposition would not know I was a girl.

When I was ten, my mother fell in love with a teacher at the school who was a decade her junior. He left his wife and children, and uprooted us to Northern Ireland, to a boarding school which felt like a prison. I missed Ashfold and yearned for it every day. We moved back to England a year later to Bradford-on-Avon, where my stepfather got a job at an all-boys prep school, the Old Ride. I was admitted as the only girl at the school. It was a *Lord of the Flies* experience, dealing with nasty boys who did not want a girl "contaminating" their school. I studied hard and was top of the class. At thirteen I won a scholarship to a coeducational school, Dean Close, in Cheltenham. I flourished at the school, excelling academically, playing in the hockey team and joining the army cadet force. For the first time in my life, I had friends who were girls. However, in my final year I rebelled against the rules and strictures, and was suspended. The headmaster, an evangelical Christian, told me that I had thrown away my life. I left school with an abiding scepticism towards organized religion.

In my gap year after school, I worked as a volunteer in Kfar Menachem kibbutz in Israel. Kibbutz life was another universe, with unimaginable freedoms, with secularism and socialism, where we discussed the meaning of life, where we drank and smoked hashish around campfires, where we listened to the Voice of Peace "from somewhere in the Eastern Mediterranean" proclaim "no more war, no more bloodshed," where people reinvented themselves and not only imagined an ideal community but tried to live in one. Getting up at dawn to round up the cows and then milk them seemed the greatest job that I could ever wish for.

On the kibbutz, I met Israelis from all backgrounds. The original founders of the kibbutz had escaped from Germany, Poland and Russia. Some were Holocaust survivors, some had lost their families, and many carried with them the fears and trauma of that experience. Their children were native-born kibbutzniks, who would typically serve in the elite units of the Israel Defence Forces as commandos and fighter pilots. The kibbutz was also a boarding school for children from poor families, mostly Jewish immigrants who had had to leave Arab countries after the foundation of the state of Israel in 1948. And there were also Israelis who divided their national service between work on a kibbutz and military service; they were very left wing and highly critical of Israel's occupation of Lebanon. People spoke of war with such horror—and such regret. There was the brilliant fighter pilot who lacked the killer instinct, the man who lost both his sons in one of Israel's wars, the youth who would injure himself to avoid national service, the middle-aged man who became increasingly unhinged whenever his reserve duty approached. And there was Yunis and his family, Arabs who lived locally, who had given their farm to the kibbutz for safe keeping, and who returned once the fighting was over to reclaim it peacefully. It was with them that I went go-karting on Shabbat when we had a day off work, and they would ride bareback on their horses. Through life on the kibbutz, I got to learn about Israeli society, how Israelis saw themselves, and their fears and yearning to live in security. It was a connection with the side of my family I had never known. I came away a humanist.

I arrived at Oxford to read Classics. The teaching fees were paid by the state, and I received a full grant for my living expenses, based on the low level of my parents' income. However, when the First Palestinian Intifada broke out in December 1987, during my first term, I decided to change to Oriental Studies with a focus on Arabic and Hebrew. My Hebrew teacher was the daughter of the remarkable Israeli writer Amos Oz.

At Oxford I was blessed with a multitude of influences. And I listened to a stream of speakers whose tales captured my imagination. I went to hear the great explorer Wilfred Thesiger speak at the Pitt Rivers Museum and got him to sign a copy of his book on the Marsh Arabs. I remember Leonard Cheshire talking about his life, his military career and his work establishing homes for disabled people. He told us that we should do something with our lives, and not make money our goal. A life of purpose. That is what I would lead. I had taken Edmund Burke's maxim as my own: "All it takes for evil to triumph is for good men to do nothing." But what would be my cause? There were Soviet Jews trying escape to the West, there was poverty in Africa. There was war to be ended in the Middle East.

The principal of Somerville College was Daphne Park. Each year, like all Somervillians, I would go to see her for a thirty-minute one-on-one, in which she would ask me what I was up to and I would stress my desire to help bring about peace in the Middle East. It always astonished me how much she remembered from our conversation the year before. She looked like a normal gran, though a very smart one. It was only years later that her illustrious career as a spy was revealed.

My second year was spent at the University of Alexandria in Egypt, and every summer vacation I went back to the region. At the height of the First Intifada, I spent my university holiday working in the West Bank town of Ramallah for a Palestinian NGO whose goal was to make Palestinians independent of Israel for food. I met a wide range of Palestinians: "48ers" whose families had fled the fighting when the State of Israel was created; West Bankers whose towns had been occupied by

Israel in 1967 following the Six Day War; and Jerusalemites who came from well-known Palestinian families. I experienced life under occupation, carrying an onion to bite on when tear-gassed and learning how to get round Israeli checkpoints. I came to understand the insecurity of Palestinians' lives and their yearning for justice.

While I was still at Oxford, my stepfather ran off with another woman, leaving my mother heartbroken, penniless and distraught. Our relationship, which was always difficult, became further strained. Oxford friends provided love and support, but I felt I was drowning. On graduating from Oxford, I set out for Timbuktu. It sounded like a magical kingdom far away, and I wanted to escape the grief and anxiety that family seemed to cause. Fear of failure and of not doing something with my life was greater than my fear of risk and danger.

I never made it to Timbuktu. I travelled through Morocco and across the Algerian Sahara. I only realized I had reached Niger when soldiers mistook the occupants of the Peugeot I had hitched a ride in for Tuareg rebels, and at gunpoint ordered us back into the desert. As the only French speaker in the car, I had to mediate with the nervous soldiers and convince them that we were simply European travellers. But I could not get from Niger into Mali because of the fighting, so I went on to Benin and Nigeria. From there I flew to Egypt and found temporary work teaching English and as a freelance journalist. I then crossed the Sinai to Jerusalem. It was two years before I set foot back in Britain.

But the return was short-lived. In September 1993, Yitzhak Rabin and Yasser Arafat shook hands on the White House lawn. I got a job working with a committee that had been established as part of the Middle East Peace Process. I travelled around the region to Palestinian refugee camps to assess their living conditions, needs and aspirations. I moved out to Jerusalem, determined to remain for the length of the Peace Process, which I envisaged would be five years. After working for Palestinian NGOs, I took a job at the British Council to manage a project aimed at improving the efficiency and effectiveness of the Palestinian Authority's public services. I went on to design and manage initiatives to help strengthen the Palestinian civil service, the Palestinian Legislative Council and Palestinian human rights organizations, and to build relationships between Palestinians and Israelis.

I was in Tel Aviv on 4 November 1995, at the peace rally where two hundred thousand Israelis gathered to show their support for Rabin, singing songs of peace, and urging him to continue moving forward with the difficult compromises for peace. It was an incredible atmosphere. But as Rabin was leaving, he was assassinated. I cried for a week. Days of hope gave way to despair. Everything then started to unravel. Suicide bombs, bombs on buses and in clubs, increased. Over the next few years, all the projects I was working on were suspended. All the progress of the Oslo Accords was lost.

I returned to the UK in 2001 to live in Manchester. When war with Iraq broke out in 2003, and I heard that the Foreign Office was looking for people to administer Iraq for a couple of months, I immediately volunteered. I was single. I had had a couple of relationships that had come to nothing. I wanted to be doing something that I felt was important, something with purpose. It seemed obvious to me that I should go to Iraq. I was excited to be heading back to the Middle East. I loved waking to the call to prayer; shopping in the markets; inhaling the smell of coffee; and sharing plates of food with complete strangers who were always so warm and hospitable.

2

SKY SOLDIERS

We, in the ages lying
In the buried past of the earth,
Built Nineveh with our sighing,
And Babel itself with our mirth;
And o'erthrew them with prophesying
To the old of the new world's worth;
For each age is a dream that is dying,
Or one that is coming to birth.

—ARTHUR WILLIAM EDGAR O'SHAUGHNESSY

I TURNED UP at the Kirkuk government building to find the US military swarming around as if they owned the place. They had put up signs on numerous doors indicating either the unit or the function. Other rooms had been given to members of the Kirkuk Provincial Council that the US military had appointed. I found a small office on the ground floor which they had allocated to the CPA—in other words, to me. Colonel Mayville had set up office in the largest room in the building, which until the invasion had served as the governor's office.

I had observed Colonel William Mayville, the US commander of the 173rd Airborne Brigade, on a couple of occasions but we had never spoken. He was of average height and athletic physique. He looked tough. I noted his distinctive way of wearing his pistol, attached to his belt on his right side, but with his shirt tucked in behind it so that it was always visible. He appeared unpredictable, sometimes a quiet and thoughtful introvert, other times bouncing with energy and enthusiasm, other times furious. I climbed up the staircase to his office and introduced myself. I remained standing near the door as he strutted around the room,

Colonel Mayville preparing to lead the 173rd Airborne Brigade in a parachute jump into northern Iraq. *Photo by Brandon Aird*

expressing his concerns about the CPA: its lack of capacity, how people flew in and out for a few hours, and how no one seemed particularly interested in Kirkuk.

"I intend to stay in Kirkuk, Colonel," I told him. "Kirkuk is of crucial importance to Iraq because it is a microcosm of Iraqi society. If we can get it right here, there is hope for the new Iraq." I left the room shaking my head. He seemed so arrogant. American soldiers seemed so out of place, running around in uniforms which looked like pyjamas, with their name tags on their chests. How on earth was I supposed to interact with such people?

Tat, tat, tat. tat, tat, tat. I awoke abruptly to the sound of automatic gunfire. I looked at my clock. It was four in the morning. *Boom.* Several colossal explosions suddenly shook the house. Paralysed by the deafening sound, I remained in bed, totally naked, curled up in a ball with my hands over my ears, shaking like a leaf, my heart pounding as I watched the dust pouring in through the sandbags. Would the walls cave in? My top-floor bedroom, a roof extension, shook so much that I feared it was going to become detached from the rest of the house, with me in it.

It was my seventh night in Kirkuk. The attack may not have lasted even half an hour—but it seemed much longer. When the noise stopped I jumped out of bed, dressed, put on my body armour and went downstairs to inspect the damage. I discovered that four rocket-propelled grenades had been fired at the house, with one exploding on impact as it passed up through the building a few feet from my bed. The kitchen and operations rooms were badly damaged, with glass blown everywhere. Fierce shooting from the Gurkhas on guard on the roof had prevented the attackers from storming the house, but they had managed to get within thirty yards.

My "home" was a large modern villa which the CPA was renting at vast expense in a residential part of town. I shared the house with staff hired by the CPA, a couple of techies, American consultants working for a firm called RTI and some engineers. However, a mortar attack soon after I arrived had led most to pack their bags and head north to the safety of Erbil. I had remained with a couple of support staff. The Gurkhas had sandbagged all the windows downstairs and upstairs. They were a team of Nepalese contracted by a private security company to protect the house. I had no bodyguards to protect me when I was away from the house, nor armoured cars to transport me, even though regulations stated that I should only go out in one.

The morning after the rocket attack, a manager of the private security company turned up. A humourless Australian, he criticized the Gurkhas for not having killed any of the attackers. The Gurkhas demanded reinforcements, more ammunition, and that the manager stay. The Australian refused. The Gurkhas then said they were not prepared to stay any longer, and one by one they threw their weapons down on the ground in a pile. The Australian proceeded to put their weapons in the back of his car parked out in the street, in full view of everyone in the neighbourhood.

At this stage I stepped in. I gathered all the Gurkhas together in one room. "I want to thank you," I said, "for saving my life last night." I told them about my visit to Pokhara in Nepal, where most of them came from. I spoke of the proud history of Gurkhas in the British Army and our respect for them as soldiers. "Please, will you continue to guard the house? I promise you that I will get reinforcements sent up from Baghdad." I also warned them that if they walked out now, it was unlikely they would ever find work in the security sector again. The Gurkhas looked at one another, exchanged a few comments, and agreed to stay.

Pleased with the result, I went out and informed the manager that the Gurkhas were staying. The Australian then made some further derogatory comments to the Gurkhas, which caused them all to resubmit their resignations. I stepped in once again. In the end the majority decided they would stay. But three, including the team leader, said they had had enough. They said they had families and they did not want to die in Iraq.

I asked the techies to charge up the "bat mobile," which was parked outside the house. This enabled me to connect to the Internet on a wireless computer. It was the first time I had come across such technology. I climbed into the van and sent an urgent message to the British ambassador, John Sawers, Bremer's deputy in Baghdad. I described the events of the last eight hours and requested that someone with experience of working with Gurkhas be sent to Kirkuk immediately. By late afternoon, the cavalry arrived in the form of an ex–British Army officer with some

Gurkha reinforcements from Baghdad. John Sawers had contacted the headquarters of the private security company in London, who had immediately responded.

The next day, Sawers appeared in person in Kirkuk. With his dark handsome looks, charm and ability to speak Arabic, John was a legend. I was astonished that he would think to drop in. He whisked me off with him for his farewell tour of Kurdistan. It was his last week and he had people to say goodbye to.

The trip was immensely enjoyable. Also in the entourage was Meghan O'Sullivan, a prominent member of Bremer's governance team in Baghdad. Meghan had red hair and wore red lipstick, and had already risen to prominence within the CPA. She was also great fun. Meghan and I mocked Sawers mercilessly for his lack of gender awareness. "Meghan, did you hear John mention women in his speech?" I asked her, in front of him. "No," she replied, "it was all about 'men and sons.' He didn't once mention 'women and daughters.'" Sawers promised to try to be more gender sensitive in his next speech. He failed.

When Sawers dropped me back in Kirkuk, I asked his advice on what I should do. He told me to become a trusted partner to all groups and to get to know the Turkmen. And that, in essence, was as far as guidance from the CPA went.

Back in Kirkuk, my first priority was to find safe accommodation. I went to see Colonel Mayville again in his office at the government building. He was reclining on a couch, with his feet up, boots on. He had heard about the RPG incident and told me he was going to hunt down my attackers. "Those who attacked my house did not know me," I told him. "They were attacking the symbols of foreign occupation, and they deserve to be given a trial if arrested." I turned up to see the Colonel the next day with the Fourth Geneva Convention on my laptop. From my years working in the Palestinian territories, I regarded the Convention as the legal framework for the conduct of any occupying army. "If I find you in violation of any of the articles," I told him, "I will take you to The Hague." I took my brown Filofax with me everywhere and began documenting everything Colonel Mayville said and did.

The next day, I moved into a tent on the airfield which I shared with seven American men who moved with me from the CPA villa. The tent was a large structure, with amazingly effective air conditioning fed through large tubes. There was a bed each, a fridge, and a couple of tables and chairs. I would get up each morning at around seven, traipse out into the scorching heat to the "Cadillac" shower block, and take a freezing-cold shower. In the shower block there were signs setting out "Cadillac etiquette." Showers should be no longer than three minutes. Thirty seconds to soap up; two and a half minutes to rinse—not ideal living accommodation, but safer than staying in the bombed-out house in town.

DESPITE OUR INITIAL ENCOUNTERS, Colonel Mayville appeared genuinely delighted at my arrival in Kirkuk. He saw me as his exit strategy, the first of the civilian wave that would replace the military. It was mid July, and he hoped to be back at the Brigade's US Army base in Vicenza, Italy, by the end of the month. He seemed to enjoy the fact that I was prepared to stand up to him—and with a British accent. He decided that in the next couple of weeks he was going to teach me all he had learnt about the province and its people. For my part, I was very wary of the military. I had never worked with the British military, let alone the US Army. However, it made sense to learn what I could from the Colonel and have him introduce me to the key Iraqi figures.

Colonel Mayville decided that I would share his office in the government building. "In Baghdad, you have Bremer and Sanchez," he told everyone, referring to General Sanchez, the most senior military commander in the country, who worked alongside Ambassador Bremer. "In Kirkuk, you have Sky and Mayville." Within hours, a desk for me had been set up in his office and a sign had appeared on the door: MAYVILLE AND SKY. At the bottom was written SKY SOLDIERS. At this point I thought the Colonel had truly lost the plot—I knew war did this to people. Everywhere we went, soldiers jumped up and shouted "Sky Soldiers!" as they saluted.

I soon discovered that the Sky Soldiers moniker had been around for a lot longer than I had. On the Internet I read that the 173rd Airborne Brigade was originally constituted in 1917 as an infantry brigade. It was on the island of Okinawa, where it had been activated in 1963 to serve as

the quick-reaction force for the Pacific Command, that Taiwanese paratroopers had dubbed them *Tien Bien,* or Sky Soldiers, due to the mass
parachute jumps they undertook in training. They were deployed to
Vietnam in 1965, and the names of more than 1,790 Sky Soldiers adorn
the Vietnam Memorial Wall in Washington, DC. The Brigade was reacti-
vated in June 2000 in Vicenza, Italy, as the US Army's airborne strategic
response force for Europe.

Colonel Mayville told me about his first months in Iraq. He had led
the 173rd Airborne Brigade on their parachute drop into Bashur in northern Iraq to open the northern front—the first wartime jump since the
1989 US invasion of Panama to overthrow Noriega. On 10 April 2003,
the 173rd Airborne Brigade, with Kurdish peshmerga forces, had seized
Kirkuk from a demoralized and fleeing Iraqi Army. Although the Iraqi
Army had the equipment and stores required to fight a protracted battle
and also severely damage the infrastructure of Kirkuk, they had opted to
bolt.

Afterwards, looters and criminals had run amok and inter-communal
fighting had broken out. By 17 April, Coalition forces had restored order
in the city and had asked the people of Kirkuk to come back to work.
By the first week of May, people had returned to their posts in the public sector. In the directorates, the heads, being senior-level Baathists,
melted away. The deputies and below tended not to be senior Baathists
and returned.

The city began to function again, with public services, including education and health care, up and running. The Coalition forces agreed to
the arrival of a group of Kurds—actively supported, and in some cases
engineered, by the KDP and PUK administrations in Erbil and Sulaymaniyah—to take over top positions in the town and to protect infrastructure. Many Arabs were appalled by this perceived "Kurdification"
of Kirkuk and decided not to go back to work. On 17 May around five
hundred armed Arabs had marched on Kirkuk and attacked the Kurdish
sectors of this city. After intense fighting in the city for a day, Coalition
forces intervened to restore calm. At the end of May, Colonel Mayville
had set up a thirty-seat Provincial Council.

Colonel Mayville and I held many conversations in what was now
our shared office in the Kirkuk government building. Our desks were

next to each other. We also had a large table and chairs, round which to meet, and sofas along the sides. Off one end of the room was a small bathroom with a toilet which occasionally flushed; and off the other end, a balcony. There was no air conditioning. On a wooden board on the wall were carved the names of former governors. The government building served as the centre for local government officials as well as military and civilian contractors.

Making this building safe from snipers and car bombs was an immediate priority. A barrier of concertina wire was used provisionally to create the required stand-off, until proper walls and gates were in place. A system of identity cards and badges was set up, in an attempt to provide quicker access to the building for government officials and other trusted Iraqis.

In those first weeks, I was a novelty as well as a sanitizing factor. Colonel Mayville's mood seemed to improve whenever I appeared. He treated me initially as his pet and spoilt me with tea and attention. He was interested in all my previous experiences in the Middle East and was willing to share insights from his own career. It felt good to be appreciated, particularly since I was virtually ignored by my civilian bosses in Baghdad.

When we were not in the government building we spent our time visiting villages and towns, meeting Sky Soldiers in their Forward Operating Bases, and getting acquainted with the leadership of the different communities. We travelled together in his big SUV, a Chevrolet Suburban, both sitting in the back seat. The military police would spin around in the turrets of their Humvees (one behind and one in front), surveying the landscape with weapons poised, a mode of travel that never made me feel safe. Our presence on the roads was obtrusive. We looked like, and were, an occupying army.

On these trips, we would talk endlessly in the car. I was the nearest thing that Colonel Mayville had to an expert on the Middle East, and he determined to learn everything he could. He wanted someone who could think "outside the box." I knew little about Iraq, but having spent over a decade in the Middle East, I knew a good deal about the history and cultures of the wider region.

For longer distances, we usually travelled by helicopter—with the doors open. There would always be two helicopters, with gunners on

either side carefully surveying the surrounding land. They would sit in
their flying suits, hands poised on their weapons, peering out across the
country. I was initially amazed at this low-tech security surveillance. We
would fly very low across the country, to lessen the chances of being hit
by rockets or mortars, but climb dramatically to evade electricity cables.
We tried to avoid the villages but we could not help being a deafening
sound overhead, particularly for those working out in the fields. I quickly
learned to avoid the "hurricane seat." Whoever sat in the back right seat
would have the wind soar through their face, with cheeks and mouth
flapping furiously.

I WAS FAST DISCOVERING how contested Kirkuk's past was, and the implications this had for its future. It was estimated that a quarter of a million Iraqis—mostly Kurds but also Turkmen—had been displaced from
Kirkuk under the Baath party project to "Arabize" the province. The
province had been renamed *Ta'mim* (Arabic for "nationalization"), its
borders had been changed to cut out Kurdish towns and villages, and
tens of thousands of Arabs, mainly Shia from the south, had been given
incentives to move to the province. The Baath party had sought to ensure
that Kirkuk—and its oil—would remain firmly under the control of central government.

The West, and the Arab world, had largely stood silent while the
ethnic cleansing had taken place. Much of it had occurred in the 1980s
during the Iran-Iraq war, in which the West had supported Saddam,
and the Kurds had received support from Iran to fight against the Iraqi
government.

Saddam had launched the *Anfal* ('Spoils of War') campaign against
the Kurds in the north, which included chemical warfare such as the
infamous 1988 attack on the town of Halabja which killed thousands of
civilians. After Saddam invaded Kuwait in 1990, there were uprisings
across Iraq. Saddam brutally crushed the rebels, with Iraqi forces regain-
ing control of Kirkuk. The establishment of a no-fly zone over northern
Iraq in 1991, at the end of the First Gulf War, enabled the development
of a Kurdish region in the provinces of Dohuk, Arbil and Sulaymaniyah,
governed by the two main Kurdish parties, the KDP and PUK. The PUK

had split from the KDP in 1975, its left-wing intellectuals frustrated with the tribal nature of the KDP. However, in 1994 competition between the two parties spilled over into civil war, before the US managed to broker a peace deal with power-sharing arrangements. Although that period was behind them, tensions still remained. But both parties agreed that Kirkuk should be incorporated into the Kurdish region. Now, in 2003, with the peshmerga having played their part in the overthrow of Saddam's forces, the Kurds saw their opportunity to achieve that goal.

One morning, Colonel Mayville took me out north of Kirkuk in his SUV in the company of two Kurdish leaders, Kemal Kirkuki from the KDP and Rizgar Ali from the PUK. We left behind the flaring gas of Kirkuk's oilfields and drove out into the countryside. Colonel Mayville had a strong relationship with the two Kurds. Only weeks before he had coordinated the capture of Kirkuk with them. But this trip was not a tour of battlefields. Instead, it was to show us the destruction that the former regime had inflicted on the Kurds.

Kemal and Rizgar pointed out the Kurdish villages that had been razed to the ground by Saddam's forces. Nothing remained except a few stones. They described the lives their families had once led in these villages. Their eyes glistened with emotion as they described the uprooting and flight. Kemal spoke of how his female relatives had been raped, male relatives murdered, and how he had lived a life on the run before seeking exile in Austria. "Kemal Kirkuki," he told us, was actually an assumed name he had taken as part of his cover.

With the overthrow of the regime, the Kurds wanted the Coalition to help families return and rebuild their villages—and to push out those Arabs who had no roots in the province before 1957, the year of the last credible census. Colonel Mayville and I visited the displaced people's camps around Kirkuk and found thousands of Kurdish families living in great poverty. Many were camped out in the city's soccer stadium, taking shelter in its alcoves: toddlers with snotty noses, covered in flies, young wives feeding dozens on meagre scraps of food, old men praying for miracles to protect their families.

We estimated that the population of the province was around one and a half million, half of whom lived in the city. But over the summer, the numbers had begun to increase significantly. We heard of people returning from Erbil and Sulaymaniyah. Rumours spread quickly among displaced communities: "Coalition forces are building houses for the winter," "families in Erbil are offered $1,000 per family to move to Kirkuk," "trucks of the Kurdistan Regional Government will transport Kurds to anywhere in the city of Kirkuk at no cost if they wish to return."

The city of Kirkuk had neither the infrastructure nor the housing stock to deal with its current inhabitants, let alone an influx. We were cautious not to register displaced people for fear it would be construed as offering assistance. We were also concerned not to encourage displaced people to move until a proper return programme had been devised. In one of many requests for information sent to Baghdad, we asked whether the authorities had identified any alternative lands that might be offered to Arabs who had been encouraged by Saddam to move to Kirkuk. Some parties to property disputes expressed a desire and intent to leave the Kirkuk area as soon as such lands became available.

We never received a reply. The Coalition policy was for displaced people to stay put while we developed a legal framework to deal with competing property claims. But it was not clear who had responsibility for organizing this. The International Organization for Migration, an organization initially established to help resettle people displaced in World War II, was contracted to set up a system to handle property claims, but was slow to get moving. The United Nations itself did not want to go near contested claims and preferred to work above the "Green Line," which supposedly delineated the border between Kurdistan and the rest of Iraq. So, inevitably, the US military filled the void.

The legacy of Saddam's policies haunted Iraq. In the government building I found lists of those who had been pressured to leave Kirkuk and the paltry amounts they had received for their homes. Arabs from Kirkuk were reluctant to talk about it. Some claimed the Kurds had "sold" their homes. But for the most part Arabs had stood by passively while the Baath party implemented its policy. The factors that led to the internal displacement of so many Iraqis went right to the heart of the struggle for power in Iraq and the fundamental issues of land, water, oil, minority rights, citizenship, identity and allegiance. No group recognized the grievances of the others. And the CPA had not developed a strategy to address past conflict, manage current conflict and prevent future conflict, nor did it have the political legitimacy to do so. It would not be right to rectify past ethnic cleansing of Kurds by facilitating the forced displacement of Arabs who had moved to the province as part of Saddam's Arabization campaign.

Colonel Mayville had instructed that a room in a two-storey barracks close to his command centre on the airfield be made ready for me. Once installed in my new hooch, I soon developed a regular "battle rhythm." I would roll out of bed at seven o'clock and go to my en suite bathroom. I would catch a drip from the tap to clean my teeth or, if that failed, use bottled water. On the occasions there was water in the bathroom, I would wedge a piece of plastic under the tap to force water to come up through the shower. There was never water for the toilet, so I would have to extend the shower head to the toilet and fill it up so it would flush.

Once dressed, I would make the three-minute walk to the command centre (the Tactical Operations Center, known as the TOC), passing the headquarters of the "Rock" (2-503rd Airborne Infantry Battalion), their rabbits, chickens and three geese named Saddam, Uday and Qusay. The commander of the Rock was the charismatic Lieutenant Colonel Dom Caracillo. He had an almost cultlike following. His executive officer, Major Andy Rohling, could have earned a living as a stand-up comedian.

The TOC was the nerve centre in which the Brigade staff planned and monitored every activity. It contained maps, large plasma screens, telephones. Around twenty staff were seated there at any time in front of their laptops, managing information, including the instructions that came down to the Brigade from the 4th Infantry Division in the form of fragmentary orders (FRAGOs). In the TOC I had been allocated a desk beside the chaplain and next to the army lawyers. I would switch on my computer, log on to my 173rd Airborne Brigade account, and check the news. In the operations room, I would examine the board to see what had happened overnight. I would make the five-minute walk to the chow hall, which was in a huge hanger, to get grits or porridge, and a muffin. At the chow hall, the TV channel AFN (American Forces Network) would be showing on a huge screen, broadcasting subliminal messages. AFN would speak of liberty, freedom and heroism. We would hear tales of great Americans who had served their country over the last three centuries, with their endeavours regaled in heroic terms. There would be commercials about training, about insurance, about fitness—the army took care of all aspects of a soldier's life. Big Brother was watching you, taking care of you.

At around eight-thirty I would go to Colonel Mayville's office to drink tea with him and discuss the day ahead. His office was at the back of the TOC, alongside those of other senior personnel.

After that, Colonel Mayville and I would either head off somewhere together, or I would go alone to the government building. Regulations stated that we should travel in two-car convoys. This was then increased to three. The UK instructed that travel should only be in fully armoured vehicles, but I did not have one in Kirkuk. My car was a white SUV. Usually, Lieutenant Lee served as my "shooter." I was happy to put to use the aggressive driving skills I had picked up in the Middle East. I would hurl the car headlong into the traffic circle, barging our way right across, so as to be as difficult a target as possible for both IEDs and snipers. On the occasions that we were not able to join a convoy, Sarmid, Colonel Mayville's interpreter, and I would travel alone. Sarmid was an American of Iraqi Assyrian origin. He had a pistol, which seemed to make him feel safer. He had been on a short course to learn to shoot.

In the government building, Lieutenant Lee would act as my secretary-guard-aide. He would arrange meetings and screen those seeking to see me. Every day, scores of Iraqis would appear at the office. Many came to request badges and weapon permits. Others offered information about Saddam's whereabouts and weapons of mass destruction in the hope of receiving rewards. Some wanted money, or contracts, or positions. Some just turned up to introduce themselves. A Sufi told me he could heal the insane and could thrust a knife through himself without harm. When he offered to demonstrate, I quickly assured him it would not be necessary. A Kurdish man of the Hamawand tribe, who was nearly blind judging from the strength of the lenses in his glasses, showed me deeds signed by the British nearly a century ago, and told me not to listen to the Kurdish political parties. One man told me he was a Kakai, which was not Shabak or Kurd, and suggested that his people needed a seat on the Provincial Council.

Lieutenant Larry Lee in front of a beautified tank at the entrance to Kirkuk.
Photo by Huseyin Kara

I received visits from different sorts of Christians: Assyrian, Chaldean, Orthodox and Catholic. A group of imams turned up to see me, introducing themselves as Kurds, Arabs and Turkmen, and both Sunni and Shia. After the initial pleasantaries, I asked them how I could help. "You know our needs," one retorted. "America would not have invaded without knowing everything about us and what we need." Seeing that the conversation was not going anywhere, I told them I merely wanted to confirm my assessment. They laid out a list of repairs for their mosques.

The brother of a judge who had been killed by Coalition forces sought "blood money." I was forever receiving requests, usually scribbled on a piece of paper, for the release of individuals from jail. NGOs asked for funds. Farmers turned up requesting new silos, or compensation for damage caused to their crops. There were new directors to be appointed to run the public services; and claims that there were two directors in the same department. Some blamed fuel shortages on the Coalition, accusing us of stealing Iraq's oil. Tribes sought contracts to guard oil pipelines. When I investigated a little, it appeared they were the same tribes responsible for blowing up the pipelines in order to get contracts to deliver the oil by truck.

There were requests for me to reassign buildings which had previously belonged to the Baath party. There were competing property claims stemming from the ethnic cleansing; and reports of what appeared to be pyramid schemes. There were displaced people who desperately needed aid; and there were grumbles about displaced people squatting in public buildings. Many complained about the Provincial Council—that it was useless and not doing anything for the province. Council members grumbled that they had not been paid. The only person who understood how the budget worked was a Christian woman who had been de-Baathified. We managed to get an exemption to bring her back to work. A number of callers asked for the police chief to be replaced, claiming that the Coalition had appointed a taxi driver. Everyone hated the political parties. I received continuous allegations about Kurds taking over control of the province and directing the police. Hundreds of Turkmen outside the government building protested the destruction of a Turkmen Shia shrine, allegedly by Kurdish youths, in Tuz, and demanded an end to "Kurdification." (Tuz was a town fifty-five miles from Kirkuk which Saddam had removed from the province when he redrew the boundaries.) The more Colonel Mayville's confidence grew that I could deal with these complaints and requests, the less he came to the government building, leaving me to run matters there. People wishing to see him would get an audience with me. And I would judge whether he needed to meet them later or not.

Lunch would be brought to my office. It would usually be rice purchased at the cafe in the government building or a sandwich bought from a nearby shop. Occasionally we would splash out and order a meal from a local restaurant: hot *tapsi* (a dish made from aubergines, peppers, onions and tomatoes), kebab, chicken. In Kirkuk there was no shortage of excellent Kurdish, Turkmen and Arab cuisine.

At around two in the afternoon I would head back to the airfield and write reports. At five I would exercise. One of the hangers had been converted into a gym, with an amazing set of fitness machines. At all hours of the day, there would be people working out. Next to the gym, a barber, laundry and tailors were operating. I found a good circuit to run which took me around the northern perimeter, past parked Bradley vehicles, and then for a sprint along the road at the back of my building.

At six-thirty I would attend the Battle Update Brief, or BUB, chaired by Colonel Mayville. Each unit would provide him with a brief report on the day's events, equipment and personnel, the weather, FRAGOs, news and the Commander's schedule for the week. Back in July, the news had been able to focus on Lance Armstrong in the Tour de France, but as the summer went on we were hearing more and more about attacks around the country. Following the BUB, it was over to the chow hall for a usually inedible dinner and another dose of AFN television. Then back to my desk to complete reports and e-mails.

In the evenings I would often sit with Colonel Mayville in his office discussing the state of the province. Our partnership developed into friendship. To my surprise I found myself growing to like the Colonel as a person, and respecting him enormously. I came to realize that behind the bravado was a deep intellect—and a wicked sense of humour. We discovered that we had read many of the same books and poems. But what impressed me the most was his interest in Iraqis. He had decorated his office with artefacts from all the different groups in Kirkuk. Behind his desk was a framed poster of a Frenchman in uniform looking stoic beneath the words *Pour la défense de l'empire*. He had been given it by a French officer early on in his career and took it with him whenever he deployed. When it became clear there were no WMD to be found in Iraq, he was left with the question of why we were here. He found the answer on the poster. On his coffee table were current affairs magazines and Siegfried Sassoon poetry. He could recite by heart Wilfred Owen's poem "Dulce et Decorum Est."

I usually fell into bed by midnight. I managed on average five hours sleep a night. Missiles were lobbed onto the airfield almost nightly, but the area was so large they never found a target and nobody was ever injured. Following each attack, the air force siren would sound telling everyone to go down to the shelter. Air force did. Army did not. I was army and remained in bed. However, the constant sound of gunfire and explosions kept all of us—Iraqis and foreigners—in a state of some nervousness.

I STARTED READING MORE about Iraq's modern history. During the First World War, Britain had led Sharif Hussein of Mecca to believe he would be granted an independent Arab kingdom in return for an Arab revolt against the Ottomans, who had sided with the Germans. Instead, under the secret Sykes-Picot Agreement of 1916, the territory was divided up between the French and the British.

The British introduced a system of direct rule, with districts run by British political officers who reported back to a central administration, similar to the set-up the CPA introduced in 2003. In 1919, the Versailles Peace Conference established the League of Nations, with Mandates for former Ottoman territories. Britain constructed the modern state of Iraq out of three provinces of the Ottoman Empire, namely Basra, Baghdad and, later, Mosul, based on historical antecedents.

News that Britain was awarded the Mandate for Iraq was met with widespread riots, as Shia, Kurds and Sunnis united in opposition to British rule. After quelling the uprisings, Britain introduced a new political system of a constitutional parliamentary monarchy, with a prime minister as head of government and a senate appointed by the king. Britain essentially decided to rule Iraq indirectly through the administrative elites who had served under the Ottomans, the officers who had joined Sharif Hussein in the Arab Revolt, and landowning notables. These people were almost exclusively Sunni Arabs. Those Iraqis who rebelled or refused to pay taxes were bombed into submission by the Royal Air Force. Britain chose Faisal, the eldest son of Sharif Hussein, to be the new king of Iraq (another son, Abdullah, became king of Transjordan).

King Faisal attempted to build an Iraqi national identity through education and the army. He worked hard to integrate Iraq's diverse peoples within the state. This was no easy task. He came into conflict with Sunni elites who wanted to maintain their privileges. He wrote in a memorandum:

"In Iraq, and I say this with a heart torn by agony, there is yet no Iraqi people, but unimaginable human masses devoid of any patriotic idea, imbued with religious traditions and superstitions, connected by no unifying tie, prone to mischief, bent on anarchy, always ready to rise against any government whatever. Of these masses we want, in this respect, to create a people whom we would refine, train and educate."

Although Iraq gained its independence in 1932, Britain maintained advisers to the king, continued training and equipping the Iraqi military, and kept RAF bases at Habbaniya and Shuaiba.

Under the monarchy, Iraq became a modern state with a bureaucracy, an infrastructure and a professional army. But after the death of Faisal in 1933, the monarchy became increasingly isolated from the population and failed to develop the necessary institutions to manage competing and dissenting views, with the military playing a key role in politics and crushing revolts with force. Britain had and intervened to restore the monarchy following the 1941 coup by Rashid Ali. The monarchy's reliance on Britain became an increasing liability, especially after the Suez crisis of 1956. The opposition dominated cultural and ideological thinking in Iraq.

A new generation of Arab nationalist officers emerged in Iraq, inspired by the Egyptian leader Gamal Abdel Nasser. Calling themselves the Free Officers, they overthrew the monarchy in 1958, killing all the royal family. Abd al-Karim Qasim, Iraq's new leader, who was of mixed Arab and Kurdish background, promised to reform and modernize Iraq and create a more just society. The revolution swept aside the old elites and brought a new middle class to power, but there was no agreement on policies. Arab nationalists wanted Iraq to become part of a larger Arab union; leftists focused on domestic issues, urging radical social and economic reforms; and Kurdish nationalists sought greater autonomy.

Qasim was overthrown and killed in 1963. After a series of coups and unstable government, the Baath party initially appeared to offer Iraqis stability when it took power in 1968. It built up a one-party state, expanding the bureaucracy, military and security forces, and bringing all aspects of civil society under its control. Saddam Hussein was the power behind the throne for a decade before he became president in 1979, placing members of his clan and people from his home town of Tikrit in key positions in the security and intelligence services, and creating a new Sunni elite based on loyalty derived from kinship.

The Islamic revolution in Iran in 1979 had a dramatic effect across the whole region. Saddam, concerned about threats to his regime from domestic unrest that he thought were orchestrated by Tehran, attacked Iran in 1980, using the pretext of a border dispute. He believed it would be a short war in which he could assert Iraq's leadership position in the region and his own status within Iraq. The war finally ended eight years later, with no changes in the border between the two countries—and a million dead. Bankrupted by the war, Saddam invaded Kuwait to get concessions from the Gulf States to pay off Iraq's debts and gain access to Kuwait's oil.

Saddam completely miscalculated how the international community would respond. In Operation Desert Storm, the US-led Coalition quickly removed Saddam's forces from Kuwait. However, President George H. W. Bush decided not to march on Baghdad. He believed that the humiliation of the defeat would lead to Saddam being replaced in a military coup, and he called on Iraqis to replace him. Heeding Bush's call, Iraqis in the south and the north rose up and took control of fourteen of Baghdad's eighteen provinces, including Kirkuk. But without Coalition support for the rebels, Saddam was quickly able to suppress them.

ONE AFTERNOON, Colonel Mayville presented me with a gift. *Kurds, Turks and Arabs: Politics, Travel and Research in North-Eastern Iraq, 1919– 1925* was written by C. J. Edmonds, a British political officer in Kirkuk during colonial times. I devoured the book, fascinated by the challenges my predecessor had faced almost a century ago. I told the Colonel that if I ever wrote a memoir about my time in Iraq, I would add a section on "the American tribe." The American tribe tended to have a less tenacious sense of history than the Iraqis, but just as strong an opinion on what was right and wrong, and how the world should be.

The soldiers viewed themselves as liberators and were angry that Iraqis were not more grateful for their liberation. When I arrived, one of the questions put to me was "What do we need to do to be loved?" I told them that people who invaded other people's countries, and killed people who were no threat to them, would never be loved. I said that after the First Gulf War of 1990–91, a decade of sanctions with its devastating effects on the health, education and the economy, and the humiliating defeat of the Second Gulf War, I could well understand why Iraqis were shooting at us. What I found harder to understand was why intelligent Americans would choose to join the army and kill other people in wars which were ideological rather than defensive. I obsessed over how many people they had killed. I would visualize the American soldiers covered in blood. What lives had they destroyed? What damage had been done to them as humans? It was not productive. I realized I needed to see them as they saw themselves.

I asked a number of soldiers why they had joined the army. I heard stories of growing up poor, with the army providing an opportunity to gain an education, to better oneself, to have status in American society. I met many who came from military families. Nearly everyone I spoke to loved the army, was very proud to serve their country and grateful for the opportunities the military provided. Most spoke of their love for America and their belief that their service in Iraq was making America safer. I heard how many Americans had joined up following 9/11. One soldier, however, explained why he had enlisted in more basic terms: "What other job pays you to knock down doors and blow up things?"

Many considered themselves righteous warriors, killing evil and bringing justice. Within the Brigade, I discovered a range of talented individuals. Some had degrees in law, public administration, international relations; some had experience of work in the Balkans. Some were believers in God, America, the War on Terror, the war with Afghanistan and the war with Iraq. Others simply said they had taken an oath to serve and would obey orders as long as they were legal and moral. They lived very disciplined lives, which included time allocated for communicating home and going to mass. The only vice I detected was "dipping," the unsightly habit of chewing tobacco and then gobbing onto the ground or into a water bottle. On the wall of the TOC was a large sheet of paper from a church back home. The congregation had pinned on pictures of the 173rd officers in uniform, with religious messages of support.

Colonel Mayville brought me into his inner circle, the closed club of the army. In response, I rolled up my sleeves, knuckled down and adapted to working within their culture. I mastered the rank structure, the fist bumps, the jokes, the code. I realized that the military was from Mars. But I studied it, found shared values and objectives, and learnt how to work with it. I came to appreciate its organization, its bureaucracy, its leadership and its resources. I found it could be flexible, adaptable and a quick learner. Importantly, the soldiers generally wanted to do the right thing.

Initially I found all the saluting and protocol absurd. But I came to understand the purpose of the etiquette and appreciate its value. It provided a framework in which everyone understood their place in the hierarchy and their role. And as nothing else in Iraq was clear, the transparency of the military command structure was refreshing. In private I addressed Mayville as "Bill," but in public I always addressed him as "Colonel." I copied Mayville's example of addressing all senior American officials as "sir." To my surprise, I found that Americans were much more formal and deferential towards people in authority than Brits were. I had to remind myself that it was totally inappropriate to address senior Brits as "sir"; ambassadors expected me to call them by their first names, and senior British generals were addressed as "General John" or "General Andrew."

My relationship with the Brigade staff was generally good. They accepted my immersion into the Brigade remarkably easily. They realized that the Colonel valued and respected my opinion. Some also appreciated that being in command was lonely and that the Colonel had found a friend in me. However, at times there was tension. "Who do you believe—a West Point graduate or a lying Arab?" one of the officers barked at me when I disagreed with him. I shot back that I did not categorize people in this way. I was red in the face and walked off.

The military could be so frustrating to work with. They had categorized Iraqis, on three-by-five-inch cards, as good guys (pro-America, Kurds) and bad guys (anti-America, Arabs). Good guys got full support: money and love. Bad guys got wrath: "kill or capture." Those we were fighting were classified as the "enemy," or by the abbreviations FRE (former regime elements), FRL (former regime loyalists) and later "insurgents" and AIF (anti-Iraqi forces). I wanted to understand who we were fighting and what they wanted. I tried to argue that how we treated people would affect how they reacted to us. But the military did not do nuance. They broke the world down into straightforward orders and simple tasks. And they were sure they were always right.

I heard soldiers speak with contempt about the Iraqi people for living in "mud huts," wearing "man dresses" and giving "man kisses"; about how being in Iraq felt like being in *Planet of the Apes* or the bar scene in *Star Wars*. The soldiers' only entertainment were DVDs, violent video games and the gym. Colonel Mayville may have been fascinated by Iraq, but inculcating respect for local culture among the soldiers was no easy matter.

I had never been part of something so violent, or something I found so morally dubious. I set red lines for myself. I would never provide information or participate in events that might lead to the death of another human being. But the closer I worked with the Brigade, the more adaptive I became and the more flexible to bringing about changes in a highly imperfect world. The world of destruction and killing was somehow sanitized by abbreviations. Dead and wounded were KIA (killed in action) and WIA. Whether I liked it or not, I was part of the occupation of Iraq. And it was the military that had all the resources. I was motivated by wanting to help improve the lives of Iraqis and to get the country back on its own feet. The ends justified the means, I convinced myself.

SINCE APRIL 2003 the Brigade had been busy running the affairs of the province, reporting on all aspects from security, to fuel, to health and education. By the time I arrived, the military already regarded civilians and their agencies as largely incompetent and impotent and were filling the vacuum, making policy on the hoof. They joked that CPA stood for "can't provide anything." I had appeared in Kirkuk, a British civilian volunteer, supposedly seconded to the CPA, but with no money and very few staff, and was reliant on the army for my basic "life support."

I could not help but marvel at the way in which the military had got stuck into trying to improve the lives of the Kirkukis. They were identifying priority projects in the province, tendering out work to local contractors, and managing large amounts of money. Tank commanders were working on economic development, paratroopers on governance, civil affairs officers on education. They were totally dedicated to the task at hand. I walked into a meeting of the Kirkuk Council to discover an American captain scolding the members for not adhering to *Robert's Rules of Order*. He held a copy of the book in his hand as he lectured them, telling them that if they wanted to speak they must stand up and wait until identified by the chair! Not only, however, were there rivalries between Coalition military units, but also between the military and civilian consultants, most of whom were funded through USAID. All groups were competing against each other for the attention and love of the Iraqis. And the Iraqis quickly learned to play one group off against another.

As THE SUMMER WORE ON, it became clear to Colonel Mayville that he was not leaving anytime soon, that the CPA document which set out positions to be filled by civilians was a fantasy and that "government in a box" (a rapidly deployable team of experts with resources and ready-made systems) was a mythical, not magical, concept. I was not going to be reinforced with a large team of civilian experts, so Colonel Mayville proposed assigning some of his officers to work for me. He agreed with me that the Brigade needed to start rating success not by all the things the military was doing, but rather by what the Iraqis were doing. We needed to empower Iraqis, not to make them dependent on the Coalition. Colonel Mayville issued a revised "Commander's Intent" instructing his soldiers to "Put an Iraqi between you and the problem."

I quickly took the decision not to set up a parallel structure to Colonel Mayville, and instead to use my skills to help the military adapt to working in Kirkuk. We were there for the same purpose: to get Kirkuk back up and running. The close brush with death in my first week in Kirkuk had been an eye-opener. I had breezed through troubled areas before in Asia, the Middle East and Africa. But for the first time in my life, I was in an environment where I was actually a target. I had learnt the hard way that there was no such thing as "humanitarian space" in Iraq. The rationale for going to war was highly contested and so the legitimacy of the intervention was disputed. Any foreigner working in Iraq was viewed as complicit with the US "project" and hence a target.

I invited all the international consultants and NGO staff who worked in the government building, military as well as civilians, to a meeting in my office. We all agreed that the rivalrous way in which we had been working was frustrating, causing unnecessary duplication and resulting in the Iraqis taking the same request to five different offices. I suggested that we turn ourselves into an integrated consultancy agency, providing training, mentoring and support to strengthen Iraqi institutions. Iraqis needed support in local government design; public services delivery; financial management and budgeting; economic development; civil society development; displaced people and resettlement; political processes and democracy development; and safety and security. We decided to call our new organization Team Government.

I ended the meeting, by addressing the group: "Every one of us is an ambassador for the US and the West. It is crucial that we bear this in mind in the way in which we conduct ourselves with the Iraqis." Addressing the military, I said, "Under no circumstances should anyone raise their voice or shout at an Iraqi. Treat them with respect at all times." I had sometimes seen them treat Iraqis as if they were children or badly behaved soldiers.

I was keen to find ways to ensure that the Kirkukis not only were consulted but also were given ownership of the development process. We established the Kirkuk Development Commission to ensure that the leadership of the province was fully involved in setting the strategic objectives for the use of development funds, prioritizing sectors and oversight of project implementation. It was co-chaired by the governor and myself and met twice a month. Reporting to the Kirkuk Development Commission was a cell which coordinated all development projects for the Province. The cell was staffed by Iraqis and supported by Team Government. It identified needs, ensured donors did not duplicate activity, provided details of quality-assured contractors and set rates.

To make ourselves more accountable to Iraqis, we established an office in the government building for Iraqis to register any complaints against Coalition forces.

The novelty for the military of having me living with them had worn off and I had definitely become one of the troops. I even started appearing on the Brigade's organizational chart, reporting to Colonel Mayville, rather than as a separate organization reporting to Ambassador Bremer. No longer did my mere presence serve as a calming factor or raise a smile.

We broke new ground, redefining civilian-military relations. We took pride in overcoming our different organizational cultures to work together to help the province of Kirkuk. Each week I drafted a political analysis on the province which Colonel Mayville submitted, with his signature, up the military chain, and I submitted, with my signature, to CPA

Baghdad. When military officials visited, I played the role of Mayville's political adviser. On the rare occasion when Ambassador Bremer visited, Mayville switched to being my military adviser. It worked well for both of us. I had little contact with the CPA in Baghdad, and none with London. I was left to my own devices to work out how best to carry out my nondefined job, with no one any the wiser.

I COULD NOT BELIEVE my eyes when I first caught sight of General Odierno. I had never seen such a large human being. He almost seemed a different species. His head was totally shaven. His hands were massive. Yet his face was strangely striking and his eyes were kind. Major General Ray Odierno was the commanding general of the 4th Infantry Division and was based in Saddam's home town of Tikrit, in the neighbouring province of Salah al-Din. He was Colonel Mayville's boss. He would regularly appear on Kirkuk airfield, with his entourage scrambling to stay ahead of him, and come to the TOC to be briefed by the Brigade. As the only nonuniformed person and the only female in the room, I stood out. But I was nevertheless surprised when General Odierno turned to me and asked why there was still instability in Kirkuk when the Baathists were either dead or had fled.

"General," I responded, "Kirkuk sits on top of 40 per cent of Iraq's oil reserves—6.7 per cent of the world's. The Kurds need Kirkuk if they are to achieve independence in the future. They have been struggling for decades to incorporate Kirkuk into Kurdistan. Central government in the past tried to prevent this by ethnic cleansing of Kurds and importing Arabs. So the instability is over where the border of Kurdistan should be."

General Odierno looked surprised and repeated back what I had told him. But I was impressed that he kept asking me so many questions. I soon realized that all his focus had been on fighting and winning a war, not on occupying a place as complicated as Kirkuk. I also noted that every time he made a comment, everyone nodded in agreement. Every time he joked, everyone laughed as if it was the funniest comment ever made. Like a Greek chorus. An interesting tribe, I thought.

The 173rd Airborne Brigade, based at Vicenza in Italy, did not belong to any division. In Iraq it had been attached to the 4th Infantry Division, commanded by General Odierno. Over the weeks and months, a deep bond developed between Odierno and the Brigade as they grew to trust, respect and value each other. General Odierno seemed to get a kick out of the relationship between me and Colonel Mayville. Sitting together in his office at the back of the TOC, Colonel Mayville responded to a sarcastic jibe I made about the military with "Go put on your orange jumpsuit!" General Odierno was shocked for a moment. "You make her wear an orange jumpsuit like the Iraqi detainees?" He roared with laughter.

"Sir," Mayville responded, "when she gets too much we lock her in the closet by the side of my desk." General Odierno walked around to examine the cupboard that Mayville was pointing to. Mayville remarked, "I can't even get my arm in there, but she can get her whole body in!" The space was incredibly small, and even I had wondered how I had managed to get in there. (Colonel Mayville had bet me that I could squeeze into his cupboard—and I had proved him right.) The food on the base was so bad that I had become even thinner than normal. I was down to 112 pounds.

To my knowledge, General Odierno never questioned the fact that one of his commanders had incorporated a British civilian woman into an American brigade nor my presence in all the meetings, no matter how sensitive the content. The relationship between military and civilians in Iraq was often tense, as each sought to exclude the other from areas deemed outside their realm. In Kirkuk we were genuinely one team. General Odierno always asked my opinion and treated me as one of his staff.

Whenever General Odierno visited, Colonel Mayville would unload on him all the issues we were facing. The three of us would sit in Mayville's room, or out the back, chatting away, always delaying Odierno's departure. The two men would smoke cigars, seemingly their only indulgence. General Odierno would listen, ask us how he could help, what we needed him to do at his level, what issues could he take up on our behalf at the highest level of the Coalition. Whenever there was trouble he would fly in to provide support. As soon as he walked into the room, we felt a sense of relief. He took the stress off our shoulders and made us feel everything was going to be okay.

GENERAL ODIERNO'S CALL SIGN was "Iron Horse 6." For months, I thought this was because he was so huge. Only later did I discover that it was the call sign assigned to the commanding general of the 4th Infantry Division. Colonel Mayville's call sign was "Bayonet 6." I started hearing people refer to "BB" and was told that it was my call sign—British Babe.

3

"OUR MISS BELL"

So you're the British woman I've heard all about, living on an air-field with thirty-five hundred American paratroopers. How have you managed to cope with them?

—COLIN POWELL TO EMMA SKY, 15 September 2003

How HAD I ENDED UP in such a role—and with an American colonel as my new best friend? I was still somewhat embarrassed to hold such a position. I did not have the qualifications nor the experience for the job. Furthermore, I had come to Iraq to apologize for the war. Now I was sitting like some colonial administrator in the office that before the war had served as the governor of Kirkuk's. I was seen as the new symbol of power, with the force of Colonel Mayville behind me. There were always lines of Iraqis wanting to see me, looking to me to help them mediate their disputes and address their issues.

From the outset, the US was faced with the difficulty of finding legitimate leaders to take charge of the new Iraq. Over the decades, Iraq had lost generation after generation of its middle classes through the effects of war, oppression and sanctions. Some had been killed by the regime, many had gone into exile. Saddam had ensured no local leaders emerged to threaten his rule. And de-Baathification removed those with managerial experience. Those who had been in political parties outside Iraq had no experience of governing and were largely unknown to those in the country.

The US had chosen to rule Iraq directly through the Coalition Provisional Authority. At the urging of Sergio Vieira de Mello, the special representative of the UN secretary general, the CPA had agreed to establish a twenty-five-member Iraqi Governing Council as an advisory body.

Determined to ensure that future leadership in Iraq was more representative of all Iraqi society, ethnicity and sect were made the primary organizing principles for the first time in Iraq's history: thirteen members
of the Governing Council were Shia Arab, five were Kurdish, five were
Sunni Arab, one was Turkmen, and one was Assyrian Christian. But the
focus on subnational identities was at the expense of building an inclusive Iraqi identity. No one at the time seemed to have any foreboding of
the disaster this would bring upon the country.

On the nerve-wracking journey by helicopter to Kirkuk, during which
I was not wearing a seat belt and the doors were left open, I had been
in the company of two women, in their mid twenties, from the CPA
Governance Team in Baghdad. The Brigade had been asked to set up
a series of meetings for them with Iraqi women and I had sat in as an
observer. During the meetings they asked the Iraqi women about their
backgrounds, what they had been doing before the war, what their aspirations were. What I discovered later was that they were looking for a
Turkmen woman to be a member of the soon-to-be formed Iraqi Governing Council. Songul Omar, who headed up a women's NGO in Kirkuk,
was the only one they met who fitted that category. It had not taken me
long to find out that Songul was not popular with other women activists
and that she was a complete unknown within the Turkmen community.
Fearing the Coalition was on the brink of making a terrible mistake, I
went down to Baghdad and lobbied against her appointment. But I was
too late. The decision had already been taken.

Following the advice of the British ambassador, John Sawers, to get
to know the Turkmen, I had spent the intervening weeks doing exactly
that. I had met a broad range of Turkmen from civil society as well as political parties. Turkmen were a minority group in Iraq, and the majority
of them lived in Kirkuk and Nineveh. Around half were Sunni and half
were Shia. Many had become totally integrated into Arab society over
the years and spoke Arabic as their mother tongue. Others spoke Turkmani, a Turkish dialect.

A number of Turkmen turned up at my office to complain of an American conspiracy against them. They were outraged that Songul, a woman
they had never heard of, had been appointed as the Turkmen representative to the Iraqi Governing Council in Baghdad. The month before,

photographs had appeared in the media of Turkish special forces detained by Sky Soldiers on 4 July, with sandbags on their heads and their hands tied behind their backs. The Turkmen viewed this incident as retaliation by the US for Turkey's refusal to allow General Odierno's 4th Infantry Division to use its territory as a launching pad for operations into Iraq. I assured them all that there was no conspiracy and that Turkmen had an important role to play in the new Iraq. But they remained deeply suspicious.

COLONEL MAYVILLE AND I met the Arab Provincial Council members in our office in the government building. The Arabs on the Council had become increasingly exasperated at what they perceived as their reversal in status, victimization and the takeover of the province by the Kurds—supported by the Coalition. Back in May 2003, the Brigade had set up the Provincial Council by allocating six seats to each of the four ethnic groups. The US military then invited three hundred people to participate in the selection of the Council. They were split into their "groups" and told to nominate six people to sit on the Council. In addition, a further six "independents" were selected, five of whom happened to be Kurdish and one Assyrian.

The focus on ethnicity led groups to complain that the Coalition was biased towards the Kurds, since the Kurds had eleven seats, the Arabs six, the Turkmen six and the Christians seven. From the day I arrived in the province, I heard complaints about the Provincial Councils. Kurds, Arabs and Turkmen all argued that they formed the majority in the province. A reliable census had not been conducted since 1957. And there had been considerable forced migration in the interim, so no one knew the ethnic and sectarian breakdown in Kirkuk.

"*Salaam aleikum,*" said each of the Arabs as they entered the room and shook our hands. Colonel Mayville and I quickly emulated their gesture and placed our hand over our heart every time we shook an Iraqi's hand. I still had not worked out how many kisses the men gave each other. Sometimes it seemed to be one on each cheek. At other times it was three or four just on the right cheek. Four of the Arabs were sheikhs and wore white *dishdashas,* with a *bisht,* a light cloak with gold embroidery along the edges, over their shoulders. On their heads they wore a *ghutrah,* a white scarf, held in place by an *agal,* a black cord headband. The other two wore suits.

The Arabs took their seats around the table. *"Allah bil kheir,"* one said. *"Allah bil kheir,"* everyone responded. Sarmid, the American Assyrian Iraqi, was there to translate. A young Iraqi man, who worked in the government building's coffee shop, served everyone *chai* in small thin glasses balanced on saucers. Colonel Mayville started the meeting by assuring the group that there was no conspiracy to give Kirkuk to the Kurds. As always, Sheikh Ghassan al-Assi of the Obeidi tribe was the first to speak. He responded, "Colonel Mayville, you speak nicely, but nothing is ever achieved." He said the situation was not good. The Arabs were putting great pressure on their Council members, saying that they had got nothing through the Council. He urged the Coalition not to erase the Arab presence in Kirkuk. Kurds were in every police station, hospital and school. There were now three powers in Kirkuk: the Coalition, the KDP and the PUK. The Arabs recognized the Coalition, but did not find it acceptable for Kurdish political parties to assert authority over Arabs.

Sheikh Ghassan said Kirkuk was the real issue and the Coalition had to "open doors to the Arabs" and make them feel welcome. Sheikh Wasfi al-Assi, who was not on speaking terms with his nephew Sheikh Ghassan, took up the baton: "Before Allah, and under international law, Coalition forces are responsible for Iraq. Actions speak louder than words."

A pained look came across Colonel Mayville's face. He threw his hands up in despair and said he was very upset to have so disappointed his Arab friends. Sheikh Ghassan shook his head from side to side, smiling as he said, "Colonel Mayville, you are the commanding officer, a wise man, and importantly a friend."

Sheikh Agar Nezal al-Tawil described in theatrical detail how he himself had been arrested, "thrown on the wires" and beaten up by the Coalition. He was a tall thin man, with a short-cropped grey beard and appeared to be in his sixties. The only Shia Arab on the Council, his origins were somewhat of a mystery. His mother was apparently from the area, but his father was not. He always wore traditional robes. He was forever coming to see us and would greet Colonel Mayville enthusiastically, kissing him on both cheeks.

He complained that the Coalition had entered Arab houses and con-fiscated the weapons they kept for their own protection. Thousands of Arabs, he claimed, were being detained on the airfield for no reason, and he requested they be released as a "goodwill gesture." Kurds were now in all the important positions in the city and "they do not even speak Arabic!" The police were his greatest concern. He said the police force in Kirkuk had become an army of three thousand Kurds.

Sheikh Agar paused at the end of his sentences for me to write down what he was saying. Nodding towards me, he grinned and said, "Our Miss Bell." I quickly realised he was referring to Gertrude Bell, who had served as the "Oriental Secretary" for the British High Commission in Baghdad, playing a major role in establishing the modern state of Iraq af-ter the First World War. Sheikh Agar extolled the wisdom and knowledge of the British, and how they worked so well with the tribes, and how they had invested in Iraq's infrastructure.

The Arabs complained of the injustice being done to them. "The whole Province is unjust," Colonel Mayville responded. "There has been injustice for thirty years. Look at Chemical Ali's house, with the skulls in the ground," he said referring to Saddam's cousin, Ali Hassan al-Majid, who had been responsible for leading the campaign against the Kurds in the late 1980s and gained his nickname from his use of poison gas. The only people causing violence at the moment, the Colonel believed, were Baathists, former regime loyalists and mercenaries from outside. They were not here because of injustice in the past. They were here to attack the Coalition and destroy everyone's lives. They were attacking Iraqis as well. There was no money in Iraq because Saddam had bled the country dry. Iraq was barely exporting half a million barrels of oil a day, which was not even enough for the streetlights of Baghdad. All the money had gone on palaces, marble and forts. There was no money to put people on the payroll.

The meeting ended. They all got up, shook hands, declared "fi aman Allah" (may God protect you) as they left the room. But not long after-wards, Sheikh Ghassan and Yehiya Hadidi stopped turning up to the Pro-vincial Council meetings in protest at what they perceived as the Kurdish takeover of the province.

ON ONE OCCASION in August, Colonel Mayville and I sat in our office in the government building discussing the situation in Kirkuk. I listened closely to his thoughts on what was required to prevent conflict breaking out in the province. I suddenly turned to him and said, "What you are describing is some form of 'special status' for Kirkuk." His face lit up. *Yes*—that was what Kirkuk needed. I drafted a paper headed "Kirkuk: A Challenge for the Coalition," and sent it down to Baghdad.

As it happened, soon after this Ambassador Bremer was unexpectedly delayed on Kirkuk airfield for a couple of hours. We took him on a tour of the ancient citadel. There was still time to kill. I discovered that his staff had not given him my paper, so I presented him with a copy. As we waited in the air-conditioned car for his helicopter, he read the paper with me sitting next to him, watching nervously as he wrote comments on particular sections. He then asked me more about special status and requested that I write a short paper outlining exactly what it would entail.

I quickly produced another paper and sent it to Baghdad. I argued that the "Kirkuk issue" could derail the national discussion on the Constitution. There was real potential for conflict within the province, which could easily spill over into other parts of the country and encourage the involvement of external actors. Some form of special status could defer the determination of Kirkuk's final standing for five years to provide the time and space to resolve the issues, the strengthening of local leadership capability and economic development.

I received a summons to appear before Bremer. Getting to Baghdad from Kirkuk was no easy matter, as transport was in heavy demand. However, Major Bill Ostlund had found a way through the red tape by having me classified as an "ambassador." This meant that whenever I needed a helicopter, they managed to find me one. I discovered this ruse when I heard the pilot say, "Good morning, Ambassador" after I had climbed on board, strapped myself in and put on the headphones. There were no other passengers in the helicopter, so I realized he must be speaking to me. I pressed the button which allowed me to speak. "Good morning, pilot, how are you?" "Couldn't be better, ma'am," he responded. "Another glorious day in I-raq."

We landed in front of the Republican Palace and I went straight to the front office. A number of the Governance Team were invited, as was

Sir Jeremy Greenstock, whom I met for the first time. He had recently arrived in Iraq as the UK's special representative. He was described as the greatest diplomat of his generation and had previously represented the UK at the United Nations. The moment came and we all walked into Bremer's office. It was a modest-size office, with a large wooden sign on the desk that read SUCCESS HAS A THOUSAND FATHERS.

Bremer indicated for me to sit on his left and told me to put the case for special status. Discussion then flowed back and forth. Greenstock set out the conditions that needed to be met if a region was to be granted such a status. One of the conditions related to whether there was the support of the local population. I was convinced there was. However, the Governance Team members said that special status recognition for Kirkuk might internationalize the problem and bring in other external players. They also felt that special status should only be given in a crisis situation, and would send out the wrong political message at this time. Their arguments prevailed.

I grabbed a couple of gin and tonics to drown my sorrows at a reception before walking from the palace to the helicopter landing zone. Once I had climbed on board, belted myself in and put on the headphones, I was apologetically told by the crew that my departure time was delayed because Secretary of Defense Donald Rumsfeld was due to depart shortly. Annoyed at losing the argument over special status, and chancing my luck, I told the crew that I was in a hurry to get back to an eight o'clock meeting in Kirkuk with Colonel Mayville. "Understood, ma'am," the pilot said. Within minutes we were airborne, looking down on Donald Rumsfeld as he made his way towards his helicopter.

AS THE WEEKS PASSED, intolerance of the Coalition presence was growing around the country, particularly among those who felt excluded from the new Iraq. Attacks against Coalition forces were on the increase. On 19 August 2003 the headquarters of the UN in Baghdad was blown up, killing over twenty people including Sergio Vieira de Mello, the Special Representative of the secretary general. The UN had been specifically targeted. Tributes flowed, testifying to the extraordinary talents and reputation of de Mello—a life led in search of peace and justice around the world, yet truncated in the most violent manner.

On 29 August, Ayatollah Mohamad Baqir al-Hakim was assassinated in Najaf in a massive car bomb explosion which killed over a hundred Iraqis. He was a prominent Shia cleric, the leader of one of the main Shia political parties, the Islamic Supreme Council, and the brother of Iraqi Governing Council member Abdul Aziz al-Hakim.

Nor was the Iraqi Governing Council helping matters. It was reviled for being a puppet of the occupation as well as for its high representation of Islamists and exiles, with links to both Iran and the US. The new leaders were determined to ensure their total control of the state, despite having a limited domestic constituency. They lobbied the CPA to carry out broad de-Baathification to punish those who had cooperated with the former regime and to prevent their return to public life. CPA Order No. 1 of 16 May 2003 stipulated that all those in the top four ranks of the Baath party should be dismissed from their jobs and never allowed to hold public office again. Apparently, the architects of this policy in Washington had studied the experience of Germany in 1945 and regarded de-Nazification as a model. The CPA handed over responsibility for de-Baathification to an Iraqi commission, headed by Ahmed Chalabi. He then politicized implementation, giving exemptions to Shia but not to Sunni Baath party members. Far more Iraqis were affected by the policy than the CPA had originally intended. As a result, many Sunnis were becoming alienated from the new Iraq and felt they were being collectively held responsible for the crimes of Saddam because he was a Sunni.

ONE MORNING IN SEPTEMBER, Provincial Council member Sheikh Wasfi al-Assi came to tell me that 540 teachers from Hawija, southwest of Kirkuk, had been expelled from their positions. His office was always brimming with people bringing their problems to him. He would then bring their issues to me. De-Baathification was taking up much of our time. I informed Sheikh Wasfi that the Coalition was no longer involved in de-Baathification and that this was now an Iraqi process. Responsibility for de-Baathification had been moved to a committee headed by Ahmed Chalabi. Sheikh Wasfi looked at me incredulously.

"If the current resistance could succeed in pushing Coalition forces out of Iraq, I and my family would join in," Sheikh Wasfi admitted to me. Increasing numbers of Sunnis were taking up arms. But Wasfi believed that attacks on the Coalition were actually prolonging the Coalition's departure.

I felt powerless. I had sent report after report to CPA Baghdad on the effect of de-Baathification in the province. But there had never been a response. The people sitting in CPA Baghdad did not have to meet the men and women in Kirkuk who could not feed their families or pay their rent. They did not feel the devastating impact of this order on people's lives. They also did not seem to realize the impact the order was having on communal relations. In the province of Kirkuk, de-Baathifcation was particularly problematic as it increased ethnic tensions between the Arabs and Kurds. It had become a witch hunt, rather than a means of achieving justice for past wrongs. It was important to remove those Baathists who were guilty of crimes against humanity. But there also needed to be some mechanism for reconciliation. If we placed large numbers of people outside the system with no means of supporting their families, this would only lead to unrest.

Colonel Mayville and I agreed that as the occupying authority we had a responsibility for ensuring that children could receive an education. I went back to the Fourth Geneva Convention. In it I found articles which set out the responsibility of occupying powers to ensure that children had access to education, and the illegality of prosecuting people for opinions they had held under a previous authority.

General Odierno understood that if de-Baathification was implemented in the areas under his control there would be hospitals without doctors and schools without teachers. The people would revolt. Without reference to higher authorities, he issued an amnesty to all level-four Baath party members in the three provinces he was responsible for in order to get teachers and doctors back to work. His decree quickly found its way into Arabic and was widely waved around.

But the payroll was controlled from Baghdad. Systematically, all those with Baath party membership in levels four and above had been removed from the payroll even if they had been granted exceptions by the Coalition or by the Kirkuk de-Baathification office. Quietly, however, the Brigade brought the teachers back to the schools, paying their salaries for a couple of months out of military funds charged to a budget item labelled "Janitors." But once those funds ran out, there was no way to pay them.

WE STARTED TO RECEIVE indications that foreign jihadis had entered the area, bringing with them their intolerant and extremist views. Fliers began appearing at the government building, warning of how the "infidel" West was spreading seeds of sectarianism and sedition against the Iraqi people.

In order to allay fears, Mayville decided to put out a media statement. I came across the "Proclamation of Baghdad," issued to the inhabitants of Baghdad on 19 March 1917 by Lieutenant General Sir Stanley Maude shortly after the occupation of the city by British forces. I showed it to Mayville and within an hour we had re-addressed it "To the people of Kirkuk Province." As Colonel Mayville pointed out, it was a "timeless" speech, and barely needed editing. We too claimed we had come "not as conquerors but as liberators." Colonel Mayville increased the presence of the US military in the streets because there was concern about the capacity of the local forces.

A STREAM OF SENIOR American officials, both military and civilian, visited Kirkuk in these months. British officials tended to go to Baghdad and Basra, where British troops were based.

Lieutenant General Sanchez, the overall commander of Coalition forces in Iraq and General Odierno's boss, visited us in midsummer. Colonel Mayville and I drove out onto the tarmac to meet him. We took him to the police headquarters to be briefed on the development of the Iraqi police force when he suddenly asked me how much money the CPA had invested in the province. I blanked and looked to Colonel Mayville for help, but he was unable to bail me out. I told General Sanchez I would get back to him on this before he left. I had written details of CPA projects in my brown Filofax which I had left behind in one of the cars. There were so many different projects. Millions were being spent and new Iraqi currency was arriving bubble-wrapped on pallets. It seemed that every time we spent the millions assigned to us, the pot was refilled—until it wasn't, and we were left strapped for cash.

We took General Sanchez on a tour of Kirkuk by car. He was impressed to see shops open and markets full of people. I started to explain the issues of Arabization and displaced people, outlining the need for careful strategies to manage expectations and maintain stability. Sanchez turned to me and asked, "What's the corruption like?" Disliking his insinuation that Kirkukis were corrupt, I responded. "Sir, the American soldiers aren't too bad." There was deadly silence. We drove on for ten minutes with no one talking, until the one-star general turned to Sanchez and said, "Sir, I think she was joking." Sanchez, relieved, turned round to me and grinned. I tried to grin back. The day couldn't get any worse.

Sanchez wanted to know what major projects needed funding in Kirkuk. We told him about the airport, the sewage systems, the Mullah Abdullah power plant and the railway, as well as schools, health centres, the government building and the cement factory. I wanted to describe how political disputes led to violence. But all General Sanchez wanted to hear about was projects and money spent. He spoke to us of the challenges in different parts of Iraq and the conditions necessary for the withdrawal of US forces. We were left slightly perplexed by his visit. Was he planning to withdraw the Brigade, or certain battalions attached to the 173rd? He was hard to read. But of one thing we were sure: he had a limited sense of humour.

Not long after, Bremer and US secretary of state Colin Powell stopped briefly in Kirkuk to change aircraft on their way to and from Halabja. Colonel Mayville and I had the task of escorting them from the C-130 to the helicopter in the morning; and from the helicopter to the C-130 in the afternoon.

"Thanks, Emma, good of you to turn up," Bremer said.

"No problem, sir, it's my job."

"You could have sent the protocol officer," Bremer responded.

I smiled. I wondered how many staff he thought I had.

Colin Powell had great presence and radiated warmth. He joked with Mayville about parachuting into northern Iraq, the appalling weather and the gutsy decision Mayville had taken at the last moment to jump. He had watched it all from the US.

Colin Powell came over to me. "So you're the British woman I've heard all about, living on an airfield with thirty-five hundred American paratroopers," he said as he shook my hand and kissed me on the cheek. "How have you managed to cope with them?"

I shrugged my shoulders and laughed in response. I thought back to when I had been the only girl in an all-boys' boarding school. It was somehow very familiar, except that these American soldiers were a lot more civilized than those British boys had been.

AFTER MY THREE MONTHS had come and gone, the British Council e-mailed to tell me I was needed back at work. I explained that I could not leave Iraq—I had important responsibilities in Kirkuk, that this was a critical time for Kirkuk and that there was no one to replace me if I left. They told me to stop exaggerating, and return as soon as possible. As requested, I had submitted an article about my work in Iraq to the British Council in-house magazine. But it had been rejected on the grounds that it would offend staff members to discover that someone from the organization was involved in the occupation of Iraq. They had agreed to second me to work on civil society development, not to be a "colonial" administrator.

I was hugely irritated by the British Council's response. I was working all hours of the day, using all the skills and knowledge I had gained whilst working for them, but they were completely uninterested. I made a quick trip back to the UK to plead with them to let me remain in Iraq for a bit longer. They acquiesced.

I was relieved to return to Iraq. I had worried constantly about the province during my week away. I worked my way through all my new clothes which I had brought back with me from the UK, as I had initially only packed for the summer. I handed the pile to Huseyin Kara to take to the laundry he had found in town, which washed, pressed and neatly folded my clothes much better than the military facility on the airfield. Kara was a Turkish-born Kurd and an American citizen, and one of the most saintly people I had ever come across.

He nervously approached me a few days later to tell me that the launderette had been blown up and my clothes destroyed. I was sure that some had to be salvageable. But not a single item ever returned. Kara raided the military stores and decked me out with brown T-shirts, brown fleece shirts, and black silk undershirts. He also got me a pair of US desert boots and a black fleece jacket, on which was sewn the 173rd patch. My wardrobe became almost military.

Kara took me out into Kirkuk city one afternoon. We ate in a restaurant and then walked through the market. It felt great to escape the cage from which I viewed Iraq and plunge once more into the Middle East, inhaling deeply the smells of coffee and vegetables, and feasting my eyes on the colours and peoples. We sat in a clothes shop drinking tea, and asked the owner about his daily life and how things differed from the Saddam era. I wanted to hear how people viewed the occupation, the governor and the Provincial Council. Kara and I walked for miles, discovering new sections of the city. We were delighted to come across a very old section of town, walking down narrowing, twisting alleys, surveying the beautiful old houses. The inhabitants in this area were mostly Turkmen, with a heritage dating back centuries. This was the first of a number of occasions when Kara and I escaped from the military and became tourists in Kirkuk.

ONE MORNING IN OCTOBER, Tahseen Ali and Abbas Bayati came to see me in my office. Abbas Bayati was a regular visitor to my office and I very much valued his counsel on how to achieve what he referred to as "balance" in Kirkuk. He was a Shia Turkmen, the leader of the Islamic Turkmen Union. Tahseen, the chair of Kirkuk Council, belonged to his party. Bayati had described Iraq as suffering from a lack of national identity. It would take a decade, he had told me, to establish political parties not based on ethnicity or religion. Smiling broadly, he had said the problem originated from the way in which the British set up the state of Iraq, favouring "one group"—the Sunnis—over all the others. He had suggested that Kirkuk could be a pilot for developing processes which went beyond ethnicity and religion.

"*Shlunkum? Shaku maku?*" (How are you? What's up?) I asked them. They sat down, their faces wracked with concern. They said there had been a terrible mistake: one of the members of their party, a Turkmen Shia and a close friend, had been arrested by Coalition forces and was being held on the airfield. His name was Hashem Jaafar and he was a Dutch citizen, the representative of the Islamic Union of Iraqi Turkmen in Holland and an opposition leader for twenty-three years.

Promising that I would do my best to sort things out, I went back to the Brigade to gather information. I was told that Hashem Jaafar and eight associates had been arrested while digging fighting positions near Tuz. Sky Soldiers had been attacked and injured from these positions in recent weeks.

I saw Tahseen again a few days later. The US Air Force hosted a show, "Tops and Stripes," to which I was invited along with the Council members. The gym was converted into a theatre for the evening and we were given front-row seats as guests of honour. This was a rare experience; no other entertainment had been organized on the base in the four months I had been there. The performance began. The dancers appeared: air force men and women whose role was to entertain the troops. Men in tight trousers, women in short skirts. The women paraded before us in the front row, flipping up their skirts as they danced and flashing their knickers. They jumped up onto the waists of their male partners.

To a Western audience it was mildly titillating. To a Muslim it was pornographic. I looked around me at the Council members. Tahseen sat staring at his knees, unable to look up. And then the whole row got up and walked out, with me following along behind. Outside in the cold air, many of them rushed for cigarettes. I apologized profusely, dying of embarrassment. "This is not our culture," one said to me. "It's not mine, either," I responded. "It is kind of the Coalition to invite us, but please don't invite us again," a Council member said.

Out of respect for our relationship with Tahseen and Abbas, and as a goodwill gesture for Ramadan, Colonel Mayville instructed that Hashem Jaafar and his team should be released, and asked me to oversee the process. I drove over to the detention facility, which was at the edge of the airfield. I had never been to this area before and needed to get directions. I passed a building, outside which men in orange jumpsuits were sitting on the ground behind a wire fence. I went up to the grill gate and asked whether anyone called Hashem Jaafar was there. A voice called out and a man came to the front. I introduced myself, telling him that Tahseen Ali and Abbas Bayati had facilitated their release. The soldiers let the group out of the holding cell. We went to another room, where they signed for their belongings and their cars.

Hashem Jaafar stood before me in a dirty *dishdasha*. Why had he been arrested, he asked angrily. Why had he been held for fifteen days in such conditions? He felt utterly humiliated by the experience. I explained that he had been found digging what looked like a fighting position. "Do we look like a bunch of terrorists?" he asked me. I looked around at his motley crew of workmen, a mixed group of Arabs and Turkmen, who wore rags and flip-flops. "Do terrorists drive a BMW?" he exclaimed, pointing at his car parked beside the building. I didn't know how to respond. What were terrorists supposed to look like? I looked down at the list of names I was holding in my hand. One name stuck out: Saddam Hussein. "We thought we had Saddam Hussein," I said. Suddenly the atmosphere changed. They all burst out laughing, pointing at Saddam Hussein, a one-eyed young man in his early twenties.

A few days later, Tahseen and Hashem came to see me in the Government Building. Hashem was wearing a smart suit, with a stylish yellow and green tie. On one hand he sported a ring with a large blue stone. I apologized once more for what had happened, and the meeting was cordial. Hashem told me of the hopes he had had for the new Iraq—he had been visiting from Holland with the intention of investing in the country. It had all gone so horribly wrong. All he wanted now was to get home to his family.

THE NAME OF Abdel-Fatah Mousawi was increasingly heard around Kirkuk. There was talk about his sermons at the al-Husseini Mosque, about fliers put out in his name and instructions issued to people demanding they appear before his Islamic court. I knew little about Mousawi other than he was a young Arab Shia from Najaf, a follower of the firebrand preacher Muqtada al-Sadr, and that he had arrived in Kirkuk after the war. Muqtada al-Sadr had been excluded from the Iraqi Governing Council and feared that he and his followers—the poor, downtrodden Shia working class—would be marginalized in the new Iraq. He was determined to oppose what he viewed as the nefarious designs of Kurdish nationalists and Shia Islamists who were aligned with the Coalition.

Muqtada stood accused of ordering the assassination of Abdul Majid al-Khoie, the son of one of the most highly respected spiritual leaders in the Shia world, in Najaf in April 2003, a week after his return to Iraq following a decade in exile in the UK.

Colonel Mayville and I decided in October that it was time to visit Mousawi in the al-Husseini Mosque. Sheikh Agar, who frequented the mosque, agreed to take us. He brought me one of his daughter's *abayas* and gave it to me as a gift. We climbed out of the car and I covered myself up in the *abaya*, much to everyone's amusement. Sheikh Agar beamed approval. "You are my daughter," he said. It was the only time in Kirkuk that I covered myself.

Opposite the mosque, two pieces of paper were pinned to a wall: DO NOT LET THE OCCUPATION FORCES APPOINT PEOPLE TO WRITE THE CONSTITUTION. YES, TO ELECTIONS and WE WANT A CONSTITUTION WRITTEN BY IRAQIS AND WITH IRAQI IDEAS—NOT FOREIGN. We walked through the door of the mosque, removed our boots and entered a modest room where we sat cross-legged on the floor, near Abdel-Fatah Mousawi.

Mousawi, who looked very relaxed and appeared to be in his mid twenties, said he was exerting every effort to preserve stability: "It is in my power and capability to maintain security. All listen to me and receive their guidance from me." "The US superpower," he continued, "favoured the Kurds in everything that it did." The governor was a Kurd. The chief of police was a Kurd. Arabs had been dismissed from their jobs. Arabs and Turkmen lived in jeopardy in Kirkuk, threatened and attacked by Kurds. Kurds were writing RESERVED and FOR SALE on the walls of Arab houses.

Colonel Mayville responded that there were many people in government who were not Kurds. The ethnic representation was much more balanced than people believed. He acknowledged that there was currently an imbalance in the police force. The Coalition was checking the payroll and it would be fixed. He said he saw the Kurdish flags, signs and names, and this upset him. The Coalition was committed, he assured Mousawi, to ensuring stability in Kirkuk and to dealing with all groups equally.

Mousawi waited for Colonel Mayville to finish. Kirkuk, he replied, had suffered from thirty-five years of injustice. The levels of security were now below zero, with Kurds coming in from Erbil and Sulaymani-yah. Everyone was fearful that they could be killed at any time. People wished for Saddam to return because of the low standard of security. But based on the teaching of Islam, they were required to treat all fairly. Kirkuk would not be taken over by any one group. "We love everyone created by Allah," Mousawi concluded.

The meeting lasted for well over an hour. We felt it had gone well. We had been welcomed into the mosque and had achieved a level of under-standing. Over the next weeks we received orders to arrest Sadrists. We always made an exemption for Mousawi. We took the decision that it was better to try to work with him for as long as we could.

We never met Mousawi again. However, not long after the meeting a man came to see me at the government building. He introduced himself as Mudhafer Yas, a messenger from Mousawi. Mousawi would not be able to meet directly with us again. After the last meeting, people had made up stories which were reported back to Najaf, the city south of Baghdad that is the centre of Shia Islam in Iraq. It was difficult to speak out against the occupation and then to be seen meeting with us. But Yas would meet me in secret, and Mousawi and I would be able to commu-nicate through him.

Yas spoke highly of Mousawi. He said that Muqtada's father, Moha-mad Sadiq al-Sadr, had created a generation of young religious men with the courage to remain in Iraq and to stand up to Saddam. Before he was martyred, Sadr II had built up a mass movement among the urban poor as well as the neglected rural and tribal population. Yas explained that the Shia leaders had not called for jihad during Saddam's time as they did not want people to be butchered for nothing. Iraqi blood was the most important commodity in Iraq. Yas described Muqtada al-Sadr as a brave man similar to his father. "Jaysh al-Mahdi [Muqtada's Shia militia] is a group of capable honest men who could run the city," he said. "They are not involved in killing or fighting."

Yas was a religious Shia Arab. He was well read and spoke good En-glish, although he had never been to the West. He was originally from Baghdad, but his family had moved to Kirkuk in 1988 as housing was much cheaper there. His father was a poorly paid teacher. Yas had studied at Baghdad University and currently worked as a computer programmer.

He had been in the Iraqi Army at the time of the war. After the fall of Saddam, everyone had thought the country would be "lovely." Now they found gambling and pornography in the streets. They had never expected it to be like this.

Yas returned a week or so later with a question from Mousawi: how long did someone have to live in Kirkuk to be considered a Kirkuki? He said that the people who had moved to Kirkuk had done so because they were poor, not because they believed all the lands in Iraq were for the Arabs. I said that, in the UK, people had the freedom to live wherever they liked by virtue of being a citizen. However, in the Middle East people were considered "new" if they did not have family origins in an area dating back over a century. I hoped that in the new Iraq people would be able to live wherever they chose.

On another occasion, Yas said that Mousawi wanted to know what I thought a Baathist was. It was an interesting question. I said that in some places around the Middle East I had observed that the dominant political party and the public administration were inextricably linked and were in effect one and the same. It was important to distinguish between those who were cogs in the system and those who committed crimes against the Iraqi people. Yas appeared to be satisfied with this answer.

DR. ISMAIL ABUDI came to see me to express his concerns about unemployment in the province. He was the director of the Employment Office. I had heard a lot about Ismail Abudi before I met him. He was a religious Shia Arab, who Provincial Council members wanted sacked for speaking out against the local government, and who US officers in the Brigade suggested we should arrest. Ismail complained that the Kurds were sending down teachers from Kurdistan, while Kirkuk had hundreds of unemployed teachers. He warned me that if I did not resolve all these matters he would lead the thirty thousand unemployed people on a demonstration against me. Having said his piece, he left the room. He made no attempt to be friendly.

Despite the hostility of our initial meeting, I asked to see Ismail again and tried to build a relationship with him. I explained our efforts to ensure open and fair recruitment for jobs and about the discussions going on with Baghdad about decentralization. I asked him about his plans for the Employment Office. We had lengthy discussions on how to link training to the job market and how to bring down unemployment. He was always brimming with ideas.

Ismail discussed the mistakes the Coalition had made. He said the Coalition had not carried out its promises to the citizens. The people had not seen improvements in electricity and water, and this was leading them to sympathize with every missile fired at the Coalition. If the situation continued, the Coalition would lose the street. Ismail said he worked for Allah and for His satisfaction. It was difficult for him to work with the occupying army and for people from a different religion. Before the invasion, all they knew about America was that it was the Great Satan. The badge he had to wear as a public-sector employee had the US flag on it and hence showed that he was an "agent" for the Americans. This was difficult for him.

I told him that I too did not like having to wear a badge with the American flag on it. I said I was not normally an "occupier" and that the focus of my work before coming to Iraq was on poverty elimination across the Muslim world. But my current job meant I had to work with Americans. And I was getting to know them as people. I had travelled to many countries and had come to realize that people were basically the same. Everywhere I had seen people struggling to earn a living to provide for their families. I believed in a common humanity. Ismail nodded and quoted to me from Imam Ali: "If you are not my brother in religion, you are my brother in creation."

ONE AFTERNOON IN OCTOBER, Colonel Mayville and I wandered around Kirkuk museum. We found that all that remained were the broken frames which had once housed the exhibits. The Colonel was down, with the loss of one of his soldiers weighing heavily on him. He had known Lieutenant David Bernstein well. Bernstein was a West Pointer, and a great athlete, renowned for his swimming. I had met him once—the day before the ambush in which he was killed. Colonel Mayville shared with me his doubts about everything we were doing, the loss of life and the impossibility of succeeding. To cheer him up, I said, "I bet you fifty dollars that we can get this museum up and running before the end of the year." He smiled and shook hands, accepting the bet.

The museum had apparently opened at this site in 1989 when the Ministry of Culture had established eight museums across Iraq. It was set within the complex of a walled two-storey barracks dating back to 1864. Facing onto a grand courtyard were cloisters which had once housed soldiers of the Ottoman Empire.

We decided to hold a cultural event to mark the reopening of the museum. Colonel Mayville and I fantasized that the cloistered rooms would one day be converted into artists' studios, as part of a municipal arts centre. I also hoped that trees would be planted in the courtyard bearing plaques to remember the young Sky Soldiers who had lost their lives in this "corner of a foreign field."

I tasked Major Heyward Hutson with the project. A space to the right of the museum, framed on two sides by the courtyard walls, was selected for conversion into a theatre. Over the next weeks, the ground was levelled, tiles laid down and an awning put up. At the far end, a platform was erected to serve as a stage. The director of the museum contacted people from all the communities to exhibit within the museum artefacts they held at home or elsewhere. There was a good response. Musicians from the different ethnic groups were approached to put on performances on the opening night.

Drawing up a guest list was no easy matter. We sent out invitations to the governor and deputy governor and all the members of the Kirkuk Council; the mayors and town councils around the province; the police chief and senior security officials; the heads of departments; the religious leaders; and the business community. Few responded, so we had no idea how many would turn up. And while most were unlikely to bring their wives along, some might. In addition to all this, we had to ensure effective security—the event would be a prime target for a terrorist attack.

The reopening of the museum took place on schedule on 23 October. Colonel Mayville and I entered the museum together. Where before it had stood derelict, it was now brimming with exhibits and buzzing with people. In each room, someone was on hand to explain the exhibits: an Arab sword, an Assyrian bible, a Turkmen painting or a Kurdish leather

Sculpture created in front of museum. *Photo by Huseyin Kara*

basket. In the Kurdish room, a wedding was being enacted, and people of all different ethnicities observed it with great enjoyment. Outside, we witnessed the unveiling of the sculpture. It was magnificent: a design depicting Kirkuk's multi-ethnic heritage and the crafts, agriculture and industry for which it was famed. The sculptor explained to the audience what each part of the piece represented. They were suitably impressed.

Colonel Mayville and I moved to the head table to join the governor, deputy governor and chair, as well as some of the members of the Kirkuk Council. General Odierno arrived from Tikrit to share the occasion with us. The food was brought out and we began to eat. We had commissioned the al-Qasr Hotel to produce Iraqi food, reflective of the tastes of all four ethnicities.

During the meal, the musical entertainment began. I recognized a voice on the microphone and looked up to discover that the Colonel's interpreter, Sarmid, had assumed the role of master of ceremonies. The first act was a Kurdish dance troupe, which rushed onto the stage in wonderful costumes. They sang traditional songs, one moment acting out harvest scenes, the next flirtations between boys and girls. Once on the stage, they didn't want to leave. I saw Sarmid go around the back and signal vigorously for them to come off.

Next on were the Assyrians. They wore feathers in their hats, and moved more sedately around the stage as they sang and danced. The Turkmen played the oud, with a singer reciting traditional songs which many in the audience knew.

Last on was the Arab group. The first part of their show consisted of a blind man in traditional clothes seated at the back of the stage, singing. The final part of the show was the traditional *dabke*, a dance loved by all four ethnicities, where men linked arms or hands and made small steps back and forth as they moved round in a circle.

I looked around. The audience was clapping and singing, as were the policemen stationed along the walls. Everyone was enjoying themselves. Ismail Hadidi, the Sunni Arab deputy governor, stood up and approached the stage. Kemal Kirkuki, the Kurdish council member, whose body bore the scars of eleven bullets, got up with him and hand in hand they went onto the stage and joined the dancers. They were joined by Turkmen, then other Kurds—all dancing together. The Arab singer sang songs in Kurdish and Turkmani. Suddenly, Colonel Mayville got up and went up onto the stage to join the dancers. The governor, Abdul Rahman Mustafa, jumped up, grabbed the microphone and declared, "This is Kirkuk! This is what Kirkuk is all about: it is a city of four ethnicities who speak each other's languages and love each other's cultures."

By the end of the week, the artefacts had been taken away and the museum was once again empty. However, the memory of that wonderful night at the museum would for ever be etched in my mind. It showed the wonders and potential of this most amazing province—the Kirkuk that all wanted to imagine. And on that evening, it seemed so right that Kurds, Arabs, Assyrians and Turkmen should be dancing hand in hand— and that an American soldier was with them.

4

SCRAMBLE FOR KIRKUK

Kirkuk is famous for Turkomans, fruit, and crude oil, all of which abound. The town, which must have a population of at least 15,000, is one of the trilingual towns of the Kurdistan borders. Turkish, Arabic and Kurdish are spoken by everyone, the first and last being used indifferently in the bazaars. Itself a Turkoman town, to its south and west are nomad Arabs, and to its east the country of the Hamavand Kurds.

—ELY BANISTER SOANE, *To Mesopotamia and Kurdistan in Disguise* (1912)

The CPA in Baghdad was totally consumed with its own affairs and unable to compute, let alone deal with the challenges in the provinces. And each governorate coordinator felt that their province was the most complex and critical to Iraq's future. This had become clear in early September 2003 when I had gone down to Baghdad with General Odierno to attend the Commanders and Coordinators Conference. The meeting had taken place in the al-Rashid Hotel. All the governorate coordinators from the other provinces and the most senior generals were seated in a square.

At the meeting, Bremer had laid out the Seven Steps on the path to Iraqi independence. Three steps had already been achieved: the establishment of an Iraqi Governing Council, the naming of a preparatory committee to determine how to write the Constitution and the appointment of Iraqi ministers to run day-to-day government operations. The plan required that a Constitution be drafted and ratified. And that national elections be held prior to the formation of an Iraqi government—a sequence likely to take a couple of years. Bremer also identified two success criteria: a decentralized government with devolved powers, with a centre setting policy guidelines; and a vibrant private sector. In his hand, Bremer held an inch-thick document that he said was the strategic plan for achieving our goals.

Major General David Petraeus, the most articulate of the generals, was the first to respond. He asked how it was possible for us to be presented with a plan to implement when none of us had been consulted on it. He did not receive a reply. In the absence of guidance from the CPA, Petraeus had been busy governing the northern province of Nineveh in the way he saw best, earning the nickname "King David," and even conducting his own foreign policy. Seated beside Petraeus at the meeting was my counterpart in Nineveh, Herro Mustafa, a multilingual American of Kurdish origin.

The timetable Bremer had laid out in September had proved too slow for Washington—as well as for the Iraqis. Members of the Iraqi Governing Council were already positioning to consolidate power.

Senior US officials kept visiting to gain "ground truth," increasingly concerned about what was happening in Iraq. We were told that Paul Wolfowitz would visit Kirkuk in late October. "Wolfie," as we referred to him among ourselves, was deputy secretary of defense, one of the most prominent of the neoconservatives and a leading advocate of the war. And it was he who had promised that the war would be self-financing, as Iraq would be able to pay for its own reconstruction. Although the numbers would later be increased upwards, Iraq was estimated at the time to have 112 billion barrels, the fifth-largest proven oil reserves in the world. But as we had quickly discovered, production was well below capacity because the infrastructure needed modernization and investment. And insurgents kept blowing up the pipelines.

Colonel Mayville met Wolfie on the airfield and took him to Kirkuk market in a Humvee with a significant escort of soldiers. Wolfie was able to get out of the Humvee, walk in the street and speak with the locals. I was waiting at the museum. I introduced him to a group of Sunni clerics—Arab, Turkmen and Kurd—who were seated outside around a table. The clerics made their usual gripes.

Before leaving, Wolfowitz made some snide comments to me about the CPA. Apparently, he did not think we should be administering Iraq. He had supported handing the country over immediately to Iraqis, in particular Ahmed Chalabi, who remained the darling of the neoconservatives.

Hillary Clinton visited Kirkuk. She asked Iraqis astute questions and took a genuine interest in their issues. A number of the Brigade officers expressed surprise that she was so impressive. She was a breath of fresh air compared to the numerous congressional delegations that had visited us. One senator had kept asking the Iraqi Provincial Council members, "Have you seen Sad-dam?" I wondered how on earth he had ever been elected.

Shortly after, Secretary of Defense Donald Rumsfeld visited Kirkuk. He came to the TOC for a briefing. A picture taken at the meeting was used by *Time* magazine to feature "The American Soldier" as Time Person of the Year. General Odierno tried to run through a series of Power-Point slides, but Rumsfeld kept interrupting, shooting questions at him. How many soldiers in theatre? How many killed? How many wounded? He turned to the map of Kirkuk and northern Iraq and asked, "Where is Iran?" I had hoped he knew that sort of thing. And why was he asking? Was that the next adventure?

Bremer was summoned back to Washington for discussions. Suddenly, out of the blue, the Seven Steps were replaced by the 15 November Agreement. It provided a speeded-up timetable that called for the negotiation of an interim constitution, a transitional national assembly that would be chosen by provincial caucuses rather than by ballot, and a transitional government to be selected by this assembly. The entire process was to be completed by mid 2004.

However, the 15 November Agreement quickly ran into opposition from Grand Ayatollah Ali al-Husseini al-Sistani, the highest *marja al-taqlid* (source of emulation) for Iraq's Shia, who rejected the caucus suggestion. The UN secretary general dispatched Lakhdar Brahimi to Iraq to mediate a way forward. Brahimi brokered an amendment to the agreement, which eliminated both the caucuses and the transitional assembly, in favour of a UN-appointed interim government to replace the CPA at the end of June 2004. Bringing forward the date of the transfer of authority intensified pressure in Kirkuk, with the Kurds in particular seeking to make as many gains as possible while the Coalition was still around. The "scramble for Kirkuk" had begun.

RAMADAN PROVIDED a change in tempo. Colonel Mayville ensured that his soldiers were briefed about the Muslim holy month, and instructed not to smoke, eat or drink in front of Iraqis during daylight hours. Work hours in the government building were now 10 a.m. to 2 p.m., as Iraqis stayed up late at night, and rested during the afternoon. Most people seemed to fast, but I noticed a few who sneaked a cigarette or a cup of tea.

We were determined to do the right thing for Ramadan. We hosted *iftar* (the meal at sunset which breaks the fast) for the Provincial Council, mullahs and children. We gave donations to mosques. We also released some of the detainees we were holding, including two of Sheikh Wasfi's relatives. And we accepted invitations from our Kirkuki friends to their houses to break the fast with them.

One evening we went to a local orphanage that we visited from time to time. We sat in the dining room with the children, eating the *iftar* of kebab and salads, which we had paid for. After the dinner, we distributed the presents that had been sent out by the soldiers' families, keen as ever to support our efforts. It was wonderful to watch the children's faces light up, loving the attention and gifts. Mayville naturally fell back into the role of father, playing with the kids.

The trust between Ismail Abudi and myself grew. And it was through Ismail that we learnt more about the Shia Arab community of Kirkuk, many of whom had been brought to Kirkuk under the Baath's Arabization process. They were dubbed the "10,000 dinar" families, the sum they had received to move to Kirkuk. During Ramadan, Ismail took us to the area of al-Hussein, a "10,000 dinar" tenement. It was an eye-opener. We had driven past on numerous occasions, but had never actually entered the area. It was run-down and densely populated. Kurdish families were squatting in the school building and there was nowhere for them to be moved to. The local children were therefore unable to go to school, and there was no bus to take them to schools elsewhere. In one hallway, a man lay very sick. We broke fast with one of the families there, sitting with them on the floor to eat the array of foods that had been prepared for *iftar*.

We knew the relationship between us had been cemented when Ismail invited Colonel Mayville and me to his own house for *iftar*. He lived in the poor Kirkuk neighbourhood of Hozerain in a modest home, where we met his wife and children. We discovered that he had a doctorate in nuclear physics and at one stage had been a successful businessman with links to Uday Hussein. But he had fallen foul of Uday, and had had to flee the country to Syria, leaving behind his family.

Not long after the *iftar*, Ismail Abudi's secretary rushed into my office and told me that he had been walking with Ismail to the government building to meet me when a car had drawn up and three people, who he believed to be Kurds from their accents, grabbed Ismail and drove off with him. Colonel Mayville and I were very concerned. We drove over to Ismail's house and, trying not to raise suspicion, asked his wife whether she had seen him. She had not, and thought he was still at the Employment Office. We went to his office, to find it closed and the staff gone. We went to the Kirkuk Bureau of Investigations to see if they had snatched him. We then went to the KDP and PUK headquarters. Colonel Mayville told the Kurds that Ismail was important to us and that we wanted him released unharmed. Both Kemal Kirkuki and Rizgar Ali had heard that Ismail had been captured but claimed they did not know by whom and said they would investigate.

We had done everything we could and now waited nervously. I kept thinking of Ismail's young wife waiting for him to come home, wondering why he was late and why we had come round to the house. The next day at the government building we received the news that Ismail was free. He came to the office to see us, looking shaken and nervous. I was so relieved and pleased to see him that I ran forward, hugged him and kissed him on the cheek. He laughed in surprise and embarrassment, shook his finger at me, and told me never to do that again!

ONE CRISP NOVEMBER MORNING, towards the end of Ramadan, we drove to Erbil and from there north-east to the airfield at Bashur. It was here that Colonel Mayville had led the Brigade in the parachute jump back in March. We got out of the car and walked along the airstrip. The airfield was surrounded by mountains, stretching up into clear skies. Colonel Mayville told me how they had dug latrines facing the mountain to the north and would squat looking up at the stunning view. To the west, he pointed out a village and then a castle. We walked on, then

suddenly he stopped. This, he told me, was the exact location where he
had hit the ground.

The weather had been terrible on the day, and there had been rain
for weeks. At the last moment, there had been a break in the cloud and
Colonel Mayville had led the jump. A thousand Sky Soldiers had jumped
out of the planes after him, floating down to land in the vicinity of the
airfield. Everyone who had done the jump always described the mud.
With mud up to their waists, some were stuck for hours trying to dig
themselves out. It was weeks before they had the opportunity to get dry,
showered and change clothes.

I asked Colonel Mayville why he had ordered a jump and not landed
the planes. Was it bravado? Was it the opportunity of a lifetime to lead
such a jump? He took me to the side of the airstrip, showing me that it
was not built to withstand the weight of heavy aircraft. There was evidence all around of the ground subsiding. Based on the information he
had about the airfield, and the location of Saddam's forces, he had calculated that a third of his soldiers should jump; the rest should come
afterwards, landing in planes.

US special forces had been operating in that area for a while, had
secured the airfield and made contact with the Kurdish leadership. Masoud Barzani came to meet Colonel Mayville on the airfield, greeting
him as a liberator. The Kurds had realized that this time the Americans
were serious about removing Saddam.

Being shown Bashur by Colonel Mayville meant a lot to me. It was
part of the 173rd's experience that I had not shared. After a few hours, we
drove on through the stunning mountainous terrain of Kurdistan, which
reminded me of the north of Morocco, heading down unpaved tracks
past villages on the Lower Zab river to Taq Taq, following the route that
some of the Sky Soldiers had taken towards Kirkuk. I wished we did this
more often. I wished we had more time to explore this beautiful land.

ON 14 DECEMBER, Colonel Mayville and I went with the governor of
Kirkuk to the village of Taza to help mediate a land dispute. News of the
capture of Saddam Hussein broke just before the meeting and the atmosphere was one of intense excitement. The PUK claimed to have caught

him in Hawija. But we didn't pay much heed initially, as we constantly received reports, which we dubbed "Elvis sightings," of Saddam driving a taxi, or in a car, or near Hawija . . .

By the time we returned to base, however, the news of Saddam's capture was running on all the satellite stations. Bremer appeared on TV saying, "Ladies and Gentlemen—*we got him!*" At last, Saddam had been caught. For nine months he had evaded capture, making the Coalition look weak and keeping Iraqis fearful that he might return.

The next day I flew to Tikrit where I connected with General Odierno, to travel on with him to the monthly Commanders and Coordinators Conference in Baghdad. On the helicopter, we chatted using our headphones. He told me that after months of searching, his troops had found Saddam down a hole near Tikrit in view of the palace where General Odierno was based. Saddam had apparently emerged from the hole proclaiming, "I am the President of Iraq and I wish to negotiate." I told General Odierno how proud we all were that it was he and the 4th Infantry Division who had got High Value Target No. 1, the Ace of Spades. With a straight face, I said to him, "Sir, I was most surprised to see you on TV giving Saddam a medical inspection." He looked at me quizzically for a moment, and then the helicopter started to shake with his laughter. The whole world had got to see the back of a large, bald-headed US soldier inspecting Saddam's eyes, ears and hair. It could well have been General Odierno!

We landed in the Green Zone. As we entered the conference room for the meeting, General Odierno was greeted as a hero. Everyone stood up clapping, rushing forward to shake his hand and to have their photo taken with him. He would for ever be known as "the General Who Caught Saddam." It was General Petraeus and the 101st who had killed Saddam's two sons, Uday and Qusay. But the biggest prize was always going to be Saddam.

In my weekly report to Bremer, I noted that in Kirkuk the news of Saddam's capture was greeted with great enthusiasm and celebratory gunfire, resulting in the deaths of half a dozen people and the wounding of around a hundred. The morale of Americans in Washington and Baghdad soared. After so many setbacks, this was a major success. But on the ground, none of the challenges we were facing had disappeared.

THE KDP HELD A LUNCH in Erbil to express gratitude to the 4th Infantry Division for its efforts in liberating Iraq. It was a splendid affair, with vast quantities of delicious food. The table was covered with lamb, rice, kebabs, salads. Given the fare we were served on the airfield, these feasts were greatly appreciated. Masoud Barzani sat at the centre of the high table. While his advisers often wore suits, he was always dressed in traditional clothes when in Kurdistan: *kurtak u sharwal* (baggy trousers, jacket and cummerbund) with a red and white *jamadani* (turban). When we had all eaten, Barzani rose to his feet and gave a short speech: "I remember the first time I saw Colonel Mayville. He descended from the sky like an angel."

The Brigade had jumped into Iraq in March 2003. They had believed they were going home when I first met them in July. But their end date had never formally been set—and it was only towards the end of the year that they heard they would go home in February 2004, nearly a year after they deployed. Fatigue and stress had taken its toll. The Brigade had been working at an incredible pace, month after month, expecting that having fought the war they would soon be brought back to Vicenza in Italy. The senior staff had no leave, no weekends, no time out. And back home, their families had to continue without them. The men missed a year of their children's lives, and went through an experience in Iraq that would be difficult to ever describe to their families.

Colonel Mayville was tired and his thoughts had turned to departure. I would find him in his office, sitting in silence staring at boats sailing across the ocean on the satellite TV in his room. Preparing to leave and getting into the mindset for going home after all these months was hard.

I spoke to a number of soldiers about how they felt about leaving Kirkuk now that the end was finally in sight. Many were going through personal crises as they thought of returning home and fitting back into their families. Some worried about how they would feel towards their wives. Others were concerned at whether their wives would understand their need for space and to be alone. A soldier's life in Iraq had its responsibilities and stresses. But it was also simpler than the complexities of life back home. Some acknowledged how much they would miss being with each other in Kirkuk. They would for ever be changed by their experiences in Iraq.

Meanwhile, life on Kirkuk airfield was not easy. Now, in winter, it was cold and wet and there was mud everywhere. I spent many an evening with Major Vincent and Sergeant Oliver, the public affairs team, where we would drink Gatorade, share snacks and be terrorized by Sergeant Oliver's kitten. Sergeant Oliver had some DVDs of the old 1970s TV series M*A*S*H*. One episode in particular stuck in my mind. The Korean War medics were freezing, and huddled around a heater. The most valued possession of all was a pair of long johns, which was traded for a high price. By this stage I too had acquired military long johns thanks to Huseyin Kara.

The block I lived in had been without electricity for weeks. The military police, who also lived in the building, did not want to complain for fear of appearing weak. Every night I would venture back to my barracks, climb up the stairs and collapse into bed. A miniature flashlight provided a small green beam, just enough for me to find my room and bed. There was no hot water. The dirt in my room accumulated from the desert dust and the mud of combat boots. Dust also gathered over my desk in the TOC. The sergeant major put up a sign saying he was holding my mail hostage until my desk was cleaned. The threat had the desired effect.

On Christmas Eve, twenty-four-year-old Sergeant Michael Yashinski electrocuted himself while trying to mend the electricity supply, and fell off a building to his death. I went to the Sky Soldier chapel for a carol service and then to the airstrip. On a cold winter's evening, soldiers lined up in formation on the airfield to perform the ritual of putting the body onto the ramp and into the plane.

It was in December that the demonstrations had started. The first one was supposed to be against terrorism, with a sizeable group of Kirkukis gathering in the square outside the employment office. I grabbed a lift to the square and mingled in the crowd. The organizer of the demonstration lamented the fact that the event had changed into a show of strength by the Kurdistan Democratic Party. Colonel Mayville and I went to see Kemal Kirkuki in the KDP office and advised him to get in touch with the Patriotic Union of Kurdistan immediately to apologize for what had happened before the PUK took some form of retaliatory action. The competition between the two Kurdish political parties was intense.

Days later, another demonstration took place outside the government building, attended by around two thousand Kurds, including women and schoolchildren. The demonstration, a joint KDP-PUK affair, was billed as a celebration of the arrest of Saddam, and there were placards calling for him to be hanged. A city fire engine, driven by a policeman, was at the centre of the demonstration, covered in banners and carrying demonstrators. Kurdish flags (red, white and green with the sun at the centre) were everywhere, along with pictures of Barzani and Talabani. There were also some American flags on display. Banners declared that Kirkuk should be part of Kurdistan; deported Kurds should come back; Chamchamal, Khanakin, Kifri should be part of Kirkuk. Rizgar Ali of the PUK and Kemal Kirkuki of the KDP addressed the crowd in Kurdish. But the governor was not to be swayed. He spoke in Arabic and stressed the importance of Kirkuk as a city of brotherhood, home to four ethnicities.

I left the government building and went outside to where the demonstrators were gathered. However, I refused to go on stage to accept the petition in case it seemed as if I was agreeing to Kurdistan's annexation of Kirkuk.

Colonel Mayville was so angry with the PUK and KDP antics that he refused to attend the PUK Christmas party. He insisted that Coalition members would only attend if other ethnicities were also present. I went along with Mayville's deputy, Lieutenant Colonel Randy George, and some other members of the Brigade. We entered a large room crammed full of people. Suddenly over the microphone I heard a voice in English declare, "We welcome the coming of our mistress, Emmasky," pronouncing both my names as one word like most Kirkukis did. I was ushered to the high table and sat down. Immediately, members of the Kirkuk Council joined me at the table, with Sheikh Naif of the Arab Jabour tribe sitting down next to me. He grinned and brought out a bottle of whisky from beneath his robes for us both to drink. I was soon merry. And it didn't take long for me to be called up to join the men as they danced around in a circle hand in hand. Various men I knew—Arab, Kurd, Turkmen, Assyrian—came forward to dance next to me. Round and round we went, laughing, singing along, all enjoying the party. This was how Kirkuk *could* be.

At 10 a.m. on 31 December, a crowd of around three thousand Arabs and Turkmen gathered in a square in Kirkuk. Many old Iraqi flags were visible, with the red, white and black tricolour, with the *takbir* ("God Is Great" in Arabic) supposedly in Saddam's handwriting between the stars of the Baath party. There were also blue Turkmen flags. There were banners declaring Arabs and Turkmen were one; and "one country, one people, no ethnic federalism." I grabbed a lift with Major Vincent, the public affairs officer, to see how the demonstration was progressing. Most of those gathered began dispersing at around 11 a.m. to head home. However, around three hundred demonstrators decided to move towards the government building. They were a fairly young crowd, well organized, with leaders ensuring that people stayed in groups.

Colonel Mayville and I had met up at the government building, with Ismail Hadidi, the deputy governor, Tahseen, the chair, and Sheikh Wasfi, when the demonstrators arrived. Some of the demonstrators moved quickly past the government building, heading down a street that had been blocked off with concertina wire. Soon after, we heard shots close by and received reports of casualties.

I felt terrible. Sheikh Wasfi had begged me not to allow the demonstration to take place, warning there could be trouble. I had met repeatedly with the Arab and Turkmen organizers to try to dissuade them. They had told me they needed to show that Arabs and Turkmen existed and had their rights; and that they had to react to the Kurdish demonstrations. Colonel Mayville and I weighed up the arguments, and in the end we had decided to let the demonstration go ahead.

Colonel Mayville called a meeting of the leadership of the political parties and tribal leaders for a frank discussion of the day's events. "If we banned demonstrations," he said, "people would not have the opportunity to express themselves, so it would be no different from Saddam's time. But today the message of innocent people was lost in the gunfire." Four people had been killed and twenty-four wounded. The day would be remembered as one of violence between ethnic groups. Colonel Mayville urged the leaders to work together to prevent the province descending into civil war.

That evening, New Year's Eve, the chow hall was converted for a party. The TV channel CNN Türk, Turkmen and Turkish newspapers were all invited along to witness the soldiers of the 173rd Brigade partying with Turkish special forces (who were now resident on the airfield) in order to improve the Coalition's relationship with Turkey. The Sky Soldiers put on an Oscar-winning performance. So after a day managing ethnic tensions and demonstrations in town, Colonel Mayville and I saw in the new year wearing funny hats, blowing whistles and drinking non-alcoholic "near" beer.

On New Year's Day, Colonel Mayville increased the presence of US soldiers in the streets to help calm the situation. He was livid at the false statements the Kurdish leadership had put out, claiming he had agreed to redraw the boundaries of the province and to remove all the "new" Arabs. Thanks to the BBC monitoring service, I received a daily readout of the media of all the groups. He told the Kurdish leaders that their behaviour was destabilizing the province and provoking attacks on US soldiers. He insisted they should each have only one political office in Kirkuk—like the other political parties. We suspected that they were using up to a hundred or so innocuous sounding civil society organisations as fronts for political activity.

A few days later, Mayville ordered the Brigade to conduct "'compliancy" inspections of Kurdish organizations across Kirkuk. In an inspection of the Kurdistan Midget Society, Lieutenant Colonel Caraccilo removed rocket-propelled grenades (RPGs) from the building. "There were no small arms here," he quipped.

I HEARD THAT Ambassador Bremer was coming north to visit Jalal Talabani and Masoud Barzani and that he would stop by Kirkuk to have lunch with us. Sure enough, Bremer's helicopter landed around lunchtime. General Odierno, who had arrived moments earlier from Tikrit to provide us with support, met him at the ramp, and Colonel Mayville and I greeted the party at the door of the TOC as we had not managed to get to the landing zone in time. Bremer was accompanied by Sir Jeremy Greenstock and Ambassador Ron Schlicher, who had recently assumed responsibility for northern issues. He also brought with him two members of the Governance Team: Meghan O'Sullivan and Roman Martinez.

Colonel Mayville and I sat side by side. We had agreed the brief beforehand and that I should lead with him in support. I started by framing the problem: "The Kurds are seeking to redress thirty-five years of ethnic cleansing in the Coalition's time frame. But the Kurdish drive to make Kirkuk part of Iraqi Kurdistan is rejected by Arabs and Turkmen—and leading them to seek allies in Turkey and Syria."

Colonel Mayville expanded: "The rapid return of the Kurdish community and the degree to which they influence provincial affairs is creating a backlash among non-Kurdish communities." He described how our strategy locally was to engage the diverse communities in Kirkuk and facilitate political dialogue, while developing a common framework for security and peace. At the national level, Kirkuk was a political football, with Erbil and Sulaymaniyah on one side and Baghdad on the other. "The Coalition acts as a referee," he said, although in practice it was "refereeing in hell."

I explained Kurdish tactics. The Kurds had assumed senior public-sector posts in the province, taken control of Kirkuk's security apparatus and had established a shadow government. They had rolled out Kurdish mother-tongue teaching, removing non-Kurdish students from previously mixed schools. They were encouraging Kurds to return to Kirkuk while at the same time pressuring "new" Arabs to leave. And they were pushing to restore the pre-1976 borders of the province. All of this was aimed at ensuring an overwhelming Kurdish majority in the province so they could annex it to Kurdistan.

Bremer asked about the Christians in Kirkuk. Although they were fewer in number than other communities, I told Bremer they had high representation on various committees, as other groups perceived them as neutral and often accepted them as compromise candidates. Iraqi Christians were one of the oldest continuous Christian communities in the world. Prior to the first Gulf war, there were an estimated one and a half million Christians in Iraq. But harsh sanctions in the nineties had pushed many to emigrate and by 2003 their numbers had halved.

Bremer then asked for recommendations on the way ahead. I proposed that the CPA in Baghdad work with senior Iraqis of all backgrounds to get their commitment to Kirkuk as a multi-ethnic community. I urged that we help Iraqis agree on the mechanism by which Kirkuk's future would be determined; and that we develop a strategy for the return and reintegration of displaced people as well as the restitution of property. On a local level, I said that we would continue to build bridges between the communities so they understood each other's perspectives and concerns. We needed to assure everyone of the Coalition's position as an honest broker.

The brief went well and Colonel Mayville and I were pleased to have this final opportunity to raise our concerns about Kirkuk at the highest level of the Coalition. At the end of the meeting, Bremer asked me to join his Governance Team in Baghdad as his adviser on Kirkuk. It was Mayville who had initially suggested to me that I go work on northern issues for Bremer in Baghdad. He had raised the issue with General Odierno. Mayville knew that I wanted to stay in Iraq. But neither he nor I wanted me to remain in Kirkuk after the Brigade departed. General Odierno, Ron Schlicher and Greenstock all beamed—they had done the groundwork to put the idea into Bremer's mind. I shook his hand and accepted. I had mixed feelings. After so much independence in Kirkuk, I was not looking forward to the constraints of Baghdad. But I would have the opportunity, I calculated, to push for the necessary national policies for Kirkuk.

OVER A THREE-MONTH PERIOD, I had held a series of negotiations with the various constituents to identify ways in which we could achieve a better "balance" on the Provincial Council. "No change" was not an option. On my desk, I had a petition supposedly signed by ten thousand people requesting that the Council be dissolved. Mayville and I had decided to keep all the current Council members, but add representatives from the different towns in the province. I hoped this move towards geographical representation might lessen ethnic tensions. There was no way of pleasing everyone in Kirkuk—but I believed that all would be able to live with the new arrangement.

Songul Omar, the Turkmen member of the Governing Council, waltzed into my office one afternoon. She claimed that Bremer had told her she needed to spend more time in Kirkuk to counter the perception that the Governing Council in Baghdad was out of touch with the people.

She demanded a house in the centre of Kirkuk, an office and funds for her NGO. Much to my concern, she announced that she herself was going to oversee the replacement of the current governor of Kirkuk. I told her that I had received loads of complaints about the Governing Council in general, and her in particular, from all over the province. Did she want me to pass these back to Bremer? She stared at me for a moment and I glared back. Then she shook her head, and walked out.

On 14 January, the evening before the refreshing ceremony of the Council, Colonel Mayville and I had dinner at the al-Qasr Hotel with the governor, deputy governor, chair and other community leaders. We had initiated this custom in midsummer, and had brought them together every couple of weeks to discuss the difficult issues that Kirkuk faced. It was the last time we would provide such a forum. As we sat enjoying the food and the conversation, I looked around the table at people I had come not only to trust and respect, but whom I cared about deeply. With tanks on the streets and Sky Soldiers out in force around the government building, the refreshing ceremony went smoothly. It took place in the freshly redecorated auditorium, with dignitaries from across the province in attendance.

I had drafted a speech for General Odierno to give. Bad weather prevented him from making the ceremony, so Colonel Mayville delivered it instead. He spoke of how he remembered standing in this very auditorium eight months ago swearing in the Council for the first time. What a different place Kirkuk was back then, when smoke still hung in the air. Saddam was now in jail and his supporters were defeated. People were going about their normal lives. Now the Kirkuk Council was being expanded to include new members representing all the towns in the province.

Colonel Mayville commended in particular the governor and deputy governor, saying they had worked tirelessly and had shown great leadership. He started clapping. The audience joined him, enabling me to "confirm" that they had received the necessary two-thirds endorsement the CPA demanded.

The chief justice swore in the governor and deputy governor, as well as the thirty-six Council members. Although we were keen to stress that all areas of the province were now represented on the Council, the communities still viewed the representation by ethnicity, with the revised

Colonel Mayville with the refreshed Kirkuk Provincial Council. *Photo by Heyward Hutson*

Council having twelve Kurds, nine Arabs, eight Turkmen and seven Assyrians. Four seats remained vacant.

For Colonel Mayville and myself the refreshing of the Council marked the culmination of our work together in Kirkuk. It was the end of our partnership and time to say farewell.

The Sky Soldiers began their handover to the 2nd Brigade of the 25th Infantry Division. It was difficult watching another brigade take over. Would they care for the Kirkukis as much? In the TOC one evening at the Battle Update Brief, Colonel Mayville stood up and spoke of all the work I had done, absorbing daily the complaints and conflicts of the Iraqis, and managing all the problems of the province. I got up and looked around the room at the soldiers I had worked so closely with over the last seven months. I said that I had never worked with any military before, let alone the US military, and that they were not as bad as I had feared. It had, in fact, been a great experience. Wars, I said, were terrible things, but I was pleased they were fought by people such as them, with their values and their sense of humanity. Afterwards, the soldiers filed by, shaking my hand and wishing me well for the future.

BEFORE STARTING MY NEW JOB, I took a week's leave back in the UK. In my house in Manchester, sitting in front of the wood fire, I was exhausted and emotionally drained. I felt so changed by this experience. I had gone to Iraq to contribute to peace-building help. And I had found myself working alongside the US military—and liking them. All my beliefs and assumptions had been challenged. I thought I would be apologizing to every Iraqi I met for the wars, hypocrisy and sanctions. Instead, I had found myself received by Iraqis with open arms and kindness. As soon as I set foot in the country, I had faced moral ambiguities on a daily basis. I was not a critic on the side, but a player in the arena, with all the challenges and compromises that entailed. But I would not have missed these last months for anything. It had been so hard and extreme, and I was only too conscious of how much more needed to be done.

When I had arrived in Kirkuk, I had quickly assessed that the way I could be most effective was through influencing the US military, rather than operating separately from them. Working with the 173rd had been so different from anything I had ever experienced. I had loved every minute of it. Colonel Mayville had brought me into the heart of his Brigade, giving me the opportunity to see the army from within, and to understand how it saw itself. I had had to learn to work in such different ways, to compromise, to pick which battles to fight. The Sky Soldiers had ensured I was fed, secured and transported. They had given me the platform from which to operate. And Iraqis who met me understood that the weight of the US Army was fully behind me. With the Brigade, I felt I had seen the best an organization can be in terms of its ability to learn and adapt—and the best of America, in terms of the quality of the individuals who put on uniform.

IN EARLY FEBRUARY, I took up my job at the Republican Palace in Baghdad. But I drove back to Kirkuk for the Transfer of Authority ceremony. I passed through Tuz, Daquq and Taza, and once again felt the tingling sensation on my lips from the flared gas as we approached Kirkuk city. The Iraqi security forces walked tall, proudly wearing their new uniforms. They were manning the checkpoints and patrolling the streets. Not a US soldier was to be seen.

I joined Colonel Mayville for dinner at Pierot Talabani's. Pierot lived in a lovely old house, next to the Talabani mosque. It had been in the

Mayville, Sky and Huseyin Kara watch dawn break at Baba Gurgur. *Photo by Robert Cornejo*

family for decades. He was a nephew of Jalal Talabani and had been jailed under Saddam for a short while. Neither he nor his sisters Hawry and Peri had ever married. A delightful family, they made us feel as if we were genuine guests in their country, not occupiers. Pierot had prepared a feast and it was fitting that Colonel Mayville should spend his last evening in Iraq at their house.

The next morning, Colonel Mayville and Huseyin Kara picked me up at six o'clock. We drove out to the Eternal Flame of Baba Gurgur. The burning flames, caused by an emission of natural gas from the rocks, had been around for centuries and were even mentioned by Herodotus. It was here that oil was first discovered in Iraq in 1927. Together we watched the sunrise over Kirkuk. We stood there drinking tea, staring at the flames and the landscape of Kirkuk that we had come to know so well.

The Transfer of Authority took place mid-morning on 19 February on the airfield. All of our Kirkuki friends came for the event. The 173rd stood in formation, alongside Iraqi security forces and the 2nd Brigade of the 25th Infantry Division. General Odierno, Colonel Mayville and Colonel Miles sat on the podium. Out of respect for General Odierno, the Brigade had put up a large patch of the 4th Infantry Division, with Airborne over the top of it—it symbolized that the orphan brigade had come to accept him as their adoptive father.

General Odierno described the achievements of the 173rd. They had parachuted into northern Iraq—the jump was the longest combat operation in airborne history, over eighteen hundred miles from Vicenza to Iraq. And to their airborne wings they could now add a gold star, known as a "mustard stain." The Brigade had lost nine soldiers during the deployment, with ninety-five wounded in action. General Odierno read out the names of the soldiers who would not be returning home: Sergeant Sean Reynolds, Corporal Justin Hebert, Specialist Craig Ivory, Specialist Kyle Thomas, First Lieutenant David Bernstein, Private First Class John Hart, Private First Class Jacob Fletcher, Sergeant Joseph Minucci II, Sergeant Michael Yashinski. General Odierno made special mention of my work with the Brigade, saying this had been a model in civil-military relations.

Colonel Mayville welcomed his successor, Colonel Miles, wishing him well for the future in the province of Kirkuk. He paid tribute to me. By this time I could not keep back the tears. I sat watching the casing of the colours of the 173rd. When it was over, Colonel Mayville, General Odierno and I went to sit at the back of the TOC for the last time, the two men smoking cigars. I walked Colonel Mayville over to the car that would take him to the plane. We said goodbye.

After Colonel Mayville departed, I sobbed unconsolably all afternoon. Months previously, I had told the Sky Soldiers that nobody could love people who invaded countries—and now I was heartbroken they had left. Kara took me out in the evening to the Kurdistan cafe north of Kirkuk. Mayville had made them take down their huge sign a few months ago but they had put it back up, along with a massive map of Kurdistan incorporating territory as far south as Baghdad, half of Turkey, a quarter of Syria and a chunk of Iran. In an e-mail to Mayville that evening, I wrote: "Perhaps, Colonel Mayville, Mesopotamia will always get the better of those who come to love her."

5

LIFE IN THE
REPUBLICAN PALACE

Ya ahl al-Iraq, ahl al-shiqaq wa al-nifaq
Oh people of Iraq, people of disunity and hypocrisy.
I am he who scattereth darkness and climbeth lofty summits
As I lift the turban from my face you will know me.
Certain I am that I see heads ripe for cutting and truly I am the
man to do it!

—AL-HAJJAJ IBN YUSUF, governor of Iraq
during the Umayyad caliphate in the seventh century, at the Kufa mosque

THE REPUBLICAN PALACE in Baghdad was now a very different place from the previous summer. There was air conditioning, both hot and cold. People no longer slept in the corridors and halls, but had all moved to trailers. And there were toilets inside the palace that actually functioned.

The Green Zone had become a bizarre, four-square-mile bubble inside Baghdad, protected by high concrete blast walls and barbed wire, with foreigners rarely venturing outside, and Iraqis only allowed in if they had the necessary US-issued badge to get through the checkpoints. In addition to the Republican Palace, the Green Zone contained the al-Rashid Hotel, the convention centre where the Governing Council met, the Ministry of Defence and numerous villas, previously belonging to Baath party members, which had been taken over by the CPA and new Iraqi officials.

The residence of the most senior British officer in Iraq was dubbed Maude House and was a villa a ten-minute walk from the Republican Palace. I was initially accommodated in a tiny trailer—shared with a fellow

Brit—in the Maude House car park, but I quickly managed to "acquire" keys to an American trailer which was reserved for the UN. In my new trailer I had my own room, a guest room, and an en suite with shower, loo, hot water. Luxury by Green Zone standards! Needless to say, I listened out intently for news of the UN's return. My unofficial residence was superbly located: two minutes from my desk, one minute from the gym and three minutes from the chow hall. The gym had an amazing array of machines and of muscular bodies. I started to work out daily, developing a routine of cardiovascular exercises and weights.

After the paucity of food on Kirkuk airfield, the quantity at the palace was a welcome change. There was breakfast, lunch, dinner and late dinner. All the food was highly processed, however, full of additives and served on plastic plates with plastic cutlery. The novelty of fried chicken and "freedom fries"—available for three out of four meals most days— soon wore off, and I diversified onto the fruit and vegetables that were flown in from overseas.

Bremer gave me a warm handshake and welcomed me to the Governance Team. This was a small group of mostly American political appointees and State Department diplomats. The team served as policy advisers to Bremer, a staff whom he could draw on at any time of the night or day on any issue. It was clear there was an inner circle. I was now responsible for coordinating policy for the north, with particular focus on Kirkuk— and would always be part of an outer circle.

The Governance Team was situated at the north end of the palace in a room which had formerly served as the kitchen. It was a long room, with desks along both walls. I had a computer, with Internet access. I also had a mobile phone, which rather peculiarly had a US number. Anyone in Iraq wishing to speak to me had to phone via the United States, which made it prohibitively expensive for most Iraqis.

EACH MORNING at nine o'clock Sir Jeremy Greenstock would hold a meeting of the senior Brits working within the CPA. Most were British civil servants from the Foreign Office and Ministry of Defence. Greenstock would provide an overview of events on the political front, and go round the room giving each of us an opportunity to feed in areas of importance and key interest. In these meetings, he shared his concerns about the developments in the country and about some of the decisions the CPA was taking.

Greenstock had an impressive breadth of knowledge gained from forty years as a diplomat, working in a range of posts including the Arab world and at the UN. Observing the way he conducted meetings, analysed political developments and negotiated was quite an education. His cynicism was in sharp contrast to the eternal optimism of Bremer who at no point expressed a moment of doubt. I wished they worked better together. It was blatantly clear that things were not going well in Iraq, but few proffered any alternative strategies. Anne Greenstock had accompanied Sir Jeremy out to Baghdad and worked on issues in the democracy team. Sir Jeremy's front office was staffed by Simon Shercliff, an impressive young diplomat, and Raad al-Kadiri, an Oxford-educated PhD whose father was Iraqi.

On my second day in Baghdad, Robert Blackwill, who was visiting Iraq, asked to see me. Blackwill was Condoleezza Rice's deputy at the National Security Council and influential on the policy of the CPA. He had a reputation for being difficult to work with.

I met Black Will, as I referred to him, in a small anteroom at the back of Bremer's office. He began by saying that Paul Wolfowitz had suggested he meet me. Black Will did not want to receive a "brief" on Kirkuk. He started by asking what language group Kurdish belonged to. Then he asked about the art and music of the different groups. What food did they eat? At one point in the conversation he asked, "If you had eight men standing in a room butt naked, would you be able to tell what ethnicity they were?" I wasn't sure this was an appropriate question, particularly coming from an American official. Flummoxed, I said that I myself would not be able to but sometimes Kirkukis could. The moment passed, and we were soon engrossed in a discussion on public policy, different concepts of justice and historical issues. It reminded me of a tutorial at Oxford. We spoke about terrorism and I said that our actions caused reactions. He asked about the chances of civil war in Iraq within five years. I said I thought the chances were high. I was thinking between Arabs and Kurds.

I SOON REALIZED that to achieve anything in Baghdad I needed to build up alliances. Information was often not easily come by and access to it was by negotiation. There were many people out to make their careers by serving in Iraq. For Kirkuk's issues to gain the attention they required, allies were needed. I walked the corridors, introducing myself to people. Among the most impressive individuals I found in the palace were three American diplomats: Ron Schlicher, Chris Ross and Ron Neumann. All three had spent a large part of their careers in the Middle East, loved the cultures and had a strong affinity for the people.

Ron Schlicher was on the point of going to Sydney as US ambassador when he agreed to come out to Iraq. He was put in charge of the Office of Provincial Outreach. While the Governance Team tended to communicate with the twenty-five members of the Governing Council, the Office of Provincial Outreach reached out to the rest of the country. As a fluent Arabic-speaker, Ron was well suited for this role. It was from Ron that I learnt about what was happening elsewhere in Iraq while I had been so immersed in the affairs of Kirkuk. He described how de-Baathification, the dissolving of the military and the closure of state-owned enterprises had left hundreds of thousands of Iraqis jobless and angry. In several parts of the country, the US military had responded to the increasing unrest by throwing out large cordons and arresting all "military-aged males." There were now tens of thousands of Iraqis in our custody, without adequate facilities to hold them in, nor systems to process their names or inform their families. Ron was constantly battling with the US military to get detained Iraqis released.

Chris Ross was a retired American ambassador and executive director of the NGO Search for Common Ground. Chris had held a succession of important posts at the State Department, including coordinator for counterterrorism, ambassador to Syria and ambassador to Algeria. He was bilingual in English and Arabic, having grown up in the region.

Ron Neumann was American ambassador to Bahrain. He was pulled from there to work with the Iraqi Ministry of Foreign Affairs. I put it to him that Kirkuk needed special treatment. We had a moral duty: we had invaded Iraq, rid it of Saddam and promised the Iraqi people a better future. If the country collapsed into civil war, no one would thank us.

We had lost nine soldiers in Kirkuk, and for their sake, the sake of their families and all who served, we should make Kirkuk succeed.

In response he told me about his friends who had died in Vietnam, and also in hostage crises. That was not a reason to act. The reason to act was because it was in the interests of the US and the UK to do so. He said we had screwed up everything else in the country, so we should at least try to get one thing right. The issue was how to get the "mandate" for special status. He said he had some ideas and would go away and explore them. My passionate concern, he told me, incentivized him and others to do something.

As THE END of February approached, discussions intensified over the interim Constitution known as the Transitional Administrative Law (TAL). I headed over to the Governing Council building. It was great to see the familiar faces of the Kurdish leaders. I chatted on the side with Jalal Talabani and Barham Salih. I did not recognize Masoud Barzani initially as he was dressed in a suit, rather than his traditional Kurdish outfit. It took me a moment to realize that the woman smiling and waving at me was Songul. She had replaced her conservative dress with a modern suit, and become a blonde. She was obviously enjoying life as a Governing Council member. And for once, I was even happy to see her.

Behind the scenes, Kirkuk had been a main focus of the TAL discussions with the Kurds. In the end, the TAL included several articles which related to Kirkuk, in particular Article 58 which said that the Iraqi Transitional Government would take steps to ensure that individuals who moved to the province under Arabization "may be resettled, may receive compensation from the state, may receive new land from the state near their residence in the governorate from which they came, or may receive compensation for the cost of moving to such areas." I knew that "may" might be interpreted as "should." But there were no Arabs on the Governing Council who were sensitive to how this might be perceived in Kirkuk.

The first deadline for the signing of the TAL at the end of February was missed and the signing ceremony was postponed until 6 March. On 6 March the press gathered at the conference centre. Governors and ministers were in attendance, along with the diplomatic community, and children were in their smartest clothes ready to sing. But the Governing Council members were nowhere to be seen. The Shia members were unhappy with Article 61C, which stated that the final Constitution could be rejected if two-thirds of the voters in three governorates voted against it. That article was of great importance to the Kurds who needed to show their people that Kurdish interests could not be ignored by the majority. The paragraph had already been agreed by the full Council. But after discussions in Najaf, the Shia feared that once again minorities would be able to impose their will on the majority Shia population.

As midnight approached, I was there to witness Bremer address the Governing Council in their building. He told them that the TAL was the most revolutionary document in modern Iraqi history. Failure to sign the TAL on time had done real damage to Iraq and to the Governing Council. But if this were corrected quickly, history would forgive them. On 8 March I went to the conference centre to witness the signing of the TAL. It was a smaller affair than that originally envisaged. In the foyer, a platform had been set up. As their names were called out, each Governing Council member stepped forward, signed and took his or her place on the platform. Speeches were made, and children sang. Masoud Barzani, in Arabic and then in Kurdish, said movingly, "For the first time in my life, I feel Iraqi."

The Governance Team was delighted that the TAL had been signed and proud of what had been written, including the Bill of Rights. However, the Iraqi public had not been consulted on, or engaged in, the process. It wasn't long before there was a raft of complaints. Muqtada al-Sadr called for the TAL to be abolished and the Governing Council dissolved. The Turkmen felt ignored. The Yazidis were upset that they were not mentioned. In response, the CPA started to develop materials to "sell" the TAL to the public. The issue was who should do the selling? It should not be the CPA. But the Governing Council was universally disliked.

ALL OF US in the Governance Team gathered around a TV on 31 March, watching in horror as the news broke of the killing of four American security contractors. They had been lured into Falluja, ambushed and dragged from their cars. Their mutilated and burnt bodies were hung from a bridge over the Euphrates.

Units from the 82nd Airborne Division had largely pulled back from patrolling Falluja in February, giving responsibility to Iraqi security forces. There was now immense American pressure for a military response. The US Marines threw a cordon of troops, tanks and artillery around the city to prepare for a battle to root out an estimated two thousand insurgents. As soon as the Marines began to go into the city, the newly formed Iraqi security forces deserted. Hundreds of Iraqis were killed before the Governing Council pressured the Coalition to agree to a ceasefire and negotiations. The siege of Falluja and the growing insurgency came to absorb the attention of the CPA. There was palpable fear, and a number of civilians left.

The level of violence in Iraq steadily increased. Attacks on the Green Zone escalated. Each time, "Big Voice" (the loudspeaker) would sound, telling everyone to take cover, people would run down to the bomb shelters. I threw myself against the wall to avoid being mowed down by the Marines who hurtled along the corridors. Medevac helicopters flew in wounded soldiers day in, day out. Contact with Iraqis decreased, and the Green Zone turned into more and more of a fortress. After a few weeks, Big Voice stopped. I didn't know whether it had broken down or was considered bad for morale. But there was no more siren or running down to the bunkers.

In the palace, rumours were rampant. There was talk of plots to smuggle weapons into the Green Zone. A soldier was brutally stabbed in the neck, with the attacker immediately framed as an insurgent. It turned out to be a spurned lover in a gay love triangle.

All Brits were moved into accommodation near the conference centre across from the al-Rashid Hotel. Rows of trailers had been placed in a car-park basement, the cement roof and sides providing protection from rockets and mortars. After running a naming competition for our quarters, "Ocean Cliffs" was deemed the wittiest. As a long-termer, I had my own trailer, close to the ablution blocks and also to the "Whine Bar."

Each morning, I would wake up to a loud boom which was either a rocket, a mortar or the air-conditioning machine in my trailer. The bus stop, where we waited every morning for transport to the palace, was hit by a mortar and the shuttle bus had ceased running. I drove a car back and forth, and was told to look underneath it for bombs every time before I climbed in. I usually forgot.

Food supplies ran low after convoys were hit. We were served food which had been cut up in different shapes and sizes for morale. We were out of fresh vegetables and fruit, as well as forks and bowls. Luckily we still had water. New security regulations were issued: body armour and helmets to be worn throughout the Green Zone; no visits to non-secure locations within the Green Zone, including the gym and the PX; no jogging or cycling around the Green Zone, day or night; carry a mobile phone at all times and a radio in a grab bag.

Fliers appeared across Iraq from different groups of mujahideen and the 1920 Revolution Brigades (named in memory of the uprising in 1920 against the British). They warned Iraqis not to collaborate with the Coalition and threatened to kill those serving in the new Iraqi security forces. They announced attacks to avenge the martyrs of Najaf and Falluja.

I set out my concerns in e-mails to Colonel Mayville, who was now back in Italy. I was becoming increasingly alarmed that the Coalition did not understand who it was fighting. There were elements in Iraq that had not been here a year ago. Local resistance to the occupation was combining with Islamist militants. And many Iraqis who had looked to us in gratitude for liberating them from Saddam now wanted us gone as soon as possible. Coalition spokesmen continued to blame the violence on former regime elements, Saddamists and "dead-enders." When US forces mistakenly bombed a wedding party, killing over forty civilians, the military spokesman glibly commented that "even bad guys have weddings."

David Richmond, who had replaced Greenstock as the senior Brit, sent out an e-mail to all Brits thanking us for our "grit and fortitude." He noted that we were all volunteers and there was no pressure on any of us to remain in Iraq. He failed to mention that the road to Baghdad airport had been declared unsafe, so there was no escape except by helicopter. I had flown to the airport a few days before, sitting next to Lakhdar Brahimi. The helicopter had dived and weaved, virtually looping the loop as it took evasive action.

Lakhdar Brahimi had become a familiar figure within the palace. Kofi Annan had appointed Brahimi—a well-respected international diplomat

of Algerian origin, credited with assembling the *loya jirga*, or grand assembly, in Afghanistan—as his special representative to Iraq with responsibility for selecting an interim government to take over from CPA.
On 9 May, I attended a dinner at Maude House that Lieutenant General
John McColl gave in honour of Brahimi, whom he knew well from his
time in Afghanistan. General McColl was newly arrived in Iraq, the most
senior British officer in-country. The next day, I accompanied General
McColl on a tour to the north. In the Khanzad Hotel in Erbil, he turned
to me and asked, "Do you think we are facing massive strategic failure?"
I said I thought it was obvious that we were. Such doubts were very rarely
raised within the CPA, and thus it was impossible to come up with alternative strategies. Anyway, the Coalition could never recover from the political and security vacuum it had allowed to emerge at the outset. Now
the goal was to hand over by 30 June—and let Iraqis take responsibility
for the country.

WITHIN THE CPA IN BAGHDAD, black humour ran rife along with premo-
nitions of another Saigon. The Governance Team all went to the gym at
six o'clock every evening. Scott Carpenter, our boss, joked that we were
building up our upper-body strength so as to hang onto the helicopters
that would be sent to rescue us; and our leg muscles to kick off others
who might try to climb aboard.

I Locked up in the Green Zone, with pandemonium breaking out outside, and constantly under attack, people searched for outlets. In addition
to the gym, release came through alcohol. There were parties around the
swimming pool and a weekly disco at the al-Rashid Hotel. A Chinese
restaurant opened in the Green Zone, run by real Chinese. It provided a
respite from the food in the chow hall.

I braved a haircut at the palace. It was free, courtesy of Kellogg Brown
& Root—but someone had estimated that it cost the American taxpayer
around $600. I attended a quiz night but scored poorly as my memory
of anything not to do with Iraq seemed to have disappeared. Everything
outside Iraq seemed irrelevant.

One night I attended a trailer party. Paula Hothersall, the political adviser to the top British general, made a very strong punch, which left me

virtually blinded and quite oblivious to the rockets whizzing overhead as I sat on top of the sandbags. I spent forty minutes looking for my car. Unable to find it, I walked back to Ocean Cliffs, the underground car park at the conference centre. Fortunately, the soldiers on the checkpoint recognized me for what I was—a drunken female, not a suicide bomber—and let me pass. The surreal nature of our lives in Iraq was captured in the increasing number of jokes about "Why did the Iraqi chicken cross the road?"

Why did the Iraqi chicken cross the road?

COALITION PROVISIONAL AUTHORITY:
The fact that the Iraqi chicken crossed the road affirmatively demonstrates that decision-making authority has been transferred to the chicken well in advance of the scheduled June 30 transition of power. From now on the chicken is responsible for its own decisions.

HALLIBURTON:
We were asked to help the chicken cross the road. Given the inherent risk of road crossing and the rarity of chickens, this operation will only cost the US government $326,004.

MUQTADA AL-SADR:
The chicken was a tool of the evil Coalition and will be killed.

US ARMY MILITARY POLICE:
We were directed to prepare the chicken to cross the road. As part of these preparations, individual soldiers ran over the chicken repeatedly and then plucked the chicken. We deeply regret the occurrence of any chicken rights violations.

PESHMERGA:
The chicken crossed the road, and will continue to cross the road, to show its independence and to transport the weapons it needs to defend itself. However, in future, to avoid problems, the chicken will be called a duck, and will wear a plastic bill.

1ST CAVALRY DIVISION:

The chicken was not authorized to cross the road without displaying two forms of picture identification. Thus, the chicken was appropriately detained and searched in accordance with current SOPs. We apologize for any embarrassment to the chicken. As a result of this unfortunate incident, the command has instituted a gender-sensitivity training program and all future chicken searches will be conducted by female soldiers.

AL JAZEERA:

The chicken was forced to cross the road multiple times at gunpoint by a large group of occupation soldiers, according to eyewitnesses. The chicken was then fired upon intentionally, in yet another example of the abuse of innocent Iraqi chickens.

BLACKWATER:

We cannot confirm any involvement in the chicken road-crossing incident.

TRANSLATORS:

Chicken he cross street because bad she tangle regulation. Future chicken table against my request.

US MARINE CORPS:

The chicken is dead.

IN THE INTERNATIONAL MEDIA, political and military figures aired their alarm about the way events in Iraq were unfolding. There was lots of criticism, but rarely was it constructive. Tensions between Americans and Brits also came to the fore. The British military expressed its concern at US tactics, the over-use of force, the treatment of Iraqis as "sub-humans," the American unwillingness to take casualties, the poor relations with the local communities.

On 29 April fifty former British ambassadors and senior officials wrote an open letter to Tony Blair saying that the conduct of the war made it clear there was no plan for the post-Saddam era. They noted that every Middle East expert had predicted that the occupation of Iraq by Coalition forces would be met with resistance. Policy needed to take into account the nature and history of Iraq. The military actions of the Coalition should be guided by political objectives. They concluded saying there was no case for supporting policies which were doomed to fail.

Bush and Blair had failed to gain consensus for the war in the international arena and were now suffering the consequences. International sceptics relished the Coalition's failures as we lurched from one crisis to another.

WITH TENSIONS around the country running high, Bremer embarked on a new "outreach strategy," inviting different communities to meet him in the Green Zone. It was now deemed too much of a security risk for him to leave the capital. I accompanied him to a meeting with over thirty high-ranking officers of the former Iraqi Army. He set out President Bush's vision for Iraq. The economy needed to be revitalized and a vibrant private sector built up. Iraq needed to move from a dictatorship to a democracy, with elections in January 2005. Iraq must come under the rule of law. Security should be in the hands of a professional police force and the new Iraqi Army. The US was spending millions to train and equip the Iraqi security forces, but the security threat at the moment was severe and these forces needed assistance.

An Iraqi general reprimanded Bremer for referring to an American vision, rather than an Iraqi vision for their country. He quoted back Bremer's words "the profession of arms is an honourable profession" and said the Coalition should have respected a defeated army—not disbanded it. "The Coalition promised regime change but instead brought about state collapse," declared another general. Iraq now had uncontrolled borders, there was a lack of security inside the country, the services were bad, the economy was suspended and many families were left without income. There was a huge army out of work. An environment for violence had been created. Democracy could not exist in such an environment or be developed under such conditions in a matter of days.

The last general to speak expressed his surprise that a country with all the knowledge and skills of America had made such mistakes, referring to the unacceptable and dishonest people on the Iraqi Governing Council, the manner in which the Transitional Administrative Law was written, the policy of de-Baathification and depriving families of incomes. The US had hurt the feelings of Iraqi society. The new Iraqi Army was not being set up in the right manner. How could it be expected to be loyal to the US—and to fight against fellow Iraqis? The main mission of the army was to protect the homeland, not to combat terrorism.

I sat quietly at the side taking notes. I had heard many similar statements while in Kirkuk. I noted that the Iraqis called us *qawaat al-ihtilal*, "occupying forces" in Arabic, whereas the interpreter translated it as "Coalition forces," which was how we referred to ourselves. Bremer rounded up saying that unemployment in Iraq was much lower than it had been at the end of the war and that the economy was improving. Members of the former army were now being recruited into the new Iraqi security services. He asserted that the de-Baathification policy was correct, but had not been implemented properly.

No matter what complaints Iraqis made, Bremer kept cool. He reminded them that they now had "freedom," at which the Iraqi officers looked mystified. He reeled off statistics about electricity production, oil exports and recruitment to the military. He never displayed any doubt these were genuine indicators of progress. He told Iraqis that Saddam had destroyed the country over a thirty-five-year period and that it could not be rebuilt in a year. They needed patience and perseverance. Bremer was trying to lead the CPA in the most difficult of circumstances and at the same time manage the competing agendas coming out of Washington. Only 150,000 US troops had been deployed to Iraq because Rumsfeld had insisted on the minimum and had wanted to downscale immediately, to avoid the US military becoming involved in "nation building." Army chief of staff Eric Shinseki had been sacked for suggesting that three times as many troops were required to stabilize Iraq, and Bremer's request to Rumsfeld for more troops had been ignored.

Moreover, pre-war inter-agency rivalries continued to plague the post-war implementation and to afflict the CPA throughout its existence. The CPA had been established from scratch and had had to develop processes, procedures and structures on the hoof. It was always undermanned and, at its peak, there were only around twelve hundred staff to administer the country. There were never enough civilians to fill the posts, so members of the military had to be assigned to them. And many of the civilians who did deploy were young, inexperienced, had no prior post-conflict-reconstruction experience and were on short-term contracts.

Bremer's deep religious faith seemed to carry him through the worst of times. He relied heavily on those who shared his convictions but lacked experience of the region, and he marginalized the experienced and skilled diplomats who had their doubts.

EFFORTS TO REACH OUT to Iraqis were dealt a dramatic blow that April by the revelation that US forces had been torturing detainees in Abu Ghraib prison. Photos of Iraqis naked, chained and in pyramids had shocked us all to the core. Among many American soldiers there was outrage at the perpetrators, a sense that they had defiled both the flag and the uniform. Among Iraqis there was a mixed response. While some were outraged, others told us that we should have treated the prisoners *worse*, that this was nothing compared with how they were treated under Saddam's regime. But in the international press, particularly in the Arab world, these photographs of torture did immeasurable damage to the image of the Coalition. Abu Ghraib, notorious for torture under Saddam, now became a symbol of the Coalition's brutality and served to recruit many more into the burgeoning insurgency.

I was one of five CPA officials sent on 5 May to visit Abu Ghraib to see what monitoring measures could be put in place. We were accompanied by a busload of journalists. We entered through the inner cordon of high walls, with American soldiers staring down on us from watchtowers. On arrival we were greeted by Major General Geoffrey Miller, who had recently arrived from Guantanamo Bay to clean up the jail.

General Miller was upbeat. "Welcome to the best-run jail in the Middle East," he said. As we stood in the burning heat, he proceeded to tell us all the "good news" about the jail. He then went on to the bad news, the accusations of torture that had recently emerged in the press. "We are appalled and embarrassed," he said. He told us that none of the soldiers here today were part of that era. They had all arrived in January. The situation was under control.

We were put on a bus and driven around the prison. I was shocked that, one year on, detainees were still in tents and not provided with shelter under hard cover. The detainees surged towards the wire barriers, shouting in Arabic, with one waving his prosthetic leg: "Down with the occupation," "Where is justice?" "Give us our rights." One of them had a megaphone and in excellent English shouted out the demands of the detainees. Apparently, a "mayor" had been nominated for each tent and given a loudhailer in order to communicate with the guards.

We were shown the medical facilities, an impressive American field hospital. Some of the detainees, wounded when insurgents had fired RPGs at the prison, were still receiving treatment. We then continued to the prison wing where the pictures of naked prisoners had been taken. It was a two-storey block, with row on row of small cells into which prisoners in the past had been crammed. The only occupants now were five women, each with a cell to herself. They screamed out at the top of their voices about the treatment they were receiving and their anxiety about what would become of them.

We went on to the interrogation cells. General Miller informed us that professional interrogators conducted the questioning using fifty-three different methods set out in a manual available on the Internet! I had thought that interrogation was a function which had to be kept within government. But no, even interrogation was contracted out.

A couple of days afterwards, I chanced upon General Sanchez and told him about my visit to the jail. When I mentioned how shocked I had been at seeing the five women locked up in one of the wings, he told me there were only three there now. "Have we killed the other two, sir?" I asked him mischievously. "No, Emma," he replied wearily, "we have not."

At Abu Ghraib I saw evidence of the worst side of human nature. With weak supervision in the jail, a number of American soldiers had used their power to create a perverse world, breaking the monotony of their days with sadistic acts on detainees under their control. It was truly sickening. Abu Ghraib was one of those places that exuded evil.

6

THE ASSASSINATION
OF SHEIKH AGAR

*Iraq is a Greek comedy that ends in tragedy. But we know all the
actors—and their deaths are not staged.*
—COLONEL MAYVILLE

I WAS AT MY DESK in the Republican Palace when I read the news that
Sheikh Agar had been assassinated on his way to the weekly meeting of
the Kirkuk Provincial Council. Early reports suggested his vehicle had
been ambushed and fired upon by people in two vehicles. His bodyguard
had returned fire but had been outgunned and also killed. Sheikh Agar,
Sheikh Agar . . . I could picture him so clearly. His smile. The way he
talked so animatedly. Sheikh Agar, in whose company I had spent so many
hours. Sheikh Agar, who had called me his daughter, Miss Bell. Sheikh
Agar dead? It could not be. I flew up to Kirkuk. I wandered through the
familiar territory of the airfield, with so many emotions swirling around.
The grass had grown, sprinkled with clusters of wild yellow flowers. It
reminded me of returning to school after graduation: I knew every bit of
the physical space, but it was no longer mine.

I went with the governor and Kirkuk Council members to Hozerain
where Sheikh Agar had lived. The tents were full of mourners, sitting
quietly, worry beads in hand, Koranic incantations in the background.
As I walked in, I heard the whisper "Emmasky has come" being passed
down the line. I spoke to the sons. The younger one, who I had often seen
around the government building, had aged years. I uttered a few words.
"Allah yarhamu" (May God have mercy on him), *"Inna lillahi wa inna ilaihi
raji'un"* (We are all from God and to him we return). Family members

105

Colonel Mayville and Sheikh Agar.
Photo by Huseyin Kara

spoke to me. "You are our sister." "You are my brother's daughter." Sheikh
Agar, bless him, had told all his family about me. And they were touched
I had made the journey from Baghdad to pay my respects.

Grief lay heavy in the air. And with that grief was fear. I sat in the tent,
the sole woman among so many men.

The tribes began dancing in circles, waving their red and black flags.
Sorrow and anger. I was then taken into a back room in one of the houses.
There I sat for three hours listening. Sheikh Agar's death had sharpened
Arab fears of intimidation and expulsion by Kurds. Sheikh Wasfi's house
had been attacked the night before, and he was afraid to return home.
Sheikh Agar in death had gained a popularity he had never had in life.

ON MY RETURN to Baghdad I arranged for a delegation of Kirkuk Arabs
to meet Bremer. I hoped this would lessen the likelihood of retaliatory
attacks, demonstrations and a boycott of the Council by Arab members.
I wanted to allay their concerns that there was some Coalition plot to
expel Arabs from the province—a fear that was pushing them to acquire
strange bedfellows and to provide passive sanctuary to those attacking
Coalition forces.

I arranged to meet the delegation at Checkpoint 2, between the al-Rashid Hotel and the conference centre. Where once had been a beautiful road, there now stood concrete blocks, large barrels, barbed wire. American soldiers gazed out from behind fortified barricades. One soldier stood with an interpreter checking the passes of Iraqis wanting to enter. I tried not to think of the snipers who might be targeting me from across the street.

Ismail Abudi was the first to turn up. We sat chatting for another thirty minutes before the other Kirkukis appeared. Sheikh Wasfi led the way, splendid in his finest robes. But accompanying Sheikh Wasfi were not only Rakan, Yahiya and Sheikh Naif, but also Sheikh Wasfi's relative Lukman (who we had jailed for over fifty days, along with his uncle Sheikh Hatem), the head of Sheikh Wasfi's office, and a policeman. I told them that it was lovely to see them all but I did not have permission to take the extra guests into the palace so they would have to wait outside.

I accompanied them through security, where they were patted down to ensure they had no weapons. The five then squeezed into my car, and I drove them towards the palace, catching up with everyone's news. I pulled up in the parking lot at the front of the palace, and walked them to yet another checkpoint where they were again searched.

I brought the group into Bremer's office, where we were also joined by Ron Schlicher. Sheikh Wasfi led off, setting out in detail how the Arabs of Kirkuk felt about the post-war situation and their concerns that the Coalition had given Kirkuk to the Kurds. The others then added their comments. Bremer listened patiently throughout. Beforehand, I had provided him with a "Read Ahead" for the meeting. He understood the complexity of the issues and announced at the end that he would send a Fact Finding Mission, consisting of Ron Schlicher and myself, to Kirkuk to investigate the security situation and measures required to reduce tensions.

After the meeting, I escorted the Kirkukis back to the edge of the Green Zone. They were bubbling with excitement, asking me how I thought the meeting had gone. I told them I thought it had gone very well and that they had expressed the concerns of their community eloquently. Sheikh Wasfi could not stop grinning. I promised I would see them all soon back in Kirkuk.

A week or so later, Ron Schlicher and I went up to Kirkuk and met all the key players. We reported back to Bremer that we were concerned at a sharp spike in ethnic tensions, which had been created by the assassination of Sheikh Agar and Kurdish triumphalism over the TAL. The Arabs had now suspended their attendance at Provincial Council meetings and had been joined by the Turkmen. The Assyrians were also boycotting the Council meetings, ostensibly in protest at the murder of an Assyrian police officer. The game of boycott and non-attendance had been played in Kirkuk before. Provincial Council members claimed their constituents were threatening them with assassination if they resumed attendance at the Council in the absence of progress in addressing perceived Kurdish excesses.

IRAQIS WERE GLUED TO their televisions, watching in horror the on-going fighting between Coalition forces and Iraqis. It was all Kirkukis could talk about when I next visited. The deputy governor even asked for the UN to intervene to protect the people of Falluja from the Coalition forces. When I met up with Ismail Abudi, he was shocked by the clashes between the Coalition and the Sadrists: "The Coalition should not focus on destroying Jaysh al-Mahdi. Jaysh al-Mahdi is not a professional army. It is more of a media and public relations stunt."

I had heard from the new US brigade in Kirkuk that Mousawi had set up fighting positions on the roof of his mosque. I sent a message to the mosque asking to meet Mudhafer Yas. He came immediately, tired and upset, to the government building. He complained that so many promises had been made by the Coalition, but none kept, and nothing delivered. He said he believed the US was in Iraq to stay. They were not here for liberation. He was horrified, he said, by all the killings. The current troubles revealed the real face of the occupation.

Yas said that Muqtada al-Sadr was calling for the US to leave and for detainees to be released. The Governing Council did not represent Iraqis. As for the Kirkuk Provincial Council, Yas complained, it had fallen apart. It had no powers and nothing to do. He said Barzani and Talabani claimed they had a deal with Bremer. There had been no response from the Coalition, so people believed it was true.

Yas told me the Sadrists were worried about security in the mosque. He said Coalition forces had taken up positions around the mosque. I tried to calm him. I repeatedly told him that the Coalition in Kirkuk was not his enemy.

ARAB MEMBERS OF the Provincial Council, led by Sheikh Wasfi, got in contact with me and insisted on meeting. They complained that they had not seen any results from the Fact Finding Mission.

"The Arabs spend all their time crying and whining and they are not able to see what has been achieved," I told them calmly and firmly, concealing the frustration I had felt for weeks. "I have sat quietly in your meetings over the last couple of months with Bremer, Schlicher and the UN—now it is my turn to speak and your turn to listen. Under the previous regime it was the Sunni Arabs who benefited the most, while others had been discriminated against. In the immediate post-war period, there has been a change in the balance of power, with others gaining and you losing. However, your position today is much better than it was a few months ago."

I commended them on their leadership and in keeping the province calm after the assassination of Sheikh Agar. "The mourning period is now over," I said, "and you should go back to the Council because the people of the province need you." The people of Kirkuk had a difficult road ahead. The leaders of Kirkuk needed to develop a vision for the future as a prosperous province, with a thriving business community and civil society, and a stable system of local government which involved power sharing. I pointed out that there were only eighty days left until the Coalition was scheduled to transfer sovereignty back to Iraqis. If they refused to return to the Council until certain preconditions were met, they were wasting valuable time when there were so many important issues that needed to be discussed.

The Arabs nodded in agreement. At the next meeting of the Council, the Kurds, Arabs, Turkmen and Assyrian members were all present. The Council was back together.

Ron Schlicher and I worked on a series of information and action memos to Ambassador Bremer and cables to Washington. We noted that for the Kurds, possession of Kirkuk would greatly increase their economic viability and was a step further towards their final dream of independence. For the same reason, the Turkish, Iranian and Arab governments were suspicious of Kurdish aspirations towards Kirkuk.

I proposed the establishment of a Kirkuk Foundation as part of the strategy to prevent conflict. The Kirkuk Foundation was intended to bring the leadership of all communities in Kirkuk together to develop a common vision for Kirkuk. And through a $100m endowment from Iraqi funds, it would provide significant resources to implement that vision, with international facilitation and oversight. The Foundation would be a principal tool in changing the political dynamic from the current timetable-driven "numbers game" to a dialogue based on finding wide-ranging mutual interests.

In a meeting with Bremer in his office, I went over again the two options for special status: heavy and light. The general consensus in the room was that we would not get buy-in for an international administration, as it would pose a glaring exception to Iraqi sovereignty. On the second option, I described how a special rapporteur could visit Kirkuk every few weeks, and serve as an honest broker to whom all the different groups could pour out their grievances. Bremer declared that he liked this option. I said to him, "Sir, you are looking for a job post-June. Maybe you would like to be considered for the post?" He laughed, flicked through the pages in his notepad and said, "Emma, looking at my list of things I want to do post-June, I just don't see this on it."

There was no response from Washington to our cables requesting guidance on the final status of Kirkuk; or on a UN Security Council Resolution (UNSCR) to grant Kirkuk special status and a special rapporteur; or on suggestions for prominent international personalities to sit on the board of the Kirkuk Foundation. Kirkuk's "special status" disappeared in revised drafts of the UNSCR.

IN MID MAY, more than three months after my arrival in Baghdad, Ambassador Bremer's meeting in Kurdistan with Talabani and Barzani to discuss Kirkuk was finally happening. The timing of this visit coincided with the arrival back in-country of Black Will to "assist" Lakhdar

Brahimi in selecting the Interim Government. Black Will established his own office and created a mantle of secrecy, apparently fearful of leaks back to Washington that could undermine the process. The request of David Richmond, the British ambassador, to accompany Bremer on his visit north was rejected. Senior Brits were now being excluded from key meetings. This was all going on above my level—and I kept my head down.

Bremer agreed that Meghan O'Sullivan and I should be the two staff to accompany him to the north, having prepared his talking points and briefing notes. I walked over to the helicopter landing zone (which had been mortared the day before) and took my place on the Black Hawk. I sat nervously waiting for Black Will to arrive, fearing that he would demand that I, the non-American, disembark. But he climbed on board looking quite innocuous in his baseball cap and did not comment.

Hours later, we descended on the town of Sari Rash. It was cold and raining, and reminded me of home. Masoud Barzani greeted us, bringing us into an anteroom for tea, before we moved into a separate meeting room. Meghan and I sat on either side of Bremer, with Barzani opposite us. Bremer kept to the script we had prepared. He spoke of the Coalition's close relationship with the Kurds, the shared vision of Iraq as a democratic and pluralistic country and the US commitment to a long-term relationship with the Kurds. He said that Kirkuk was of great geostrategic interest to Iraq, the region, the US and the international community.

Bremer described how some of the "aggressive behaviour" on the part of the PUK and KDP had increased tensions in Kirkuk. Bremer recognized the injustices done in Kirkuk by the previous regime, including the displacement of Kurds, forcing people to change their ethnicities, and the denial of jobs and livelihoods. He spoke of the need to integrate the Kurdish "shadow government" into the local administration of Kirkuk. He acknowledged that these issues would not be resolved overnight.

Barzani sat quietly throughout, his eyes shifting between Bremer and myself. He thanked us for our concern and hoped the relationship between the Kurds and Americans would continue and deepen into the future. He said he and Jalal Talabani were both under a lot of pressure from the Kurdish people over Kirkuk. It was important to find the right solution. We went to the KDP guest house for lunch. Lakhdar Brahimi

was there with his team, involved in backroom deliberations over candidates for the new Interim Government.

After we had eaten, we flew on to Lake Dukan, the resort where we
had celebrated US Independence Day the previous year. Jalal Talabani
and Barham Salih greeted us at the helipad and we went immediately
to the PUK guest house where we got down to business. Bremer did not
have his script in front of him, but he had handled the Barzani meeting
so well that I felt no reason to worry. He began by stating how much the
Coalition loved the Kurds, but he then skipped the whole of the next
section—the part where he was supposed to empathize with Kurdish suffering—and moved straight to Kurd misbehaviour.

Jalal Talabani sat fidgeting. As soon as Bremer had finished speaking, Talabani turned to me and blurted out, "You are pro-Arab and pro-
Turkmen!" Then he bombarded us with details of Kurdish suffering, destroyed villages and marginalization. He spoke of how the 1920 Treaty
of Sèvres between the Ottoman Empire and the Allies had offered the
Kurds the hope of independence but it had never been ratified, and it
had been replaced by the 1923 Treaty of Lausanne with no mention of the
Kurds. The British had never managed to suppress the Kurds. Churchill,
who wanted to give them independence, then went on to bomb them.
The British had tried to rule the Kurds through Sheikh Mahmud, but
he then led a series of uprisings against them. "Do you know what they
call you?" he asked me. "Gertrude Bell!" Unlike Sheikh Agar, he did not
mean it as a compliment. He blamed her for incorporating the Kurds
into Iraq. "You are anti-Kurd!" Talabani shouted.

Bremer sat back in astonishment. Talabani and I then embarked on
a historical "discussion," during which Bremer stood up and wandered
to the table to collect a plate of sweets and fruit. He quickly got tired
when Iraqis went back over history. He wanted them to look to the future. Talabani went on to complain of Baathists in the security forces,
and the alliance that Muqtada al-Sadr, the Iraqi Turkmen Front and the
Arabization Arabs had formed against the Kurds. Arabization Arabs must
leave, he said. He claimed the PUK had seven thousand "good Arabs" on
its payroll. He admitted there were Kurdish extremists making trouble
in Kirkuk, painting Kurdistan flags everywhere and making him mad. He
was prepared to compromise by allowing Kirkuk to be an "independent

governorate" for now, but they would ask for independence in five or six years.

Having got that off his chest, Talabani felt much better. As I left the meeting, he came over and put his arm around me. "Emma . . . Emma . . . what is your name?" "Emma Bell," I dutifully replied, much to his delight. "Yes," he said, "Emma Bell." Before dinner, Black Will, Barham and I wandered outside and stood by the hotel swimming pool, taking in the panoramic view over Lake Dukan. Barham turned to me and said that I should agree to give Kirkuk to the Kurds. "In the past deals have always been made in this way, over drinks on balconies," he teased.

At dinner, Bremer, Barham and I sat on one side, opposite Talabani, Black Will and Meghan. Talabani was on fighting form—and I his target. "You must give us Kirkuk!" he announced to me and off he went once more, back into history, to C. J. Edmonds and whirling dervishes. "Kirkuk is part of Kurdistan, you must give it to us!" As the evening wore on, large amounts of alcohol were consumed. Even Bremer, who never usually drank, allowed himself to indulge a bit and relax. Barham implored me, "You, the Brits, gave me an education, a passport . . . give me Kirkuk." Black Will joked that he had witnessed Barham and me shaking on the deal on the balcony before dinner. Barham noted how everyone had predicted Kirkuk would descend into civil war but it had not happened. "Emma did stop Kirkuk from becoming a dogfight," he acknowledged.

Towards the end of dinner, Talabani stood up and toasted President Bush, saying that he hoped he would win the election. Everyone jumped to their feet and shouted, "Hear, hear!" I looked at Barham in horror. He giggled and whispered to me, "One should not interfere in the internal affairs of other countries" and raised his glass, "To Her Majesty." We toasted the queen together.

At the end of the meal I said, "Mam Jalal, on behalf of Her Majesty's Government, I would like to apologize firstly for creating the state of Iraq, and secondly for putting the Kurds in it." Talabani beamed, hugged and kissed me. And gave me a beautiful chess set.

I RETURNED TO KIRKUK one afternoon towards the end of May. Ismail Abudi came round to see me at the Northern Oil Company in Kirkuk

Sky, Barham Salih, Meghan O'Sullivan and Jalal Talabani at Dukan. *Photo by the Patriotic Union of Kurdistan*

where I was staying the night. We sat up on the roof chatting. He recalled the first time we had met. He said I had only given him three minutes of my time. I did not remember that encounter, but expected it was when we had hundreds come each day to the government building to report Saddam's whereabouts, weapons of mass destruction and Baathists. We reflected on how in those early days Ismail was an angry radical Shia Arab, speaking out against the governor, the Council, and the occupation. Everyone, including the Coalition forces, wanted him locked up.

We reminisced about his kidnapping, and how Colonel Mayville and I had charged all over town looking for him. And how after his release, I had thrown my arms around him and kissed him and he had laughed, happy and embarrassed, and told me never to do that again.

Ismail Abudi remembered Mr Saha, his friend who was a journalist. He had recently borrowed Ismail's car and had been assassinated by people who presumably thought he was Ismail. We discussed the recent arrest of a group of Arab Shia. A few days previously, Coalition forces in Kirkuk had raided twelve different sites in the city, including the al-Husseini Mosque. Mousawi was not there at the time. The US soldiers seized AK-47s, machine guns and grenades from the mosque. Ismail claimed they were not planning an armed insurrection. Yas, the messenger between me and Mousawi, was one of those arrested. Ismail pleaded with me to try to get the Sadrists released.

Ismail spoke about his work at the Employment Office. There were fifty thousand people currently registered unemployed. Jobs had been found for ten thousand so far, and the vocational training centre attached to the Employment Office was providing training for lots of the unemployed. He grinned broadly as I praised his efforts.

We discussed the 30 June deadline and the end of the occupation. I told him that I too would be leaving. "No . . . tell me it is not true," he said. We sat on the roof in total darkness with tears streaming down both our faces. "This year has totally changed my life and my ideas," he told me. And he went on to describe how he came to realize that the Coalition was here to help rebuild Iraq, and how I was the first female friend he had ever had. And I described how I too had been completely changed by my year in Iraq. I told him our friendship would last for years and that we would write, phone and visit each other regularly in our different countries.

THE NEXT MORNING at eight o'clock as scheduled, Ismail Hadidi, Kirkuk's Sunni Arab deputy governor, picked me up in his car. I was breaking all regulations once again and going out into the Sunni Triangle, the Sunni heartland where the insurgency was now raging. Our companions were Ismail's assistant (a Turkmen Sunni), who was driving, and the director of electricity, Abu Kahraba, a Turkmen Shia. Following behind us was a ragamuffin group of government building security people, with whom we were able to communicate via radio. We travelled the side roads, passing farmers out with their flocks. At times we saw people we knew, stopped the car and got out to greet them. I was seeing their world through their eyes. There were no Coalition forces in sight. The police were manning the checkpoints in their new uniforms. A sense of normality had descended.

We turned up at the Hawija Council meeting. The deputy governor took the seat of honour beside the mayor, Abu Saddam. I sat to the side.

"*Allah bil kheir*," I said. "Hello, Emmasky," voices called out. I lifted my right hand to my forehead in salute, bringing it down over my chest. The deputy governor opened the meeting. He started by saying that in the new Iraq everyone had a role to play. No one was to be marginalized. He said. "We have a visitor today, Emmasky, who you all know and who works so hard for you all." There was a chorus of "*Ahlan wa sahlan*, Emmasky, thank you for your efforts." And the meeting proceeded, with a discussion about electricity and agricultural prices. No mention of the Coalition, the occupation . . . All so normal.

The meeting finished and we went off to see an asphalt factory, which was working well; sewage works funded by USAID; and a football stadium, being prepared through an NGO. They discussed how matches would be played against neighbouring Arab towns. Ismail said they should also play the Kurdish towns of Dibbis and Altun Kopri, in the north of the province. We got lost driving around Hawija, and Ismail said I would cost them dear. We all laughed—but we knew that I was a prime target for assassination.

We drove on to Riyadh. We sang along to the radio. We laughed at our ethnic mix in the car: Arab, Turkmen and English. "Are you Sunni or Shia?" they asked me. "Jew," I responded. They burst out laughing, smacking their hands together. "*Ya, Sharon!*" Ismail exclaimed—a "joke" that was constantly repeated. In Riyadh, we met with the Council, discussed the electricity situation and listened to their needs.

On arrival at Sheikh Ghassan's house, we discovered that he and his brother Burhan were apparently in Kirkuk taking possession—at long last—of a building for the Arab bloc. Their other brother Qais assured us they would be back *hassa* (right now), and we should wait to have lunch with them. We sat chatting in the large room, lounging on the cushions. An hour went by. And one by one we fell asleep. Two hours later Sheikh Ghassan entered his home to find me curled up in a ball in his living room.

"Miss Emma, how nice to see you," he said laughing. Food was brought in. We sat together to eat, oblivious of everyone else in the room. The last time I had seen him was three months ago at a meeting of the Arab tribes, both Sunni and Shia, in this very room. We had much to catch up on. I asked him how he was. "*Mo zein*" (Not well), he replied, shaking his head from side to side. He was very worried.

Sheikh Ghassan repeated the complaint that while the Kurds had Talabani and Barzani, there was no one in Baghdad to represent the Kirkuk Arabs. I assured him that the voice of the Arabs was heard and understood. I suggested he look at forming a new party which represented all Kirkukis and had a positive vision of the future. There were many independent Kurds, Arab Sunni and Shia, and Turkmen he could attract. "Talabani has invited me to visit him," Sheikh Ghassan told me. "You must go," I encouraged him.

I told him that many of his Kurdish brothers were expelled from the province and they wanted to return. And he should welcome them back, help them rebuild their villages and work with them. He nodded, saying, "We have nothing against them."

Sheikh Ghassan asked me for news of Colonel Mayville. I told him that I had spoken to the Colonel recently, that he was home with his family in Italy. There was a glint in Ghassan's eyes. "Colonel Mayville is my friend. I love Colonel Mayville . . ." And we both chimed in, ". . . too much." I told him the Colonel always asked after him and wanted to hear his news.

I could have spent many more hours with Sheikh Ghassan but my companions dragged me away. Sheikh Ghassan promised to come and see me in Baghdad before I left. We were well fed and well rested and in an upbeat mood as we headed south towards the house of Ghassan's uncle, Sheikh Anwar, the paramount sheikh of the Obeidis. We passed a traffic control point, with the police fast asleep—it was siesta time. The countryside turned more and more to desert as we approached the Hamrin mountain range. We were travelling on the Tikrit road. No one from the Coalition had used this road for months. It was too dangerous. After a forty-minute drive, we turned down a track towards the village of Riml and got out at the main house. It was around five in the afternoon and all was quiet. Everyone was sleeping.

Ismail Hadidi entered the house, announcing that "Emmasky" was here to visit. I took off my boots and stood in the entrance. Sheikh Anwar came out and started to shake with laughter. "*Ahlan wa sahlan*, Emmasky. *Ahlan wa sahlan!*" He asked me what I was doing in the area. I told him I was here as a tourist. "A tourist! A tourist! There is nothing to see here except sand!" And we laughed together. I told him I had come to visit him as a guest, and not as an occupier.

Sheikh Anwar al-Asi,
paramount sheikh of
the Obeidi tribe.
Photo by the author

Sheikh Wasfi entered the room and I got up to greet him. I told him I had been to Hawija, Riyadh and Yiachi today—he had already heard the news—and that I had not been killed despite the fact I was travelling with Ismail Hadidi, who Sheikh Wasfi referred to as a friend of the Kurds. Sheikh Anwar said I could travel where I liked in the area and no harm would come to me. He said that if I were an American, it would be a different story! But what kept me safe was my Iraqi friends. No one imagined they had a foreigner in the car. Two Japanese diplomats I knew had been murdered a few months ago travelling in their own vehicle.

We were once more into a discussion about the differences between the British and the Americans. He said the British had understood the Iraqis and worked well with the tribes, but the Americans understood nothing. I pointed out that my countrymen had not done so well last time in Iraq; that Iraq was a difficult country; and that the Americans would get better at it with more experience. "Oh, please no!" they groaned.

It had been a year since the occupation began and I asked them their opinion. They gave me their usual rendition of the Coalition's mistakes. They asked me my thoughts. I told them that I did not think an occupation by foreign forces of another country could be successful in the modern era. I added the hope that the people of Iraq would have a future better than the past had been. They asked me about life in Baghdad. I said it was *"mo zein"* and described how I lived underground.

Sheikh Anwar recalled the first time he had met me. It was in the government building. He said that Colonel Mayville had done all the talking and I had not spoken. He did not mention that the meeting was about the arrest of his relatives, Sheikh Hatem and Lukman.

Ismail Hadidi sang the praises of Colonel Mayville, extolling his qualities as a leader. Sheikh Anwar nodded in agreement and then declared, "Colonel Mayville gave me a headache!" We all laughed. Mayville had indeed put a lot of pressure on him, even flying planes over his house at one stage to persuade him to stop attacking Coalition forces! Sheikh Anwar said he was actually grateful that Colonel Mayville had prevented one of his officers from destroying all their villages. He reported that relations with the new Coalition forces were good. Their footprint was lighter. He mentioned that Colonel Mayville had invited him to the US to see democracy at work. "If this is democracy," Sheikh Anwar declared, referring to the chaos in Iraq, "we don't want to see any more of it."

Everyone came out to wave us goodbye as I put my US Army boots back on. Sheikh Anwar said, "She comes as a guest, but she still wears the boots of the occupation!" I laughed and told him that these too would go in thirty days when the CPA dissolved. Sheikh Anwar said, "You will always be welcome to visit us in friendship, Emmasky. Go in peace."

Heading back towards Kirkuk, we passed through Rashad where we stopped to watch a soccer match. Both teams were wearing shiny bright new kits and were cheered on by eager fans. We dropped by the electricity department to test the systems. There was a problem in a neighbouring area, but all was well in this district. As we drove home, Abu Kahraba surveyed the surrounding countryside, the pastoral idyll, and remarked, "The most important thing in life is security. Not water or electricity.

It is security. *Alhamdulillah* [Thank God] that this region is a safe one."
But few Sunni Arab areas would escape the winds of violence ripping
through the country.

THE NEXT DAY, around a hundred people gathered in the government
building to discuss the election process with Carlos Venezuela, the representative from the UN's electoral team. I stayed for half an hour before
creeping out with the deputy governor. We were off to visit displaced
Kurds and to assess their living conditions. The governor decided he
would come with us. We headed out in a convoy, led by a policeman on a
blue-flashing motorbike. I was in the car with the deputy governor, Abu
Kahraba and Abu Baladiya of the PUK. We crossed over the bridge, drove
past the tenement buildings on our left, home to Shia Arab families, and
turned right into a district covered in PUK and KDP graffiti before heading into the stadium.

The sign at the entrance to the stadium read KURDISTAN STADIUM. I
walked around with the governor surveying the living conditions. The
situation had deteriorated a lot since I had last visited. Sick, listless children sat in filthy tents, surrounded by excrement and covered in flies. No
sign of NGOs. The press were with us as we walked from shack to shack.
The governor asked people where they were from. Abu Baladiya translated from Kurdish to Arabic for me. CPA had been urging displaced people to "stay put" for a year, promising to put in place return programmes,
housing projects and assistance to rebuild the villages that Saddam had
destroyed. I realized sadly that we never would.

We left the governor and headed off to Qaranjir, a village on the border with Sulaymaniyah province which Kurds were busy rebuilding. We
entered the office of the local mayor. As Ismail Hadidi sat talking with
him, I looked around the room taking in the map of Kurdistan, covering
northern Iraq down to the Jebel Hamrin mountains, half of Turkey and
northern Syria.

Ismail dropped me back in Kirkuk. He pointed to our police escort
and told me with a big smile that they were all originally peshmerga. "*Zor
spas, ya peshmerga,*" I thanked them in Kurdish, raising my hand once

more to my forehead and then to my heart. And I bade farewell to my travelling companions, Arab, Kurd and Turkmen. "*Allo, allo, allo,*" Ismail said, as he shook my hand. Iraq was the only country where hello meant goodbye.

7

GOODBYE
TO ALL THAT

Out of the South came Famine.
Out of the West came Strife.
Out of the North came a storm cone
And out of the East came a warrior wind
And it struck you like a knife.
—JAMES FENTON

As THE SECURITY SITUATION in Iraq continued to deteriorate, we seemed powerless to do anything about it. No longer able to affect the direction in which Iraq was heading, people drank and counted the days to departure. My thoughts turned to life post-Iraq—my own home rather than a trailer, old friends, sushi . . . I knew there would be no hero's welcome for me. I feared I would return to the UK like a Vietnam vet, ostracized for participating in a highly unpopular war.

The farewell-to-CPA party was held by the Republican Palace's swimming pool. It was held early because people would be leaving at various times through June, including most of the Governance team. I helped myself to food from the barbeque and enjoyed the party atmosphere. David Richmond read out a letter from Tony Blair, thanking us all for our hard work. A video from President Bush was played, praising the good work of Americans. Bremer took to the platform and started by mentioning the Brits. There was a loud cheer from this vocal minority. In a humorous speech, which he had obviously written himself, he referred to everything we had endured, from the food and accommodation through to the constant attacks. For the rest of our lives, he said, we would remember how we had contributed to building democracy in Iraq.

The sound of gunfire and explosions could be heard in the background. There were many things I would remember about my time in Iraq, but building democracy was not one of them.

THE GOVERNING COUNCIL, which was having difficulties coming to terms with its own dissolution, insisted that Sheikh Ghazi, rather than the US choice of Adnan Pachachi, be made president of Iraq. Ahmed Chalabi had completely fallen from grace with the Americans. In May, news broke that Iranian intelligence had been manipulating the US to get rid of Saddam Hussein by providing false information through Chalabi. Chalabi's Information Collection Program had also kept the Iranians informed of what the US was up to by passing on classified information. The Defense Department halted its monthly payment of $340,000 to Chalabi, and he was not selected for a key position in the Interim Government.

On 1 June, the swearing-in of the Interim Government took place. I was tasked with escorting Iraqi officials who had come up from the provinces to the ceremony, whose location had been kept secret until the last moment. I met up with Ismail Hadidi, the deputy governor of Kirkuk and Tahseen, the chair of the Provincial Council. We were deep in conversation when a loud explosion went off very close by. We were used to these by now, but it was enough to cause the departure of some of the foreign diplomats, muttering that the Coalition was unable to provide the necessary security.

Watching the new Interim Government being sworn in, there was a great sense of relief. Iraqis were officially back in charge of their country. And the CPA was less than a month away from dissolving.

I ACCOMPANIED BREMER to a meeting with Sheikh Ghazi al-Yawar. A few weeks earlier, I had travelled to Mosul with Bremer and Ghazi. When we landed back in Baghdad, Bremer's car was waiting for him, but there

Sky asleep on Sheikh Ghazi al-Yawar, president of Iraq, aboard a C-130 plane.
Photo by Ali Khedery

was no sign of Sheikh Ghazi's. I told Sheikh Ghazi that we would have to hitch-hike. He pulled up his *dishdasha*, revealing his left leg, while hopping on his right, and waved a thumb at Bremer's car as it flashed past. We had laughed so much. Now Sheikh Ghazi was president of Iraq.

Bremer began the meeting by referring to Ghazi's recent attendance at the G-8 summit in the US. Ghazi said he had thoroughly enjoyed himself. He had never imagined that he would one day be president of Iraq, and within a week would get to meet the president of the United States. Bremer brought up the matter of the Kirkuk Foundation and invited Ghazi to accompany him to Kirkuk to announce its establishment. Sheikh Ghazi was excited by the concept and immediately understood that he could play a role as president in bringing about reconciliation in Kirkuk. He himself was from Mosul, so he had a good grasp of the complexities.

I left the meeting and bumped into Ayad Allawi in the corridor. We smiled at each other. I had recently had dinner at his house in Baghdad, outside the Green Zone, drinking and chatting while gunfire went off all around as Iraqis celebrated a victory of their soccer team. And now Allawi was prime minister.

ON 23 JUNE, I flew with Bremer and Ghazi to Kirkuk. We landed on the airfield and walked to a large container which served as a meeting venue—Bremer's security detail would not allow him to venture to the government building. The great and the good of Kirkuk had gathered for the event, which had been shrouded in secrecy. I stood at the side, looking at the familiar faces.

Bremer spoke from the podium. I had worked with his speechwriter over the last week or so, making sure that key phrases appeared and removing the mentions of "evildoers" that were prone to pepper his speeches. He described how all of Iraq's peoples, who made up the country's rich human tapestry, were in Kirkuk: Kurds and Arabs, Turkmen and Christians. He told them the people of Kirkuk were the province's greatest asset and that they were the eternal flame that lit this city. He announced the establishment of the Kirkuk Foundation, with an initial endowment of $100m from the Iraqi budget. He ended the speech with his hallmark slogans: "*Mabrouk al-Iraq al-Jadeed. Aash al-Iraq!*" (Congratulations on the new Iraq. Long live Iraq!)

After he had given his speech, Bremer exited with his entourage, a symbolic act of "out with the Coalition, in with the new Interim Government." I remained with Sheikh Ghazi and listened to him speak without notes for about an hour. He happily took questions from the Kirkukis and answered eloquently, calling for peaceful coexistence among the different communities.

For me, it was a final opportunity to say goodbye to the people of the province. I did not know when I would see any of them again. But I had promised myself that one day I would return, and reminisce with them about this bizarre period of their history when our lives had been so intertwined.

We flew back to Baghdad on separate helicopters. When Sheikh Ghazi emerged from his helicopter he called for me and Dan Senor, the CPA spokesman, to come over, and he proceeded to spit venom. He had travelled back in a helicopter with the doors open. The wind had blown off his headdress, totally dishevelling his robes. He shouted at us for the humiliation caused not to him as a person but as the president of Iraq. He was absolutely furious. I apologized profusely for what had happened, saying it was obviously a mistake and no slight had been intended. Later I went over to the president's office, to be told that as a result of the trip he had a bad leg, bad hearing, sinus problems and was refusing to take any calls.

After a couple of days recovering, the president reappeared and hosted the first meeting of the board of the Kirkuk Foundation. The board needed to move quickly to establish the foundation in Delaware and to transfer the $100m to a bank account in the UK before the transfer of authority on 30 June. (I only found out weeks after I had left Iraq that the funds had not been transferred in time. It was infuriating that after all those months of planning, the foundation would never be established. It was yet another one of our good intentions that came to nothing.)

Sheikh Ghazi phoned me one afternoon. "Hello, Mr. President," I said. "Please stop calling me that," he responded. "Call me Ghazi." I laughed. He was upset that his security guards, who had recently received training from American navy SEALs, had been thrown to the ground by American soldiers. I apologized yet again for the helicopter trip. I encouraged him to be patient. It was only a matter of days until the restoration of Iraqi sovereignty and the end of the CPA. He mentioned the Republican Palace. It was a symbol of Iraqi sovereignty, but the Americans were not handing it over. They were transforming it into the American embassy. So many humiliations, he lamented.

THE 30 JUNE DEADLINE loomed ahead of us and attacks on the Green Zone increased another notch; but as usual we received little information about where the rockets and mortars were landing. Iraqi security forces were now more visible, but restaurants were out of bounds and travel even within the Green Zone was prohibited except in armoured vehicles.

I packed my goods away on Sunday 27 June. Mementos of the 173rd Airborne Brigade were carefully stored among old leather Kurdish weighing-scales (to be converted into hanging baskets), the chess set from Jalal Talabani and gifts from the people of Kirkuk. DHL Express had warned us that Sunday was the last day they would be working until after the transfer of authority—everyone was expecting insurgents to launch spectacular attacks on Sovereignty Day.

That evening, in whispered tones outside the bar at Ocean Cliffs, I was told I would be leaving in the morning with Bremer and a select crowd. Our departure had been brought forward two days. I rushed into the palace early the next morning. There were e-mails to respond to, documents to be saved onto memory sticks and files to be moved to the shared drive. And goodbyes. But how to say goodbye when our departure was secret?

I stood at the helicopter landing zone. One Chinook helicopter for journalists; another for Bremer's party. Barham Salih, now deputy prime minister, arrived. We hugged. "Are you leaving, too?" he asked me. I nodded. "I'm going to miss you," he said.

Within a quarter of an hour, Bremer, David Richmond and the others were on board. The Chinook took off. I had tears streaming down my face. I was weeping to be leaving *bilad al-rafidayn* (the land between the two rivers). I was weeping for the Iraqi people who had had the yoke of Saddam's tyranny lifted from them, only to see their country collapse, feel the humiliation of foreign rule and suffer random acts of terrible violence. I was weeping for Kirkuk and my Iraqi friends who lived in hope of a better future, and in fear of assassination. I could so clearly picture the faces of the Kirkuk Council members who had died: Sheikh Agar, Sheikh Naif and Yahiya Hadidi, all murdered; and Mustapha Kemal and Nizam al-Din Gali, killed in car crashes.

Barham took out a piece of paper and wrote me a note that today marked the departure of Iraq's occupiers, in the company of their "former masters," as Talabani was fond of calling the Brits. He then showed the note to Bremer. We all laughed. A camera captured the moment. We arrived at Baghdad airport. There it was the final farewell to General Sanchez. We all hung around chatting. I joked that we were the Family von Trapp from *The Sound of Music*—at the end everyone was waiting for the big performance, but it was not going to happen because we, like the von Trapp family, had run off.

Ambasador Bremer, Barham Salih and Sky. The great escape, 28 June 2003, on a Chinook to Baghdad airport. *Photo by Coalition Provisional Authority*

I turned to Jerry Bremer to say farewell. He commended me for all my hard work, particularly with regards to Kirkuk. I could not think of what on earth to say. So I simply thanked him for the opportunity to work on his staff. It was over in seconds. I then watched him walk out with Barham Salih to a plane, shake hands and wave goodbye. That image was beamed around the world. What was not shown was Bremer walking through that plane, down the steps and onto another plane. Operational security.

I flew off in an RAF C-130 to Kuwait. Once we were up in the air, and the danger of being shot down had subsided, my thoughts turned to the Coalition I had been part of, a modern-day Crusade of ideologues and idealists, and the ignorance, arrogance and naivety: people who believed they could bring liberal democracy to Iraq and hence to the Middle East; that Saddam and Bin Laden were connected, and that this war was an essential part of the War on Terror; that Iraqis would be eternally grateful for their freedom from tyranny; and that Iraqis would love America.

Many young Americans had volunteered to come to Iraq in response to 9/11, as a way to serve their country, to make America safer, to stop blood being spilt again on America's soil. And I began to cry for all those who had been killed in this war.

Hours later, I was sitting in a luxurious room at the Sheraton Hotel in Kuwait. My days of flying in C-130s were over. The next day I sat in the comfort of British Airways business class, bound for London. I picked up an English-language newspaper. The front page showed Saddam in court. He was wearing a suit and had a cropped beard. He looked much better than when he was first arrested. I stared at the picture wondering how he could have committed such crimes against humanity, burying Iraqis by the tens of thousands in mass graves which were now being discovered.

I wondered what impact this trial was going to have on Iraq and the Middle East. Would it be cathartic? Would it help the Iraqis deal with the terror they had experienced under Saddam's reign, while the rest of the region had remained silent? Or would it widen the rifts between Arabs and Kurds, and Sunnis and Shia? So much blood had been spilt in this land. When would it ever stop flowing? No matter how many statues of Saddam were removed, and posters torn down, a sense of Saddam remained in the psyche of every Iraqi. His overwhelming presence would be felt long after his death.

I FINALLY ARRIVED at my house in Manchester. When I had initially gone out to Iraq, it was only supposed to be for three months until we handed back sovereignty to Iraqis. In the end, the CPA existed for over a year before it disbanded, handing over authority to an Iraqi Interim Government. But tens of thousands of Coalition forces remained in Iraq to prevent the overthrow of the government and to keep a lid on the increasing violence inflicting the country. I changed into my black US Army shorts and brown T-shirt and went for a run down the overgrown lanes and up onto the banks of the River Mersey. I inhaled the fresh damp air. I relished the bright-green fields and the sight of ducks floating in the water. I had survived. I was free. And I was home.

PART II

SURGE

JANUARY–DECEMBER 2007

8

BACK TO BAGHDAD

We are the Pilgrims, master; we shall go
Always a little further: it may be
Beyond the last blue mountain barred with snow,
Across that angry or that glimmering sea,
White on a throne or guarded in a cave
There lives a prophet who can understand
Why men were born: but surely we are brave,
Who make the Golden Journey to Samarkand.
—JAMES ELROY FLECKER

AT THE END OF JUNE 2004 I returned to my old job—and sat at my old desk—at the British Council in Manchester. But I could not settle back into it. Nobody wanted to talk about Iraq or hear about my experiences there. And with the wars still going on in Iraq and Afghanistan, everything else felt irrelevant. The British Council agreed to second me to the Post Conflict Reconstruction Unit (PCRU) in London. It was a newly established interdepartmental unit, belonging jointly to the Foreign Office, the Ministry of Defence and the Department for International Development (DFID.) Its purpose was to ensure that the UK had capable and trained civilians able to deploy with the military into conflict zones so that we would not face the problems we had suffered in Iraq staffing the Coalition Provisional Authority.

It was good to be working among others who had served in Iraq and who cared about what was happening in the news. But after a few weeks in London, I was already becoming disillusioned with the bureaucratic infighting between the three different departments that frustrated the work of the PCRU at every turn. As it happened, the PCRU was asked to

recruit an adviser to go to Jerusalem for six weeks as the UK contribution
to a new US-led mission in support of the Middle East Peace Process. I
seemed the obvious choice as I had lived there for a decade and had experience of working with the US military.

Following the death of Yasser Arafat, the US had decided to re-engage
with the Palestinians by appointing a security coordinator for the Middle East Peace Process: General Kip Ward. I ended up spending nine
months in Jerusalem serving as General Ward's political adviser—POLAD
in army-speak. We monitored Israel's disengagement from the Gaza Strip
and the removal of Jewish settlers. But the decision by Israel to unilaterally
withdraw from Gaza, without an agreement with the Palestinian Authority, enabled armed groups to claim the credit for ridding Gaza of Israelis.

When General Ward's mission came to an end, I went to Kabul in early
2006 to serve as the Development Adviser to General Del Vecchio, the
Italian commander of International Security Assistance Forces (ISAF)
in Afghanistan. DFID determined to put an adviser into the Italian-led
NATO headquarters that had taken over from the Turks, and which in
due course would hand over to the British. By this stage, the British
Council was no longer prepared to second me to do such work. So to
take up the short-term DFID contract, I had to leave my permanent and
pensionable job. It was a gamble. I had no idea what I would do when my
Afghanistan tour ended in six months.

It was my first time in Afghanistan. I arrived in freezing-cold weather:
minus 13°F. I was met at the airport by an Italian colonel, who greeted
me with a big smile: "We are five hundred Italian men with no women
to dance with." What had I let myself in for, I wondered. Within hours of
arrival in Kabul, I sought escape from the Italians. My old friend Colonel
Mayville was serving as the chief of staff of a two-star US general on Ba-
gram airfield. He immediately sent a car to collect me. We had not seen
each other for two years and had much catching up to do. Colonel Mayville then put me on a plane down to join the Sky Soldiers in Kandahar.

The nervousness and dislocation disappeared the moment I was back
among familiar faces, flying on helicopters and riding in Humvees. The
173rd were keen to give me a thorough introduction to their area of responsibility. I flew in a Black Hawk helicopter to Lashkar Gar, the capital
of Helmand province, hovering low over the fields. There was no need

to go up and down to avoid the power lines, as we had done in Iraq—in Afghanistan only 6 per cent of the country had electricity. I looked down on the fields below, wondering whether they were full of poppy. I wore thermal long johns and top, corduroy trousers, a big woollen jumper, and a North Face inner and outer coat, as well as a hat and scarf. Despite this, I shivered all the way. The journey was about half an hour—much longer and I was sure I would have come down with hypothermia.

The 173rd took me along to a meeting with the governors of Helmand, Kandahar and Zabul provinces. After the initial pleasantries and drinking of green tea, the security chiefs briefed the governors on the security situation. They described facing the enemy without enough weapons or fast enough cars. I asked the governor of Kandahar, who the "enemy" was, to which they referred. Were we fighting al-Qaeda, drug smugglers, Taliban, criminals, poverty, weak government? I would spend the next months trying to find the answer.

While the Italians were unlikely to win any prizes for their soldiering, they certainly would for morale and welfare. The quality of the food— pasta and pig—was exceptional. Kiosks on the base sold pizzas and cappuccinos. A superb new gym had been constructed and the soldiers paraded round in their Gucci-styled military jackets, comedy beards and plucked eyebrows. The language of communication was English, or rather an Italian version of English. One communiqué explained at length why there was no water on the base and ended: "Please be patient, we are hardly working." Another announced that the car park would temporarily be closed and apologized for "the incontinence."

The Italians were replaced by the Allied Rapid Reaction Corps, headed by British Lieutenant General David Richards. On my last evening, General Richards invited me to join him for dinner, along with the command group and the ISAF leadership from the regions. He generously made a toast in my honour, and I looked round the room at the raised glasses and smiling faces. I could not help but marvel at how soldiers of the UK, Germany, France, Italy and the other countries interacted with each other as if it were the most natural thing on earth. Only two generations ago, these soldiers would have been fighting each other. And few then could have dreamt of a time when the soldiers of Europe— and America—would work together side by side on peace-keeping and stability operations around the world. Surely there could be no greater inspiration that peoples with a history of war can put the past behind them, live together in peace and cooperate in other ventures.

After completing my tour with ISAF, I returned to spend a glorious month working with Rory Stewart at his Turquoise Mountain Foundation, living in the fort he rented in Kabul and travelling around the country. It gave me a totally different sense of Afghanistan from the one I had gained through the lens of the military. I first met Rory in Iraq, after he had walked across Afghanistan following the fall of the Taliban. He was so scarred by his experience of working with the Coalition Provisional Authority that he had come to believe that grandiose nation-building schemes could never succeed in societies such as Iraq and Afghanistan. He was now focused on helping to restore historic parts of Kabul and to resuscitate Afghan traditions of arts and crafts.

ON MY RETURN to the UK in August, I moved into a tiny Victorian maisonette I had bought in London from the sale of my house in Manchester, and threw myself into restoring it. Sanding floors and installing a kitchen proved the perfect antidote to war. I visited friends. I exercised regularly. I cooked. I started as a research fellow at the War Studies Department of King's College, London. I began to embark on life after war. Or so I thought.

Into this world arrived an e-mail, out of the blue, from General Ray Odierno, who was now a three-star general: "Dear Emma. I'm headed back to Baghdad. Will you be my POLAD?"

It was the very last thing on my mind. I went for a long walk along the Thames as I deliberated how to respond to Odierno. There were plenty of reasons to decline, not least that I was only a month out of Afghanistan and not ready for a year-long deployment. Unlike military guys who had to go where they were ordered, I could choose. And why would anyone in their right mind choose to go to Iraq when it was clearly such a disaster? But Odierno had directly requested my help. If anyone else had asked I would probably have refused. But he felt he needed me and I did not want to disappoint him. I did not want to miss the opportunity to help him make the situation in Iraq a little less worse.

It took me a couple of days before I reached the decision to return, just a few weeks later, to Iraq—and only for three months. I asked the DFID if they would be interested in contracting me for this role. They agreed.

The first time I had gone to Iraq was to apologize to Iraqis for the war and to help them rebuild their country. I had fallen in love with Iraq, and had learnt to work with the US military. I agreed to go back not because I was optimistic that things would get better in Iraq, but because a man I greatly respected, and liked immensely, had asked me to.

In the intervening years I had sought to learn more about the US military, to understand their culture and traditions, and the way in which they viewed the world. I had gone through their recommended reading lists, pouring over books on counter-insurgency, the autobiographies of respected Generals such as Anthony Zinni and Colin Powell, as well as one of their fictional favourites, *Once an Eagle* by Anton Myrer.

AT THE BEGINNING of January 2007, I found myself back at Brize Norton RAF base. The flight, delayed for hours, was a charter one with Monarch Airlines, taking three hundred British soldiers to Qatar and on to Iraq. On board, the air hostess passed through the cabin offering duty-free goods. And on landing, the pilot thanked us for flying with Monarch Airlines and wished us a safe onward journey. It was surreally ordinary. If this had been an American plane, it would have been full of stars and stripes, and air hostesses wishing the guys good luck and praying for their safety.

From Qatar I flew by C-130 Hercules to Basra. And from there, I flew onwards to Baghdad with Major General Berragan, the new British deputy commanding general of Multi-National Corps—Iraq (MNC-I). We arrived at 4 a.m., to be driven the half hour to Camp Victory before walking the last ten minutes through deep mud to my trailer. I had forgotten about the mud. Later that morning, when I was settling in to my office, General Odierno dropped by and gave me a big hug, welcoming me back. We had not seen each other for a year and a half, when we had dined in Jerusalem during his visit to that city as military adviser to Condoleezza Rice, the secretary of state.

General O, as he was widely known, asked me to attend a meeting in his office with the US assistant secretary of state on economic

development, who had brought with him a bunch of American businessmen interested in investing in Iraq. One of the US officials asked
why Iraqis in particular and Muslims in general were not more grateful for what the US was doing for them in Iraq and around the world.
General O leant back in his chair and said, "Emma, can you answer this
one?" I jumped right in. Studies showed that Muslims had respect for
the US and its achievements. But they did not like US foreign policy. I
described the gap between US rhetoric (of freedom and democracy) and
US actions (invading two Muslim countries and propping up authoritarian regimes). The man looked stunned. In his world-view, anybody who
thought badly about Americans had to be bad themselves.

General O told me he wanted me to attend all his meetings and
accompany him everywhere he went. He made this clear to his staff,
explaining that I brought a different perspective. But I knew I had to
prove my mettle, to show that I was worthy of the confidence he placed
in me. Given how bad the situation was in Iraq, it meant a lot to General O that I had come back. I had agreed to return—and to put myself
in harm's way—because he had asked me. Loyalty meant everything to
General O.

By EARLY 2007, the violence in Iraq was spinning out of control. Tens
of thousands of Iraqis had been killed and hundreds of thousands had
fled their homes. Security in Baghdad had degenerated and the city was
divided into armed sectarian enclaves. Meanwhile, back in the United
States, public support for the war was waning, and in the UK it was more
unpopular than ever.

On 30 November 2006 in Amman, Jordan, President Bush had met
Nuri al-Maliki, the Iraqi prime minister, and informed him of his intention to make a dramatic change in policy, surging extra US forces into
Iraq in an effort to break the violence. This went against the recommendations of most experts including the Iraq Study Group, a high-powered
bipartisan US panel headed by former secretary of state James Baker.
But Bush reasoned that the prevailing US strategy of transfering responsibility for security to the Iraqi security forces was destined to fail, and
something new needed to be tried.

In the news conference after his Amman meeting, Bush said he was reassured by Maliki's determination to hold to account those who break the law, "whether those people be criminals, al-Qaeda, militia, whoever." Bush strongly endorsed Maliki, calling him "the right guy for Iraq." "He's been in power for six months, and I've been able to watch a leader emerge," Bush observed. Maliki was a member of the Dawa party, chosen as a compromise candidate to be prime minister. He was from the mid-Euphrates, and had spent years in exile in Iran and Syria before returning to Iraq in 2003.

Maliki promised there would be no political interference in the military operations, and that extremists of all persuasions would be targeted by Iraqi and Coalition forces. Having executed Saddam at the end of 2006, he felt he had firmly established his authority—and according to Iraq's new Constitution, the prime minister was both the chief executive and the commander-in-chief of the armed forces. For Maliki, the basic cause of violence in Iraq was the refusal of Baathists to accept Shia rule. He believed the strength of Shia militias was exaggerated. He needed US support to build and train the Iraqi security forces. But the presence of US forces caused him difficulties, not least by complicating Iraq's "understanding" with Iran. So the surge in US forces would only be temporary and the first step towards reducing the US presence.

On 10 January, Bush formally announced the commitment of an additional twenty thousand US troops to Iraq and a change in strategy. General O had fully supported the decision, against the judgement of most senior US military, who argued that the US troop presence was the problem and that the US should continue to transition to the Iraqi security forces.

IT WAS V CORPS that had first established its base at al-Faw Palace in 2003 near Baghdad airport and dubbed it Camp Victory. The name had stuck, without any sense of irony, long after Iraq had begun to unravel. Saddam had commissioned the palace to celebrate the retaking of al-Faw peninsula during the Iran-Iraq war. It was a sterile place. I heard no birdsong, nor laughter of children, and saw no flowers. An artificial lake surrounded the palace. In the lake were carp that had become piranha-like during our tenure due to the power bars and leftover food the soldiers

al-Faw Palace at Camp Victory. *Photo by the author*

had fed them. One soldier had used his phone to film the little ducklings in the lake and had captured the moment when the carp had come up underneath them and gobbled them up.

The palace was situated within a landscaped resort whose numerous villas, formerly second homes to Iraq's elites, now housed Coalition generals. The rest of us lived in trailers. As with the colonels, I was assigned a "wet CHU," a "containerized housing unit" where I had a room to myself and shared an indoor bathroom with one other who I heard but never met. Lower ranks shared trailers and outside bathrooms.

Camp Victory had become a city in itself, inhabited by around twenty thousand Coalition military and contractors. Only a small percentage ever left the "wire" and ventured out into Iraq. The camp was a twenty-five-minute drive, or a ten-minute helicopter ride, from the Green Zone.

In some ways Camp Victory was like a prison, wired in with checkpoints to prevent people leaving or coming in. In other respects it was more like a rehabilitation centre, where all our "needs" were taken

Trailer accommodation at Camp Victory. *Photo by the author*

care of. Clothes taken to the laundrette would be washed and ready for pick-up a few days later. There was a giant dining facility (DFAC), which served the thousands who lived on-camp with an atmosphere of American excess. There were vast quantities of food—and variety. In addition to the all-American hamburgers and fries, there were salads and "Middle Eastern" cuisine (actually Indian). Close by was a large gym, which was always full of soldiers pumping weights and running on treadmills. Connected to Camp Victory was Camp Liberty—another incongruous name. It hosted the PX as well as a Pizza Hut, a Burger King, a Green Bean cafe and a "Hajji market." American soldiers were now banned from referring to Iraqis as Hajjis, but the name had stuck for "local" shops.

The American Forces Network (AFN) blared out across the base and its announcements still seemed geared towards those with subnormal IQs. Don't drink and drive. Speed kills. Always wear a seat belt. Remember the military code. Don't commit suicide. Never leave a fallen comrade in the field. The nation is grateful to you for defending freedom. Greatest military in the greatest country in the world. Army strong.

Hooah! America the great. America the beautiful. Endless jingoistic messages, intermingled with sports coverage. Beautiful plastic women in short skirts churned out a parochial and paranoid picture of the world.

The military had to comply with a myriad of rules. They were obsessive about pornography, sex and alcohol—all banned by General Order No. 1. There was no prohibition on killing. As "warriors" the use of violence was their profession. There were sets of rules governing when it was permitted to kill, laid out in the "Rules of Engagement" and referred to by euphemisms such as "kinetic" and "contact."

The military strode around purposefully in their pyjama-type uniforms. Up close, ranks were discernable on collars and tribal markings on sleeves. A patch on the left sleeve indicated current unit and any special qualifications such as Airborne, Ranger or Special Forces. On the right sleeve a patch indicated previous combat service. They saluted each other continually around the base, but were exempt from doing so indoors. Sometimes they called out the mottos of their units. *"Shoot them in the face, sir." "Climb to glory, Sergeant."* It seemed to boost morale and camaraderie.

The lowest form of life was the contractors. They did not have to wear uniforms but typically imposed one on themselves of cargo pants and polo tops. They lived on the edges of the base and among them there were various subspecies. Some were techies and intelligence analysts, others ran the cafes and laundry.

Scattered across the camp were "duck and covers," concrete structures in which to take shelter from the rockets which were frequently lobbed at the base. I never responded to the frequent calls in the middle of the night to go to the shelter. Sleep was a precious commodity. On one of my first nights there, I jumped out of bed startled out of my wits by an ear-shattering, bone-jangling boom. Later, I discovered it was the C-RAM going off. The Counter-Rocket, Artillery and Mortar system was supposed to detect and destroy incoming missiles before they hit the ground. Judging by the amount of times we were hit, the C-RAM didn't seem to have a high success rate.

I looked around for the 173rd paratroopers but there were none. Most soldiers were cavalry, artillery, tankers, different clans from the one I had come to know well. I was given a regulation military green book in which to write notes. I then acquired the camouflaged sleeve in which to keep it. Everyone else had their name and unit patches sewn onto the cover. I thought it cool and copied it. I wanted to show that I had served in Iraq previously, and with one of the most elite units in the US military. I asked the deputy chief of staff, Colonel Volesky, for one of his name tabs. I cut off all but the last three letters, creating my name as I imagined British immigration had once done to my Eastern European forebears. I asked Major Ostlund from the 173rd to send me a unit patch. He did so along with a ranger tab. "173rd," he wrote to me, "are always ranger qualified." I went to one of the stores on base to have the name and patches sewn on. Later, I fixed my name patch to my body armour and helmet, with B+ to indicate my blood group.

I observed that the inhabitants of this world were very accommodating if I conformed to protocol. Protocol was held in the highest regard. It translated to respect. I was referred to as "ma'am," but insisted on being called Emma. For some of the Texans this was hard. They could not help but call me "Miss Emma." I told them it made me sound ancient, like Miss Daisy. "Ma'am, it's just our southern ways," they responded.

I made a point of not learning the rules, and got by fine most of the time. But the one rule I ran foul of was running with headphones. I would go jogging around the "lost lake," in the eastern part of Camp Victory, with my headphones on, listening to music. There was hardly any traffic around the lake, and most of the way I ran off-road, winding through palm groves, imagining myself somewhere else. But a number of times I was stopped and a note of reprimand sent up my "chain of command." "It's a stupid rule, Sergeant Major," I complained to Command Sergeant Major Neil Ciotola. He insisted it was for my own safety. "I jog through the streets of London with headphones and I haven't been run over," I told him. "There are many ways I could get hurt in Iraq—I think this is very low-risk." In the end he pleaded, "Please, Miss Emma, just do it for me."

EACH MORNING I walked from my trailer to the DFAC, grabbed a plastic box and filled it with bacon and fruit, and walked to al-Faw Palace, showing my badge to two sets of guards in order to get in. I quickly ate my breakfast while checking e-mails. After General O had received an intelligence brief, he walked from his office, across the foyer of al-Faw Palace and into the Joint Operations Command (JOC), a large auditorium. I listened out for the sound of his movement, scuttled out of my office and walked behind him into the JOC. Seated there, in row after row, were staff and liaison officers from the different organizations that constituted Multi-National Corps—Iraq, the organization that General O headed. There were hundreds upon hundreds of staff at Camp Victory. I had no idea what they all did. The Corps consisted of a number of divisions: Multi-National Division—South East (MND-SE), run by the British; MND—Central, run by the Poles; MND—Baghdad and MND—North, run by the US Army; and MND—West, run by the US Marines. Each division had a number of brigades subordinate to it.

When General O entered the JOC, everyone jumped to attention until he sat down. Major Jeremy Wilson, his aide, brought him his coffee. The Battle Update Assessment, the BUA, began at seven-thirty, connecting Multi-National Force—Iraq with corps and divisions. Down at brigade level with the 173rd in 2003-4, I had attended the daily BUB, the Battle Update Brief, so I was used to the concept. But what I was not used to was the size of the headquarters and the huge amounts of facts and figures that came up through the system to the corps.

General O had an extraordinary ability to absorb the vast quantities of information from all the subordinate commands. I did not. The reports meant little to me initially. I had mastered the lingo at brigade level. But now there were new terms, abbreviations and concepts to learn. They assigned their own names to roads—the airport road, for instance, was Route Irish. And they pronounced the names of Iraqi towns in ways unrecognizable to the inhabitants. Mosul became "Mo-zoooool." Taqaddam was referred to as "TQ." There was endless data and statistics quantifying enemy killed, operations conducted and our own casualties.

After a while I feared that the quantity of information would cause my brain to overload and explode. Iraq was unrecognizable to me through this prism of data, divorced from the human aspect. I found the most useful information came from the Iraqi media, from the interrogation reports of insurgents we had detained and from the Friday sermons in the mosques, which the Coalition recorded and translated.

Chief of Staff Joe Anderson; Colonel Jerry Tait; Karim Sinjari, minister of interior of Kurdistan Regional Government (KRG); Lieutenant Colonel Gary Volesky; Falah Mustafa, chief of protocol for KRG; Fuad Hussein, chief of staff for President Barzani. *Photo by the Kurdistan Democratic Party*

At the end of the BUA, everyone jumped up, saluted and chanted in unison *"Phantom Warriors,"* the motto of the Phantom Corps from Fort Hood, Texas, from which the headquarters in Iraq was derived. After the BUA, General O went off into a side room for "Small Group" followed by "Small Small Group" with the commanding general of MNF-I. Then he returned to his own office for Senior Leadership Huddle, feeding back discussions from his previous meetings.

On the walls of his office were maps of Iraq and photos of soldiers in combat. General O sat at the head of the table, with his chief of staff, General Joe Anderson, at the opposite end. I soon learned that General

Anderson was an excellent support to General O, a master at converting General O's intent into tasks for the multitude of staff. Seated around the table were the heads of the branches. Others sat in the seats behind. This meeting was frequently in two parts, with those in the cheap seats removed for the discussions on the more sensitive issues. In this highly compartmentalized world I was given a seat at the table next to the chief of staff and was included in all the "stay-behind" meetings. Even the small meetings ended with everyone saluting and repeating, *"Phantom Warriors."*

After the meeting I returned to my office, but kept my ears peeled. Once General O had finished going through his e-mails, his aide Major Wilson passed the message that the CG, the commanding general, was moving. He contacted the private security detail (PSD), the car drew up at the front of al-Faw Palace, I threw on my body armour and rushed out. I had to get to the car before the General, and climb into the far back seat. General O then got in. Jeremy rushed around and jumped in on the other side. And off we drove to the helicopter landing zone. General O boarded the helicopter first. I got in after him, sitting diagonally opposite, as the seat facing him had been removed to give him more leg room. It was a morning routine that we all perfected.

Each week in "calendar scrub," every hour of the day from dawn to dusk was allocated for some meeting or activity. There was no "down time." General O said where he wanted to go. And the staff went ahead and planned the "Battle Field Circulation." The unit on the ground was given time to prepare its brief and what it wanted to show the General. Usually we received an operations and intelligence brief, an "O&I," at the unit's base. And sometimes we drove out in a convoy to visit other units and projects. On other days, we flew to the Green Zone for meetings with Iraqis.

We returned in the late afternoon for the Corps BUA, to be updated on operations across the country. Then there were more internal meetings. Afterwards I generally went to the DFAC, filled a box with food, and brought it back to my desk to read e-mails and write up the notes of the General's meetings, to keep the staff informed and to identify follow-up tasks. At the end of the day, around ten o'clock, I walked out of al-Faw, across the moat and over to my trailer. I usually collapsed into bed exhausted and fell asleep within minutes. Such was my normal "battle rhythm." But no day in Iraq was ever normal.

DURING THOSE FIRST WEEKS, I wound up most evenings with General O, in his office or out on the balcony with him while he smoked a cigar. On one occasion I blurted right out, "Sir, this is the greatest strategic failure since the foundation of the United States." He responded, "What are we going to do about it? We're not leaving it like this." There was none of the happy talk that had defined the Coalition during my previous tour.

We got to know more about each other, and discovered we had little in common. If not for Iraq, our worlds would never have intersected. We came from different planets, but found much to laugh about. He had grown up in New Jersey, in a stable, middle-class, close-knit Italian American family. He had gone to West Point to play football, at which he had excelled until he had been forced to quit through injury. He graduated in 1976 and had spent years in Germany, training for the Cold War. He had never expected to stay long in the military but it had somehow turned into a full career. He had married his "high school sweetheart." General O spoke no foreign languages, was not widely read and had not really travelled outside the military context. He liked beer and sport.

He asked me about myself. I told him about Oxford, my travels across Africa and the Middle East, and a decade living among Israelis and Palestinians. In the 1991 Gulf War he had been with tanks in the deserts of Saudi Arabia. I had been at anti-war demonstrations in London and had signed up to be a human shield (although never deployed). He looked at me in amazement. He had never known anyone who had done such things or held such views. While he had been killing the "enemy," I had been glued to the TV, tears streaming down my face at the footage of Iraqi conscripts being mowed down as they fled along the Basra road. "Look at me now," I told him. "I am part of the occupation of Iraq, working as the adviser to a modern-day Genghis Khan!"

We recognized that we were both idealists, but of different types. He had total faith in America, in the government, in the system. He believed in serving his country and defending it with his life against all enemies "both foreign and domestic." I defined myself as an internationalist, who

was dedicated to fighting injustice and promoting peace. I spoke to him
of state terrorism, of Western foreign policy which propped up oppres-
sive regimes and of ordinary people in distant lands. I believed our policies were creating enemies.

"Their politicians lie," General O declared one day.

"And American politicians don't?"

"No, ours don't. Not deliberately."

"How about Saddam's WMD?"

"They didn't lie about it. They were mistaken."

I tried another tack. "How about the Virgin Mary?"

"What do you mean?"

"Don't you think she lied to Joseph? Have you ever heard of a woman
getting pregnant without having sex?"

He put his head in his hands. "Where do such thoughts come from?"

General O loved the army. He regarded it as his second family and
cherished it almost as much as his first. He also loved Texas, where the
4th Infantry Division and Phantom Corps were both based at Fort Hood.
I had never been to Texas. I viewed it as a State of cowboys, electric
chairs and right-wing zealots who spent their weekends down by the
border shooting Mexicans who tried to cross illegally. I had watched a
documentary on this once, and the images had stuck.

General O confessed that in his first tour he had learned the limits
of military might, as well as the importance of understanding other cultures and the need to seek advice from outside the military. He had seen
how Colonel Mayville and I had worked closely together. He admitted
that he had not had anyone on his first tour who could tell him frankly
when he was screwing up. This was why he had asked me to go back to
Iraq with him. But whereas Mayville and I had been peers, General O
and I were definitely not. General O was clearly my boss and my role
was to support him as best I could. This meant becoming his confidante
and speaking "truth to power"—to be his "conscience." In 2006 a best-
selling book by Tom Ricks, *Fiasco: The American Military Adventure in
Iraq*, had been scathing about the US military in Iraq in 2003–4. Ricks
was particularly harsh on Odierno, accusing him of causing the insurgency through his harsh tactics of breaking down doors and mass arrests.

The allegations had hurt. It was an exaggerated portrayal which had tarnished his reputation.

I spoke to General O about his son, Captain Tony Odierno, who had had his arm blown off fighting in Baghdad in 2004. It had brought the cost of war home to him personally. Soldiers feared injury, feared losing limbs more than anything else. He had had to confront the dreaded phone call; the worry of losing a son; the endless visits to the hospital; the long rehabilitation; sitting with other parents as a parent rather than as a general. I asked him if he felt guilty that his son had followed him into the army and then been injured. He did not. Tony loved the army and had already gained a great reputation as a soldier. He was currently serving as the aide to General Peter Pace, the chairman of the joint chiefs of staff, but his injury was forcing him to consider a career outside the military. Tony had told his father that he now lived each day for his driver, who had been killed in the RPG attack which had injured him.

We had a heated discussion one evening about an article in which a US soldier had condemned those protesting against the Iraq war and called for all Americans to get behind the president, the war and the selfless efforts of young Americans to "kill the evil" in Iraq. What I valued most about Western society was the freedom to take to the streets to protest our policies. What General O valued most was the willingness of soldiers to go around the world to defend what he saw as freedom.

General O told me, "'I have found that there are very few people who have actually fought wars that glorify them or like them, which is why so many will never talk about it. Those who glorify it tend to be those who have not experienced it. Today, television and Internet stories can immediately impact what goes on. Our opponents, unbound by any rule of law, have learned to use these tools to increase hatred, violence and promote intimidation and death. People should remember this when they speak. It has nothing to do with the freedom to do it. It is understanding and taking responsibility for your actions. There is no one who understands more the importance of liberty and freedom in all its forms than those who travel the world to defend it."

I told him, "One day, I will have you admit that the war was a bad idea, that the administration was led by a radical neocon programme, that the US's standing in the world has gone down greatly, and that we are far less safe than we were before 9/11 . . ."

He responded, "It will never happen while I'm the commander of soldiers in Iraq." To lead soldiers into battle, a commander had to believe in the cause.

THE VIOLENCE WAS EVERYWHERE around us. Death hung in the air. It affected my every sense: the constant boom of explosions, the *pat-patter* of small-arms fire; the smell of burning cars, and much worse, of burning flesh; the deserted streets, shuttered shops and roaming dogs; and the grisly coverage on the news.

The deaths of our soldiers appeared as news items and statistics on charts. In January 2007, the death count for the Multi-National Forces was eighty-six. Each one received full honours and a ramp ceremony to send them home. Each American was transported on an "Angel flight" to Dover Air Force Base in Delaware, the body meticulously cleansed and redressed in best uniform, before being escorted to the final destination for burial.

At the end of the BUA each day, we stood for the Hero Tribute. Photos of the dead were shown, in uniform and in front of the flag, and the chaplain read a short description of the person killed, how the soldier loved family, army, America and God. Little was gleaned of the person, the manner in which he or she was killed or of the family ripped apart by the tragedy. Then we prayed for them, their families and for ourselves and our own safety. Their deaths motivated us to try harder to achieve the "mission."

On 20 January 2007, five US soldiers were killed in Karbala. It was a shocking incident. A dozen Shia militia had disguised themselves as US soldiers and driven past the guards into the Provincial Joint Coordination Center in Karbala. They had killed one US soldier at the centre, wounded three and driven off with four others. The kidnapped soldiers were later found dead and dying in an abandoned vehicle. That same day, twelve more US soldiers were killed when their helicopter was ambushed. Insurgents had hit the helicopter with small-arms fire, forcing it to make a crash landing and had then blown it up with an RPG, killing all on board.

Those who were supposedly insurgents were registered as EKIA—enemy killed in action. One day in the BUA, the briefer reported five EKIA in an operation in Diyala. He went on to explain, "Sir, we killed the IED emplacer."

"Good job," General O responded.

"The atmospherics were positive," continued the briefer, implying that the local population was pleased.

"Who were the other four people killed?"

"Four children, sir, who were in the vicinity."

Silence. Afterwards, I said to General O, "Sir, I noted the briefer said that the atmospherics were good. Do you think they were fat children, or they were doing badly at school?" General O shook his head, but black humour was the only way to deal with this absurdity. We had killed someone who had probably been paid a $100 to place an IED. In the act, we had also killed four children. How many more enemies had we created?

Daily, we would receive reports of dead Iraqis who would then become statistics in the BUA. An estimated three thousand Iraqis died that month, but the precise numbers were never known and many families never had the opportunity to bury their loved ones. The most extensive figures were those produced by the Iraq Body Count, an NGO that meticulously collated the numbers of Iraqi dead from reports of the MNF-I, the Iraqi government, hospitals and media. In Vietnam, the US had erroneously associated the number of enemy dead with winning the war. So in this war the US Army had not tracked Iraqi deaths from the outset. This had now changed, but the figures were incomplete.

The majority of Iraqis victims were killed in bombings or assassinations. On 22 January, two car bombs exploded in Bab al-Sharqi market in Baghdad. This was reported as "88 LN KIA"—eighty-eight local nationals killed in action. They were ordinary Iraqis, whose lives were blown apart while out shopping. So many bodies were found floating in the Tigris that some Iraqis stopped eating fish, claiming its flavour had changed from nibbling on human flesh. Dead animals were used to conceal roadside bombs. Bodies of dead Iraqis were booby-trapped to blow up relatives who approached them. Mentally disabled children were turned into suicide bombers. Funerals were frequently the target of attacks. The morgues were full of mutilated bodies: if the head was cut off, it was

Shia; if the head was drilled through, it was Sunni. Iraq was in the midst
of civil war. But we were not allowed to acknowledge it because it was
not what Washington wanted to hear.

I thought continually about how to understand the violence in Iraq.
Some argued that it was because of "ancient hatreds" between Sunni and
Shia. The schism in Islam stemmed from disagreement over the succession to the Prophet Muhammad, and whether it should be through the
bloodline, or the person most suitable to rule. Those who believed the
rightful successor was Ali—Muhammad's cousin and son-in-law—became known as Shiat Ali (the Partisans of Ali), while the others were
called Sunnis. After being passed over three times, Ali became the fourth
caliph and established his caliphate at Kufa in Iraq. He was assassinated
in 661 and buried in Najaf. After Ali's death, his main rival, Muawiyah,
claimed the caliphate and founded the Umayyad dynasty, ruling from
Damascus. His son and heir, Yazid, defeated Ali's sons Hussein and Abbas in 680 at Karbala.

Yet despite this historic struggle, Sunni and Shia had for the most
part coexisted in Iraq throughout their history with very few periods
of sectarian violence. It was the Islamic Revolution in Iran in 1979 that
had led to fears of the spread of radical Shia Islamism. The overthrow of
Saddam's regime in 2003 had brought about Shia empowerment and a
sense of Sunni loss. But still an estimated 30 per cent of those who lived
in Baghdad were intermarried.

Were Iraqis inherently a violent people? Some argued that Iraq could
only be ruled by leaders such as Saddam Hussein who were prepared to
use total violence. Saddam's legacy of fear and hatred hung over Iraq.
During the three decades of Baath party rule, Iraqis were subjected to
three wars, the militarization of society, the brutal crushing of dissent
and impoverishment under sanctions. Policies of exclusion deepened
divisions in society. Saddam had begun his reign as president by purg-
ing his own party, killing numerous members to ensure the loyalty of
the others. After Iraqis rose up in response to President George H. W.
Bush's speech in 1991, after the Kuwait (or First Gulf) War, calling on
them to overthrow their regime, Saddam had retaliated, killing hundreds of thousands of Shia in the south while the West only protected
the Kurds in the north with a no-fly zone. Saddam had created a nation

of informants, making all who remained complicit in his rule, and gaining their acquiescence through fear. And many of those who belonged to opposition groups had received support from Iran to fight the Iraqi regime.

Following the invasion in 2003, the Coalition had collapsed the state through de-Baathification and disbanding the military. In the resulting vacuum had emerged a world of everyone for himself. Furthermore, the elite pact put in place by the Coalition Provisional Authority was not inclusive. The ill-fated Governing Council had determined who the winners were—excluding Sadrists and Sunni mainstream. The new political process emerged in an atmosphere of violence and under foreign occupation. The allocation of posts based on ethnicity and sect undermined any hope of building a "nation," institutionalizing sectarianism rather than pluralism. The emphasis had been on identifying communal representatives rather than bridging communal divides. Those excluded sought to overthrow the new order and drive out the Coalition. Returning exiled politicians, who had little base in the country, had used sectarianism to mobilize constituents.

Shia Islamists swept the January 2005 elections on an all-Shia list (which now included the Sadrists), blessed by Ayatollah Sistani. They then formed a coalition with the Kurdish political parties of the PUK and KDP, their old allies against Saddam. The electoral system, in which the whole of Iraq was treated as a single electoral district of 275 seats, favoured the large, organized political parties. Secular and liberal parties had neither funds nor militias to promote their vision of a non-sectarian Iraq. The majority of Sunnis boycotted the elections. The only "Sunni" party in existence was the Islamic party, which few Sunnis related to. Sunnis mobilized to try to veto the Constitution, which had been drafted by Shia Islamists and Kurdish nationalists based on the TAL—but failed. Sunnis turned out to vote in the December 2005 elections, but by that time the Shia and Kurds had already "captured" the state.

The insurgency against the occupiers and their allies morphed into civil war between Sunni and Shia. Foreign jihadis entered Iraq to fight the "infidel" US forces, collapse the state and replace it with a Sunni caliphate. Abu Musab al-Zarqawi, the leader of al-Qaeda in Iraq, accused Shia of being Safavids, agents of Iran, and of collaborating with the US invaders. He regarded Shia as "rejectionists" and deliberately targeted their holy places, leaders and civilians. Through suicide bombings, kidnappings, assassinations and beheadings, Zarqawi sought to provoke Shia to retaliate against Sunnis.

With increasing levels of violence, and with insufficient US troops to maintain security, the Coalition embarked on the rapid recruitment of new Iraqi security forces. The new recruits were poorly vetted and received minimal training. Sunnis viewed the new security forces as the tool of the Shia and Kurds. The Shia militias, which had fought on Iran's side against Iraq, were integrated into the new Iraqi security forces, while Sunni members of the old Iraqi Army joined the insurgency.

In February 2006, the blowing up by al-Qaeda in Iraq of the golden dome of the al-Askari Mosque, one of the holiest sites in Shia Islam, in Samarra north of Baghdad, further accelerated the spiral of sectarian killings. Iran increased its support to Shia militias to fight Sunnis and to pressure US forces to leave Iraq. Feeling threatened by the presence of US troops to its east in Afghanistan and to its west in Iraq, Iran sought to ensure the failure of the US "project" in Iraq. With support from Iran, the Badr Corps assassinated those they associated with the former regime; the Sadrists carried out revenge attacks on the Sunni population, clearing whole areas of Baghdad; and "special groups" deliberately targeted US forces.

Towards the end of January, after many nightly discussions, I set out my thoughts in writing for General O, in what I termed a "no shit" assessment of the situation. We had to stop framing the conflict in terms of the "enemy" with all the violent actors lumped together as AIF (anti-Iraqi forces) or ACF (anti-Coalition forces). We needed to identify who the different groups were and what motivated them, and to acknowledge that the Iraqi government and Iraqi security forces were also parties to the conflict and involved in sectarian killings.

I proposed that our focus should be on creating stability, that we should draw up different strategies to mitigate the various drivers of "instability" in every location. With the majority of the violence caused by sectarian conflict, our efforts should focus on protecting the population, suppressing the violent actors and brokering agreements between the different groups.

AN AUSTRALIAN who sat behind me in the JOC said to me, "These Yanks are not like us Aussies and Brits. They pray more often than the Muslims do." I knew what he meant. There were prayers in the morning BUA, prayers in the afternoon BUA and chaplains everywhere. In the DFAC, soldiers prayed, blessing their food before devouring it. And on Sundays various rooms of the palace held services for the multitude of different churches represented in the military. Their God was also different from the one I had grown up with, more Old Testament than New—with American can-do. The chaplains prayed for victory over our enemies rather than for peace.

On one occasion, General O appeared in the BUA with a big black smudge on his forehead. I wanted to spit on a tissue and wipe it off. But I looked around and noticed a number of senior officers with the same marks on their foreheads. In shock, I realized they were black crosses. I was horrified. What was going on? Was this some masonic cult? Were they Crusaders? Then someone told me it was Ash Wednesday and this was an American Catholic tradition.

At one BUA, the soldiers passed around a flier with a photo of Muqtada al-Sadr, dubbed "Ayatollah Asshola" on a milk carton, like a missing child in the US. He had not been seen for weeks and we did not know where he was. The Australian said to me, "Just wait till you see their reaction to some of the video footage." I did not have long to wait. Aerial footage was shown of a "target" under surveillance, apparently laying IEDs, and then being blown up. The whole JOC roared with applause, as if the home team had won a game rather than a human being had just been killed.

In the Senior Leadership Huddle, General O mentioned the video footage that had been shown at the BUA. It had been released to the media and was gaining wide coverage. "It's great, sir," one of the senior officers said. "This will really show the enemy! We must get more out onto the news networks." Everyone agreed.

I couldn't let this go. I hit back: "These are American jihadi videos, just like the videos al-Qaeda puts out of its fighters shooting down helos. All around the world, people will watch this footage. Is this what we want to show? Us killing people? Are we not supposed to be different from our enemy? Are we not supposed to be morally better than our enemy?" They all scoffed and scorned, mocking my outburst.

"I feel I am in an American jihadi camp, surrounded by violent extremists," I retaliated. The meeting ended and I went back to my office. I was livid. What on earth was I doing here? Not long after, Sergeant Major Ciotola came to my office and gave me a big hug. I looked at him, surprised. "Miss Emma, I stayed behind with the General to discuss what you said. We think you are right." General O had decided not to release any more video footage to the media.

9

FARD AL-QANUN

"All my life," Dienekes began, "one question has haunted me. What is the opposite of fear?" . . .

"When a warrior fights not for himself, but for his brothers, when his most passionately sought goal is neither glory nor his own life's preservation, but to spend his substance for them, his comrades, not to abandon them, not to prove unworthy of them . . ."

"The opposite of fear," Dienekes said, "is love."

—STEVEN PRESSFIELD, *Gates of Fire*

THE CORNERSTONE OF the Surge was to be a new Baghdad Security Plan. In order to gain Kurdish support for the new plan, General O flew up to Erbil towards the end of January to meet Masoud Barzani, who had been sworn in as president of Kurdistan in June 2005, following regional elections. It was great to be back in Kurdistan. Barzani greeted us, dressed as ever in traditional Kurdish clothes. I followed General O down the line, smiling at the familiar faces as we shook hands. Kemal Kirkuki hugged me. It had been almost three years since I had last seen them. Barzani was a gracious host and served a banquet in General O's honour: kebabs, lamb biryani, fresh bread.

General O briefed Barzani on the Baghdad Security Plan, describing how we were bringing in an extra twenty thousand US forces. It was to

General Odierno and Masoud Barzani, president of Iraq's Kurdistan Regional Government. *Photo by Curt Cashour*

be an Iraqi-led operation and he was helping to set up the new Baghdad Operations Command. He was hoping to get enough Iraqi security forces (ISF) into Baghdad, moving some units there from elsewhere in the country. There were 500–600,000 ISF on the books, but no one knew how many there were in reality.

"Americans are growing impatient with the situation in Iraq," General O admitted. "But President Bush is dedicated to making this a success. This will be our last chance." General O said he would appreciate Barzani's help as he was someone that people listened to and respected.

Barzani said he had spent the last month in Baghdad. He had urged Maliki to behave as prime minister for all Iraqis and not as the leader of a sect. Moderates from all groups who believed in the political process needed to be brought into the government—and extremists removed. Iraq could not have people who participated in the government during the day, and conducted violence by night. Disputes had broken out within and between the leaders of different communities because they had no trust in each other. In the meantime, the Iraqi people were suffering on a daily basis.

Barzani told us he had gone to Baghdad to show that the Kurds did care, not only for humanitarian reasons but also because they had taken the decision to stay within the framework of the state of Iraq, to protect and maintain the unity of Iraq. However, he said the Kurds could not continue to be part of a government which, infiltrated by Shia militia, carried out all these killings. Jaysh al-Mahdi was the centre of terrorism, and criminals had gravitated towards it.

"I told Maliki," Barzani said, "that never in the history of Iraq has a ruler had so much backing as he, and support both inside and outside the country. Even the American president, who others in the world spent ages trying to meet, came all the way to Jordan to meet him." Barzani acknowledged the disappointment Americans felt in the internal Sunni-Shia war, particularly after having made so many sacrifices. The Kurds had agreed to send down peshmerga to Baghdad but what were they supposed to fight? If it was to fight terrorism, that would not be a problem. But what to do in an internal war between Sunni and Shia?

Barzani described how after the cessation of hostilities in 1991, those Kurds who had previously fought as auxiliary forces for Saddam's regime had been granted amnesty, and captured Arab forces had been treated with respect. This had made him so proud to be a Kurd and a peshmerga. Back at the London conference in 2003, he had urged everyone to think about national reconciliation, pointing out how this had been achieved within Kurdistan. He lamented that his advice had not been heeded, noting that "Shia have a complex about the past; Sunnis are afraid about the future." As for the Kurds, he told us, they feared both the past and the future.

GENERAL O ESTABLISHED an "initiatives group" to help him define the nature of the threat facing Iraq and how Coalition forces should respond. It consisted of four colonels—Derek Harvey, Mike Meese, Robert Taylor and Gary Volesky—and me. We met General O in the evenings for a further couple of weeks. We redefined "success" in a much more modest way as "sustainable stability" and identified different *drivers of instability,* namely sectarian violence, al-Qaeda in Iraq (AQI), Sunni insurgency, Shia extremists, Kurdish expansionism, Shia-on-Shia violence, external subversion, criminality and weak state institutions. The group plotted on a map the different threats to stability in different areas around the country, and noted the diverse tactics required to deal with these threats.

We knew that failure to identify the various causes of instability appropriately would result in the wrong response and hence cause greater instability. For instance, there was a risk that the Coalition could be used by one group to "cleanse" another; or that the Coalition could capture or kill the very leaders needed to broker cease-fires. We described the conflict in Iraq as a struggle between different communities for power and resources—and not simply an insurgency. We acknowledged that the government was part of the problem. Iraq was a fragile state with weak legitimacy. We set out how we would decrease the violence, using the extra forces of the Surge, and by changing tactics.

To much fanfare, General Petraeus assumed command of Multi-National Force—Iraq from General Casey on 10 February 2007. The new religion was Counter Insurgency, which we called COIN, and its sacred text FM 3-24, a counter-insurgency field manual whose development Petraeus had overseen while at Fort Leavenworth. Its central thesis reaffirmed the old adage that the "population is the prize."

President Bush had appointed Petraeus to lead the Surge. The media reported how he was bringing with him a "brains trust," officers with PhDs who had been top of their class at West Point. Petraeus, who was two years older than General O, was promoted to four stars to take up this post and was to be General O's boss. And General O had not been looking forward to it. He had not been having an easy time with General Casey, who did not support the Surge. And he was irritated by all the publicity Petraeus was receiving.

Petraeus turned up to General O's office for their first meeting, accompanied by Pete Mansoor, his executive officer and Bill Rapp, chief of his initiatives group. He did a double take when he saw me standing beside General O. "Emma Sky, what a surprise to see you here!" he said as we shook hands. He remembered me from the CPA days back in 2003.

General O briefed his analysis of the situation and his concept of operations for the Surge, based on the work of his initiatives group. He used his favourite PowerPoint slide—the "gap slide"—to describe the complexity of the problems facing Iraq and how the power vacuum in the aftermath of the fall of the regime had been filled by armed groups. Coalition forces were needed to displace the armed groups and fill the "gap" until the Iraqi government had developed the capacity to do so. The goal of the surge was to buy the time and space for the government of Iraq to move forward with national reconciliation and the delivery of public services.

Petraeus asked a few questions and we all had a good discussion. At the end of the meeting, Petraeus said he thought our approach was right and told General O to go ahead and implement. We knew this would be our last chance to break the back of the violence. Although it was rarely mentioned, we were well aware of the consequences if we did not succeed. But for the military, failure was "not an option."

General O's initiatives group was now disbanded and the planners, led by Colonel Mike Murray, turned the concept that General O had briefed Petraeus on into a detailed operational plan. Hours of discussions each week determined which units should go where. I watched in fascination. The size of the endeavour was huge. Battalions and brigades were separated from their home divisions and attached to headquarters they had never previously worked for or trained with. Were they all compatible? How to know what units—cavalry, infantry, artillery—could do? Which units had vehicles too big for the streets of Baghdad? I observed General O's feel for the different capabilities of the units and his instinct on how and where to apply them. It was part art, part science.

We had captured an al-Qaeda diagram depicting their plan to stage attacks in Baghdad from the surrounding areas. And from studying Saddam's tactics, we saw how he had tried to defend the city by placing forces around it. General O therefore designated two extra brigades to be brought into Baghdad; and three other brigades to be based in the "belts" around the city to eliminate insurgent safe havens, logistical support areas and launching pads into Baghdad. More forces would also be sent west into Anbar to help the tribes in their battle against al-Qaeda in Iraq.

Coalition forces would move out of large bases to live among the local population. Together, Coalition and Iraqi security forces would help protect the Iraqi people by establishing Joint Security Stations, hardening markets, setting up checkpoints and establishing "gated communities." Coalition forces would help develop the capacity of Iraqi security forces through mentoring, training, partnering and embedded advisers, setting an example in terms of standards of uniform, conduct and performance. ISF leadership would improve its ability to exert command and control, and to plan and implement complex operations.

By patrolling the neighbourhoods together, Coalition and Iraqi forces would build up a better understanding of the local population and forge ties with local leaders. Once the public felt more protected, they were more likely to provide information about the extremists and criminals.

As we were driving along in the car one day, General O asked, "Emma, did you ever dream you would end up working on a military campaign plan?"

"No, sir."

"How does it feel?" he queried, turning to look at me.

"Sir, I hope God will forgive me for the things you forced me to become involved in." He laughed.

WITHIN WEEKS, I had firmly established myself in the role of General O's POLAD and had been accepted as a permanent, if somewhat unusual, feature within the headquarters. In the US system, POLADs were typically State Department foreign service officers—whose careers were not going anywhere. In the UK system, they tended to be high-flying Ministry of Defence civilians. Contracted-in for the post, I had no home organization whose interests I was supposed to represent, and no reporting lines other than to General O.

General O took me with him everywhere, no matter how dangerous the situation or sensitive the topic. I had access and influence. In the car, on helicopters and in the office, we constantly discussed issues, prepared for meetings and analysed them afterwards. General O used these private exchanges to help himself strategize.

We had such different instincts. A six-foot-five military man, who was always part of the most powerful pack, was bound to have a different approach to a five-foot-four civilian female, who had travelled on her own around the world. A Palestinian man in the West Bank had told me once that I had no idea what it was like to walk down the street with eleven brothers by my side. He was right. I was an only child from a broken-down family. I recalled his words while walking through Iraqi villages with General O and his troops. It certainly gave me a different outlook on life. The soldiers formed a protective ring around General O, surveying every angle as we walked along. If we were attacked, I knew that every one of them would spring into action without a moment's hesitation and fight to the death to protect him. And me.

I observed General O's leadership style up close. He listened and took advice. He led through making clear his "intent," setting the "left and right limits." He was hard on his staff, and regularly gave "ass-chewings." But he was greatly empowering of his commanders. He placed his trust in them and did not micromanage. He encouraged them to take calculated risks. He used his visits to units to hear first-hand what was happening on the ground, to clarify his thinking and to ensure soldiers of his support. He could not write well, struggled with typing, and his handwritten scrawls on memos were illegible to everyone except Sergeant Erika Strong, who had learned to decipher them after years of practice. But he was a strong oral communicator. His sincerity shone through. And the strength of his personality carried everyone along. The mission was so much greater than any of us as individuals. General O was our undisputed boss. He was so big, so confident, so decisive and so determined. I was in awe of him. I thought he was indestructible. As I was sure he could not be killed, I felt totally safe when I was with him—no matter where we went or how dangerous the situation.

In the civilian world from which I came, it was all about management, bureaucracy and competencies. Such environments did not nurture compelling leadership. In the military, leadership was valued and developed. Leading soldiers was seen as a great privilege. And experience and power created charismatic leaders.

I noticed that America's civilian leaders continually praised the US military and wanted to be photographed with the troops. It played well back at home. But I never had a sense that they really knew what the military was capable of, nor the cost of using it. Few had served, so they had little sense of the furies unleashed when soldiers went into action—nor the impact of that violence on the perpetrators.

To DIFFERENTIATE THIS Baghdad Security Plan from previous ones that had failed, and to send the message that it was an Iraqi plan, we called it by its Iraqi name, *Fard al-Qanun* (Impose the Law). It was soon abbreviated to FAQ.

Relationships with Iraqi security forces had to be built at all levels. General O's main partner was General Abud Qanbar, who had been selected by Maliki to head up the new Baghdad Operations Command (BOC). The BOC was set up in the Adnan Palace, just inside the Green Zone. All Iraqi Army, local and national police operating in Baghdad would come under General Abud's command. US officers were assigned to work in the BOC. The last thing we needed was for our forces to fire on each other by mistake.

Finding a good interpreter for General O had been a challenge. It was a difficult and skilled job, and very few self-respecting and educated American Arabs would agree to be part of the US mission in Iraq. The Coalition had also hired "locals." While they spoke Iraqi dialect, the downside was that their lives were put in danger, their families could be intimidated and some had links to political parties.

At one meeting, I had been impressed by General Casey's interpreter, who simultaneously translated from Arabic to English and back without any hesitation. I went up to speak to him afterwards. Mike Juaidi was of Palestinian origin, but a naturalized American. I asked him whether he would be interested in working for General O once General Casey had departed. He agreed, and he became an inseparable part of the cabal that went everywhere with General O.

General O went to the BOC a couple of times a week to meet General Abud. General Abud had been dismissed from the military in 2003 along with everyone else, and had sat at home depressed doing nothing until strings were pulled to bring him back into service. He was apparently related to Maliki, but he proved to be a good choice. He was a decent and honest man, and a career officer. He had a long, serious face, and was totally sincere.

In charge of the national police was Hussein al-Awadi. He was a brilliant commander, and the smartest of the Iraqi military leadership. He had had part of his intestines removed which apparently was the reason he was very skinny. He did not believe Abud had the qualifications or experience to be the overall commander of the operation. But the Coalition officers worked hard to ensure close cooperation between them.

General Ali Ghaidan was appointed the head of Iraqi ground forces. General O did not care for him at all and found him annoying. General O's British deputy, General Berragan, invested his energies in building close relations with the different Iraqi generals. General J. C. Campbell, the deputy commander of 1st Cavalry Division, which was responsible for Baghdad, spent the most time with the Iraqi leaders, mentoring them. He practically moved into the BOC. The Iraqi officers admired and respected him, recognizing his qualities as a soldier and leader.

General O attended several meetings a week on *Fard al-Qanun* to ensure that the military operations tied in to the overall strategy. I went along with General O, sitting in a chair behind him and General Petraeus, taking notes, identifying what needed follow-up, and responding to any messages General O passed to me. The meetings were important in terms of building Iraqi confidence. But they were often long and tedious, and my mind sometimes wandered. The generals brought along their own reading material, while keeping a headphone in one ear to listen out for the translation.

At one Sunday afternoon meeting of the Ministerial Committee for National Security, it was agreed that once military operations had cleared neighbourhoods in Baghdad, services would be delivered to show the presence of the government. This was easier said than done. The government had very little capacity to deliver anything. Most professionals had been dismissed from their posts through de-Baathification, were dead or had fled the country. Barham Salih, the deputy prime minister, said it was crucial that the Iraqi government succeeded this time. "If not," he said, "we will all be toast." Ahmed Chalabi was getting back into the political game after his fall from grace with the US back in 2004. He was supposed to mobilize popular backing for *Fard al-Qanun* but, ever the schemer, saw the opportunity to muster support for himself.

The scale of the task ahead was immense. For example, Baghdad at night was totally dark. The insurgents had taken out all the lights. It was a fearful place, leaving to one's imagination the events that produced the dead bodies found in the morning in the streets or washed up on the banks of the Tigris. The lack of electricity was a constant theme in the Iraqi meetings. How could the government show success if Baghdad remained in darkness? The Ministry of Electricity official lamented that whenever he laid lines, citizens dug them up, disconnected wires and tapped electricity supplies for themselves. *Fard al-Qanun* would not succeed unless Baghdad could be lit. He recommended using solar units, which would require four months to set up; and requested our help to bring in seven thousand solar-powered street lights.

It was not only the electricity situation that was bad. The hospitals were a nightmare. The Sadrists ran the Ministry of Health and there were numerous reports that the guards on hospitals were members of Jaysh al-Mahdi. Sunnis were terrified to go to hospitals in Baghdad after some had been murdered in their hospital beds.

The Crisis Action Cell took place on Mondays in Adnan Palace. It was chaired by National Security Advisor Mowaffak al-Rubaie and attended by Minister of Interior Jawad Boulani, Minister of Defence Abdul Qadir al-Obeidi, Iraqi generals, General Petraeus, General O, General Joseph Fil as commander of 1st Cavalry Division, and his deputy, General Campbell.

The minister of interior, Jawad Boulani, seemed a decent, honest man. He lived and worked in Adnan Palace, which also served as the headquarters of the BOC. It was too dangerous to go to the Ministry of Interior; it was outside the Green Zone, and every floor was run by a different militia. The minister of defence, Abdul Qadir al-Obeidi, had formerly been in the old Iraqi Army but had been jailed by Saddam. He had been nominated for his post by Sunni politicians, but they had lost confidence in him and wanted him removed.

In meeting after meeting, the details of the operational plan to secure Baghdad were discussed. There were concerns about the strength of Iraqi forces. There were not enough forces in Baghdad so units needed to be rotated in. But would they actually turn up and would they fight? And what to do about the hundreds of thousands of displaced Iraqis?

Despite the assertion by Maliki that politicians were not to interfere in the plan, they already were. Abdul Qadir complained that Chalabi was causing problems, phoning him, asking why certain people had been targeted and where particular detainees were being held.

There were constant exchanges of fire across the Tigris in Baghdad between the areas of Adhamiya, the former bastion of Arab nationalism and a stronghold of the Sunni insurgency, and Kadhimiya, which was an enclave of Shia fighters. We feared what might happen if either of the great mosques were hit: the Kadhimiya mosque housed the shrines of two Shia imams, Mousa Kadhim and his grandson Imam Mohamad al-Taqi; and the Abu Hanifa Mosque in Adhamiya was built around the tomb of the Sunni Imam Abu Hanifa al-Numan, the founder of the Hanafi school of Islamic jurisprudence.

The challenges ahead were daunting. I rose at dawn each day, attended all the US military meetings, ran around with General O to Iraqi meetings, and then wrote up the notes before going to bed.

ONCE A MONTH, General O and I dined with Dominic Asquith, the British ambassador. Dominic was the great-grandson of the former British prime minister Herbert Asquith. He was tall and handsome, with the most wonderful manners and a dry wit. His residence was in a villa in the Green Zone, near the United Nations.

I loved these evenings. They were our monthly treat. We would fly in from some trip to the battlefield, dirty and tired. But in the ambassador's residence we relaxed in comfortable chairs, surrounded by paintings and photos and various artefacts that spoke of culture and life away from war. I always started with gin and tonic before proceeding to red wine, happy in British sovereign territory to violate General Order No. 1, which prohibited alcohol. We were served a three-course meal, seated around a table that had once belonged to Gertrude Bell. Never had food tasted so good. We ate off china with metal cutlery, a welcome change from plastic and Styrofoam.

For General O, it was an opportunity to probe Dominic's insights into what was happening in Iraqi politics. It was the chance to delve deep, to speculate on the future. I had first met Dominic back in CPA days when we had lived in trailers in the same underground car park. He was witty and cynical—and completely disillusioned by our whole endeavour in Iraq. But as a loyal servant of the Crown, he toiled away.

I had informed General O that I would soon be leaving, as my three-month contract to serve as his POLAD—issued in the UK by the Department for International Development (DFID)—was expiring. He had looked at me in shock. "You are not leaving," he said. It was a statement of fact rather than a question. "I really appreciate everything that you are doing. You are making a real difference." I was embarrassed and didn't know what to say. I responded, "Are you feeling ill, sir? You're not just saying this because I make you laugh?" With a deadly serious face, he stared at me and said, "I need you."

At dinner, General O requested that the UK extend my contract until the end of the year. Dominic promised he would instruct the DFID to do so. I said I would agree to stay on as General O's POLAD on condition that he gave me a satellite TV without American Forces Network. General O hit back, "You are dreaming! I will never give you a TV without AFN."

THE RIVALRY BETWEEN General O and Petraeus dated back to 2003 when they had both served as division commanders in Iraq. The staff went out of their way to lessen the points of friction between the two by trying to ensure General O was informed ahead of Petraeus about everything taking place on the ground.

This was put to the test daily in the morning BUA. Petraeus would ask a question via videoconference. Then General O would pop up like jack-in-the-box on Petraeus's screen to deliver the answer. Moments before, he might have been shouting at CHOPS (the chief of operations), but he was total composure the second he appeared on Petraeus's screen. On the few occasions where there was a question raised that General O did not immediately know the answer to, the staff scrambled to get it to him before the screen was raised. He was our boss—we were all on his team. It took me a while to realize that Petraeus was only a few feet away in another room at al-Faw Palace.

Petraeus understood the importance of getting the big ideas right and communicating them not only throughout the military but also to the public. He brought an aura of confidence that we could succeed. He effectively managed expectations, telling us, "Iraq is hard. But hard is not hopeless." He urged commanders to be "first with the truth" whenever they spoke to the media. He knew that winning the narrative was critical. The military needed to regain the credibility it had lost from all the over-optimistic reporting in the past.

In mid March, General Petraeus brought out a joint strategic assessment team for a month to help himself and Ryan Crocker, who had just taken up his post as the US ambassador, to develop the Strategic Campaign Plan. The twenty-strong team was led by the highly gifted Colonel H. R. McMaster and included diplomats, military and academics. The process helped raise confidence in the new strategy. By bringing in the critics to help formulate the new strategy, Petraeus turned them into advocates back in Washington.

Military planners and State Department diplomats worked together to formulate a joint campaign plan which put politics as the main line of operation, and economics, governance and information in support. For the first time since 2003, the different US inputs were coordinated coherently. This was a major achievement. However, Iraqis were not involved in the process—and had no idea we had a plan to "develop" them. The American-centric planning assumed we knew what was best for Iraqis and that they wanted the same outcomes as we did.

In early April 2007, General O took Ambassador Crocker out to see parts of Baghdad. We flew by helicopter to Falcon, a base in southern Baghdad, to receive a brief from Lieutenant Colonel Steve Michael, who I had served with on General Ward's team in Jerusalem. It was good to see Steve. He was in command, empowered and loving things—but he had lost two of his soldiers the day before, which hit him hard.

We then headed off in Humvees to Doura market. It was a chance for General O to show Ambassador Crocker first-hand how the troops had moved out to live among the population, converting an abandoned building into an outpost with Hesco barriers (defensive fortifications) and sniper screens for protection. Walls had been built around the market, and the entrance and exit were controlled to make it harder for al-Qaeda to plant bombs, or for Jaysh al-Mahdi to dominate an area and displace Sunnis. Our units were competing over how many T-walls (concrete blast walls) they had erected, joking that the surge of troops had been accompanied by a surge of cement.

Steve Michael, Crocker, Odierno, Sky in Doura Market. *Photo by Curt Cashour*

We went out "on foot patrol'" with Steve Michael, wandering through the market. Crocker greeted the Iraqis in Arabic and asked them how business was doing. He spoke to Iraqis with respect and as equals. He cut a tiny figure beside General O, but Iraqis were keen to talk to him. One of the shopowners requested the security barriers be removed. The ambassador asked him, "Are you not afraid of bombs?" He responded, "I am worried that I will have no customers." Round a back alley, we sat at a cafe and drank tea. Lovely, sweet Arabic tea.

GENERAL ODIERNO MADE frequent visits to Taji, a camp twenty miles north of Baghdad, where incoming units were schooled in counter-insurgency. He spoke about the overall situation in Iraq and about leadership: "No matter what you do, you must be morally and ethically upright. You will see things that anger you. You will see people hurt and killed. You will be let down by people you thought you could trust. But never let your soldiers and marines lose their moral and ethical compass." He went on: "Our army, our marine corps, is based on morals and ethics. We must teach what this means at all times. It is much harder when in combat and under stress. But you must talk about it all the time." He urged them to communicate constantly. "You need to be communicating up and down the chain of command, and horizontally. Talk to your soldiers and marines." And he stressed the importance of maintaining standards. "Standards save lives. Start early with the little things. If you don't enforce standards, discipline goes down and accidents occur."

Sergeant Major Ciotola frequently accompanied the General on battlefield circulation and to the COIN Academy. An extraordinary man, he became something of a legend among the troops. He travelled the length and breadth of the country in his Humvee, visiting all the units, listening to them, talking about the mission and boosting their morale. And ensuring standards were enforced. He told the soldiers it was important to wear eye protection at all times. "Do you like looking at titties?" he would ask. "Yes, Sergeant Major," came the response. "Then always wear eye pro, otherwise you will lose your eyes." But he insisted they wore clear eye protection when dealing with Iraqis rather than dark sunglasses. "It is important that Iraqis can see your eyes," he instructed them, explaining that "eyes are the gateway to the soul." He told them that in Iraq, as everywhere around the world, there were many good people. "We need to greet everyone with a smile and a handshake—and yet be prepared to kill."

To get the soldiers to wear their fire-resistant gloves even in the heat of summer, he would ask, "Do you like feeling titties?" "Yes, Sergeant Major," the soldiers responded. "Then wear your gloves," he insisted. "If not, your hands will be burned stubs and no woman is going to want them feeling her titties."

Sergeant Major Ciotola was concerned that I did not wear gloves and gave me a pair one day on the helicopter. "Miss Emma," he said, "you must wear gloves." I took them, not wanting to hear which parts of the male anatomy I would not be able to caress if my hands got burned.

I loved travelling with General O and the Sergeant Major. There was so much warmth between the three of us, and respect for what we each brought to the mission. General O and I would talk about the situation in Iraq. Sergeant Major Ciotola would mull over how to interpret this for soldiers, and regale us with stories from his trips around the country. And I would listen to General O and the Sergeant Major talk about

US marines led by General Walter Gaskin and General John Allen brief General Odierno and Sky on the situation in Anbar at Camp Fallujah. *Photo by Curt Cashour*

the soldiers, fascinated by the different leadership roles of officers and non-commissioned officers, and how this caste system continued to be effective in modern armies.

Sergeant Major Ciotola turned to me one day and said, "When the CG [Commanding General] speaks I can hear a bit of me in him—and a bit of you." He smiled and said, "Isn't that a wonderful thing?"

WE MADE REGULAR TRIPS out to Anbar, Iraq's huge western province. The marines were pleased to show the progress they were making since Sunni tribes had started turning against al-Qaeda. Before leaving the base, they gathered everyone in the convoy for a security briefing, indicating who the medics were and what to do in case of attack. If the Humvee became disabled and the door could not open, push out the window and climb out. I looked at General O and raised an eyebrow. He grinned back. He knew what I was thinking. There was no way he would be able to squeeze through a Humvee window.

Sky walking through a market in Baghdad with Odierno. *Photo by Curt Cashour*

We drove through Ramadi in Humvees past bombed-out buildings and bullet-ridden walls. With barbed wire and concrete barriers everywhere, the place had an eerie feeling. On one wall the graffiti read *Long live the Mujahideen*. But there was no one on the streets. The town was deserted. We visited a Joint Security Station where the US battalion commander introduced us to the chief of police and the Iraqi Army commander. Afterwards, I spoke to some of the Iraqi soldiers. None of them were from Ramadi. They told me all the citizens of Ramadi had fled because of al-Qaeda.

On another occasion, as we drove to an outpost on the outskirts of Falluja, I noted that every Iraqi vehicle stopped as we passed. In the helo, Sergeant Major Ciotola explained to me that this lessened the likelihood of US troops shooting Iraqis out of the mistaken belief they were attacking rather than just driving badly. In other places, I heard that golf balls were thrown at Iraqi vehicles so they would keep their distance. On the back of US military vehicles were placards saying STAY BACK 50 METERS OR YOU WILL BE SHOT, which could only be read twenty metres away.

None of this endeared us to the local population—nor did US patrols driving against the flow of traffic.

It was common when we flew by helicopter for it to set off volleys of flares as a defensive measure to confuse heat-sensing weapons. But Iraqis on the ground often thought the helicopters were firing at them.

THE INSURGENTS were not going to let Coalition forces move back out among the population unchallenged. On 5 March, a bomb in Mutanabbi Street ripped into Baghdad's cultural heartland, killing thirty people. Named after the famed tenth-century Arab poet, this street was where Baghdad's intellectuals gathered at its bookstores and cafes. "They are even killing the books," one man lamented. The following day, over a hundred Shia pilgrims were killed as they prepared to converge on Karbala for the commemoration of Arbaeen, which marked the end of the forty-day mourning period for Imam Hussein, the Shia martyr. (Under Saddam, observance of Arbaeen had been forbidden.)

Confidence in *Fard al-Qanun* took another severe knock with two attacks on 12 April 2007. A truck bomb exploded on the Sarafiya bridge in the morning. Ten Iraqis were killed and several cars were blown into the water. The bridge had been built by the British in the 1940s and was regarded as a Baghdad monument. It was one of the busiest links across the Tigris in the northern part of the city, connecting Waziriya and Utafiyah. At lunchtime on the same day, a suicide bomber blew himself up in the canteen of the Council of Representatives, killing one parliamentarian and wounding more than twenty.

When General O went to meet with Abdul Qadir, the minister of defence was very down and depressed at the extent to which the insurgents were fighting back. He feared they would derail this security plan as they had done others. The attacks had a massive psychological impact on Iraqis. He worried that it marked a turning point. But General O refused to even contemplate this and assured him we would not be defeated.

In April alone we lost 117 Coalition soldiers. Everywhere we went, Major Wilson would come into the meeting and pass a piece of paper to General O notifying him of attacks and casualties. It was a terrible time.

It was his plan that the troops were risking their lives for. And they were dying for it by the dozen.

Senior officers, whom we met regularly, were also getting injured. On 3 May, we received word that Colonel Billy Don Farris had been shot by a sniper while surveying the construction of the three-mile concrete wall to protect a Sunni Arab enclave in the eastern Adhamiya area of Baghdad. We drove straight to the hospital. I hovered in the background while General O spoke with Farris's sergeant major, who had rushed him there, worried that he would bleed to death en route. Farris was flown back to the US but returned to Iraq a few months later to resume command of his brigade. On the night of 7 May, while returning from a memorial service for two soldiers from his brigade, Lieutenant Colonel Greg Gadson was blown up by a roadside bomb in Baghdad. He lost both his legs and severely injured his right arm.

Flying over Baghdad one day in May, General O saw a burning Humvee. He directed our helicopter to land in the middle of the main road. Telling me to stay on the helicopter, he jumped off with a few of his bodyguards to go tend to the soldiers. I remained in my seat. It was not long before dozens of Iraqis started to move towards the helicopter. Over my headphones, I heard the pilot say, "Three o'clock, three o'clock, coming down the alley." I turned my head round to the left to look at the Iraqis. I prayed they were not armed. "Nine o'clock, nine o'clock," the pilot called out. I turned my head the other way. I became increasingly nervous, fearing this would turn into a scene reminiscent of *Black Hawk Down* in Somalia. My heart was pounding. I would much rather be out in the street with General O than sitting in a helicopter in the middle of a main road in Baghdad encircled by hostile-looking Iraqis. Suddenly, and not a moment too soon, General O reappeared. The soldiers on the Humvee had been rescued by another unit. "Sir, you must never leave me again!" I reprimanded him. We took off and I looked down anxiously at the crowds of Iraqis who had surrounded our helo.

The death of every soldier made General O more determined to succeed, to ensure that their sacrifice had been for something. Most days of the week we were out visiting units. Everywhere we went, General O shook hands with soldiers, gave awards and pinned on Purple Hearts for those who had been wounded. I could see how his presence motivated and lifted morale. He would gather the soldiers around him. "What you are doing is making a difference," he told them. "Every tactical success you have contributes to the overall strategic success of the mission." He realized it was hard going out day after day, in the heat, with body armour, climbing over walls, getting shot at and taking casualties. "We are going to win," he assured them. And he believed it.

I was riddled with doubts. As I looked into the faces of the young soldiers gathered around General O, I was not at all sure their increased presence and constant raids could break the cycle of violence in Iraq; in fact, I worried that it could escalate it. It was not force numbers that mattered—it was a change in tactics. Would Iraqis understand that the US military had changed and would they see us as their protectors from each other? But even in the quietest moments, when it was just the two of us, and we spoke of the loss of the soldiers and he revealed how heavy the weight of responsibility of leadership was, General O never once expressed fear that the plan would not work. It had to work. For him, there was no other conceivable outcome.

10

AWAKENING TO RECONCILIATION

You can't kill your way out of an insurgency.
—GENERAL PETRAEUS

IT HAD FINALLY DAWNED on the US military that they could not win by force alone. Sustainable stability would only come when Iraqis determined to stop fighting. Back in 2006, Sunni tribes in Anbar, led by Sheikh Sitar Abu Risha, had started turning against al-Qaeda, and had sought support from US forces. The sahwa (Arabic for "awakening") had opened up new opportunities, and shown it was possible to work with Iraqis who had previously been fighting us.

Among General Odierno's intelligence officers, one in particular stood out: Lieutenant Colonel Nycki Brooks. She was tall, with a thin chiselled face, made more pronounced by her tied-back hair. Brooks spoke at a hundred miles an hour, the pace at which her brain worked. She seemed to have encyclopedic knowledge of armed groups, in particular the Shia ones. What set Brooks apart from other intelligence officers was a much more sophisticated understanding of Iraqis and what motivated them. In briefing after briefing given to General O, the image of the different groups emerged. She would unroll a large chart identifying the different leaders, and who they were connected to.

Brooks was ably assisted by two other women, Major Ketti Davison and Lieutenant Colonel Monica Miller. Their unit was headed by Colonel Jerry Tait, who I admired for the way he empowered his all-female team, without feeling the least intimidated by their intellect. I knew little about their backgrounds or their lives outside the military. But there

Colonel Jerry Tait with Major Ketti Davison, Lieutenant Colonel Nycki
Brooks, Lieutenant Colonel Monica Miller and Major Michelle Krawczyk.
Photo by Vanessa Jackson

was an unspoken sense of sisterhood among us. We backed each other
up in meetings, built on each other's ideas and looked out for each other.

General O viewed the armed groups as accelerants to the sectarian
violence. Sunni extremists' networks ran from the towns on the outskirts
of the capital and into the city itself. Shia militias had cleansed areas
of Baghdad of Sunnis and behaved as mafia units, financing themselves
through their control of gas stations. But how to deal with the fighters?
Mass arrests had put many innocent Iraqis into our detention camps, the
most notorious of which was Bucca down near Basra. Many detainees
became radicalized as they languished in our jails without any due process or sense of how long they would be kept.

General Graeme Lamb, the British deputy to General Petraeus, had
been given the task of exploring outreach to insurgents. This was not an
easy matter, as it meant dealing with people who had killed our soldiers.

But "Lambo," as he was known to all, had served as commander of the SAS, and with his experiences in Northern Ireland and elsewhere he couldn't be accused of being soft on terrorists. To those senior officers who said we should not deal with people who had blood on their hands, Lambo pointed out that he and others had very bloody hands.

Every encounter with Lambo was memorable. Walking out of al-Faw Palace, he bumped into Mike Juaidi, the interpreter who had recently moved to Camp Victory from the Green Zone. "How are you doing, Mike?" Lambo asked, shaking his hand. "I'm okay, but I haven't got myself a car yet," Mike replied, "and my trailer isn't as good as the one at the Palace . . ." "Mike," Lambo interrupted him, "do I look like the sort of guy who gives a shit about your problems?" When Mike told me about the encounter, he had tears of mirth running down his face. There was only one General Lamb—and he was like no other.

Lambo would never have survived in the US military culture of political correctness. His e-mails were usually a stream of consciousness. He frequently sent me words of advice: "Take a tip from the head of the bad ass and resident president of the bunch of bastards club—do not have friends. PS: you're doing alright for a bird." Every six weeks, Lambo announced he was heading back to the UK to "spank the wife." General O shook his head. He, like all US military, was permitted just a week off in a fifteen-month tour. Strutting around, sleeves rolled up, swearing, Lambo looked and behaved like a thug. But it was all theatre, all an act, to make the Americans confront the need to change their approach and to take calculated risks. By the sheer strength of his personality, Graeme Lamb won over others to his ideas.

Lambo used his residence at Maude House in the Green Zone to convene discussions on how to get insurgents to stop fighting, a process that we now dubbed "reconciliation." He invited for dinner General O, General Dempsey, who was responsible for training and equipping the new Iraqi Army, and General Stan McChrystal, who was in charge of special forces in Iraq. Lambo always included me in the discussions and e-mails. He had few staff of his own, needed allies and sensed that I could be a useful one. Leaning over General O, I explained to Lambo who was seated on his other side that we had just got back from the COIN Academy at Taji. I told him that in his speech General O had encouraged his soldiers not to live like pigs, which made me feel guilty as I was untidy. Lambo asked, "Have you heard my pig story?" I hadn't, I admitted. "There I was on the eve of battle in 2003," he said, "talking to the boys. I gave a rip-roaring address and ended with 'Never forget, the faint-hearted have never fucked a pig.'" General O looked at Lambo, then at me. I shrugged my shoulders. What could I possibly say?

Lambo appeared in General O's office one day with his small team. He sketched out a diagram on a white board, referring to a "squeeze box," "pipe-swingers" and "wedges." No one had a clue what he meant. When he lost his train of thought, Lambo would repeat "fuck, fuck, fuck" as if he had Tourette's syndrome, until he remembered what he wanted to say. He responded to General O's questions with anecdotes that went off in all directions and left us more perplexed than when he had started. But the need to separate those who were prepared to stop using violence from those we deemed "irreconcilables" resonated. The question was how to do it.

A few days later, we went up to the US military base at Balad, north of Baghdad, to discuss with General Stan McChrystal how to convince insurgents to stop fighting. His team had placed themselves at the centre of reconciliation. It was reconcile—or die! General O did not agree. It was his troops that would be taking the risk and therefore should be the lead on reconciliation. Reconciliation had to be about both persuasion and coercion. Those who refused to take the opportunity to stop fighting should then be left to McChrystal's forces.

Lambo had a range of ideas on how to get armed groups to stop fighting Coalition forces. One of his schemes involved releasing insurgents from our detention camps if they agreed to try to persuade members of their group to stop attacking us. This approach was obviously fraught with risk. How was it possible to assess whether we had genuinely "turned" these insurgents?

General O was sceptical about releasing captured insurgents who had killed Americans, fearing it would only lead to the deaths of more US soldiers. He was also concerned that it would be perceived by soldiers as a "catch and release" programme, hence providing greater incentives for the US troops to kill, rather than to detain. "I have not experienced anyone who has been able to deliver what they have promised in Iraq," he said. "It will be hard for me to agree with the release of Iraqis who have killed US soldiers."

But the differences between General O and Lambo were narrowing. I worked with Lambo and his staff to help them understand General O's concerns and to seek ways to address them. General O wanted a policy and strategic framework in which to work. What was our position on those who had killed US military? What were our red lines? Lambo viewed the release of detainees as a confidence-building measure. But General O wanted to see a reduction in violence, and the building of a local Joint Security Station, before the release of detainees.

In e-mails I urged Lambo and his team to integrate their work within the main effort, rather than keeping it as a separate British initiative. "This work at the moment appears to be a Lambo one-man show," I warned. "It needs to be brought into the fold. And it must not be seen as a Brit thing (remove the Union Jack flag on the cover!) if it is to gain traction." Lambo responded: "Emma, How could you possibly suggest that we haul down the Union Flag—my dear girl we do not do that sort of thing. You have obviously spent too long in the company of Americans, but since I know how sensitive the female sex is to any 'upset' messages, we will in this case condescend and remove the offending symbol which we should not forget flew over an Empire on which the sun never set etc., etc."

I wrote back: "General Lamb. I know it may be hard for you to come to terms with, but Great Britain lost Her Empire (as well as the Great) some years ago. These days we have to be more skilled and subtle, and rule indirectly through our cousins. We should therefore embrace the Stars and Stripes as our own."

Once we were close to consensus, Lambo convened a session in Maude House with the top US generals. The dashing British major Charlie Williams gave the brief, impressing all with his intellect and charm. At dinner, Lamb seated Petraeus between Charlie and myself, with General McChrystal opposite me. It was the first time I had had a proper conversation with General McChrystal. I was impressed by how thoughtful, liberal and well read he was—for someone who specialized in hunting down humans. He spoke to me about the effect of counter-terrorism operations on those who prosecute them. He asked how I could participate in the work in Iraq if I did not believe in the whole premise of the Global

War on Terror, the GWOT. I told him I could have remained an arm-
chair critic in the UK. But I had chosen to be here on the ground trying
to shape our approach. I recognized that working with the military was
changing me. But if I wanted to influence others, I had to be prepared to
change my own ideas.

WE FLEW TO TIKRIT and drove by Humvee to the government building. I
sauntered out of the vehicle and took off my helmet only to be shouted
at to put it back on as snipers were targeting the entrance. Inside, we sat
down to a meeting with the governor, deputy governor and the Grand
Mufti, Sheikh Jamal al-Dabban, who was considered one of the most
influential Sunni leaders in Iraq. He had been detained, briefly, by US
forces the year before in a case of "mistaken identity."

The Grand Mufti said that both the corruption and the killing needed
to stop. Employment opportunities would draw young men out of violence and into the workforce. He hoped the de-Baathification law would
be abolished. "A great number of those involved in the resistance and
jihad could be persuaded to move from the fighting side to the political
side," he told us, "except for al-Qaeda." He said he did not know all the
insurgent groups, but he had met some. They were willing to be part of
the solution. He handed us the insurgents' suggestions for the way forward in Iraq.

Back on the helicopter, I mentioned to General O the graffiti I had
seen on the wall of a building: *The hero, the martyr Saddam Hussein*. He
commented that the dead dictator was a mass murderer. I said, "We still
don't know who killed more Iraqis: you or Saddam, sir." There was total
silence on the helicopter. Everyone froze. I thought this time I really had
gone too far. Then General O shouted, "Open the doors, pilots. Throw
her out!"

ON ST PATRICK'S DAY, Lambo invited us over to Maude House. We sat in
the garden, drinking tea while the bagpipes played in the background.
General O lounged in a chair, smoking a cigar. Lambo reflected on his
outreach to the Sadrists. It was not going well, he told us, "Skinny has

been whacked and the Sadr City Mayor wounded." (Lambo could not pronounce Arabic names easily so had given nicknames to the people he worked with.) He complained that he was short-staffed: "I only have five blokes and a bird doing all this shit." "One bird," I reminded him, "is worth ten blokes."

A couple of days later, General O wandered out of his office looking for me. He had just received notification that our special forces had picked up Layth Khazali in Basra, along with his brother Qais. This was big news. Qais Khazali was on the prime minister's "no touch" list, but we had detained him unintentionally and were not going to let him go. Maliki knew Qais personally, claimed that he was anti-Iranian, an alternative leader to Muqtada al-Sadr and argued that Qais was not attacking Coalition forces. We suspected the Khazali brothers had been responsible for the complex attack in Karbala in January when five US soldiers had been killed. It would be weeks before we discovered the full extent of the Khazali brothers' involvement in attacks and had built up a clear picture of their organization, Asaib Ahl al-Haqq—and the extent of Iranian activity in Iraq. (One of those detained with them claimed for over a month to be dumb and was dubbed "Hamed the Mute." It turned out he was Ali Musa Daqduq, a Lebanese Hezbollah operative.)

DURING OUR TRAVELS around Iraq it was clear there had been a shift among the Sunni population. In several areas, Sunnis who had been fighting us had got in contact with our local commanders. They wanted to switch sides and fight with us against al-Qaeda. The US decision to "surge" additional forces into Iraq was having a big psychological impact on the Sunnis, who realized they could not defeat the United States militarily. Instead they sought protection from the Shia militias and they wanted to work with us to push back on their greatest threat: Iran.

It was a bottom-up phenomenon—and highly localized. In Anbar, Sheikh Sitar Abu Risha had brought with him a whole tribe; in other places insurgent leaders had hundreds rather than thousands loyal to them. A number of US commanders on the ground were following the example set by Colonel Sean MacFarland in Anbar, doing deals with previously hostile Sunnis.

For the US military, the Sunni Awakening was a lifesaver. Insurgents who had been fighting us were switching over to our side and helping us fight other insurgents. Spokesmen waxed lyrical about how the Sunni population was rejecting al-Qaeda due to its perverse interpretation of Islam. The US military started referring to the former insurgents as Concerned Local Citizens. The term "CLCs" stuck for months and lists were collated of the thousands on our payroll.

Of particular importance were developments in Abu Ghraib. Just west of Baghdad, Abu Ghraib was the gateway to the capital and was heavily contested. We met with sheikhs who declared that Abu Ghraib was in the hands of the terrorists and not the law because tribal leaders had been weakened; that the Iraqi Army behaved badly, and that both the Iraqi government and the Coalition assumed all the people in the area were terrorists. Despite all this, the sheikhs claimed that a local leader called Abu Azzam and his group were fighting al-Qaeda without help from the Coalition or the Iraqi government—and had lost many sons. The discussion revealed the complexity of the dynamics in this area. Seeing how intently we were listening, one of the sheikhs said, "Iraqis like foreigners. We just don't like being occupied!" I was convinced it had to be possible to get these people on our side.

Lieutenant Colonel Kurt Pinkerton was the battalion commander of 2-5 Cavalry responsible for Abu Ghraib. We visited him a number of times. An impressive and innovative commander, he described how he had started working with Abu Azzam's group, giving them lights and reflective belts so the Coalition could recognize them when they were manning checkpoints. In return they provided us with information about significant al-Qaeda leaders and factories that produced car bombs. Abu Azzam's group wanted to become the official security forces for the area, but the Iraqi government refused. Pinkerton found himself in the unenviable position of having to negotiate between the Iraqi Army and the tribes.

General O went to meet Prime Minister Maliki in May to try to persuade him to accept Abu Azzam's group into the Iraqi security forces. He said he understood how difficult it was to deal with these people because of some of the things they had done in the past, but there was an opportunity to "reconcile." General O pointed out that in the last thirty days, there had hardly been any attacks in the Abu Ghraib area. Maliki,

General Odierno greets Iraqi prime minister Nuri al-Maliki. *Photo by Curt Cashour*

however, feared that Abu Azzam was forming a Sunni brigade. He did not want to recruit these groups into the security forces, only to become afraid of them later. Abu Azzam was tricky as a fox, he cautioned, a chameleon who changed his colour according to his environment. He warned against arming everyone who claimed they were fighting al-Qaeda. As we began making deals with former insurgents, I could see that the Iraqi government was becoming increasingly nervous.

THE US MILITARY was frustrated by what they viewed as the schemes of Maliki and his inner circle to actively sabotage our efforts to draw Sunnis out of the insurgency and to recruit them to guard their own locales. Worse, the military feared that Maliki's office was interfering to prevent us from building up credible national security forces, and was complicit in the operations of Shia militias. US officers began briefing against the Office of the Commander-in-Chief (OCINC).

I feared that if we continued down our current path, with Maliki and his advisers opposed to our initiatives, we would create a whole new host of problems. I wanted to understand what was going on inside OCINC, to try to improve relations and see if we could reach some form of compromise.

Fortunately, with the arrival of Colonel J. T. Thomson to take over as General O's executive officer, I was relieved of some of my duties, including writing up the minutes of General O's meetings and drafting his daily report to Petraeus. There had been no chemistry between General O and his previous executive officer, so he had not taken him out of Camp Victory. JT, on the other hand, had worked for General O for years and was trusted by him. We now both accompanied General O to his meetings. I now had more energy and headspace to pursue meetings of my own after we returned from "battlefield circulation."

My first step was to meet Dr. Tareq Najim, Prime Minister Maliki's chief of staff. Tareq was a Shia Islamist and a Dawa party member who had studied in Egypt and lived in the UK. I had accompanied General O to meetings with him, but he had remained something of an enigma. I reached out to him and he invited me to join him for lunch in his office at the White House (as the prime minister's building was called).

I asked his opinion of America. Dr. Tareq said that up until the 1970s people had genuinely believed the US stood for democracy and freedom. The US had been on the Arab side in the 1956 Suez issue, against France, the UK and Israel. In the 1970s this changed, due to US attitudes towards the Palestinian problem and US support for Saddam, especially after the Islamic Revolution, when the US supported Saddam in his war against Iran. Attitudes changed again when the US helped Iraq to get rid of Saddam. But they had now swung back once more. Many believed the US was helping Sunnis against Shia. The killing of Shia gave the Sadrists the opportunity to retaliate, claiming they were the defenders of the Shia community. But these people, he insisted, were really criminals and outlaws.

I informed Dr. Tareq that in recent days we had lost eleven soldiers, nine of whom had been killed by Jaysh al-Mahdi (JAM). This was totally unacceptable and must stop. The Shia were not our enemy. I urged the Iraqi government to try to persuade the Sadrists to stop attacking us.

Dr. Tareq said Iranian support for JAM served to undermine and challenge the authority of the Iraqi government. Rockets landing in the Green Zone were having a big psychological impression on people in the city. "If the government and the Coalition are unable to protect themselves, how on earth can they protect the public? People think it is a conspiracy," he told me. "Saddam would have stopped this in a day!"

I told him about a recent ceremony I had attended in which Major Jim Gant was awarded the silver star for bravery. Major Gant had spoken passionately about his role training Iraqi security forces and the importance of the US staying to complete its mission. I read out an extract from his speech:

> The best friend I have ever had is an Iraqi . . . If you knew Colonel Dha-fer, a great commander and leader . . . one of the best friends I have ever had, if you knew Major Fadil, who pulled me out of a burning Humvee . . . if you knew Captain Khais, if you knew Salaam, or Abbas, or Ali; all are brave warriors who fought with incredible courage that day and I would gladly and without hesitation lay my life down for all of them.

No one, I said, had believed that Americans and Iraqis would create such bonds.

Dr. Tareq was moved, and said, "The blood of our sons is mixed with the blood of your sons."

HIGH UP ON THE US MILITARY'S LIST of those contributing to sectarian violence was Dr. Basima Jadiri, a religious Shia woman in her late thirties, and the military adviser to the prime minister. US assessments described her as a malign sectarian actor, a satanical figure. I decided to make up my own mind about her, but it was a few days before we were able to meet, as she was not answering her phone. It took the interpreter Mike Juaidi and myself thirty minutes to get through the outer security cordon and to her office, when normally members of the Coalition were able to waltz into any building in Iraq.

In my first glimpse of Dr. Basima, she was holding court around a large table with a group of sheikhs, discussing Falluja. She spoke firmly and loudly. She was wearing a *jilbab* with *hijab*, rather than a traditional Shia cloak or *abaya*, and high heels. She was clearly the authority figure at the table. Mike and I sat off to the side, along with some other Iraqis who were waiting their turn.

Her meeting over, I introduced myself and explained that I was General O's political adviser. I said she and I might have much in common as we were both female, civilians and working with the military—and military men were not easy to work with. She laughed, threw her hands up in the air and said, "Yes, this is the tragedy!" A sheikh interjected, "The difference between you and her is that she has real power—she rules!"

I explained that General O had asked me to pass on his apologies for comments made about her in the international media by US officers, claiming that she was directing Shia death squads and sacking Sunni officers. "The *Washington Post* article did me a great injustice," she responded. "It made problems for me that I really do not need." She thanked me for passing on the apology. "I now want to meet General Odierno," she said. "He sounds very nice." I smiled.

The meeting had only lasted twenty minutes. But we had connected. Dr. Basima told me I was welcome to visit her any time—and she would instruct the guards to let me enter quickly in future.

At our second meeting a week later she only had one other person with her, General Abu Mohamad, the director of intelligence and security at the Office of the Commander-in-Chief (OCINC). Abu Mohamad was a well-built man with a cheeky grin and a strong handshake, who smoked incessantly. Dr. Basima was pleased to see me again. She hoped these meetings would bear fruit. The US and Iraq would succeed together or would fail together—the blood of our sons was being shed together.

She explained that neither she nor Abu Mohamad belonged to a political party and therefore did not have top cover, which meant that people could put out negative reports about them. Being responsible for the security file in OCINC, they had to deal with officers who had inherited the culture of the previous regime. She complained that lots of US advisers working with the Iraqi security forces suffered from "clientitis" and repeated the lies of the Iraqis they were advising, hence the reason why the Coalition had a negative picture of OCINC.

I asked them both about their backgrounds. General Abu Mohamad told me about his military career and his experience in the Iran-Iraq war. After 2003, he was appointed to the Ministry of National Security. He said "political parties" then entered the ministry and "things changed." Some of those appointed were loyal to Iran. Abu Mohamad said because he was an Iraqi nationalist and a patriot he had trouble with them. He moved to OCINC in November 2006.

Dr. Basima had been born in Sadr City. She had been one of the best in her class at Mosul University, where she had studied statistics. She went to Baghdad University to do postgraduate studies in management and economy. However, as her education was government-funded—and she was neither in the military nor an engineer—she had to conduct research that was relevant to the military. Influenced by the writings of Professor Bar Shalom of Haifa University on the accuracy of rockets, she had studied launching pads, rockets and surface-to-air missiles. After 9/11 and the US invasion of Afghanistan, Saddam required all academic research to be related to military manufacturing, and she had concentrated on network radars, "Kalman filters" and the accuracy of targeting. She had presented her research in 2004 and received her doctorate.

In 2005 the Sadrists had decided to enter the political process. As she was a follower of Muqtada's father, the Sadrists had approached her to run on their list as part of the quota set aside for women. In the National Assembly she was the only woman on the twelve-member defence and security committee. Initially they had tried to stop her joining, but she had not given up. She refused to accept that it should be an exclusively male club. She first met Nuri al-Maliki on this committee. She described him as "a patriot, brave, and a decision-maker." The Sadrists complained that Maliki had influenced her against them. She described Maliki as her mentor, and the only person she was afraid of. "He is a leader," she said, "of the stature of Nelson Mandela." I thought to myself that Mandela had defined leadership as doing what was in the best interests of the country as a whole, not following populist instincts. There were no such statesmen in Iraq.

As I got up to leave, General Abu Mohamad declared, "It"s not fair. Dr. Basima is a dictator. She took up most of the meeting!"

"Remind Dr. Basima what happens to dictators," I told him. She laughed. At least, I thought, Basima and Abu Mohamad wanted me understand them—and to like them.

Over copious cups of sweet tea in Basima's office it became apparent that they were deeply suspicious of America's intent. They had never travelled outside Iraq nor met any Americans before the invasion. Given what had occurred since 2003, they had concluded that America had deliberately planned not just to remove Saddam, but to destroy Iraq and create a civil war.

I tried to explain the emergence, after the end of the Cold War, of a neoconservative movement in the US which advocated a "muscular" foreign policy. Influenced by Iraqi exiles, the neoconservatives became convinced that the removal of Saddam would result in Iraq becoming a democracy which would transform the Middle East and bring about regional peace with Israel. Following his election, President George W. Bush brought the neoconservatives into government. In the immediate aftermath of the 9/11 attacks, senior US officials portrayed Saddam as an imminent threat due to his supposed possession of weapons of mass destruction. Rumsfeld was put in charge of the post-war phase and wanted to immediately hand over the country to Ahmed Chalabi and draw down the troops. He discarded the analysis of the State Department, as he was adamant that the US was not going to get involved in "nation-building."

Basima stared at me incredulously. "How can a country such as America, a country that can put a man on the moon, not know what it is doing? How can the US not have had a plan for Iraq after removing Saddam?" she asked. It was difficult to convince her of the Coalition's incompetence. But she was fascinated to learn that the US government was not monolithic, that there were disagreements between different departments and individuals. That was certainly something she could relate to! I promised I would always be totally honest with her. It was important that we trusted each other.

We had a lengthy discussion about how Iraqi society had become more sectarian following the fall of the previous regime. For centuries they had lived without this differentiation. There used to be lots of inter-marriage. Basima's sister-in-law, for instance, was a Sunni from Falluja. And General Abu Mohamad's wife was Sunni.

"The Coalition has not lived up to its responsibilities as defined by the Geneva Conventions," Dr. Basima complained. "The Coalition allowed lawlessness and stood back as spectators while the Shia were pushed to seek shelter with the militia and the Sunnis with al-Qaeda."

"The battle is with terror and should be an intelligence battle," General Abu Mohamad observed. "Even if five more US divisions came to Iraq, they will not be able to achieve their mission. Large numbers of Iraqis are being detained. Inside prison, they are being trained by al-Qaeda. The US is doing al-Qaeda's work for it. Does the US not understand this problem?" I assured him we were well aware of the issue.

I brought the discussion back to JAM. General Abu Mohamad said JAM were originally a group of unemployed young men. He said criminals had infiltrated JAM, as had Iran. The best solution was to provide them with jobs, but not in the security forces. He was optimistic because people were starting to turn against JAM, just as Sunnis were turning against al-Qaeda.

I QUICKLY REALIZED there were two main camps within OCINC, one headed by Dr. Basima, the other by Lieutenant General Farouq al-Araji. I wasn't sure whether the differences were personality related or to do with policies. So I determined to meet General Farouq to ensure good communications with both sides. "OCINC's role," he told me "is to give advice on military issues to the Commander-in-Chief; to pass on his orders to divisions and to security ministries; and to follow up on the execution of those orders." He said OCINC itself had no authority to give orders.

"Dr. Basima is the security adviser for the prime minister," General Farouq told me, "but not a part of OCINC. She has an office in the building as a guest, but has never been an employee." Dr. Basima, he said, gave advice to the prime minister on security issues, but through another channel, not through the office. He didn't know why people called her the Iron Lady when she was "quiet, generous, with good manners." I tried to keep a straight face at his description of Basima, who was known for her temper. It was clear that he was lying through his teeth. He loathed her.

General Abud, Basima, Faruq al-Araji. *Photo by Office of the Commander-in-Chief*

"There is no misunderstanding between the Coalition and Iraqis," Farouq insisted. "We are all working together to build the new Iraq and to fight terrorism in Iraq, in the region and globally." Somehow I never felt totally at ease with General Farouq. He kept saying that I was like a daughter to him, that the door would always be open to me. But behind the pleasantries, I detected little honesty.

HAVING CONVINCED Dr. Basima that the US had not purposefully set out to create civil war in Iraq, I suggested we work together to promote reconciliation. She explained what she and her colleagues had been doing. They had sent out application forms to members of the old Iraqi Army through the banking system, over the Internet and through embassies, offering three options: to return to service, retire or take civilian jobs. The cabinet had taken a decision that officers from the rank of major through to general could receive retirement payments if they did not wish to return to work. Retirement pay was equal to current military salaries.

"Basima, this is amazing!" I said. "Why have you not shared this with the Coalition?" The Coalition's hostile attitude towards OCINC, she replied, and the nasty articles about them in the media had led them to believe that the Coalition was opposed to national reconciliation. "This is crazy," I responded. "We are totally committed to reconciliation. Your work is hugely important."

"We are now focusing on the military manufacturing file: a hundred and ten thousand people. It was these people who had rebuilt Iraq after 1991," she continued. "Saddam had rebuilt a hundred and three bridges in six months. Whereas today," she complained, "there has been little progress in five weeks in rebuilding the Sarafiyya Bridge." They were also, she said, investigating the previous intelligence agencies, reaching out to those who had operated across the Middle East, Europe and Iran. They wanted them to work for the government, not for the terrorists.

I raised the issue of Abu Azzam's fighters in Abu Ghraib, who had been fighting against al-Qaeda and had submitted their names to the Ministry of Defence to join the Iraqi Army. But Basima said she believed these people were members of the 1920 Revolution Brigades under the leadership of Harith al-Dari. "They continue to play both sides." She went on, "Some tribal leaders have approached the Iraqi government asking for protection from those same people who wish to join the Iraqi Army. If people want to join the Iraqi security forces they should do so under a Tribal Awakening. It is important that the government has someone to deal with. Iraq is a tribal society and an agreement with tribal sheikhs is a contract." She told me they had files on many members of parliament. "When relations are tense between particular Sunni and Shia politicians, this is reflected by killings in the streets. Is this the parliament we want?" she asked. "We need to clean up from the top down." Some politicians had militias who carried out murders but operated under the cover of the political process.

"There is not really any al-Qaeda in Iraq," Dr. Basima asserted. "Armed groups just adopt that name but they are not reliable nor loyal to al-Qaeda. They vacillate constantly, siding with whichever group is stronger. There is a continual flow of people in and out of their ranks.

Iraqis are fickle," she announced. "If we had realized the problems we would inherit, we would have hung on to Saddam!"

I tried again. Around the country, there were many Sunnis who wished to join the Iraqi security forces but were being prevented from doing so. This might be due to sluggish bureaucracy; or it might be due to sectarianism. In recent weeks there had been a decrease in violence in Abu Ghraib and the killing of significant numbers of al-Qaeda. If the sons of Abu Ghraib did not join the security forces, there was a danger they would go back to the armed groups. But Dr. Basima replied that the Coalition only thought about itself, not about the future of the country.

I tried another tack: "Dr. Basima, throughout history, kings carefully married off their daughters to end feuding or cement relations. Perhaps national reconciliation in Iraq could be achieved by Maliki marrying you off to a suitable person?" She roared with laughter. "Perhaps Izzat al-Douri, Muhamad Yunis Ahmed or Harith al-Dari are suitable candidates?" I said, naming some of the leaders of the Sunni insurgency. Dr. Basima chose Harith al-Dari and asked me to raise this issue with Maliki when I next saw him.

ONE DAY, DR. BASIMA TOLD ME Maliki had asked her about the messages that ran along the bottom of the screen on the satellite TV channels. Men seeking women. Women seeking men. How did this work?

I explained that this was a relatively new phenomenon of the last decade. There were now Internet sites where people could look for potential partners. People wrote short descriptions of themselves, sometimes submitted photos and described what they were looking for in a partner. Basima was intrigued. "Have you tried this?" she asked.

"Yes, once."

"What happened?"

I said that I had put up a profile of myself on the Internet. A number of interested men had contacted me. I eliminated those who spelt badly, had poor grammar or seemed dull. I decided to meet in a pub with the one whose e-mails I found the funniest.

"So what happened?" Dr. Basima was eager to hear more.

"Well, he had mentioned on the Internet that he was small. I'm short. So I hadn't thought much of it."

"How small was he?"

"He was very short . . ." I was finding it hard to keep a straight face. "And he was a flame-throwing juggler on a circus boat. But he was ever so funny."

"He was a dwarf!" Dr. Basima announced. Tears poured down her face. She and Abu Mohamad were bent double in hysterical laughter. By now I too was laughing uncontrollably. Between gulps of air, Dr. Basima declared, "Emma, you are not destined to get married."

DEALING WITH DR. BASIMA was always tricky. It depended on her mood. She frequently took offence with the Coalition where none was intended. And she always fought with her colleagues. But she had the ear of the prime minister and he obviously trusted her. She went over to his office most days to see him, and they were forever texting each other. The nature of their relationship was never clear. Iraqis used to joke about the "*muta'a*," the temporary marriage between the two.

But whatever one thought of Dr. Basima, she was capable and got things done. And there were not many within the Iraqi government of whom one could say that. I felt we could find ways to work together. The level of mistrust, however, between the Coalition and the prime minister and his office was such that we always interpreted the worst from the other's actions. I was continually up against US officers who remained antagonistic towards the prime minister's advisers and argued that we should push ahead with our deals with Sunni groups regardless of the Iraqi government.

I argued that if we continued to support all the Sunnis who claimed they would fight al-Qaeda while ignoring the concerns of the Iraqi government, we would fuel Maliki's paranoia that we were seeking to overthrow him; we would be creating more militias; and we would weaken the state by creating alternative power centres. We should learn from similar US government initiatives in Afghanistan and Central America— and avoid the pitfalls.

I urged that we try to reach a compromise on the way ahead. But I was not winning the argument. Things came to a head one morning in the Senior Leadership Huddle, in a discussion about arming the tribes to fight al-Qaeda. I said it was an "*inshallah* plan," based on wishful thinking.

After the meeting, General O summoned me back to his office. I walked in. He was sitting at his desk. He turned to me and proceeded to give me the strongest scolding of my life. He shouted at me about being too negative and not believing in what we were doing. He accused me of going over to the Iraqi side ever since I had started working with OCINC. I stood with my arms folded, glaring back at him like a sulky teenager. But I was trembling as he raged at me and too frightened to answer back. He ended with, "We need to talk." I replied, "Yes" and turned around and left the room. We were both too furious to have a civilized conversation at that moment. I had not received such a telling-off since school.

Bastard, bastard, bastard, I thought to myself, still simmering as we drove in the car together to the helicopter landing zone, neither of us speaking. Once I had begun to calm down, however, I realized I had not handled the situation well. I believed I was right in terms of substance, but not in terms of approach. I was General O's closest adviser—and I had made him feel that I had abandoned him.

On the helicopter, he offered an olive branch, starting up a conversation. I looked at him and said I was sorry. I was angry and frustrated. Everyone was constantly attacking the very Iraqis with whom I was trying to improve our relations. How could I get the Iraqis to change their behaviour if they felt such hostility from the Coalition? "Look," said General O, "I value your support. I need you to help me think through all this shit."

I felt contrite. And that evening I e-mailed General O, proposing a number of measures. We needed to understand the real motives of the different groups coming forward. For some, it was about money: they wanted salaries from the Coalition in return for providing security. For others, it was an opportunity to realign with the Coalition in preparation for the real battle against what they viewed as the Iranian-backed Shia government. We could broker ceasefires, and work at incorporating the armed groups into the security forces. But without a political process, there was a danger that the security forces would not be national ones but serve as political party militias, trained and equipped by us, and potentially forces for instability in the future. We needed our senior leaders to push the Iraqi government towards national dialogue. And we needed to set a time limit for these groups to be incorporated into the Iraqi security forces or be disbanded.

In the days that followed, General O and I discussed how we could take advantage of the Sunni Awakening—and get the Iraqi government on our side. He had been so angry with me that I thought he was going to sack me. We had got through it, and were closer than ever as a result. It was an important lesson for me. I was on General O's team. And no matter how badly we disagreed or argued, he was not going to throw me out. This was a family that worked through its problems and did not break down.

TONY BLAIR PAID HIS FAREWELL VISIT to Iraq in mid May. Lambo invited me over to Maude House to be part of a small group to meet him. "I will have my tomatoes ready to throw," I said. "And I have warned the guards to shoot you on sight and claim that you had a shifty look," Lambo responded.

The British embassy was rocketed in the morning, minutes before Blair arrived—he was running ten minutes late. Two vehicles were destroyed. At Maude House, I stood in line waiting my turn. Lambo introduced me, saying I was a star and that I looked after the Big Man. There was no mistaking who the Big Man was, as he was standing right there. Petraeus came forward and told Blair that I was "a national treasure." General O explained that I had been working with the US military since 2003. At this stage, Blair got confused. "Are you British?" he asked. I assured him that I was British born and bred. "What are you doing working with the American military?" I shrugged my shoulders. "Stockholm syndrome," I offered.

At that moment, the sirens went off. "*Incoming. Incoming. Take cover,*" boomed the big voice. Everyone moved away from the windows. Blair's security team took him off to the safe room. "*Stay under cover.*" We heard a thud—the rocket landed close by. The "enemy" was fully aware of Blair's itinerary. We found out how, when Jalal Talabani, who was now president of Iraq, phoned to apologize that he might have made a mistake in

As General Odierno and General Petraeus look on, British prime minister Tony Blair talks with Emma Sky. *Photo by Curt Cashour*

informing the Iranian ambassador about Blair's visit. So in my one and only interaction with Blair, I never did get to have a discussion with him about the decision to go to war.

GENERAL O SENT ME to reassure Dr. Basima that the Coalition was not arming the Sunni tribes. She was satisfied: "This is what I want to hear." I described General O's recent visits to Diyala and Arab Jabour and the need for local police there. In certain areas we had reached agreement with armed groups for them to turn their weapons away from us and towards al-Qaeda.

Lambo left Iraq in style. At his farewell at the BUA he stood up on a chair and removed his shirt, revealing his muscular and incredibly hirsute torso. It was not immediately clear that he was trying to show off the Texan belt buckle General O had given as a farewell gift. He ended by saying, *"One Team!"* flicked the finger at us all and strode out of the room.

The work that Lambo had begun had now become institutionalized within the Force Strategic Engagement Cell, which was headed up by Major General Paul Newton and State Department foreign service officer Don Blome. Maliki agreed to establish a counterpart committee, with Basima and Abu Mohamad as the key staff. They were given responsibility for vetting all the volunteers who wished to join the Iraqi security forces.

I continued to drop by Basima's office to check on how she and Abu Mohamad were doing. She told me there had been a transformation in their relationship with the Coalition: "There is clarity, transparency, and trust." "But," she warned, "we don't like to be told what to do!" Basima confided that Maliki had got angry with her for becoming too close to the Americans. "Men!" she said, holding up her hands in despair.

GENERAL O CALLED ME INTO HIS OFFICE. He was very unhappy with the Abu Ghraib situation. We were hoping to have around seventeen hundred accepted into the Iraqi security forces; but had just heard that Basima's committee had only agreed to consider seven hundred. None of those from the Sunni insurgent group Jaysh Islami had been accepted, a decision that would push them back into the insurgency.

"This is a red line," General O declared. "If the Iraqi government does not reconcile with the armed groups, the Coalition will leave." He knew that if Petraeus and Crocker were unable to point to any progress in reconciliation when they testified in September, Congress would call for US troops to pull out.

General O told me that Petraeus and Crocker were going to see Maliki the next day to withdraw support from him on the grounds that he was not serious about reconciling with Sunnis. He told me to head over to OCINC the next morning for one last try to get them to accept the Abu Ghraib recruits.

I found Dr. Basima in her office with Abu Mohamad. She looked angry.

"I don't want to talk about Abu Ghraib," said Basima. "I have really had enough of this issue."

"Well, I'm really sorry that you didn't agree to accept Abu Azzam's group into the Iraqi security forces. It was very important to us—"

Basima interrupted me: "I don't want to talk about it. I never want to talk about this subject again." I had heard that she had had a bad meeting with the Coalition team who had pushed her to process the applications, and she had refused.

Abu Mohamad looked up. "We approved seventeen hundred thirty-eight names from Abu Ghraib to join the Iraqi security forces."

I looked at him incredulously. "Abu Mohamad, are you serious?"

"Yes," he said. "Here are the files. We processed them." He smiled at me and said, "Abu Ghraib is an experiment. We must be brave and take the risk."

"Did you tell the prime minister?" I asked Basima. She shook her head. I could tell she was still angry.

"Basima, listen to me. Petraeus and Crocker are on their way to meet Maliki at twelve. It is now gone past eleven. They believe that Maliki has refused to accept Abu Azzam's group into the Iraqi security forces, and are going to tell him that they do not have confidence that he is prepared to reconcile with Sunnis. This is very serious." (In fact, I'd been told that Petraeus was going to push Maliki "under the bus.") "Dr. Basima, we need to get the information to them before they go into the meeting. Can you get hold of the PM, and I'll try to get through to Petraeus?"

From the look on my face and the tone of my voice, she realized I was serious. She texted Maliki and then called him. I phoned Sadi Othman, Petraeus's charismatic adviser and interpreter, who I knew would be accompanying Petraeus to the meeting. I told him that the prime minster's office had accepted Abu Azzam's group into the ISF—1,738 names. Petraeus came on the phone.

"Emma, has Abu Azzam's group really been accepted into the ISF?"

"Yes, sir," I replied. "I am over at OCINC with Basima and Abu Mohamad. They have approved 1,738 names from Abu Ghraib to join the ISF." Basima was busy shredding paper and I had to shout over the noise of the machine.

"Do those names include Jaysh Islami members?"

"Yes, sir. They do."

"That is great news. Please pass on my thanks and best wishes to Basima and Abu Mohamad."

"Wilco, sir."

"What do I talk to the PM about now!" Petraeus asked me rhetorically. I got off the phone.

"I never want to discuss Abu Ghraib again," Basima announced. I agreed with her.

That evening Petraeus invited me to dinner at his villa in Camp Victory. It was the first time we had really had a conversation. He asked me about my education, what languages I spoke and which countries I had visited. He was impressed that I had gone to Oxford. He told me he loved academia and wanted to be a professor when he retired. Talking to him, I realized that he really was extremely smart. It was the most relaxed I had ever seen him. He told me that the cooperation I had engineered from the Iraqis had helped him understand how Britain had ruled half the world with a handful of Foreign Office folks and the odd sergeant major. Embarrassed, I told him it was just about relationships, building trust and listening.

The next morning at the BUA, with thousands of soldiers listening in, General Petraeus mentioned that he had a great meeting with Maliki and had congratulated him on his courageous decision to "reconcile" with Abu Azzam and his men.

"Ray, your POLAD saved the day," General Petraeus said.

General O replied, "Sir, she is not my POLAD." There was a pause. "She is an insurgent!"

There was a roar of laughter around the JOC.

ONE OF THE BIGGEST CARROTS we had was the discretion to hand out badges to Iraqis to get in and out of the Green Zone. They were like gold dust, and Basima and Abu Mohamad had been requesting them for months.

"Dr. Basima, I received an e-mail from Petraeus asking whether you have received your badge yet?"

She scowled at me. "I do not want to discuss this matter further. It's quite clear that America does not want to give me a badge."

I apologized for the delay. I had been assured they would both be issued badges. I suspected that somewhere in the system someone was quite deliberately obstructing Petraeus's instruction, but I said it was probably some bureaucratic hold-up. I told Dr. Basima how my badge had recently expired and I had been caught trying to enter the US embassy "illegally." I had been taken away to a room where I had endured two hours of hell until someone had vouched that I really was who I claimed to be and did indeed work for General O. She enjoyed the story. Hearing about my misfortune cheered her up a lot. "It's not personal," I insisted.

A few days later, I turned up at her office with a couple of American civilians who constituted "the mobile biometrics unit." I told her this was special treatment for close advisers to the prime minister, to save them from having to appear at the US embassy. Dr. Basima and Abu Mohamad obediently looked into the camera for their iris scans and mugshots, dipping their fingers in ink and rolling them on a piece of paper to take fingerprints.

I sent Petraeus a copy of Dr. Basima's badge as proof that she had finally got it. He responded, "A face that could launch a thousand Sunnis, Emma!"

When I next saw Dr. Basima I told her that Petraeus was pleased to hear that she now had her badge. "What did he say?" she asked.

I wasn't sure how she would respond to the Helen of Troy analogy, so I fabricated, referring to our detention facility near Basra.

"He rubbed his hands and said, 'Send her to Bucca!'" She roared with laughter.

11

SURGING THROUGH
THE SUMMER

Stelios: It's an honor to die at your side.
King Leonidas: It's an honor to have lived at yours.
—*300* (film)

THE SUMMER OF 2007 was a long hot one—hot even for Iraqis who were born and bred in "the land between the two rivers," and hotter still for us occupiers in our body armour and Kevlar helmets. Iraqis, most of whom did not have electricity for more than a couple of hours, tried to stay inside during the hottest part of the day and slept outside on their roofs at night.

General O's battle rhythm did not relent for a moment. In every meeting, in every brief, he urged commanders to be aggressive, to take risks, to be relentless in going after the enemy. There were times when I despaired that the cycle of violence would ever end. But even in private moments, General O never doubted what his soldiers could do. He was a man with a mission. And this permeated down throughout the Corps. What he did fear, however, was that Congress might pull the plug on the Surge and not give us the time we needed.

General O had used the initial Surge brigades to secure Baghdad. It was not until the other additional forces arrived that he could launch Operation Phantom Thunder in mid June. This was a Corps-level operation to secure the "belts" around Baghdad. By midsummer, there was a total of seven brigades in the belts.

Operations in Anbar and Baghdad had displaced insurgents to Diyala province in the east. It was in this province that Zarqawi had sought sanctuary and had been killed by General McChrystal's men back in 2006. It had become the most violent part of Iraq. A darkness had descended on a province which had hitherto been known only for its date palms. Al-Qaeda had banned smoking. It also forbade cucumbers and tomatoes from being sold together, bestowing on them opposite genders and regarding their mixing as lascivious.

Colonel Sutherland, the commander of the 3rd Brigade Combat Team of the 1st Cavalry Division, took us on an aerial tour of the Diyala River Valley. It was clear we had inadequate numbers of troops to clear territory and hold the ground. Whenever we flew over the palm groves of Diyala, General O stared intently at the ground. It was as if he could feel the eyes of insurgents looking up at him. In April, a few days after a unit of the 82nd Airborne lost nine of its soldiers in an attack, we had flown to visit them at their outpost in an abandoned school in as-Sada, a Sunni Arab village north of Baqubah. Captain Jesse Stewart described to General O how a dump truck had rammed the gate and a second one had driven through the gap that was created, causing the building to collapse with the soldiers inside. After the attack, the soldiers had found and destroyed al-Qaeda training camps and a logistics base in the palm groves. Captain Stewart said his unit was determined to rebuild the destroyed school and to show the local community their commitment. The sheikhs in the area had all signed a document taking responsibility for ensuring that bombs were not planted on their land.

We saw that military operations inside Baqubah, the provincial capital, were dislodging insurgents up the Diyala River Valley. Al-Qaeda were taking up positions in houses there. Lieutenant Colonel Poppas tried to contain them from coming back into Baqubah; they responded with a car bomb at the gate of his base. The areas that the US military cleared of al-Qaeda were then back-filled by Jaysh al-Mahdi, as there were insufficient Iraqi security forces.

General O's operational reserve was the 3rd Brigade Combat Team of the 2nd Infantry Division, led by Colonel Townsend. This Stryker brigade had initially deployed to Nineveh in the north. Five months later, they had received orders to move to Baghdad, where they served as a strike force, disrupting insurgent activity, smashing their way through ambushes in their eight-wheeled armoured fighting vehicles and clearing

General Odierno and Sky listen to Lieutenant Colonel Bruce Antonia, commander of the 5th Battalion, 20th Infantry Regiment, 3rd Stryker Brigade Combat Team, 2nd Infantry Division, talk about the progress of Operation Arrowhead Ripper at an abandoned medical clinic in Baqubah, Diyala. *Photo by Curt Cashour*

areas of the capital. Now, in June, General O deployed the brigade to Diyala to focus on Baqubah in order to free up Colonel Sutherland to focus on clearing the Diyala River Valley.

The fighting in Diyala was relentless. We met up one day in June in a bombed-out clinic in Baqubah. We sat on cartons as Lieutenant Colonel Bruce Antonia briefed us on the battle, pointing with a stick at a map to show where the battle lines were. He was responsible for south Baqubah, and was trying to stop insurgents getting into the town from Baghdad. His unit was in constant fire-fights and bomb-clearing just to move along small stretches of road. They discussed enemy strength and enemy tactics. General O asked what additional support he could provide in order to destroy the enemy. It was a scene that could have come from any war. At the front line, war was still an inherently human endeavour. I peered into the corridor. Soldiers were sleeping propped up against walls or

General Odierno, Sergeant Major Neil Ciotola and Sky after patrol with
Colonel Steve Townsend and members of the 3rd Stryker Brigade Combat
Team, 2nd Infantry Division, at Forward Operating Base Warhorse in
Baqubah, Diyala. *Photo by Curt Cashour*

leaning on each other. They had been fighting for days, clearing house by
house and street by street.

Colonel Townsend stood out among the pack. He was a paratrooper,
from the ranger regiment, and a seasoned fighter. His subordinates wor-
shipped him. He was empowering and inclusive, and made everything
seem fun. He was tactically savvy and prepared to take risks. He had re-
sorted to dropping his own bombs on the road to clear it of the explosives
insurgents had buried.

I knew the situation in Baqubah was even more dangerous than usual
when General O loaded his 9mm pistol. We boarded a Stryker vehicle and
General O took up a position, standing out of the turret. I was crouched
in the bowels of the vehicle unable to see anything except for his legs.

We met up with Sergeant Major Ciotola in Baqubah. He had been going out on raids with a unit in Diyala. He told us that jumping over walls
in full battle rattle in the midday heat had nearly killed him. He was su-
premely fit—but no longer eighteen. He provided General O with ground
truth on how soldiers were feeling and how they were performing.

Colonel Sutherland was investing considerable amounts of time with
Iraqi leaders, so that they would be able to take over in the future. But his
armoured mechanized brigade was taking heavy casualties—each one
of them seemed to kill a part of him. He truly cared for his soldiers. He
appeared deeply religious, and in his office I noted biblical quotations on
the wall. He described to General O how the head of a suicide bomber
who had tried to kill him bounced off the bonnet of his vehicle. Sutherland and Townsend managed their relationship brilliantly, working together to ensure a security bubble inside Baqubah, then pushing it out up
into the Diyala River Valley. Lieutenant Colonel Mark Landes's Stryker
battalion was sent to clear the valley, starting north in Muqdadiya and
working back down it towards Baqubah. The soldiers were constantly
shot at by enemy fire throughout the operation.

General O visited one of the main coalition hospitals in Balad. As
I followed him around, wounded soldiers saluted him. One wanted to
get back into the fight as soon as possible. Another wanted to re-enlist
before he was medically evacuated out of the country. The quietness
and sterility of the hospital was suddenly broken by the rush of medics
unloading more wounded soldiers from Diyala. We pressed our backs
against the wall as medics rushed through with stretchers carrying the
young, bloodied men off the helicopters, some writhing in agony, others
unconscious—the horrible reality of war. I steeled myself to look at their
faces. I said a silent prayer that they would recover from their wounds
and return safely to their families. And that their sacrifices would not be
in vain.

WE MADE REGULAR VISITS to units in and around Baghdad. As a gesture
of goodwill, General O invited Dr. Basima to join us on a visit to one of
the Awakening leaders in Amiriya in western Baghdad, Abu Abed. Abu

General Odierno at Patrol Base Hawkes near Arab Jabour. *Photo by Curt Cashour*

Abed was a member of the old Iraqi Army. Two of his brothers had been killed by Shia militias and their tortured bodies dumped on the Iran-Iraq border. The killing of a well-respected local leader had driven him to take action against al-Qaeda. When al-Qaeda retaliated, Abu Abed had called the local battalion commander, Lieutenant Colonel Kuehl, for help. Kuehl had responded and together they had cleared Amiriya of al-Qaeda.

Dr. Basima came along on the trip, riding in a Humvee in her high heels. Abu Abed recounted how his group had pushed al-Qaeda out of the area, but complained that he received no support from the Iraqi government and the Iraqi Army was reluctant to work with them. Dr. Basima commended him on his work, said he was doing a much better job than the Iraqi security forces, and offered to cook food for him herself! I had no idea if she could cook.

WE FLEW NORTH to Mosul on a C-130. As the plane took off from Baghdad, shots were fired at it, and it took evasive action. The ramp at the back of the plane began to drop open and crew hurried to secure it. If this had been a civilian plane, everyone would have been screaming. But the military was unperturbed. I turned to General O. He looked completely calm, and gave me a reassuring smile. We could not speak above the noise of the plane.

On landing, we set out in a convoy through Mosul. A roadside bomb exploded, blackening the window of the vehicle I was travelling in. Fortunately, it had gone off a second or two early, so did not do much damage to the Humvee. The unit spotted the young men who had detonated the bomb and gave chase. I was relieved when we landed safely back in Baghdad. Although I generally felt safe when I was with General O, the trip to Mosul had tested my faith.

On another day, we flew south to Jurf al-Sakr, a small town on the Euphrates about thirty-seven miles south-west of Baghdad and in an area which the US military had dubbed the "Triangle of Death." The helicopter landed on a dusty road. We got out and quickly walked towards the outpost, protected by US soldiers in the palm trees either side. There, the young captain proceeded in an animated fashion to explain how his base had come under attack from insurgents the week before but his troops had managed to repel them. As we walked back to the helicopter I expected insurgents to ambush us at any moment.

In July we visited Bayji, Iraq's biggest oil refinery, about 130 miles north of Baghdad. Captain Kuhlman, who was responsible for the security of the refinery, explained that the most complex issue he was dealing with was corruption, which affected production and distribution. He gave an example. Militiamen were driving up to Bayji in an oil tanker, filling it up and then selling it on the black market to an Iraqi official who had set up his own personal petrol station.

NOW THAT OUR TROOPS were out living among the population, we had far greater interaction with Iraqis. When we visited areas, it was not uncommon for an Iraqi to request that a particular American NCO or officer have his tour extended so he could stay on in the area.

One day we as were walking down a dirty street on the outskirts of Tarmiyya, a small town north of Baghdad which had recently been cleared of al-Qaeda, a group of kids suddenly ran up to us. I was eating freshly baked diamond-shaped *samoon* bread which Mike Juaidi had bought for me from a bakery we had just passed.

"Look at the little girl," General O said, pointing at her. I looked down at her. Her hair was matted from the dust. She had spotted me among all the American soldiers. She stared intently at me—and then lifted her arms towards me.

"She wants to touch your hair," General O observed. I bent down towards the girl. She ran her fingers through my hair.

"What's your name?" I asked her. "How old are you?" She answered me shyly. I held her hand and we walked along for a few steps together. I wanted to stay with her longer but I had to leave, and so I waved her goodbye.

As we took off, I could not get the image of the little girl and her piercing green eyes out of my mind. Did she have anyone to look after her? I imagined picking her up, continuing down the street carrying her on my hip. I wanted to apologize for leaving her and to explain that I had to look after generals, not children.

On 29 July I sat glued to the TV watching the final of the Asia Cup soccer tournament in Jakarta. Iraq's team, known as the Lions of the Two Rivers, was made up of players from all of Iraq's communities. The security situation had prevented them from training in Iraq. Over fifty Iraqi fans had been killed in two suicide bombings in Baghdad the previous week when they had been celebrating Iraq's victory in the semi-finals against South Korea.

That day the team played their hearts out for Iraq. And the whole country willed them on to victory against Saudi Arabia. In the seventy-first minute, Iraq's captain, Younis Mahmoud (a Sunni Arab from Kirkuk), scored the winning goal with a header from a ball passed to him by a Kurd from Mosul.

Tears rolled down my face when the final whistle blew and I listened to the sound of celebratory gunfire rippling across Baghdad. Nothing could kill the joy of Iraqis celebrating across the entire country. I found myself daring to believe that Iraq just might actually pull together.

ONE MORNING IN THE BUA, a US colonel approached me and informed me that our special forces had picked up a "friend" of mine: Ismail Abudi from Kirkuk. He was accused of buying weapons from Iran for Jaysh al-Mahdi. The recommended punishment was life imprisonment or death. During his interrogation, he had kept repeating that he knew General O and me. I did not for a second believe the allegations. Ismail had been arrested on the basis of two sworn statements. It was a system wide open to abuse, enabling Iraqis to take revenge or simply make false accusations against someone in return for a bribe.

I wrote a statement setting out what I knew about Ismail and why I believed he was not buying weapons for JAM. I also suggested a motive for others to make false accusations against him. As an Arab Shia living in Kirkuk, he was vulnerable to pressure from Kurdish political parties seeking to compel those Arabs without historical roots in the province to leave as part of the "normalization" process set out in Article 140 of the Constitution. Ismail's wife called me in tears. I promised her that I was doing everything I could. I followed up on a daily basis, and after a couple of weeks he was released.

Ismail came down to Baghdad to see me. We met in the al-Rashid Hotel. "You saved my life again!" He grinned as we shook hands warmly. He described how US special forces had descended on his house in the night and arrested him in front of his family. He had been taken to a detention facility where he was interrogated.

"Ismail, I am so sorry," I said.

"Oh, don't be," he said. "The US military treated me very well. It was much better than when I was jailed during Saddam's time." He recalled how I had helped save his life when he was kidnapped back in 2003. "I might not be around to do it a third time," I warned him.

He gave me news of Kirkuk. "Sheikh Wasfi has married Saddam's daughter!"—his way of saying that Sheikh Wasfi, the member of the Kirkuk Provincial Council who I had escorted to meet Bremer in Baghdad, had joined the insurgency and was now based in Syria.

Not long after his release, Ismail packed up his family and home in Kirkuk and moved south to Nasiriyah, where his family had historical roots, to begin a new life. He was a survivor and I knew he would be able to make a fresh start.

ONE DAY IN AUGUST, we flew west to Anbar and made a series of stops to visit troops across the province. By the time we visited the final outpost, in a remote spot in the middle of nowhere, I was exhausted and dehydrated. I lay down on the ground, and announced I could go no further. No one was concerned or sympathetic. Major Wilson, the aide, gave me a bottle of Gatorade. "Drink," he insisted. I did so. And by the time I had drunk the Gatorade and two litres of water, I had come back to life.

When we got back to Camp Victory, General O reminded me that I was dining with him that evening as he had invited some journalists to his quarters. "Sir," I protested, "I nearly died today. I need to go lie down." "You are coming to dinner," he responded. "I don't want to," I replied, pointing out that my hair was matted and had turned to straw from all the sweat and dust of the trip. "You are coming," he ordered. He did not relent. I was shoved once more into the back seat of the car behind him.

The journalists were, as ever, good company. We listened to them describing what they had seen around the country. And in turn, General O gave them his assessment. We now had all the Surge forces in-country. Our forces in Anbar and Baghdad had forced al-Qaeda out east to Diyala province. There was intense fighting still going on there. "As I go around the country, I am hearing from my soldiers on the ground that they have a sense that the tide is turning."

US fatalities had finally started to drop. We had lost 131 troops in May, 108 in June, and 89 in July. "As our military operations continue and our soldiers push back out into population centres and clear them of insurgents, we are hiring locals to man checkpoints in areas where there are no security forces," Odierno explained to them. For many Iraqis, this was an opportunity to make money to look after their families—and it made them less susceptible to being paid by insurgent groups to lay roadside bombs. As trust between the Coalition and Iraqis grew, we were receiving more information from Iraqis about the terrorists. The blowing-up of the remaining minarets of the ninth-century Samarra mosque on 13 June had not set the country back as it had done in 2006, when sectarian violence had spiralled out of control. "The Surge is working," Odierno insisted. It really was.

By MIDSUMMER, the majority of US casualties were being caused by Shia militia using their signature weapon, EFPs. The explosively formed projectiles were able to pierce the armour of US vehicles. During the past year, Iran had increased its provision of weapons, ammunition, funding and training to Shia militia.

Some units of the Iraqi security forces were heavily infiltrated by Shia militia. I was sitting at the OCINC chatting to General Abu Mohamad one afternoon when Iraqi Brigadier General Falah arrived, accompanied by US Lieutenant Colonel Steve Miska, who was based at Camp Justice in Kadhimiya, a northern neighbourhood of Baghdad. General Falah described in graphic detail how he had survived an assassination attempt in which Hazem al-Araji (the brother of a member of parliament) and an Iraqi battalion commander were clearly complicit. General Falah painted a picture of a gangster-land around the Kadhimiya shrine. The director of the Sadrist office claimed he personally had phoned Condoleezza Rice to get the US troops withdrawn from the area, and Jaysh al-Mahdi were bragging that they were stronger than the Iraqi security forces. General Falah said he had inherited the brigade from an officer who had recently been reassigned to sort out Basra but who should really be jailed for his collusion with Jaysh al-Mahdi, and for all the missing weapons and ammunition. He named a couple of subordinate officers who he described as extremely bad, involved with terrorists and corrupt.

On a visit to one of our units in the Rashid neighbourhood of west Baghdad, we received a brief on how an Iraqi national police unit, known as the Wolf Brigade, was cleansing areas of Sunnis, tipping off Jaysh al-Mahdi about Coalition raids and failing to prevent militia attacks on the Coalition. General O met the Iraqi Wolf Brigade commander. Towering over him, he warned him of the consequences if the national police did not clean up its act.

Fortunately, the national police commander, General Hussein al-Awadi, was a courageous leader. He replaced the two divisional commanders, the nine brigade commanders, and eighteen of the twenty-seven battalion commanders. With strong leadership, supported by training from the Italian *carabinieri*, we saw the national police transform itself into a more reliable and professional force.

In early September 2007, only days before Crocker and Petraeus were due to testify before Congress on the progress of the Surge, General O flew by helicopter to the government centre in Ramadi, the capital of Anbar province and its largest city.

The province had completely turned around during the last year, thanks to the tribes swapping sides to work with the Coalition against al-Qaeda. To reward the tribes for their efforts, and to demonstrate a level of progress in Iraq, we had helped engineer a conference to bring senior Iraqi officials out to Anbar to show their commitment to reconciliation. Maliki did not come. But Adel Abdul Mahdi, Barham Salih and Tareq al-Hashimi did. Crocker was accompanied by Senator Joe Biden, who happened to be visiting Iraq as part of a congressional delegation.

Dozens of sheikhs were seated around the long table in Ramadi's newly renovated Provincial Council Chambers, along with the representatives of the Iraqi government and the senior US officials. Governor Ma'mun opened the event. As ever, the sheikhs surpassed each other with their rhetoric and hyperbole. The most prominent of them was Sheikh Sitar Abu Risha. He had a quick wit, and was said to have been previously involved in oil smuggling, although no one really knew for certain. He had come forward and established the Awakening after his father and two brothers were killed by al-Qaeda.

During the conference, the Iraqi government representatives pledged $70 million in reconstruction funds and $50 million to repair homes destroyed in the war. There were also commitments of six thousand new government jobs and new generators. Crocker marvelled that the conference could take place in Anbar, without security even being a topic of conversation. But Senator Biden warned that American patience with the Iraqi government was wearing thin. If the Iraqi government did not do more, then US forces would be withdrawn.

DESPITE THE FACT that the Iraqi government had failed to meet most of the eighteen benchmarks established by the White House to measure success in Iraq, Petraeus and Crocker were able to provide some indicators of progress when they testified before Congress in Washington on 10 September 2007.

"The situation in Iraq remains complex, difficult and sometimes downright frustrating," Petraeus said. "I also believe that it is possible to achieve our objectives in Iraq over time, although doing so will be neither quick nor easy." Ambassador Crocker argued that Iraqi leaders "are capable of coming together and thrashing out issues in a serious and deliberate manner."

It was a shock for us in Iraq to see how Petraeus was treated in Washington. In Iraq, he was on such a pedestal, revered by all. Back in the US, the *New York Times* ran a large advertisement by an anti-war group called MoveOn.org with the headline GENERAL BETRAY US. Hillary Clinton responded to his testimony by saying, "The reports that you provide to us really require the willing suspension of disbelief."

Petraeus gave evidence of the Iraqi government's commitment to reconciliation. He highlighted the recruitment into the Iraqi security forces of members of the former Iraqi Army and former insurgents in Abu Ghraib—and the prospect of "conditional immunity." When I went round to see Basima and Abu Mohamad, they told me they had been following the news closely and were genuinely surprised at the level of recognition of their work. They were busy turning bombed-out rooms in OCINC into offices for staff working on reconciliation. Basima asked me for help in choosing new wallpaper!

Petraeus and Crocker managed to convince Congress that the Surge was having a positive impact and that the US should not pull the plug on Iraq. They had succeeded in putting more time on the Iraqi clock. But Iraq was never going to become easy. A few days after their testimony, on 13 September, al-Qaeda assassinated Sheikh Sitar Abu Risha in a roadside bombing. He had done more than anyone else to show that the sands of Mesopotamia were constantly moving. It was his shift in alliances and the establishment of the Anbar Awakening that had provided Sunnis with an honourable exit from the insurgency and a new platform from which to participate in the future of Iraq.

12

SADRIST CEASEFIRE

To do this job you have to be more of a missionary than a soldier.
—CAPTAIN BRIAN DUCOTE, US ARMY

AT THE END OF AUGUST, we were completely taken by surprise when Muqtada al-Sadr announced the suspension of the activities of his Shia militia, Jaysh al-Mahdi (JAM). Recognizing there were different groups operating under his name but not under his jurisdiction, he announced that anyone who continued to conduct attacks was not a real member of Jaysh al-Mahdi.

The ceasefire came at the end of a month in which power struggles between Shia groups had escalated. The governors of Muthanna province and Qadisiya province, who were members of the Islamic Supreme Council of Iraq, were both killed in separate roadside bombings only a few days apart. Tensions had culminated when clashes in Karbala between Sadrists and Badr left over fifty dead, shocking the Shia public.

The Coalition considered the different options. Our targeting of Shia extremists had been having an effect, and some argued for continuing to inflict maximum damage on JAM. But in the end General Petraeus and Crocker decided that the Coalition would welcome Muqtada's declaration—and monitor the ceasefire closely. Petraeus began referring to *Sayyid* Muqtada in public, using the honorific.

But reconciliation with the Sadrists was a different ball game to reconciliation with Sunnis. The Sunnis and the Coalition had come together to fight against al-Qaeda. Former Sunni insurgents now took shelter behind the Coalition and saw common cause with us against Iran. The Coalition felt that the Shia should be grateful for their liberation from Saddam; instead, Shia militia attacked our troops and bases. In their case there was no common cause we could come together around. They wanted us to leave.

IT WAS IN AUGUST that I first got to know Safa al-Sheikh. He had been appointed the head of the Implementation and Follow-up Committee of National Reconciliation, and hence the boss of Dr. Basima and General Abu Mohamad. He was mild-mannered, courteous and genuine, and I admired his skill in managing Dr. Basima. In itself, that was quite a feat.

A devout Shia Muslim who had lived all his life in Iraq, Safa had been educated at Baghdad College, the high school set up by Jesuits from Boston College, which graduated generations of Iraq's elites. He had become religious as a young man and had joined the underground Dawa party. The ideological founder of the Dawa party was Mohamad Baqir al-Sadr, Muqtada al-Sadr's father-in-law, who wrote important works on philosophy and economics before he was executed by Saddam's regime along with his sister Bint al-Huda. As Dawa was a secret organization, and Safa was an officer in the air force, he limited his contact to members in his own cell. But others in his cell had been identified by the Baath regime and executed. Safa had become a member of the Baath party as cover. He had initially been involved on the de-Baathification committee and had told the Americans and the Iraqi exiles it was wrong to view this in the same way as de-Nazification. The Baath party had moved far from ideology, and most people had joined it simply to enhance their career prospects. Safa had two Sunni wives, one of whom lived with him in Baghdad. The other, who had become Shia, was in Sweden where she had taken their children to escape the violence in Iraq.

Safa went to great lengths to help me understand the thinking of the prime minister and his inner circle. He complained that the Coalition did not have a real policy on national reconciliation and did not appreciate that reconciliation took time. He criticized the Coalition for assessing the threat to Iraq simply in terms of al-Qaeda and Jaysh al-Mahdi. The Coalition was too binary in its thinking, when the environment was so complex. National reconciliation was not just about ceasefires and deals with tribal sheikhs. He also criticized the Coalition's limited understanding of Jaysh al-Mahdi: "Things which are known to Iraqi children do not seem to be understood by US policy-makers." The Coalition used the term "JAM" to encompass what were many factions within the Sadrist movement.

Following Muqtada's announcement, Safa was exploring how to reach out to the Sadrists. They seemed to trust him; he had remained in Iraq all along and had never lived in exile. He told me about meetings he had had with some members of JAM. For the most part, Jaysh al-Mahdi was anti-Iranian although it had been infiltrated by Iran. Muqtada represented the largely poor, downtrodden Shia, who remained in Iraq during Saddam's time, hence his conflict with the Hakim family, which headed the Islamic Supreme Council of Iraq, and who were more elitist and had been based in Iran. The intent of the ceasefire, however, was not clear. For some it was about reconciliation; for others it was about reorganization.

Safa invited me to join him one afternoon to meet two Sadrists from Sadr City, the Shia neighbourhood of eastern Baghdad. Lack of opportunities had driven thousands of poor Shia to migrate there from the countryside in the south. It had become a densely populated slum area, with its residents maintaining their distinctive rural culture, isolated from urbane Baghdadis. Following the fall of the regime, the area, which originally had been called Thawra City and then later Saddam City, had changed its name to Sadr City, in honour of the father of Muqtada al-Sadr. But those who lived there referred to it as *al-madina*, "the city." Safa introduced me to the two local government officials as a true friend of Iraq whom he completely trusted. The two Sadrists said that after Muqtada's declaration JAM members had suspended military activities. They welcomed the Coalition's public response to Muqtada's declaration but complained that the Coalition continued to conduct raids and aerial attacks. Each time the Coalition pursued someone, they destroyed several houses and traumatized people.

"The Coalition welcomes the declaration by Muqtada," I said. The Iraqi government had asked us to reduce our raids against JAM. Since the declaration we had only conducted one raid into Sadr City. There were often false reports in the media, accusing the Coalition of things we had not done. I gave them my phone number and said any time they heard of a raid in Sadr City, they should phone me and give me details. I would then check and phone them back.

The Sadrists told me that, in Sadr City at least, there was cooperation between the police and JAM to provide security. JAM also protected religious events and cleaned the streets. JAM was putting on plays to get the community to reject violence. They acknowledged, however, that there were some rogue elements who operated under the banner of JAM.

"There is a misunderstanding between the Coalition and the Sadrists, due to the lack of trust," I explained. "America was built by people who had fled oppression. Americans have no desire to occupy another country. We will leave as soon as the Iraqi government is able to manage the country and has a monopoly on the use of force." The Sadrists said they wished this meeting with me had happened four years ago. They concluded by complimenting me on my humanistic outlook. "You have all the qualities to be a member of Jaysh al-Mahdi!" one told me, a comment I decided not to report back to General O!

WITH PETRAEUS still in the US being grilled by Congress, General O went to meet with President Talabani to discuss Muqtada's declaration. Talabani met us on the steps of the presidential palace. After shaking hands with General O, he kissed me on both cheeks. "How are you, Miss Bell?"

Talabani told us he had good relations with the Sadrists. Before the declaration, he had called the Iranian ambassador in Baghdad and told him that the Iranian policy was undermining Iraq. He recommended to Iran that they dissolve JAM and stop attacks on Coalition forces for a year. He had received a letter from the Iranians saying they had ordered JAM to cease activity; and that they would keep Muqtada in Iran. Talabani described some of the tensions between the Shia in Iraq and Iran. Iraqi Shia viewed their "Vatican" as Najaf, the city in southern Iraq which housed the famous *hawza* (Shia seminary) and followed the "quietist" school of Ayatollah Sistani. And this detracted from the prestige of the Iranian city of Qom, the other distinguished *hawza*, and the rule by jurists, *wilayet al-faqih*, promulgated by Ayatollah Khomeini's Islamic Revolution.

There was no way to have a short meeting with Talabani. We were taken off to a side room where the table was laden with food. "Have some more kebab, Miss Bell," he said, as he spooned even more food on to my plate. He obviously believed I needed fattening up. He himself had put

on so much weight in recent years that his doctor was increasingly worried about him. A young Kurd, who had been instructed to monitor the
president's food intake, hovered behind him at meal times.

Afterwards, General O went to meet Maliki. He told him we had
greatly reduced our operations in Sadr City since Muqtada's declaration
and were trying to build relations with the community there. But we were
still being attacked with Iranian-made EFPs as well as Iranian-supplied
240mm rockets. While attacks on the Green Zone had decreased, they
had increased against Camp Victory, and all the rockets were fired from
Sadrist strongholds in Baghdad. General O said we understood that it
was criminal elements behind such attacks, not mainstream Jaysh al-
Mahdi, and we were only targeting those people.

"When the Coalition undertakes raids, we sometimes get fired on
from the tops of buildings and have to respond in self-defence," General
O explained. "Even so," Maliki replied, "the response should be propor-
tionate. Excessive use of force by the Coalition makes the public hate the
government." He went on: "The deaths of a handful or more innocent
civilians to kill one terrorist or criminal undermines support for both
the government and the Coalition." Maliki suggested that the Coalition
provide the names of targets to the Iraqi government, and maybe the
Iraqi security forces could make the arrests without anyone being killed.

Unfortunately, not long afterwards a special forces raid into Sadr City
on 20 October created outcry. The unit had come under fire and had
called in attack helicopters. The US military claimed forty-nine gunmen
were killed. But Iraqi television showed footage of dead women and children. There was uproar in the parliament. This latest raid came only
weeks after Blackwater private security contractors had opened fire in
Nisour Square, killing seventeen Iraqis. Maliki was furious. He threatened not to sign the strategic partnership declaration with the US nor to
support the renewal of the UN Security Council resolution that provided
the legal basis for Coalition forces.

THE SITUATION WAS CONFUSING and chaotic. Negotiations with the Sadrists were never going to be easy. Safa became a main mediator with
JAM and kept us informed of how his discussions were going. Due to

an "intercept" of a conversation between Safa and a Sadrist, a US colonel made the ludicrous claim that Safa himself was a member of JAM. I banged my head against the wall.

General O remained cautious about dealing with the Sadrists. He agreed that we had to be willing to talk to anyone, but we had to be careful not to give representatives legitimacy, resources or immunity until they produced more than promises. We had been down this road multiple times with the Sadrists since 2003. Muqtada suggested engagement opportunities through a range of Iraqi government, religious and tribal interests in order to cause paralysis in our decision-making and thus buy himself breathing space. We were at our strongest now. JAM was losing popular support. But in the first week of October, there already had been fourteen EFP attacks. These were clearly from special groups linked to Iran, and caused a visceral reaction from US commanders. And there was a steady increase in indirect fire coming from Sadr City. General O had seen nothing to make him believe they would stop these attacks. Overtures to Sadrists in Sadr City came to nothing. The Sadrists there did not feel the need to negotiate or compromise. And Coalition raids into Sadr City had further alienated the community.

Not to be put off by the setback in Sadr City, Safa brought to my attention a reconciliation meeting he had heard about in Jihad, a mixed Sunni-Shia district in south-west Baghdad. Safa wanted to explore using Jihad as a pilot for reconciliation with the Sadrists. The Sadrist community in Jihad felt under threat from Sunni insurgents. They realized they needed to reach a deal if they were to survive. I dug around and found out that Lieutenant Colonel Patrick Frank, the battalion commander of 1-28 "Black Lions," had indeed hosted such a face-to-face reconciliation meeting. This was very interesting. But the information had not been considered relevant to pass up the chain to General O.

General O called for a meeting with Lieutenant Colonel Frank and his brigade and division commanders. Frank was very articulate and spoke in detail about the situation in his neighbourhood. His soldiers were living out among the population and had built up a thorough understanding of the area's dynamics. They had spent five months aggressively going after al-Qaeda and Jaysh al-Mahdi leaders. Frank now felt they were in a position to exploit the differences between militants and moderates.

A couple of months previously, General O had asked commanders in Baghdad, "Is any one talking with the enemy? Has anyone reached out to Jaysh al-Mahdi?" In response, Frank had written a letter to Abu Duma, the Jaysh al-Mahdi brigade commander for the area, inviting him to talk. Abu Duma accepted the offer by allowing Shia community leaders to attend reconciliation meetings, sponsored by Frank. It was clear that Lieutenant Colonel Frank was much more progressive than his superior officers. General O gave permission for me to deal with him directly, rather than go down through the chain of command, and to link him up with the Iraqi government officials.

I spent some time with Frank in Jihad, getting to know him and some of his tightly knit group of officers. He was another idealist, a slightly built redhead, full of energy and ideas. A highly intelligent and well-educated officer, what struck me most about him was his willingness to take risks. He truly believed that American soldiers could change the world. He told me that every time he deployed, American soldiers had been embraced by those who supposedly hated them. For him, the liberals and academics got it wrong, and the "muddy boots guys" were the ones who got it right. He believed in American exceptionalism—in America as the crusading nation bringing freedom to oppressed peoples around the world.

At one point, I stood on the corner of a street in Jihad talking to Captain Brian Ducote. He spoke about the local people: their strength of character, their pride, dignity, sense of honour. He told me, "To do this job you have to be more of a missionary than a soldier." Captain Ducote was receiving dozens of phone calls a day from Iraqis requesting assistance. His comrades had dubbed him the "insurgent whisperer." It was wonderful to watch the way he interacted with Iraqis. When I saw the level of respect the Black Lions had for the Iraqis, I understood why they were being successful.

I got Lieutenant Colonel Frank to come to the Green Zone to meet Safa and Dr. Basima. We were all excited about the possibilities of taking forward this initiative in Jihad. To generate goodwill, and to build up Safa's reputation as someone who could deliver concessions from the Coalition, in exchange for JAM stopping their attacks, General O agreed to go ahead with a detainee release in Jihad. Previous releases of prominent

Shia detainees had neither helped end attacks on the Coalition nor progressed reconciliation with Sunnis. This time, General O wanted to ensure that those released were very low-level detainees.

I waited for news of how the release had gone. It was not what I had expected. Safa recounted how families in Jihad had prepared a welcoming-home ceremony for their returning sons. But none had returned. Only one of the detainees released was actually from Jihad, and he was not involved with Jaysh al-Mahdi. And three (of the nine) were Sunnis. Safa and I both convulsed with laughter over this. He knew the Coalition had not done this deliberately; it was an unintentional mistake. He told me the Jihad families were dealing with it stoically. But we had to move quickly to rectify it.

Lieutenant Colonel Frank set 18 October as the date for a big reconciliation conference for all the community leaders from Jihad. I went over to the Green Zone to collect Safa and Dr. Basima. We loaded Dr. Basima into a Humvee, with lots of giggles. The doors were small and heavy, and there were American soldiers in the other seats. She was dressed in her normal *abaya* and heels. We drove to Baghdad airport, where Frank had arranged to hold the conference in the business centre. When we arrived, I confiscated Dr. Basima's phone so she would focus completely on the events in hand.

Safa and Dr. Basima addressed the fifty or so community leaders on the importance of reconciliation, the interest of Maliki in Jihad, the positive aspects of Shia and Sunni working together, and a vision for a united Iraq. The district chairman responded that this was the first time Iraqi government officials had come out to assist in reconciliation and they were most welcome. Safa stated that Muqtada had called for a freeze. Anyone who still carried weapons was therefore not a member of Jaysh al-Mahdi. He spoke of the need for trust, including with the Coalition.

Sounding like a charismatic young headmaster, Pat Frank addressed the group, urging them to reach an agreement. Jihad was leading the way for all Baghdad. "You are the hope for the entire city. If you do not agree, it will diminish people's hopes. You feel the pressure of the three hundred thousand citizens of Jihad—but the hopes of seven million Iraqis are also on your shoulders."

The leaders chose two Sunnis and two Shia to go into a separate room. In the end, Safa and Dr. Basima managed to broker an agreement that the Coalition and Iraqi Army had the right to conduct raids, but they would only target those who continued to use violence. It was agreed that "conditional immunity" would be granted for those who had stopped using violence. After five hours of discussions and negotiations, the amended draft was presented and signed. There was much laughter and joking, and taking of photos.

Safa and Dr Basima both gave interviews to the media. Dr. Basima told the *Washington Post*, "'I believe that reconciliation is the only solution to save Iraq from violence and terrorism. Where it has happened in other areas, we see the curve of violence going down. Reconciliation is the only solution, not military operations." In describing the day's events, Safa told the same newspaper, "These are members of Sunni and Shiite tribes who were involved in fighting each other, but they agreed to look to the future and forget the past. I think it's the beginning of a success story." I returned Dr Basima's phone to her. She then called Maliki and updated him on what had been agreed.

Days such as this gave me hope it was possible to get Iraq on the right track. It just required huge amounts of effort—and the right people with the necessary relationships to push everything in the right direction. Pat Frank was all charm and chocolates. And Dr. Basima loved him. He was thoughtful and kind. While many US officers tried to bulldoze their way past her, he treated her with respect. In the absence of progress at the national level on reconciliation, we were brokering local agreements. Safa and Dr. Basima had even argued for the right of the Coalition to undertake raids in Shia neighbourhoods against those conducting attacks. We had come a long way.

To SHOW HIS SUPPORT for the Jihad initiative, and to help to reduce the fallout from the 20 October raid on Sadr City by special forces, General O agreed to escort an Iraqi government team to Jihad, led by General Abu Mohamad, showcasing the Coalition and the government working together to help ordinary Iraqis. The Iraqi media also came along. Lieutenant Colonel Frank carefully planned the itinerary.

On arrival in Jihad, General Abu Mohamad told the gathered group of Jihad leaders that in response to their reconciliation efforts, Maliki had sent this government team to look at ways of improving services. But he warned them, "Reconciliation is being targeted. Do not be puppets for rumours. Rumours are spread to ruin reconciliation." Rumours were certainly rife across Baghdad. A report that two Shia men had been beheaded by al-Qaeda turned out to be false when they reappeared after being released by their Shia kidnappers.

We visited a sewage station that was in working order but not actually running. It needed local people to manage it and secure it. General Abu Mohamad noted that the Ministry of Oil claimed it was supplying oil, but the residents had not received it. General O explained that the issue of oil assigned but not reaching the people was a problem across Baghdad. He said the Coalition could help to ensure the security of trucks and workers.

At the Red Crescent facility in Jihad, General Abu Mohamad presented fifteen wheelchairs (which had been purchased by the Coalition) to disabled and infirm Iraqis. One of the recipients, Sinan Kemal, was a former policeman in his twenties who had been wounded twice before losing both legs to a roadside bomb in Dora, when he had gone to the aid of a pregnant woman. He told me he had been engaged before his accident, but his fiancée's family had made them break off the engagement. He wanted to get prosthetic limbs so he could be mobile and then go back and ask permission to marry her, as they were very much in love.

General O had been really impressed by Abu Mohamad during the visit. He had had strong reservations about him, given the intelligence reports he had received. But Abu Mohamad had delivered. He had gathered together the necessary ministry representatives, and had got their agreement to cooperate with the local leaders and the Coalition to bring services to this area.

ONE NOVEMBER AFTERNOON when I visited their office, Abu Mohamad told me that Badr, the militia of the Islamic Supreme Council of Iraq, sometimes carried out attacks claiming to be JAM. He said the Coalition was naïve and did not realize what was going on. He explained that there was a struggle between Sadrists and the Islamic Supreme Council. It was an ideological struggle between the Arab and Iranian *hawza*, between the quietist and the activist schools of Shia Islam. Abu Mohamad claimed that the members of Badr were brainwashed from their time as prisoners of war in Iran and were married to Iranian women. Dr. Basima lamented that the Coalition had put exiles into leadership positions in Iraq. She complained that Iraq was currently ruled by the Supreme Council and Badr, which were linked to Iran, and by Kurds, who did not really want to be part of Iraq.

Safa visited Najaf to meet the Political Committee of the Sadrist Trend, who were worried that the government interpreted the ceasefire as a sign of weakness. They were under great pressure from internal dynamics among the Shia. They believed Maliki had moved closer to the Supreme Council. Safa told them the Sadrists were partly to blame for this situation as they had withdrawn from government, leaving Maliki with only the Kurds and the Supreme Council as allies. He explained that the Coalition—like the Sadrists—also had different "trends" within it. Not all the Coalition were focused on killing Iraqis. Some were dedicated to rebuilding Iraq. I smiled when I heard this. I knew that Iraqis often found it difficult to comprehend the Coalition.

As I was walking back from the dining facility to al-Faw Palace, carrying my food in a container, I heard a big boom, then another and another. Everyone shouted for people outside to take cover. News started to arrive in dribs and drabs as we began the weekly meeting with the Baghdad Division. General Fil came in late. He said a rocket had hit one of the dining facilities, wounding several soldiers. One had a sucking chest wound; another, a female, was badly wounded in the back. Soldiers had thrown themselves onto the wounded to protect them, rather than taking cover themselves. "The soldiers are amazing," General Fil said repeatedly, tears in his eyes. General O's eyes welled up. And then we were back to the brief. Later in the meeting, a captain passed General Fil a note saying two soldiers had died and another twenty-five were apparently wounded.

The attacks on Camp Victory continued, coming from the very area of western Baghdad where I was engaged in negotiations on reconciliation.

One morning in the BUA, details of another overnight attack were briefed.

"CHOPS, give Emma the POO," General O directed. I got up and walked behind the seated generals to Ryan Gonsalves, chief of operations, to get the slide with the point of origin (the POO) of the attacks.

"Give me the POO," I calmly requested.

Gonsalves stood there, arms folded, and said, "Your friends keep attacking us. We've just got to go kill them."

"CHOPS, give me the POO."

General O turned round to see what the commotion was behind him. "Sir, tell CHOPS to give me the POO," I said.

"CHOPS, I told you to give Emma the POO."

Gonsalves threw the slide at me. I took it and scuttled back to where I squatted on the stairs during the BUA.

As soon as the BUA was over, I phoned Safa. I told him the precise area the attacks had emanated from. We needed his help to prevent these attacks. The patience of the Coalition was running out fast, I warned him.

Not long after, Safa approached me and told me that Abu Ali, a key Sadrist leader in Jihad, was prepared to meet with Lieutenant Colonel Frank in secret to help "locate or neutralize" the rocketeers. Safa said that these people did not trust the Coalition in general, but they did trust Frank because of the reputation he had built up.

SAFA RECOMMENDED that the Coalition put Abu Miriam on our Restricted Target List (which meant that we would not detain him) and allow him to return to Jihad to play a positive role in reconciliation. Abu Miriam was a cleric, with good administrative skills, who had set up and run an NGO. But according to our intelligence, he was also a senior Jaysh al-Mahdi leader in west Baghdad.

I argued that we now had a leading Jaysh al-Mahdi guy who wanted to "reconcile" and was reaching out to us via the government, and we should reach back. He was believed to have influence and could make a difference. Reconciliation meant dealing with the activists and extremists, not just the moderates. The Baghdad Division advised against it. But

Pat Frank was willing to take the risk, and General O backed him up and overrode the division commander.

Safa arranged for Abu Miriam to come to his office in the Green Zone. When I met him he looked nervous, perhaps, I thought, because he had never met a member of the Coalition before. Post-2003, he told me, he had cooperated with the American officer responsible for the area. That had worked well. But after he left, the new American commander had not developed the same relationships with the Iraqis. The area plunged into sectarian violence. The *husseiniyas* and mosques were blown up. This set off a spate of revenge killings. He claimed he had been blamed for activities which he did not conduct. Currently, the Coalition was offering a reward of $10,000 for him.

I asked Abu Miriam whether he was willing to return to Jihad and to contribute to rebuilding the religious shrines and repairing community relations. He said he very much wanted to do so. I explained that, on Safa's recommendation, we were prepared to put him on a Restricted Target List.

"If this works out," he said, "I will take you as my second wife." Not sure how to answer this, I smiled back as sweetly as I could manage in response.

General O now arrived at the building. I left the room to brief him on the discussion and then introduced him to Abu Miriam. It was a short meeting to seal the deal. Abu Miriam continually fidgeted. General O then left and I stayed behind to finalize the details.

Abu Miriam turned to me. "I must apologise. When I saw the size of him, I was too terrified to ask him for you as my second wife."

WITHIN A VERY SHORT period of time, the cooperation of the Shia community increased, bringing about a dramatic decrease in attacks on Camp Victory.

Although Pat Frank graciously thanked me for my support, it was he who had made it happen. He understood his area and had earned the trust of the locals. General O had been prepared to underwrite the risk, against the recommendation of the Baghdad Division. I had helped connect Lieutenant Colonel Frank with the Iraqi government. Jihad showed what was possible at a local level when we all worked together.

Over the course of this initiative, I had spent lots of time with Lieutenant Colonel Frank and his battalion, the Black Lions. He had lost nineteen of his soldiers. He told me that "each death inspired us to continue the fight, to ensure that we defeated the enemy, and left our area dramatically better." I told General O about how impressed I was by their efforts. He said he was slowly learning that many of the young company commanders "got it." They had witnessed it, and therefore understood the importance of reconciliation. It always started with the battalion commander. It was he who shaped the leaders and attitudes of the unit.

As impressed as I was by many of the junior officers I met, I could not say the same about a number of the senior commanders, who did not get the nature of the "fight" in Iraq. They were much more comfortable in a conventional war setting, where the "enemy" was clearly defined as the opposing army. There was something in the American psyche about good and evil—good guys and bad guys—that made it difficult for many to cope with the greyness of Iraq. I never saw any senior officer removed for incompetence. One senior commander went through six aides in less than a year, indicative of his abusive behaviour towards subordinates. The 9mm pistol alongside the Bible on his desk scared me.

WHILE COALITION DEATHS had started to decrease from midsummer 2007, Iraqi deaths began to decline only from September when Muqtada's freeze went into effect. The number of Iraqi casualties dropped to 1,294 that month—down from 2,405 in August, according to the Iraq Body Count.

It was true that by this stage most of the sectarian displacement had already occurred. But Jaysh al-Mahdi had overstepped the mark with its violence and criminality and lost the support of the Shia population. They could no longer claim to be the defenders of the Shia, particularly as the Shia were less threatened by al-Qaeda attacks, thanks in large part to the Sunni sahwa, which the Coalition had helped to spread. The Coalition had seriously degraded JAM's capacity. And with the help of Coalition forces, the Iraqi security forces were growing in strength and gaining the trust of the population.

13

VICTORY

Say a prayer for peace
For every fallen son
Set my spirit free
Let me lay down my gun
Sweet mother Mary I'm so tired
But I can't come home 'til the last shot's fired
—TRACE ADKINS

TIME IN IRAQ ebbed and flowed. So much happened each day that the days seemed endless. But then weeks flew by. Suddenly, the end of the year was rapidly approaching. The season of transfer of authorities was upon us and different units, including General O's Phantom Corps, were reaching the end of their tours and new units were coming in to replace them.

We flew up to Tikrit at the end of November to bid farewell to Major General Randy Mixon and his division, which covered the north of Iraq. In his speech, General O referred to the heroic efforts of the troops. They had lost over two hundred soldiers, half of them under Colonel Dave Sutherland's command in Diyala. And thousands more had been injured. But they had succeeded in pacifying the province. On the way back to Baghdad we made a number of stops so General O could pin awards for heroism on individual soldiers. He felt strongly about recognizing the efforts of the troops.

That evening, the British chief of the defence staff, Sir Jock Stirrup, paid General O an office call. "I have nothing but admiration for what US soldiers have done and the way that they have done it," he said. "Congratulations on a great job. Astonishing difference over these six to eight months." It was a different tone from the first meeting of the year. Then he had pointed at me and said, "I can't believe you hired her!" I had waited for a diatribe about tree-hugging female types. Instead, he had said, "Look at the size of her. What happens if you get into a spot of difficulty and have to eat your aide? You need someone sturdier, with more meat on them!" He had then explained that the UK would not be following the US example of surging forces into Iraq. Her Majesty's Government had decided there was more chance of success in Afghanistan and they were moving troops over there, as it was to be the main UK effort.

This time Stirrup was much more humble. He agreed to maintain a UK brigade headquarters in Basra, headed by a two-star general. "We will continue as long as you want or value us," he said. "Thanks for everything you are doing for our folks." I sensed he was embarrassed that the Brits had given Iraq up for lost, while the Americans had refused to accept failure.

PRIME MINISTER MALIKI summoned General O for a meeting. He said he was shocked to hear of armed groups, wearing Coalition-style unit patches, searching people and setting up checkpoints in Saidiya, in southern Baghdad. They had their faces covered and no one knew who they were—some were not even from Saidiya. Maliki said it was dangerous to have armed people presenting themselves as the 1st Brigade of the sahwa, the Awakening. The behaviour of these Sunni "volunteers" was encouraging sectarian strife and creating tensions, even down in Najaf. The government and General Abud did not know about this. Was the Coalition hiding information? How could a sovereign Iraqi government accept armed people on the streets?

General O thanked Maliki for being forthright. He said the matter was one of miscommunication. Coalition commanders believed they were keeping local Iraqi commanders informed of what they were doing but the information appeared not to have been passed up the chain of command. The checkpoints in Saidiya were run jointly by Iraqi security forces and Concerned Local Citizens. He said Saidiya was probably the most contentious area in Baghdad because al-Qaeda and Jaysh al-Mahdi were trying to gain control of it. This might be causing the misrepresentation from both communities about what was happening there.

General O affirmed that Coalition priority was to provide security and stability across Iraq. The CLCs had really helped with this. Yes, the majority of CLCs were Sunni, but this was a way of getting Sunnis into the security forces, as it allowed them to show their goodwill towards the government and be vetted. General O had personally met most groups of CLCs and believed they were sincere, although this sincerity needed to be watched.

"General Odierno, you may not be paying attention to politics as you are a military man," Maliki suggested, "but the volunteers are not only causing problems on the ground, they are also causing political problems for me."

THE COALITION RECRUITMENT and payment of CLCs had already expanded considerably. Every time the Coalition briefed the Iraqi government, the numbers had increased: 50,000, 60,000, 70,000 . . . and then they climbed up to 130,000. General O had asked units to provide him with "good news" stories about the CLCs. In every brief to the government, he showed slides depicting the great work of CLCs and the decline in violence. He even brought in large boards with photographs of earnest-looking CLCs guarding checkpoints.

Maliki, in complete contrast, viewed the volunteers as insurgents who might turn on him at any moment. He wondered, understandably, why the Coalition insisted on preferential recruitment into the police of insurgents over ordinary Iraqis. He was constantly fed information about nefarious acts involving volunteers. The Coalition's relentlessly positive reporting added to his paranoia.

On one occasion when I dropped by OCINC for lunch, Abu Mohamad took me off into a small room. He was very concerned. Maliki had been briefed about a conspiracy being hatched by "volunteers," who were really insurgents in cahoots with the Coalition, to conduct a coup against himself. The plot involved volunteers taking up positions at the gates of Baghdad: Taji, Abu Ghraib, Doura, Albuaitha, Madain and Rashidiya. He showed me a piece of paper on which a map of the attack was sketched

out. They would bring car bombs and weapons into Baghdad. Their goal
was to create chaos in the city, enabling the plotters to enter the Green
Zone. The Coalition would leave checkpoints open for two hours, to allow the plotters through.

General Abu Mohamad told me General Farouq had briefed Maliki
about this conspiracy and had gathered Iraqi commanders together to
plan how to combat the coup.

"What on earth is driving General Farouq?" I asked. "General Farouq
wants to appear as the hero who saves the country from the conspiracy."
Abu Mohamad also said Farouq was driven by animosity towards Dr. Basima and wanted to undermine the credit she was getting for reconciliation, a main focus of which was the "volunteers."

I headed back to Camp Victory and went straight to brief General
O. "How can Maliki believe this shit?" he said, shaking his head. "What
bothers me is that while I stand up for him constantly in public, in my
heart I think he is truly sectarian."

BACK AT MY DESK, I discovered that British Major General Paul Newton had written an e-mail to General Petraeus, copied to General O and
myself, complaining that Dr. Basima was being rude and aggressive towards Iraqi generals. I knew that Basima was frustrated with the ISF. The
ISF did not know how to deal with the "volunteers" and Basima had requested Coalition help to develop procedures. She wanted to shame the
ISF into action. She was upset at the way former Iraqi Army members
were being treated when they rejoined the army. There were rumours
that recruitment centres were illegally charging them $500–$600 application fees.

I assumed Dr. Basima had had another go at the ISF in the presence
of General Newton. Petraeus responded to the e-mail: "Please put your
arm around her, Emma—noting that we want to confirm her excellence
as a diplomat, in addition to being a combatant!"

I replied to all: "Sir, I will do my best with Basima. I have had my arm
around Big Ray for nine months. Have you noticed a gentler, kinder, less
kinetic, more diplomatic man?"

Petraeus answered back: "True transformation, Emma!"

General O replied to me only with "Unbelievable!!" I giggled, imagining him banging his fist on the table and shouting at the computer as he hammered his one-word response with two fingers in blue font size 14.

GENERAL O INVITED ME to join his meeting with Ambassador Crocker at al-Faw Palace. I explained that every time we spoke to the Iraqi government, the numbers of CLCs had grown. Dr. Basima said she wanted a clear layout of Concerned Local Citizens in Baghdad, with threat assessment, Iraqi security force lay-down and ethnic/sect breakdown. I had told her that General O was losing sleep over the CLC issue. She replied, "If he had hair, he would have gone bald over this!"

"We need to extend you for a year, Emma, in order to help Basima implement all her great plans," Crocker declared. I laughed. My time in Iraq was nearly done. I was certain I would not stay in Iraq after General O returned to the US.

WE WENT OVER to the Iraqi White House to meet Maliki. Before the meeting, General O and I had sat chatting with Ryan Crocker. The day before, in the video conference with President Bush, they had discussed Maliki's premature optimism about declaring victory due to the dramatic decline in violence. Bush had joked that he still had the MISSION ACCOMPLISHED banner that had appeared behind him when he had delivered the ill-fated speech aboard the aircraft carrier USS *Abraham Lincoln* on 1 May 2003. Crocker seemed to have little confidence in Maliki. "Maybe you should ask him about his retirement plans," I said. Crocker laughed and said Maliki would probably need help with that too.

The meeting was extremely painful. Crocker pushed for Maliki to get the Strategic Partnership Declaration between the Iraqi and American governments signed by 20 November. Maliki pushed back, saying it would be politically difficult to get it approved by the parliament. Later with Safa, I reiterated how important the Strategic Partnership Declaration was for both Iraq and for the US government. Safa said Maliki was concerned that Iraqi parties and Arab countries were suspicious of what "partnership" and "cooperation" with the US actually meant. There was mistrust about the US vision for Iraq and concern that the US was trying to undermine the power the Shia had gained since 2003.

In the end, no agreement was reached between the US and Iraq. Instead, the Iraqi government requested, and received before the end of the year, an extension of the UN Security Council resolution to permit Coalition forces to operate in Iraq in 2008.

I TURNED UP at Abu Mohamad's office to find him in the process of interrogating a "volunteer" who had been detained for using a false name. In order to save himself, he had agreed to provide information on other volunteers. He had been recruited by Jaysh Islami, with promises of money, a house and a wife. He described his visits to Syria, where Sunni leaders sat in cafes telling people to join the volunteers in order "to build the house brick by brick" in preparation for a coup against the Iraqi government.

I left Abu Mohamad and went in search of Basima. She was depressed. She complained that people around the prime minister were creating problems. General Farouq was not disbursing the necessary funds for the tribes. Basima could not understand how the prime minister, a man she respected, could employ General Farouq, a man she regarded as totally useless. She said the prime minister's advisers, particularly Dawa party people, fed Maliki rumours, such as those about volunteers plotting coups. It was obvious that some volunteers would be infiltrated, but she said we could deal with this. "Reconciliation is succeeding," she told me.

Basima had recently had dinner with a friend from Abu Ghraib. He told her that a year ago the whole area was under the control of the 1920 Revolution Brigades, a Sunni insurgent group. Now the security situation had improved greatly. We were witnessing a big psychological change. Now that the door of national reconciliation was open, people were walking through it. But she was convinced that Iran was disrupting the efforts. She then dropped a bombshell: she was leaving her job.

AT HIS FINAL commander's conference in December, General O kicked off with a discussion on CLCs and how we must provide active oversight.

He had revised his Information Requirements to include bad as well as good reports about volunteers. He now had a fuller picture.

General O went on to discuss his revised Commander's Intent—he put up two versions: on the right, the more military-focused operations (the planners' version); and on the left, the one which made reconciliation the main effort (my version). He had presented my version at the planners' meeting the night before. General Anderson, the chief of staff, had turned to me, mimicking the slitting of my throat and a bullet through my heart. I had wanted the ground to swallow me up.

I realized that General O wanted to ensure everyone was on the same page. Those at headquarters had not witnessed how fast things were changing on the ground. At the conference, the commanders, who had flown in from across the country, pointed to my draft as the one which reflected the changes taking place and which pushed them to adapt in the necessary manner. General O sent out further guidance to his commanders: "reconciliation" was increasingly becoming the main effort. More and more, he told them, we would be playing the role of "honest broker," trying to bring different groups to the table.

I WENT TO SEE Safa and Basima to discuss the brief on the volunteers that General O planned to give at the upcoming meeting of the Iraqi National Security Council. They suggested a number of changes. General O should start by mentioning the problems the Coalition had found with the CLC programme, the "bad apples" that had been discovered and the risks involved. Only after that should he go on to the successes and how the CLCs had contributed to the significant drop in violence. And finally, he should set out the plan to transfer the CLCs from the Coalition's payroll to that of the government. Twenty percent would be recruited into the ISF and the remainder given public-sector employment. General O took the advice and changed his slides, and the order, accordingly.

On 2 December 2007, General O stood up at the meeting and delivered his brief. Everyone expected another painful discussion in which the Coalition and the Iraqi government would speak at cross-purposes. But when he was finished, Maliki declared, "I agree with everything that General Odierno laid out!"

Later, Basima told me how delighted Maliki had been with the meeting. For once, the Coalition and the Iraqi government were on the same page. She had explained to him that she and her "friend, Emma" had worked on General Odierno's brief and together we had reached a compromise that satisfied both sides. Maliki said we now needed to work hard on the implementation.

Basima was glowing with pride at the outcome and she decided to stay on at work. "Will you remember me when you are awarded the Nobel Peace Prize?" she asked.

I told her that whenever her name was mentioned people turned to look at me. At his quarterly commander's conference—seven hours of PowerPoint briefs—Petraeus had made me stand up in front of everyone and pointed me out as Basima's personal mentor.

"I will never ever forget you, Dr. Basima!" How could I forget our tour of Amiriya, with her wearing high heels?

WE LOST 25 SOLDIERS in December (compared with 131 in May). Iraq Body Count estimated 963 Iraqis were killed that month—down from a monthly total of 3,000 fatalities before the Surge. Iraqis felt that the worst was behind them: fewer bombs were going off and militias were gone from their streets.

The civil war in Iraq appeared to have run its course. Realizing they were losing the war, and disturbed by the excesses of al-Qaeda, Sunnis had realigned with the US for protection from the Shia militias. The Anbar Awakening had spread to other parts of the country during the surge of US forces. When Shia observed that the Sunnis were preventing al-Qaeda attacks on their communities, they became less tolerant of the Shia militias they no longer regarded as necessary for their protection. The US, through the Surge and a change in tactics to focus on population security and reconciliation, had helped bring about a change in the strategic calculus of the various groups.

The most important challenge we would face in the future was to develop the political space to allow the different communities to compete for power and resources without resorting to violence. I feared that the

Command Sergeant Major Neil Ciotola distributes toys to a family in
Baghdad's Hurriyah neighbourhood. *Photo by Curt Cashour*

local ceasefires would not hold unless there was some sort of political
agreement among the elites.

GENERAL O WAS IN A GOOD MOOD. We had recently flown over Baghdad at night and he had noted how it was no longer in darkness. There
were many solar lights. Everything seemed to be heading in the right
direction. He turned to me and said, "It is kinda cool the way they issue
fatwas. I wish I could issue fatwas." I laughed. "But you do, sir," I told
him. He looked at me quizzically. "You issue FRAGOs," I said. "FRAGOs
are like fatwas. You issue these decrees—FRAGOs—and everyone has to
implement them." He liked that.

We started off early one December morning in six Humvees, pooling
General O's and Sergeant Major Ciotola's vehicles. We were all excited: a
road trip around Baghdad. I asked our photographer, Sergeant Cashour,
what the music for the trip would be. He said we would start with Jimmy
Hendrix—the early years.

We drove through the streets to Doura market. I remembered when we had visited the market for the first time early in the year. It had been dead. And US soldiers had patrolled the streets daily trying to stop al-Qaeda from attacking the population. Today, the market was flourishing. A fresh coat of pink and blue paint had spruced the place up. Patrol Base Gator, which had been established next to a cafe within the market area, was no more. We met up with Lieutenant Colonel Steve Michael and Iraqi Army soldiers. They were all very proud of what they had achieved.

Then we drove on to the east side of town. We walked along Abu Nuwas Street, which I had first visited back in June 2003. We went into an art gallery. A bronze of a Baghdadi woman carrying a water jug on her head caught my eye. I did not have enough money on me. The shop-owner took what I had, handed me the bronze and told me to send over the rest of the money as and when I could.

At Shurta market, we got out and walked again. The streets were brimming. A man passed us, pushing an old woman on a cart. Fruit was being sold. I scanned the high buildings on either side, but there were no signs of armed men with weapons pointing down. I was wearing body armour but no Kevlar helmet.

Mutanabbi Street was not looking so good. It had yet to be rebuilt after the bombing in March which had ripped it apart, blowing up all the booksellers with their books. Haifa Street looked better. I felt I could be in Amman or Cairo. Life was coming back to Baghdad. Even though it was winter, it felt like spring.

WE GATHERED ON THE BALCONY at al-Faw Palace for the Hail and Farewell. It was freezing. The hails were done first. Then the farewells. General O got up and told me to stand there beside him. He was giving me a US military bag, he said, because my red "pizza" bag from North Face was so embarrassing. And in it was a Phantom Corps flask, knife, pen, reflector belt for running and baseball cap. "Emma has been extremely annoying," he said, "but worth the pain." He spoke about all the work I had done for him, how I advised him on the politics, the culture, the strategy . . . I had mentored him. "She didn't have to do this job," he said.

"She is here because I asked her to work for me." He spoke of how much I loved the Iraqi people—and American soldiers. And I stood there, embarrassed, as he extolled my virtues in such a sincere way, and did not mention my flaws. His loyalty towards me was extraordinary. And I knew, if ever called on again, I would follow him to the ends of the world—and that he would listen to my advice on how to get there.

Then it was my turn to speak. I recalled how I had received an e-mail from General O asking me to come and be his special adviser. I ignored the e-mail for three days, until pictures of my house on Google Earth, with rockets pointing at it, were sent to me. "Before coming out," I told them, "I had worried about whether I would fit in as a foreigner, civilian, female, and whether people would like me—because as a woman I worry about such things." But I had joined an extraordinary team. I highlighted a few of the key members: "Sarky Bastard—the chief, General Anderson—who organized the staff incredibly efficiently but was so sarcastic; Grumpy Bastard, Mike Murray, who had nearly had a hernia from all the changes he had had to make to the plan—if he is not selected to be a general there is something wrong with the system; Sergeant Major Ciotola, the model sergeant major who should be immortalized in movies, who drove across Iraq, inspiring every single soldier to be a Great American." I then turned to General O: "And finally the Bad Bastard, who makes Genghis Khan look like a moderate, but who underneath is wonderfully warm, and with whom I have travelled the length and breadth of the country and learned so much from him in the process."

I told them I had never worked so hard in all my life, nor slept so little. "General O's leadership," I said, "maintained troop morale through the most difficult times, drove changes in the way in which the military operated, and helped turn around the situation in Iraq." I ended by saying that it had been an honour and a privilege to be part of such a team. I meant it. Amidst the horror of war, I had experienced more love and camaraderie than I had ever known.

General O gave me a photo album of our time together that everyone had signed. In it he had written that this served as irrefutable proof that I had worked with the US military in Iraq—I would never be able to deny it. He also presented me with a miniature concrete T-wall on which he had signed his name: the Bad Bastard.

Lieutenant General Odierno presenting Sky with photo album of her time as his political adviser in Iraq. *Photo by Curt Cashour*

The US military strove to embody the ideals and values of the Founding Fathers that America should be a place for different peoples regardless of background and creed. They had accepted me into their tribe. I had become part of their band of brothers. I felt that everything in my life had been in preparation for this work in Iraq. They had allowed me to be myself, a non-compliant force, and had given me the platform to be all that I could be. It was now the end of the season—and against the odds we had won. We were disbanding and heading home.

PART III

DRAWDOWN

MAY 2008–SEPTEMBER 2010

14

MELIAN DIALOGUE

The strong do as they can—and the weak suffer what they must.
—THUCIDIDES, Melian Dialogue

A HOLIDAY IN NEW ZEALAND with a friend helped me to unwind. New Zealand was far away from the world of violence and almost never in the news. Long walks over high hills served to displace the mental-wallpaper images of destruction and war. I kayaked among baby penguins, and watched dolphins, whales and seals. I rediscovered trust that unknown trails would lead to breathtaking vistas; and that every stranger I met would be welcoming and non-threatening. I was once more responsible for what I ate. No longer was food simply fuel I consumed to survive. I relished the touch of fruit and vegetables in markets. I could choose what to buy, and how to cook it. My senses, which had been so crushed by war, began to reawaken.

London was more difficult. I constantly woke up in the night, my mind working overtime. I was anxious, but did not know about what. My level of awareness was far too high. When I walked down Oxford Street, I found myself scanning crowds for would-be suicide bombers. A car back-firing registered in my mind as an explosion. I found myself trembling in ways I never did in Iraq. My house became my sanctuary. It was only there that I felt safe. I did not want to hang out with friends. There was nothing to talk about. They could not relate to me, nor I to them. I could not simply pick up where I had left off.

I read books and worked on articles, processing and digesting the experience of war. For civilians, there are no victory parades when they return home, and little recognition. DFID had contracted me to serve as General O's POLAD, but had no real interest in what I had been doing.

There was no debriefing when I arrived back in the UK, nor any letter of thanks.

The US government flew me over to Washington to speak at the Pentagon and to think tanks. I was well received. It meant a lot to me.

Back in the UK, I was invited to Wilton Park, in the South Downs, to speak on behalf of the US military at an international conference on counter-insurgency. I said that perhaps the most important aspect of the Surge was the huge psychological impact it had on us—and on Iraqis. "We proved to ourselves, and to our critics, that we are not defeated; and we enabled the Iraqi people to choose different paths. Our mindset changed. And so did that of Iraqis. In 2007, the Coalition had leadership which redefined success in much more pragmatic terms; was prepared to make deals with Sunni insurgents with blood on their hands; pressured the GOI to target Shia as well as Sunni extremists; and welcomed the JAM freeze." After my presentation, I was surprised by the spontaneous applause.

I answered a wide variety of questions on troop numbers; logistical challenges of the Surge; public relations; the importance of governance of the security sector; how to win hearts and minds; negotiations with reconcilables; how to ensure that deals with insurgent groups do not undermine central government; and dealing with neighbouring countries. The feedback from participants acknowledged how far ahead the US military was of other nations in its practices, doctrine and training for this kind of warfare. Even the French came up to me afterwards to express their admiration for the US military.

I might once have aspired to speak at Wilton Park on relations between Islam and the West or on international development assistance for fragile states. But never in my wildest dreams had I imagined myself speaking on behalf of the US military on counter-insurgency, or sitting at high table with a bunch of generals, senior defence officials and security analysts.

I WAS ONLY a few months into my post-war life when the doorbell rang one morning. I opened my front door to find a courier with a large box. "I'm not expecting a parcel," I told him. "Who is it from?" The courier read out the sender's name: "General David Petraeus . . . Commanding

General." I hurriedly took the parcel, signed the delivery form and closed the door. Intrigued, I unwrapped the package to find a photo of myself and General Petraeus, in front of the Christmas tree at his quarters in Camp Victory. He had signed it *From a kindred spirit.*

This was so General Petraeus! I e-mailed him to thank him, and promptly received a response asking me when I was returning to Iraq. There were problems with the reconciliation work. Dr. Basima was in trouble. And there was no one taking forward the reintegration of the Concerned Local Citizens (who had been renamed the "Sons of Iraq") into the Iraqi security forces and civilian jobs. Would I come back for a few months to advise him on reconciliation?

My first reaction was, what would General O think? I was one of his people, and my loyalty lay with him. But General O was about to become the vice chief of the army, a job which he was excited about. So I e-mailed him, explaining Petraeus's request, and he gave me his blessing. I agreed with Petraeus that I would return and work for him for two months. I had not yet integrated back into life in the UK, and I leapt at the opportunity to help once more with the mission in Iraq.

Not long after, I received another e-mail from Petraeus. Admiral Fallon had resigned as commander of US Central Command following an article—which seemed deliberately suicidal—in which he claimed he had tried hard to prevent Bush from attacking Iran. Petraeus was replacing him as CENTCOM commander and would therefore have responsibility for the wars in both Iraq and Afghanistan. He needed a replacement in Baghdad, and General O was his first choice. Petraeus asked me, how could General O be persuaded to become the next MNF-I commander—at short notice?

As INSTRUCTED, I turned up at the Dorchester Hotel on Park Lane in London, where Petraeus was staying on a stopover from testifying in Washington. I quickly recognized members of his entourage in the hotel. Soon I was shaking hands, back among familiar faces. "Great to have you back, Emma," Ambassador Crocker said. "We need you." We were told to load up the vehicles to the airport. Everett Spain, Petraeus's superb aide, informed me that I would be riding with Petraeus and him.

We drove through the streets of London, passing Tower Bridge, and out into the countryside past fields of bright-yellow rape. "What a beautiful country," Petraeus remarked. "This is the landscape that so inspired British soldiers on the battlefield." We spoke of poetry and war, of Britain and America, of the state of the world. Before long our conversation switched to Iraq: the progress that was being made and the challenges ahead. I wished the journey could have lasted longer but after an hour or so we reached the airport, boarded the US military flight and were in the air.

I felt excited to be going back. I would work for Petraeus for May and June 2008, and then for General O from September 2008 when he would arrive as Petraeus's replacement. I had no idea of an end date to the deployment. All I knew was that my life in Iraq had purpose. Petraeus and General O both recognized my worth and requested I work for them. I had no inkling of the challenges that would lie in store.

I WAS ASSIGNED a tiny room in a concrete building in the Green Zone, behind the Ibn Sina hospital. It had a shower and air conditioning. I was given a car so I could drive myself back and forth to the US embassy, five minutes away. The embassy was full of familiar faces. General Petraeus's team welcomed me on board. He had numerous advisers, some of whom I knew, working on specific projects. Major Joel Rayburn, a military intelligence officer who had taught at West Point and was very close to Petraeus, helped me settle back in.

Mike Juaidi, the interpreter, quickly made contact with Dr. Basima and Abu Mohamad for me and arranged for us to meet them. I kissed Basima on both cheeks and presented her with a leather handbag. I then kissed Abu Mohamad—while Basima squealed in shock and delight— and gave him a silk tie. It felt like a reunion of old friends. I told them how I had received an e-mail from General Petraeus informing me that the two of them were in trouble and how he had summoned me back to try to help. Impressed that Petraeus was so concerned about them, they unburdened themselves to me. Basima and Abu Mohamad were both under investigation, and as a result their reconciliation committee had become dysfunctional. Safa, who had headed up the team, had returned to the National Security Council.

Dr. Basima al-Jadiri, Safa al-Sheikh and Sky. *Photo by Curt Cashour*

Their office politics had always been bad, but had taken a turn for the worse in the months I had been gone. With great drama, Basima recounted how General Farouq had issued a statement that she, Basima, be investigated for treason. "He wants me handcuffed and put in jail for twenty years—or hanged," she said with emotion. She had told Maliki that he had to choose between her and General Farouq. She had previously viewed General Farouq as useless and incompetent; now she saw him as a direct threat.

Abu Mohamad was convinced the Iranians were behind the scheme to get them removed from their jobs within the reconciliation committee. He believed he had got into trouble due to his investigation into Iranian infiltration of the Ministry of State for National Security.

One evening soon after, I went round to Abu Mohamad's apartment in the Green Zone. His life had been turned upside down and he now lived in fear. Steps were under way to evict him from his home. On his table, he had a coin which Petraeus had given him after the trip they had made together to Jihad. He recalled how Petraeus had walked the streets without body armour, talked to the children and had taken Iraqi dinars from his own pocket to buy products in the market. He described him as a highly skilled soldier as well as a diplomat and a politician. "We don't have leaders like that in Iraq," he lamented.

When I first met Abu Mohamad a year before, he had been deeply suspicious of the US, and the Coalition was hostile towards him. Now he felt betrayed by the Iraqi government and it was the Coalition who he saw as his friends.

With Basima and Abu Mohamad effectively removed from their jobs, our plans for the CLC, the Sons of Iraq, were stalled. We still had 106,000 volunteers on our books, and planned to reduce this to 60,000 by the end of the year. But Maliki was working off different figures. He claimed there was a total cap of 57,000 on the number of volunteers, and that the Iraqi security forces had already absorbed the agreed 20 per cent. While he was hammering Jaysh al-Mahdi, Maliki was loathe to move forward on integrating any more of the Sons of Iraq. The transition of the volunteers into the Iraqi security forces and civilian jobs had ground to a halt.

I was amazed by how much Maliki had changed in the few months I had been away. He was growing into power, and for the first time appeared to relish it. Previously, he had been viewed as a weak sectarian leader. But his willingness to battle Sadrists in Basra and Baghdad was welcomed by the Coalition—and by Iraqis. Many Iraqis believed he was developing into a strong leader, who would impose the law, through force, on the country.

In 2007 for *Fard al-Qanun*, the Coalition had helped Maliki establish the Baghdad Operations Command, bringing army, police and federal police under the control of a general who reported directly to the prime minister. This arrangement was supposed to be a temporary one for the emergency situation. But Maliki liked it and decided to expand the concept of Operations Commands across the country. Instead of working through the normal security architecture the Coalition had helped to establish, command and control was now exercised by individual phone calls from the prime minister's office. It was a worrying development that we were monitoring, but Maliki always had explanations for his actions and we needed to maintain good relations with him.

I DROVE OVER to see Safa in his office at the National Security Council in the Green Zone. He had e-mailed me while I was away, describing a "serious deterioration" in the relationship between the government and the Sadrists. He explained that after General O and I had left, the Coalition and what he described as "factions within the government" had failed to maintain the outreach to the Sadrists and had instead taken a hard line against them. Military operations against "special groups" of Shia extremists in Basra and Sadr City had dragged Jaysh al-Mahdi into the fight. This was exactly what the Special Groups had wanted. The Coalition had not understood what was happening and had therefore supported the government to do the wrong thing.

As I was mulling over his words and parking the car, I heard a *whoosh* then a boom, as a mortar landed about thirty feet in front of me in wasteland. The car rocked back and forth, and a flurry of sand and stone engulfed it. In response to the ongoing fighting in Sadr City, Jaysh al-Mahdi was rocketing the Green Zone repeatedly. It was totally random where the rockets and mortars landed. I had no time to get out of the car, let alone take cover in one of the concrete shelters scattered around the Green Zone.

I entered the government building, greeting the security officials. "Did you hear the mortar?" I asked them. "Yes, they go off all the time," an official replied, quite unperturbed. In London, I had trembled when a car backfired; yet back in Iraq, I hadn't even flinched when a bomb exploded right in front of me. I took the lift up to the floor where Safa had his office as deputy national security adviser.

"Welcome back to Iraq!" Safa said as he shook my hand.

"The mortar just missed me—it feels as if I never left."

"That was lucky. It's our friends, the Sadrists."

Over cups of *chai numi Basra*, dried lemon tea, he explained what was going on, with Sadr City besieged by Iraqi and Coalition security forces. I asked Safa what "narrative" was coming out of Sadr City—who did the residents claim was attacking them? Initially, he said, they had accused the US. But now they were blaming Badr, the militia of the Supreme Council which was close to Iran. The military operations were having a terrible impact on the everyday lives of the residents. There were reports

of hundreds of casualties. Day labourers in particular were having difficulty getting to work. Emotive songs about Shia suffering were played on
the radio. Sadrists accused Maliki of being another Saddam.

IN MY NEW ROLE I was left to my own devices to meet Iraqis, and to attend any meetings at the US embassy. I went to General Petraeus's planners' meeting in his office to discuss ongoing operations in Sadr City.
Petraeus acknowledged that Maliki appeared unwilling to negotiate with
the Sadrists and was fighting on.

"The strong do as they can and the weak suffer what they must," Petraeus quoted. "Who said that?" No one in the room knew.

He looked at me and said, "You should know, you went to Oxford. It
was Thucydides. The Melian Dialogue."

"I didn't recognize your translation, sir," I said, hoping that the reputation of my alma mater would fool people into thinking I knew it in its
Greek original.

QASIM SULEIMANI, the leader of the Iranian Revolutionary Guard Corps
sent a message to Petraeus telling him that he was responsible for Iran's
policy in Iraq and proposing they meet. Petraeus declined. He told me
the only thing Iran really cared about was the survival of its regime. Its
al-Quds Force bribed politicians, armed militias, created organizations
such as Hezbollah, trained fighters, and assassinated and intimidated
opposition, pushing everyone towards greater violence. "How does one
negotiate with folks like that?" he asked me. "They'll pocket what we
give them, bide their time and come back more lethal."

As in Basra a few months earlier, Iran stepped in and negotiated a
ceasefire between the government and Sadr City. Iran, it appeared, had
been supporting all sides in the fighting.

DURING THAT SUMMER, I met a wide range of Iraqis who expressed a
desire to participate in the provincial elections scheduled for later in
the year. I believed these elections—which the ruling parties conspired

to delay—and the national elections scheduled for the year after, might well be the Coalition's last opportunity to ensure the inclusion in the political process of those who had been excluded up till now.

With security much improved, Iraqis were now frustrated at the dearth of public services and the incompetence of the government. There were complaints about lack of electricity, and about sewage and water. Tribal sheikhs told me they wanted to put forward members of their tribes who were educated technocrats to replace those whose only qualification was their membership of one of the ruling political parties.

I began to get a sense that there was a large grouping that could constitute a "Third Way." I e-mailed my thoughts to Petraeus, noting, "I am working on the assumption that our long-term interests lie in a credible and capable state in Iraq—not in maintaining a clique of former exiles, Islamists and Iranian proxies indefinitely in power, through manipulation of the political process and use of ISF to crush competition!!!"

Petraeus assured me my assumption was correct. He was on a short visit to Washington and told me he had just had lunch with Sir Nigel Sheinwald, the British ambassador, whom he described as a gracious host. I wrote back: "He is bound to be gracious to the Master of the Universe, with a chest full of medals, and an industrial scale killing machine behind you." To be otherwise would be foolish.

Petraeus asked Major Rayburn and me to escort Vali Nasr, an American of Iranian origin who had recently published a book on the rise of Shia Islam, and Peter Bergen, an American expert on al-Qaeda—two witty, intelligent men—to meet Ayatollah Hussein al-Sadr, the uncle of Muqtada al-Sadr, in his house next to the Kadhimiya shrine.

Ayatollah Hussein al-Sadr was totally different from his rash and irascible nephew. He welcomed us into his home and brought us into his library. We sat in a semicircle, surrounded by books. I passed on Petraeus's high regard for his leadership, vision and moderation. Vali Nasr displayed his wonderful manners and diplomatic skills with the cleric, who appeared delighted to talk to him.

I shifted the conversation onto the elections, saying that we believed it important for Sadrists to participate in the new Iraq. Hussein al-Sadr said he did not like Muqtada's group being called the Sadrist Trend because the group was an affront to the values that his father, the Martyr, had espoused. He referred to the psychological problems Muqtada had had as a child, witnessing the murder of his father and brothers in 1999. He described many of Muqtada's followers as criminals or unemployed. If they had jobs, he believed, many would get back on the right track.

Hussein al-Sadr told us that he recently held a conference for over six hundred sheikhs of different sects, ethnicities and religions. Tribes had a major role in supporting the government and strengthening the rule of law. He described how Iraqis were tired of political parties and imported politicians. The day before, he had met a delegation of Sunnis from Falluja. He told them people had the right to be proud of their ethnicity and sect, but within a national framework. They should serve not only their sect and ethnicity, but all Iraqis.

Over dinner, Hussein al-Sadr told us his Council intended to participate in the elections. Their message would be "no to sectarianism, no to ethnicity, yes to a united Iraq." I asked him about representation of women in his Council. Smiling broadly, he responded: "Women may only be fifty per cent of the population; but they have a hundred per cent of the influence!"

With his long white beard and twinkling eyes, Ayatollah Hussein al-Sadr was a mesmerising, spiritual presence. His words were of peaceful coexistence and acceptance of all faiths and communities. "However impressive you found Sayyed Hussein al-Sadr," an Iraqi friend told me later, "Ayatollah Sistani is more so." It was an insight into the heart of Shia Islam, the intellectual world of analysis of sacred texts and spiritual joy.

The calm that Hussein al-Sadr had instilled in me quickly wore off on a nightmare journey back to the Green Zone. We got lost for hours. There were no communications between the five vehicles in our convoy as the "blue tracker," the system that was supposed to monitor our positions, had broken down. We ran out of fuel and had to buy some from Iraqis. We took every wrong turn imaginable, at one stage asking a drunken Iraqi policeman for directions. The gunner in my Humvee had yelled at one point, "We're gonna die!" "Shut the fuck up," I yelled back at him. "We are not going to die!"

When we finally reached the safety of the Green Zone, I asked to see the NCO responsible for the convoy. The soldiers pointed to a small, elderly man. It was clear that no one on his team had any respect for him. He shuffled forward towards me. I took the sergeant aside so that others couldn't hear. "You are in charge of the lives of your men," I told him, furious, "and General Petraeus's visitors." We were incredibly fortunate, I went on, that the security situation had improved so much—a year ago, we might all have been murdered. He stood at attention as I berated him. Travelling in convoy was a bread-and-butter activity for all units, and they did it with professionalism and pride. I was shocked that such a poorly trained unit existed in the US Army. The sergeant told me they were a National Guard unit. I told him to reflect on all the mistakes made and write an after-action report for his chain of command. His unit needed to learn from this, and retrain, before they went out beyond the wire again. "Yes, ma'am," the sergeant said. He looked wretched. I wondered what civilian life he had been dragged away from and sent as a reservist into a war zone.

MAJOR RAYBURN AND I went out to Anbar province in western Iraq. There we met a group of sheikhs who spoke of the need for continued partnership—not occupation—between Iraq and the US. They complained that Iran was helping extremist organizations in the south and weakening government institutions. One Sheikh burst out, "Why can't you just bomb Iran and get it over with!" He said the Arab street believed there was a secret deal between the US and Iran.

"The Iraqi government is sectarian," another sheikh argued. "That is why it has not absorbed the sahwa and the US still has to pay the salaries." Referring to the Iraqi parliament, a sheikh complained that it slept all the time and had turned into a Shia mosque! "It needs awakening!" he said. He described the frustration of getting money, fuel allocation and basic services from Baghdad. The sheikhs believed the elections would lessen many of the problems facing Iraq. "Imported" politicians would decline in power; and tribes would help Iraq regain its former status.

Many of the tribes in the south had converted from Sunni Islam to Shia in the late eighteenth century. This had turned Iraq into a Shia-majority country by the time the British invaded and modern Iraq was created. Many tribes therefore had members who were Sunnis and Shia—and tribal affiliation remained strong.

One afternoon in June, I met with a group of Shia sheikhs from the mid Euphrates who spoke of how they were mobilizing for elections. They told me they sought to win their sons back from the Badr Corps, in the same way as Sunni sheikhs had won theirs back from al-Qaeda.

From different parts of Iraq, and different communities, I was hearing the same refrain: "No to sectarianism, no to ethnicity, yes to a united Iraq." They were drawing on models and memories from the beginning of the twentieth century. It was a contest for the future of Iraq, and a struggle to put an end to sectarian religious government. It was a battle for the legitimacy of the state. There were businessmen, teachers, doctors all wanting to contribute to the betterment of the country. But it was also clear that the ruling parties would seek to use their funds and intimidation to co-opt and subvert this threat to their continuing rule.

GENERAL PETRAEUS ASKED ME to look at how we defined success in Iraq. Senator Obama had recently asked him this question and he didn't feel he had answered it well. He instructed me to go through the Joint Campaign Plan and other key documents.

After I had read the multitude of documents, I sent him a paper explaining that, actually, I did not believe there was an overall strategy which explained why we were not good at defining when the job would be done and the troops could go home. We had developed pragmatic tactics in-country to bring down the violence, but there was not an overarching strategy set at a level above us to which our Joint Campaign Plan contributed.

Petraeus responded, quickly as ever, that "strategy . . . traditionally links ways and means to achieve desired ends." He described how he and Ambassador Crocker had produced the Joint Campaign Plan which set out different "lines of operation" and which subordinate organizations had then produced plans to implement. He reminded me how the first action he had taken on arrival in February 2007 was to rewrite the opening part of the Joint Campaign Plan to convey the changes we needed to make, even as we also made a quick revision of the Plan, sought the input of the Joint Strategic Assessment Team and then completed a more substantive rewrite of the Plan. He also sought to emphasize the change in intent and narrative in a variety of other ways, from the change of command speech, and commander's conference briefings, to comments at the Battle Update Assessments (the morning BUAs), and visits with commanders.

Petraeus politely pointed out that military leaders were somewhat sensitive to being told they did not have a strategy, particularly when they had worked rather hard on one! But it was not Petraeus I was criticizing—it was Washington. They assumed that once the violence dropped, the Iraqi elites would take forward national reconciliation and state building. But it was these very same politicians who had instigated much of the violence in order to serve their own narrow interests. They had not reached a basic consensus on the nature of the state and the distribution of power and resources. There seemed little chance the Iraqi parliament would pass the specific legislation which Washington had identified as indicators of success.

PETRAEUS WAS MOST PARTICULAR about everything. I had never known anyone with such discipline. He appeared to have no "down time." Every morning he would exercise, and much younger officers struggled to keep up with him. Every Friday, he had his hair cut. Even on helicopter journeys, he did not allow himself to nod off like everyone else. Out would come a laptop and he would respond to his e-mails. On landing, his aide would plug it in and an avalanche of e-mails would be dispatched.

Most of Petraeus's interaction with Iraqis was through Sadi Othman, his tall Palestinian adviser and interpreter. Petraeus also received reports directly from US officers who served as advisers to Iraqi officials. He had an insatiable appetite for information. And in response, the machinery generated more and more data; data that would then be presented at the morning BUA. There were slides which depicted progress on the building of electricity towers; graphs on "Operation Speedo," showing the opening of swimming pools across Baghdad; photos of the chicken factory, displaying eggs one week, and hatched chicks the next. Soldiers needed to be kept busy, and all this activity appeared good for morale if nothing else. It raised Petraeus's stature among the troops as the all-knowing, all-caring leader for whom even the smallest projects were important.

At one of the meetings that brought together the senior military leadership on Fridays in Camp Victory, Petraeus described a recent conversation with a female captain who had told him about an obscure issue
affecting the supply chain. "Lloyd," Petraeus said, turning to General
Lloyd Austin, who had replaced General O as the Corps commander,
"you should go talk to this captain. You might find it useful."

"I will speak to her, sir," General Austin had replied. "And to her replacement." The room erupted into laughter at General Austin's unex-
pected wisecrack. It was this aspect of Petraeus that irked his peers the
most: he always had to know more than everyone else. The supply issue
in question was a very minor matter, not one that would have normally
been brought to the attention of a general officer, let alone a four-star one.

Our monthly and quarterly conferences were truly an ordeal: hours
and hours of PowerPoint presentations. Petraeus set out the great progress that had been made on the security front. Violence continued to
drop, even if Iraqis often failed to acknowledge what we had done for
them and constantly complained. (I was sometimes reminded of the
sketch from Monty Python's *Life of Brian* when the People's Front of Ju-
dea ask, "What have the Romans ever done for us?" before acknowledg-
ing a litany of accomplishments that would have been very familiar to
anyone who had been serving in Iraq: "The aqueduct, sanitation, the
roads, education . . .")

Oil was fundamental to the economic recovery of Iraq and in holding the country together. However, the parliament had not agreed on a
Hydrocarbons Law and there were strong differences between Erbil and
Baghdad over how the sector should be managed. Oil majors were in direct discussions with the Iraqi government about the capital investment
and technology needed to upgrade Iraq's obsolescent infrastructure. The
Iraqi government was highly sensitive about sovereignty over its oil—
and the Coalition was highly sensitive to the criticism that the war was
about oil. The Coalition's role was limited to ensuring the security of the
pipelines, installations and oil export facilities.

The highlight of the marathon sessions, for me, were Ambassador
Crocker's insights. As soon as he began speaking in his quiet, hesitant
manner, everyone took notes. Crocker described how the enormous security gains were transforming the environment. We were witnessing

Ambassador Ryan Crocker discusses an issue with General David Petraeus
in the US embassy in Baghdad, early May 2008. Colonel Peter Mansoor,
executive officer to General Petraeus, is at left; Sadi Othman, senior adviser to
General Petraeus, is at right; Ali Khedery, special assistant to Crocker, is in the
center. *Photo by Staff Sergeant Lorie Jewell*

a major political shift as Iraqis were becoming much more sensitive to
the Coalition intruding on their sovereignty. The Iraqi government was
increasingly in control, and we continued to seek to foster its legitimacy.
How we were perceived to conduct ourselves was important. When the
security situation was dire, there was more tolerance towards our misbehaviour. Today, issues such as the Koran being used by soldiers for
target practice had "negative effects of strategic consequence." Symbols
counted, hence the importance of moving the US embassy out of the
Republican Palace.

ON 26 JUNE 2008, hours after Crocker and Petraeus had met Prime
Minister Maliki to assure him of our support and our respect for Iraqi

sovereignty, US special forces conducted an operation in the village of Hindiya in southern Iraq. They entered a house and detained two bodyguards. On hearing the commotion, a man came out of the house with an AK-47. The special operators shot him dead.

In many aspects, this was a typical raid conducted by US special forces. But critical pieces of information had been missing from the documentation submitted up the chain of command for authorization. Hindiya was Maliki's home town. The house entered was that of Maliki's sister, who was at home at the time. And the man shot dead was a cousin of Maliki's.

Maliki was understandably furious. He cancelled all meetings with the Coalition. The humiliation of US forces entering his sister's home was huge. He wanted to keep it quiet, but news of the raid leaked out to the media. It followed on the heels of US soldiers at a checkpoint shooting dead Baghdad airport's bank manager and the two women who were in the car with him. Maliki put out a statement condemning Coalition forces and demanding that those "who committed these crimes in cold blood" be brought to justice. As Crocker had warned, Maliki's tolerance with Coalition mistakes was waning.

15

UNCOMFORTABLE SOFA

Remember always that your foundations are very sandy ones.
—T. E. LAWRENCE

GENERAL O RETURNED TO IRAQ in September 2008. I immediately went over to Camp Victory to see him. It had been nine months since we had last met, but it felt like days. We quickly caught up on each other's news before moving on to discuss the situation in Iraq and the challenges facing the mission. On 16 September I attended a small ceremony in a side room in al-Faw Palace in which Robert Gates, the US secretary of defense, promoted General O to a four-star general. Immediately afterwards, General Petraeus handed over command to him.

General O was based out of Camp Victory, but he wanted me to continue to be located at the US embassy in the Green Zone so that I could interact on his behalf with the embassy and the Iraqis. I was assigned a container in the grounds of the Republican Palace. The military's day started before the embassy's. I would join the BUA, Small Group and Small Small Group via videoconference; I would then go to Ambassador Crocker's staff meeting. After that I joined up with General O for his visits to troops and meetings with Iraqis.

By the time General O returned, negotiations on the Status of Forces Agreement between Iraq and the US—the SOFA—were not going well. The UN Security Council resolution authorizing the presence of US forces in Iraq was set to expire in December 2008. US forces would have to depart the country immediately if a new legal framework for their presence was not agreed. Earlier in the year, the US had thought the SOFA was a done deal. But its optimism had been premature. Points of contention included the US Army's right to conduct operations and detain Iraqis, as well as immunity for military personnel and contractors. The US team sent out from Washington earlier in the year had not handled the negotiations well. On the military side, there was concern that no one in uniform was allowed in the negotiations, and that those negotiating might "give away the farm" in order to get an agreement—given that a SOFA was crucial to the Bush legacy.

The drumbeat against the SOFA had picked up, with strong opposition from the Iranians, with the Sadrists calling for demonstrations, and with hostile fatwas issued by clerics. US SOFAs were normally negotiated with stable countries in time of peace, rather than ones in Iraq's situation. The US had SOFAs with a number of countries in the region but the details had never been made public. But in Iraq the US was pushing for an agreement that would be approved by the country's parliament.

Maliki was also only too aware of the fate suffered by Salih Jabr, Iraq's first Shia prime minister, who had been forced to resign in the wake of fierce opposition to the 1948 Anglo-Iraqi Treaty known as the Portsmouth Agreement. And the signing of a SOFA agreement between the US and Iran in 1964, granting legal immunity to US personnel and their dependants, had produced a fierce anti-American backlash. Ayatollah Khomeini had condemned the agreement, saying it reduced Iranians to lower than American dogs.

Crocker asked General O for me to join his small team for the SOFA negotiations. It was a way of keeping General O involved—but not too involved. It brought me into the heart of the most sensitive deliberations on US policy in Iraq, and it was a great opportunity to observe Crocker up close. A master diplomat, he was a good listener and displayed sound judgement. And he often thought out loud, giving us insights into his knowledge of Iraqi history, and why Iraqi politicians were so fearful. He was not a warm man, but he was kind and modest. He was also greatly respectful of the US military and service to country. He came from an air force family and espoused many of the values that the military held dear. He knew which battles to pick with the military and which to avoid. It was a revelation to me of the way the personality of a leader can shape a whole organization, which became very clear after he was gone and relations broke down.

While Crocker was focused on SOFA negotiations, General O's energies were on fighting to keep the resources he needed in Iraq. A number of senior officers back in the US were claiming the war in Iraq was won, and troops and assets should be moved to Afghanistan. The marines, in particular, were pushing to rapidly redeploy their forces. In his new role, General O went back to Washington every other month or so for consultations and to ensure that Iraq was not forgotten.

I helped General O craft a narrative that moved away from that of counter-insurgency and towards helping Iraq fully exercise its sovereignty. The greatest threat to Iraq's stability was now the legitimacy and capability of government, rather than attacks by insurgents. As security improved, jobs and public services had become the major concern for Iraqis. Iraq remained fragile because there was no national vision for the country; public-service provision was poor; and al-Qaeda and Shia "special groups" were still capable of conducting terrorist activities. Iraq needed continued US support to help broker an agreement among its leaders, to protect the political process and to build up its institutions.

General O's team was not as close-knit as the one on his previous tour, and had not trained and deployed together. He inherited most of the staff from his predecessor, but brought out some of his old crew with him. There were often tensions, particularly over access to General O. Closest to General O were General Joe Anderson, Colonel J. T. Thomson and Colonel Ryan Gonsalves. Throughout his time in Iraq, at least one of them was always on his staff to look after him, and to ensure his intent was fully understood and communicated appropriately.

Many of the staff knew me from my previous tour but others did not and some were resentful of the influence I had. One warned me, "Stop sending e-mails directly to General O or I will destroy you." Another accused me of parking my "tanks" on his "lawn." One told me bitterly that General O needed me more than him. I was tempted to reply that this was because he acted like a Neanderthal, but suggested instead that we were both needed but in different ways and fulfilled different roles. He replied, "I hate you—so does everyone else." It was my birthday.

Boarding school had hardened me to cope with bullying. I tried not to let their comments get to me. I knew their tours would be over in months, whereas I would remain. I tried to focus on what General O wanted me to do, and to block out their noise. And there was always Mike Juaidi, the interpreter. He was the only other constant on the team. Mike was a humble man, who avoided confrontation and who always kept an eye out for me. I could rant about my frustrations to him, and he would always listen. He was a kind, generous and loyal friend.

ALI KHEDERY, the special assistant to Ambassador Crocker, strode purposefully over to my desk in the Republican Palace one evening at the beginning of October. It was nearly midnight, but we were both still at work. Our desks were in the outer offices of our respective bosses, across the hall from each other.

"Come quickly," he said, "there's an emergency at Checkpoint 2. I just got a phone call from Mashhadani's aide—Mashhadani and his guards are marching on the checkpoint. He is threatening to break off the SOFA negotiations!" Ali was an American whose parents originated from Iraq. He was one of the very few educated Arab Americans who had been prepared to be part of the Coalition effort in Iraq. Still in his twenties, he had worked as an assistant to ambassadors Khalilzad and Crocker and had got to know all the Iraqi elite.

I followed Ali out of the palace to the parking lot. We jumped in a vehicle and drove over to the checkpoint. Mahmoud Mashhadani was the Speaker of the Iraqi parliament and key to driving through the SOFA. It was the last day of Eid and Mashhadani had been celebrating his son's wedding when he heard of the incident at the checkpoint and had headed right there.

We reached the checkpoint and immediately sensed the tension. US soldiers were standing with their weapons at the ready. Ali spotted Mashhandani's son, Abdul Basit, standing with a group of other Iraqis looking furious and aggressive. We went up to him and asked what the problem was. "One of the soldiers," he spat out, "called my sister a whore!"

To calm the situation down, we asked Abdul Basit to persuade his father and bodyguards to return home, and for him to represent the family. We then went over to the US soldiers and asked them to assume a less aggressive posture. It turned out that the unit had recently changed over. So we asked one of them to go and wake up the soldier who had been involved in the fracas. We waited patiently until a baby-faced soldier appeared about an hour later.

"This man accuses you of calling his sister a whore," I said to the soldier. "Ma'am," he said, looking shocked, "I would never call a woman a whore." The soldier seemed earnest and well mannered. Abdul Basit calmed down and suggested that the interpreter must have mistranslated what the soldier had said. We persuaded the two to shake hands, and the young soldier apologized for any offence that had been caused. Abdul Basit accepted the apology and agreed to go home. It was around three in the morning by this stage and we all wanted to get to bed.

As Ali and I walked back towards our vehicle, I asked the young soldier what had actually occurred: "You must have said something to her. You must have had some sort of conversation for there to be such a misunderstanding."

"Yes, ma'am, we did. She was really rude and annoying when I asked to see her badge. She had a really bad attitude."

"And? What did you say to her?"

"Ma'am, I called her a fucking bitch!"

I nearly choked. The translator had interpreted the soldier's insult as *charmuta*, a common Arabic term of abuse which meant prostitute.

The next morning, General O ended the BUA as he always did: "May God bless all our soldiers, sailors, airmen, marines, coastguards and civilians. Lion 6 out." In Small Group after the BUA, General O said he had heard there had been a problem last night at a checkpoint. I explained that Speaker Mashhadani had accused one of our soldiers of calling his daughter a whore. The soldier had denied insulting the woman. Mashhadani's son accepted there had been a misunderstanding, had shaken hands with the soldier and gone home.

"Why do Iraqis always think the worst of our soldiers?" one of the generals in the meeting asked, shaking his head. I said I had pressed the soldier for an explanation. In my best American accent, I mimicked the soldier's response: "Ma'am, I would never call a woman a whore. I called her a fucking bitch."

There was a moment of stunned silence. Then the room erupted in laughter—a casual, thoughtless insult to a young woman had almost jeopardized the legal future of the US troops in Iraq.

TOWARDS THE END OF OCTOBER, Washington became increasingly worried at the prospect of not reaching agreement on the SOFA. I headed off to Ambassador Crocker's morning staff meeting. His wit was becoming increasingly acerbic (Bush had dubbed him "Sunshine" in ironic reference to his dour descriptions of Iraq).

Crocker's small SOFA team consisted of David Satterfield, Brett McGurk, Robert Ford, Meghan O'Sullivan, an intelligence guy, Ali Khedery and myself. Each day, he allocated key figures for us to engage with in order to push the Iraqi politicians closer to signing the SOFA.

Crocker went around the room, getting feedback on the overnight meetings with Iraqi leaders. Crocker explained that Speaker Mashhadani felt it was a political imperative that the SOFA be passed in the Iraqi parliament by an absolute majority of all the members, not just a relative one. "When have there ever been a hundred and thirty-eight votes in favour of anything?" Crocker asked. The key was getting the agreement through parliament with enough support so that Sistani would not issue a fatwa against it.

The intelligence guy chirped up, "Sistani does not have a vote in the parliament." Crocker stared at him incredulously. "Sweet Jesus! Do you think I am fucking stupid?" I looked down at my toes. I had never seen Crocker so stressed. He had really begun to doubt that we would get a SOFA. He could not stop nervously scratching the back of his head.

In the afternoon, we went off to see Maliki. As General O and Crocker waited in Maliki's reception room, we exchanged the latest gossip out of Washington. President Bush had apparently invited Petraeus on a bicycle ride. Petraeus had sent his guys out to measure the track and was busy training so he could beat the president. Bush got wind of this, and decided to change which track he used. "Someone had better advise Petraeus that one does not smoke the president!" Crocker mused.

THE US MADE significant concessions during the SOFA negotiations. Iraqi officials insisted on greater control, with the removal of US troops from population centres by end June 2009, and the withdrawal of all US forces from Iraq by the end of 2011. The US even agreed to allow Iraq the "primary right to exercise jurisdiction" over US military members who committed "grave premeditated felonies" such as rape. The US military reacted apprehensively to the idea of US soldiers falling under foreign legal authority, but it was understood by senior US officials that if any US soldier did commit heinous offences, he would be spirited out of the country and put on trial in the US. There was no way he would go before the Iraqi judicial system.

We told Iraqi officials that we were disappointed that having spent so much blood and treasure in Iraq, the government was unwilling to sign an agreement with us; that the government openly condemned the US in the media—but never Iran; and that we needed to start planning for the eventuality of "no SOFA."

General O outlined to Iraqi officials that all US support would cease unless they reached an agreement on the legal authority for US forces. Iraq would then not be able to protect itself against internal terrorism or external threats. The Iraqi security forces still relied on the US for logistics and basic life support. They were not yet ready to stand on their own. However, we quickly learned such threats did not spur the Iraqi leaders into action. Instead, they retreated into their shells and went into paralysis.

It became clear that the negotiations were not so much about the future of Iraq-US relations as about internal Iraqi politics. With the income from oil and the strengthened security forces, Maliki had found instruments with which to consolidate his own power and to project it beyond the Green Zone. There was concern among political elites that he was emerging as an authoritarian leader. And some feared that, under the SOFA, US forces would come under Maliki's control, further strengthening his regime.

The different parties were increasingly distrustful of Maliki and plotted his downfall. But US officials urged them to not let their internal disputes cloud their judgement on supporting the Agreement. None of the other Iraqi leaders believed Maliki actually wanted a SOFA. Maliki overestimated the capacity of Iraqi forces, and saw US forces as a limit on his power.

After considerable arm-twisting and haggling, the Iraqi cabinet finally approved the Agreement on 16 November, with the foreign minister, Hoshyar Zebari, and Ambassador Crocker, signing it the following day. There was a moment of relief. But we were not out of the woods yet. It still had to get through the Iraqi parliament.

Consensus within the parliament to pass the Agreement was only reached after the political blocs had negotiated a resolution demanding political reform, with greater consultation within government and the building of democratic institutions; and after they agreed to hold a referendum on the SOFA by 30 July 2009. If the referendum went against the SOFA, US troops would be required to leave Iraq within a year. The elites also demanded reassurances of the US's commitment to protect the democratic process, which they received in the form of letters from Crocker.

I went along to the parliament with Meghan O'Sullivan on 27 November for the debate on the SOFA. We were given little cubicles in the rafters at the back of the chamber from which we could observe the proceedings below. Iraq was the first country in the Middle East to publicly debate the terms of a Status of Forces Agreement with the US, and the session was televised live. As the vote came in, I e-mailed General O the news from my BlackBerry: 149 out of 275 members had voted in support of the Agreement. It was approved! Thirty-five members had opposed it, mostly from the Sadrist bloc. The non-binding reform resolution and the referendum were ratified by the Iraqi parliament alongside the SOFA and the Strategic Framework Agreement, which set out the terms of a long-term relationship between the US and Iraq.

PRESIDENT BUSH FLEW into Baghdad for a farewell visit on 14 December 2008. The signing of the SOFA and the Strategic Framework Agreement appeared to mark a new era in Iraqi-US relations. Bush had spoken almost weekly to Maliki ever since he became prime minister and had built up relations with a number of Iraqi politicians. He wanted to come in person to congratulate Iraqis and to say goodbye.

The trip had been planned in great secrecy. But it broke in the Iraqi media the day before, when Talabani announced he had to leave Kirkuk and get back to Baghdad to meet President Bush. In the press conference following the signing, one of the Iraqi journalists took off his shoes and hurled them, one after the other, at President Bush. They were well aimed. But Bush had impressive reflexes and dodged both, while Maliki haplessly waved his arm in a feeble attempt to protect him.

Inevitably, the shoe-throwing incident became the lasting image of the visit. The journalist was dragged off and beaten up. In the BUA, there was, of course, no mention of the incident. A Saudi offered $10m for the shoe, which he claimed restored the honour of the Arab world. The Speaker of parliament, Mashhadani, who was erratic at the best of times, refused to allow debate on the fate of the shoe-thrower, who he dubbed the "pride" of Iraq. He then called members of parliament "sons of dogs," before tendering his resignation, saying he wept for the state of Iraq.

I accompanied Crocker and General O to see the prime minister that evening. Maliki was very happy with the president's visit. But the "incident" had shocked him. This was not in keeping with Arab and Muslim customs. "In the West you may throw eggs and tomatoes at leaders," he noted, "but this is not our custom. No one treats a guest that way." He described the journalist as a Baathist, whose mother had been a "dancer"— it implied very loose morals—during the days of Saddam. "Please present our apologies to the American people and the president." "This incident," Maliki continued, visibly upset by what had occurred, "was condemned by Iraqi reporters. Only the Baathists expressed support."

Maliki then said, "Most of the trouble brewing at the moment is due to Baathists." He claimed to have information of a "Black Day." Zero hour on the day would be 19:37, the year of Saddam's birth. He alleged that Baathists had infiltrated the Ministry of Interior and would try to blow it up. He suspected that a member of his personal security detail was linked to Syrian intelligence and was plotting to assassinate him. The conspiracy involved Shia in Karbala, Najaf and Diwaniya. His people had arrested some of the network, including a woman from his own tribe. The Baath party had so many members, he asserted, with elements of the Iraqi security forces coordinating with the former Iraqi Army outside the country. Maliki saw Baathists everywhere. He had surrounded himself with people who fed such fears—and then claimed credit for saving him from these spectres.

We left the meeting, shaking our heads at Maliki's paranoia. But, for now, what was important was that the US had a SOFA with Iraq. (The US referred to it as the Security Agreement and claimed it as a major success of US policy, an indication of US influence with the Iraqi elites and a defeat for the Iranians who had tried to scupper it.)

US officials were certain the Iraqis would extend it beyond 2011 or negotiate a new agreement with the US, in much the same way as South Korea. They paid less attention to the fact that Iraqis referred to it as the "withdrawal agreement" and that Maliki had boosted his reputation by taking a hard line with America, insisting on the removal of all US forces by the end of 2011.

16

OUT OF THE CITIES

O those who pass between fleeting words
Carry your names, and be gone
—MAHMOUD DARWISH

SENATOR BIDEN, by then vice president–elect, returned to Baghdad in January 2009, accompanied by a Republican senator, Lindsey Graham. I recognized his adviser, Puneet Talwar, in his entourage and went over to say hello. I explained to Biden that I had met Puneet at a party in the Old City of Jerusalem. "I told Puneet to sort out that problem!" Biden joked. Crocker, who was standing next to Biden, chipped in, "The Brits are responsible for all the problems in the world: Pakistan, Palestine . . ." I interrupted him: "And America." Momentary shock on their faces was quickly replaced by laughter.

In the new American embassy Crocker and General O briefed the visitors on the situation in Iraq. We had moved out of the Republican Palace at the end of 2008 and into the new embassy, a purpose-built, Stalinist complex on the banks of the Tigris that resembled a maximum-security prison, with high walls and guard towers. It was the largest and most expensive US embassy in the world, with on-site housing for families and a school—all of which then had to be converted to meet the requirements of its actual inhabitants, who were government officials and contractors unaccompanied by spouses and children for the foreseeable future.

I had moved out of the trailer at the palace into an apartment in the new embassy which I shared with a lovely Lebanese American woman who worked as an interpreter, trying to save enough money to support her family and pay off debts. With its solid walls and bullet-proof windows, I could at least finally sleep without the risk of stray rounds coming in.

Biden laid out the facts as he saw them: the new Obama administration was walking into a $1.3 trillion deficit. The American people had run out of patience. They did not see the difference between Iraq and Afghanistan—they wanted the troops home. Obama was really popular at present: he had a 75 per cent approval rate. When Obama visited the Lincoln Memorial, people were really moved. Biden said that when he went into a restaurant, he received a standing ovation—this had never happened to him before! He reckoned the incoming administration probably had about a year to show progress before the far left in the Democratic party called for the soldiers to be withdrawn. With the surge of thirty-five thousand extra troops to Afghanistan, and "taking the fight to the enemy" there, US casualties were bound to go up. This was likely to diminish public support. "Iraq was Bush's war," he said. "Afghanistan is Obama's war." The Republican party lost the election because of the Iraq war. Sitting behind General O, I felt I was witnessing an important moment. The change of policy, which we had been expecting, was coming. A new era was about to begin.

The new US administration, Biden went on, was going to be more focused on supporting institutions, not individuals. If there was no progress on a political agreement, the US might as well cut and run, because there was no point delaying the inevitable. What could be done? he asked. Crocker replied that the Iraqis had tried to remove Maliki on previous occasions but the Bush administration had insisted on keeping him in place. Maliki felt he had Bush's unconditional support. General O stressed we should invest our energies in trying to help the Iraqi institutions function better, in particular the parliament.

Once the internal meetings were complete, the delegation went off for meetings in the Green Zone with senior Iraqi officials, with me tagging along as ever behind General O. Vice President Tareq al-Hashimi sparred with the US vice president–elect over the so-called Biden Plan, in which he had previously proposed to divide Iraq into three separate parts for Kurds, Sunnis and Shia. Only the Kurds had supported such an idea. Iraq's Arabs had vociferously condemned it, fearing a plot by the US to destroy their country.

When Biden met Maliki, Maliki told him that Iraq was interested in a long-term strategic relationship with the US. He commented that the violence in Iraq was now over, and the US could meet its commitments elsewhere by drawing down its troops here. "The Iraqi security forces are ready!" he boasted.

ON 20 JANUARY 2009, a few days after Biden's visit, Barack Obama was sworn in as president of the United States. In his inauguration address he declared, "We will begin to responsibly leave Iraq to its people." The next day, we received the order to "end the war in Iraq."

Over the next two weeks, we frantically put together papers for Obama. The chief of plans was Admiral Dave Buss, a strategic thinker and one of the most impressive senior officers I ever met. Colonel Mike Meese, the head of the social science department at West Point, was filling in temporarily as head of General O's initiative group and helped coordinate the different inputs. The papers outlined how we would draw down to a residual force of fifty thousand troops over sixteen, nineteen or twenty-three months, and that the mission of these remaining troops would be to "advise and assist" rather than "combat operations." I didn't for a moment imagine that when Obama announced he would remove all combat forces he meant he would accept keeping fifty thousand troops in Iraq, even if their mission was a non-combat one. But my military colleagues were convinced Obama would accept their recommendations. And they were right.

After weighing up the options, Obama came back and committed to implementing the terms of the Security Agreement, with all troops out of the cities by end June 2009 and out of Iraq by end December 2011. He added an extra stipulation to meet his campaign promise: combat operations would cease on 31 August 2010, after which he would maintain fifty thousand troops to undertake "advise and assist" missions. We did not know it at the time, but the end of combat operations would also mark the end date for General O—and me. It was nineteen months away. And in Iraq, that was a lifetime.

IN HIS WRITTEN GUIDANCE, briefings and discussions with his commanders, General O made clear that the drawdown of forces should not become the overriding focus of the mission. Poor public services, non-state armed groups, foreign fighters and malign foreign influence remained symptoms of a state that was fragile and did not have full sovereignty capabilities. In order to transition from a fragile state to a stable one, the US needed to help the Iraqi government further develop its capacity and credibility.

"US forces need to embrace enhanced Iraqi sovereignty as an indicator of success," General O clarified. This required another change in the mindset of US forces, who were more accustomed to being in charge. The Security Agreement set out what sovereignty meant to Iraqis. With the improved security situation, Iraqis were no longer tolerant of US forces operating under the "rule of war" and wanted to see greater adherence to the "rule of law." This meant that all arrests should be warranted, and detainees held within Iraqi facilities, not American ones. Those detainees in US custody for whom there were warrants had to be transferred to Iraqi custody; the others had to be released over time in a "safe and orderly manner."

From being in the lead, US forces needed to move to partnering and advising the Iraqi security forces—"by, with and through" became the new bumper sticker. No operations should be unilateral. Embracing Iraqi sovereignty meant allowing Iraqis to make their own mistakes, but being there to help them recover. The Iraqis needed to see that the US was true to its word and that its forces adhered to the terms of the Security Agreement. Joint committees were established to deal with any issues between Iraqis and Americans that arose from this process. It was a credit to all that very few did.

As General O went around the country visiting units, he urged commanders, "Don't let the tactical be the enemy of the strategic." He continuously engaged with them to help them internalize the changing situation, and to interpret Iraqi successes as US successes. It became clear which commanders grasped the significance of the new guidance and looked at creative ways to implement it. These commanders would show a sophisticated understanding of what was causing insecurity, and worked closely with the State Department, NGOs and local government to address the issues using the full array of tools at their disposal. They would also describe the progress being made by Iraqi security forces in terms of building up relations with the local population, the operations they conducted, where they had asked for US assistance and what further training they required.

DESPITE THE EFFORTS of the ruling parties to postpone the provincial elections, they finally went ahead. On 31 January 2009, Iraqis went to the polls. Crocker's guidance had been clear: we would not pick winners; elections would be Iraqi led, managed and financed; the United Nations Assistance Mission for Iraq (UNAMI) would lead the international backing to the management of the elections, with the US supporting and monitoring. The US military would help ensure security for the elections.

I went with General O to the Iraqi National Operations Centre in the Green Zone, to see how the Iraqi security forces were coping on the day. General Ayden, a Turkmen, met us there with warm handshakes and cups of tea. He briefed us on the incidents across the country, what was going on at the polling stations and how the ballots were being managed.

In all, 14,431 candidates, including 3,912 women, contested the 440 seats that were available in fourteen of Iraq's eighteen provinces. (Kirkuk did not participate in the elections as there was no agreement on who was eligible to vote, and the Kurdistan region held provincial elections on a different schedule for its three provinces.) The candidates represented over four hundred parties, three-quarters of which were newly established. Some of them had been active in the insurgency and had now decided to give politics a chance.

I could not help but marvel at how much the situation in Iraq had changed, and with it our role. As we flew over Baghdad and Baqubah on the helicopter, General O said to me, "If things continue like this, I'm going to recommend we leave in less than sixteen months!" The elections went off smoothly. It was a great day for Iraq, a day that so many people had worked so hard to make happen.

Maliki's campaign had focused on imposing the law and national reconciliation. This appealed to Iraqis who were fed up with sectarianism. His party, the State of Law Coalition, created for this election, won 126 out of the 440 seats. It was a significant victory for him. We believed he was emerging as a nationalist leader of the country.

With the SOFA signed and the provincial elections held, Ryan Crocker finished his tour as ambassador in February 2009. He had served in the role for nearly two years and had helped steer Iraq through the most turbulent of times. I escorted him from the embassy over to Camp Victory for a farewell dinner at General O's villa. Every US general from across the country had flown to Baghdad for the occasion, to show their respect for him. He had provided the strategic direction and guidance the military so craved from civilian leaders, and so rarely received. Even while his health was suffering from a neurological disorder, he had soldiered on.

IRAQ WAS CHANGING. I needed to get out and see things for myself in order to give General O a better feel for the developing situation. So I set up a system with Safa al-Sheikh. On a prearranged evening, he would drive his car near to the embassy, park at the side of the road and text me. I would walk out of the embassy, down the street, into the darkness of the night. His car would flash its headlights. I would walk towards it and get in. And Safa would take me out into the "Red Zone."

Going out without security was against every regulation, and very few did it. The risks of being kidnapped were high. But as a British national, hired by the US Army but living within the US embassy, no one was quite sure whose regulations I came under. And I never sought to find out.

On one occasion, I got into the car to find Dr. Basima also in the back seat. I exclaimed, "Ya Allah," as I leant over to kiss her warmly on both cheeks. She giggled. We were like naughty schoolgirls playing truant. Safa took us to Saidiya, a neighbourhood which in 2007 had been fiercely fought over by rival militias. The neighbourhood was surrounded by concrete T-walls (on some of which were painted colourful murals), and the entry and exit were controlled by Iraqi security forces.

I initially mistook the ISF for US soldiers as they all were wearing smart uniforms, body armour and helmets (and some had knee-pads around their ankles, a style that seemed prevalent among US soldiers). They were conducting themselves in a professional manner. But when I saw one walk alongside a vehicle holding a wand with a telescopic antenna on a swivel that was supposed to detect bombs, I knew they were Iraqis. "The magic wands don't work, Safa," I told him. They were nothing more than glorified divining rods. "Dogs are the most reliable way of detecting explosives." The Ministry of Interior had bought over fifteen hundred of the wands, for thousands of dollars each, from a disreputable British company, with some officials making lots of money on the contract. "I know," he replied. "But at least it keeps the security forces at the checkpoints busy. And if people think they work, it serves as some sort of deterrent."

Through the car window, I saw women walking down the streets without male escorts and many without veils. Cafes were busy serving customers. Shops were lit up by private generators. As with other parts of Baghdad, life had started to return to the streets.

Over the weeks and months, we visited different parts of the city, frequently returning to some areas to observe progress. Once we went to Jihad in south-west Baghdad. Safa told the driver to stop on the corner. Abu Ali opened the door and got in. When he turned around and saw me in the back seat, he could not believe his eyes. "Welcome, welcome!" he said, shaking my hand. He proudly took us on a tour, showing us the progress that had been made in the area following the reconciliation agreement Colonel Pat Frank had helped to broker at the end of 2007.

On another occasion, we went into Sadr City. "You'll never come back alive," Maliki had warned me when I told him Basima and I were going there. But in fact the only incident occurred as we emerged from the neighbourhood and were driven off the road by a US MRAP (mine-resistant ambush-protected) vehicle which was far too large for the narrow street.

During these trips, I learned much from Safa about Iraqi society and history. He was a great fan of Ali al-Wardi, the Iraqi historian and

sociologist, who had written about the dual personalities of Iraqis. We
spent hours discussing how to foster a new Iraqi identity that was inclusive of all the groups within Iraq. He described the efforts to build
Iraqi society under the monarchy, and later, after the royal family had
been brutally murdered in 1958, under the republic. Sectarian identity
in those days was much less prominent. He spoke of the battles between
Arab nationalists who wanted Iraq to be part of the Arab world and those
who pursued Iraq-first policies; the struggles between Nasserites and
Baathists; the power of the communists; and the rise, in response to the
influence of the leftists, of Shia Islamists who were then inspired by the
Islamic Revolution in Iran. Safa described to me the devastating impact
of sanctions on Iraq society. Respectable members of the middle class
such as teachers were reduced to begging. Bribes became widespread.
It was during this period that Saddam introduced his "faith campaign,"
hoping that Iraqis would find solace in religion so as to deflect their anger. Sectarian identity became stronger. We discussed the different political parties in today's Iraq. None of them had an overall vision for the
country. The new leaders were simply concerned with gaining power,
and the resources that came with it.

LIVING IN THE GREEN ZONE, I was able to have some sort of social life.
Lieutenant General John Cooper, General O's British deputy, regularly
hosted Scottish dancing at Maude House for the international community. I would go there with Robert Ford, the head of the US embassy's
political section, and meet up with the UN's Andrew Gilmour, who was
working on special status options for Kirkuk. We would do reel after reel.
All the stress of the day was forgotten, as we linked arms and whirled
around the floor.

General Nasier Abadi regularly hosted parties in his house in the
Green Zone on Thursday evenings. Typically, Admiral Dave Buss and I
would go there and mingle with Iraqi elites and members of the diplomatic community. It was at General Abadi's house that I met Sharif Ali
bin al-Hussein (a descendant of the Iraqi royal family that had been brutally overthrown in 1958 who had returned from the UK to Iraq in 2003
hoping to restore the monarchy), and other Iraqi notables who painted

General Nasier Abadi entertaining in his garden. *Photo by the author*

for me a picture of life in Baghdad in a bygone era. In winter we sat inside, where the walls were adorned with photos of family members; and when it warmed up, we moved out into the beautiful walled garden. General Abadi was a wonderful host and loved entertaining. A fighter pilot in the old Iraqi Air Force, he had been brought back into service as the vice chief of staff of the Iraqi joint forces. His grandfather, a former Iraqi prime minister, had married his three daughters to a Sunni, a Shia and a Turkmen. General Abadi's home was always a sectarian-free zone, frequented by friends and family. Some, like him, drank alcohol; others did not. It was an island of tolerance, an image of what Iraq could be.

On a number of occasions, I went out to dinner with Western journalists based in Baghdad. I particularly admired Anthony Shadid, who won two Pulitzer Prizes for his Iraq reporting, and Alissa Rubin of the *New York Times*, for the empathy they brought to their writing and for their bravery in pursuing stories. Ned Parker of the *Los Angeles Times* dug deep into stories of human rights abuses and the fate of the sahwa, the Sunni Awakening. Ernesto Londono of the *Washington Post* produced acute insights into the lives of US soldiers fighting the war. As an openly gay, and very attractive, man he had poignant tales of life under the shadow of "Don't Ask, Don't Tell" and regaled us with wild tales about what he affectionately called Baghdad's underground gay mafia.

The relationship between the military and the media was not always easy. The military sought positive coverage of what was happening in Iraq and were sometimes upset by stories that the journalists would write. "Push back!" was a frequent command at the BUA when a negative comment in an article was regarded as unjustified. The media had become part of the battlefield for "information operations." Journalists who delivered critical reporting were often seen as an enemy of sorts, people who did not want us to win the war. Those reporters who could be trusted to grant greater weight to the military narrative were given priority for embed slots with military units. For their part, the media also needed support from the military: access to bases, emergency care and intelligence to inform their risk-mitigation strategies.

I watched General O's view of the media evolve during his time in Iraq. From initial mistrust, he grew to appreciate the courage of journalists and the in-depth knowledge that some had developed about Iraq. At regular intervals, General O invited key members of the media over to dine with him at Camp Victory to help build trust between them. The discussions were off the record. And both sides benefited.

UK FOREIGN SECRETARY David Miliband visited Iraq and requested a meeting with General O. I was instructed to meet him in the Green Zone and escort him to Camp Victory. The weather was touch and go, due to the winds. But we were told the "birds" could fly. I stood waiting in the drizzle at the Green Zone helicopter pad for the British delegation to arrive. As soon as the car pulled up, I directed Miliband and the British ambassador, Christopher Prentice, to the first bird. I got them to remove their helmets and earplugs and put on the headphones that were always available on General O's helicopters. We were now linked up and I explained to them how they could communicate by pressing the button on the wire attached to the headset and moving the microphone very close to the mouth.

I wondered why we still had not taken off and asked the pilot. Over the headset, the pilot explained there were mechanical issues with the second bird. We had a forty-minute delay while we waited to find another helicopter to escort us.

Miliband was expecting General O's POLAD to be American, so was surprised to discover I was British. He asked me how on earth I had ended up working for the US military. I told him it was a long story, and gave him a short version. He asked my opinion about the decision to go to war, how the occupation had been handled and about the Surge. He then asked me what the Americans thought of the British. "To be honest with you," I replied, "the Americans don't spend much time sitting around discussing what they think of the Brits." I told him that, at the highest level, US officials had respect and gratitude towards the UK for being such a loyal ally; but in the mid ranks of the US military the criticisms that Brits had made about the Americans in the early years had rankled. The British military had been very arrogant, believing they knew the ultimate truth about counter-insurgency from Malaya and Northern Ireland. Every situation, however, was different. And the American military had proved themselves faster learners than the Brits. At times, it appeared that the British military in Basra had given assessments of the situation to meet political agendas back in London. Miliband asked me to drop by his office when I was next in London.

We eventually made it to al-Faw Palace. Miliband was impressive in the meeting. Perhaps one day he would head the Labour party, I thought. And maybe he would even become prime minister. He seemed to have what it took.

At the end of March, we went down to Basra for a farewell ceremony for the British troops. Over the last six years 179 British soldiers had died in Iraq. It had not been the most glorious chapter of British history. But Basra that day was doing quite well. Sir Jock Stirrup, the chief of defence staff, and Major General Andy Salmon, the commander of the British brigade, gave fitting speeches. And General O spoke of the shared heritage and the blood Brits and Americans had shed together.

WITH CROCKER GONE, the US embassy was leaderless and felt overwhelmed by the military. I met up for dinners and evening drinks with some of the senior staff: Robert Ford, Tom Dougherty, Tom Krajeski and

Michael Corbin. They were good people. For them the military was a strange subculture that they had had minimal interaction with back in the US.

I also hung out with Greta Holtz who was responsible for the Provincial Reconstruction Team (PRT) programme. The military loved the PRTs because they provided a platform to put civilians out in the provinces interacting with local government and managing projects. In the military's eyes, it showed commitment of civilians to the mission. Whenever General O visited units, he asked to meet the PRTs. He constantly heard how they were short staffed. As part of their draw-down strategy, the military wanted to hand over to civilians. But PRTs were drawing down quicker than the military. Greta constantly faced difficulties in finding enough people to fill the slots. There simply wasn't a cadre of qualified civilians experienced in working in developing countries and who were available to deploy to Iraq. She regaled me with stories of some of the misfits. One sent out in Anbar turned out to have a fetish for public masturbation. The PRT team leader's response was to put him on night duty. One evening, a female marine caught him playing with himself in the common room and told him, "Put it away or I'll shoot it off!" It was not a threat to be taken lightly. He was eventually sent home.

Tom Dougherty, the embassy spokesman, told the military he did not support their initiative to establish an English-language academy for the Iraqi security forces in Baghdad. He argued that it did not have backing from an Iraqi ministry, hence the running costs would not be supported, and that it would be impossible to find English-language teachers to work in Baghdad. The military continued to berate him, with one general apoplectic that Tom was making such a fuss over a project which "only" cost $30m. Sitting with Greta Holtz and myself one evening for "wine and whine," Tom said with humour, "The military thinks the embassy does not support democracy and hates the English language!"

I explained to General O the anxieties of the embassy. A random comment that General O made at the BUA about the rule of law, for instance, had set in motion countless taskings and requests for meetings which the embassy simply could not keep up with. The military was the eight-hundred-pound gorilla in the room. The military responded to General O as if he were a god. "You are not a god, sir," I told him. "You are just a general." And I described how he had a massive tail, which meant that wherever he went, his tail swished and knocked a lot of people over.

General O invited the senior embassy people to have dinner with him at Camp Victory so they could air their concerns directly. He seemed to disarm them with his openness and willingness to listen. In a candid exchange, Tom Krajeski, who was responsible for helping mediate tensions between the Kurds and Baghdad, explained, "It has taken me years to build up my expertise and experience as a diplomat. The military barges in and thinks it can just do my job, as if it does not require any particular skill." Others nodded in agreement. The military officers were so confident and arrogant: they believed they could do anything and everything. Tom went on, "And what makes it more painful, is that some of these officers make impressive diplomats." It was a frank admission. Tom told me he was amazed how much General O had changed since his first encounter with him back in 2003.

General O understood that the military needed to let go and follow the embassy's lead. But he was not convinced the embassy had the political will and capability to actually take the lead. Things would be better, he assumed, as soon as a new ambassador arrived. But he was not sure who that would be. First, General Anthony Zinni's name had been floated. And then Christopher Hill, a career diplomat, had been nominated, but his confirmation was being held up by Congress.

AT THE END OF MARCH 2009, the Iraqi security forces undertook an operation to arrest Adel Mashhadani, a leader of the Sons of Iraq in the Fadhl neighbourhood of Baghdad. Fighting broke out between the Iraqi Army and the sahwa group. US forces intervened on the side of the Iraqi Army, helping to arrest Mashhadani.

There was plenty of evidence that Adel Mashhadani was involved in criminal activity. But he had cleared al-Qaeda out of his neighbourhood. Now that the security situation was improved, the government had issued a warrant for his arrest. It was only when we later visited the US unit on the ground that we heard a more complex story. Apparently a woman had made a number of allegations against Mashhadani and they had been used to obtain the warrant. This woman turned out to be the wife of the al-Qaeda leader of the area, who was currently in jail, and who wanted to exact revenge.

Colonel Raad of the Ghazaliya Guardians was also detained. He was an officer in the former Iraqi Army, and one of the most professional Sons of Iraq leaders the US military worked with. We had met him on numerous occasions. We successfully pushed for his immediate release.

By this stage, General O had become concerned about what was going on with the Sons of Iraq. We were trying to assure everyone that the sahwa were not being targeted by the government, but now we were beginning to have our doubts. General O instructed us to start tracking the leaders of the Sons of Iraq and report back to him. It appeared that a number of leaders had been arrested on account of previous insurgent activity which should have been forgiven under the new amnesty law. A few, such as Abu Abed, had fled the country. And some had been killed.

Another issue General O had to worry about was detainee releases. In order to get Sunni support for the SOFA, Crocker had signed letters to senior leaders explicitly stating that we would release fifteen hundred detainees a month. General O did not believe we could process the releases fast enough. There were several layers of US and Iraqi bureaucracy to go through to collect satisfactory evidence to generate warrants for those who should be transferred to Iraqi custody. A lot of those we were holding were detained on the basis of intelligence that would not hold up in an Iraqi court. The US military was more concerned about releasing those who were potential threats than about keeping in detention someone who might be innocent.

AT THE BEGINNING of the year, Sheikh Wasfi al-Assi, the former member of Kirkuk Provincial Council and brother of the paramount sheikh of the Obeidi tribe, had contacted me. We had stayed in touch throughout his time in Syria when he was active in what he referred to as the "peaceful, honourable resistance." Now that there was a SOFA, and US forces had agreed to leave Iraq, he told me the Obeidi tribe were coming out of the insurgency. His tribe, he said, had not been active in the sahwa. They did not believe Iraqis should fight Iraqis. But they would be active in rebuilding Iraq.

Sheikh Wasfi had been communicating with Maliki's office and had got agreement to his return to Iraq from Syria. The minister of defence, Abdul Qadir, who was a member of the Obeidi tribe, approached General O and told him that Wasfi wished to return to Iraq, and asked that we not arrest him—US forces in Kirkuk had frequently threatened to "roll him up" if he stepped foot back in Iraq. General O gave his word that Wasfi would not be detained.

Wasfi took up residence in the Green Zone in the guest house of the minister of defence. He invited me over to meet him and his elder brother Anwar, the paramount sheikh. They told me about their plans to hold a national conference of the Obeidis in March and invited me to attend.

I accepted the invitation and turned up at the al-Rashid Hotel for the Obeidi conference. The only foreigner and the only female, I was ushered onto the platform at the front with the dignitaries, who included Maliki and the minister of defence. In front of us were seated hundreds of Obeidis. I did not know what to expect. One stood up and regaled us with the heroic stance taken by the Obeidis in the 1920 rebellion against the British. All heads turned towards me, nodding and smiling. I nodded and smiled back. Two Obeidis got up and jousted with each other in poems. "You are a *shrugi* from the south," declared one, using the abusive Iraqi term for lower-class peasants south of Baghdad. The other replied, "You are a terrorist from the north." The humour was very Iraqi, and the audience loved it. The Obeidis were both Sunni and Shia, and active within both Shia militia and Sunni insurgent groups.

I met Wasfi and Anwar a few days after the conference. They were pleased with how it had gone and were exploring what to do next. They wanted to know who the next prime minister would be so that they could pledge allegiance to him. I told them I really did not know; it depended on the national elections. They looked at me as if I were being disingenuous. So I told them we had technology that saw into people's brains and read how they intended to vote. They laughed.

"I do not like democracy. It does not seem to be the right system of government for Iraq," Sheikh Anwar admitted.

GENERAL O MET MALIKI on a weekly basis, taking along with him Colonel Becker, the new head of his Initiatives Group, and myself. At one meeting, General O brought out photos of a downed Iranian unmanned aerial vehicle (UAV), saying it had crashed due to "mechanical failure." I stared at General O in shock—this was really stretching the truth. Maliki took the photos and looked at them with interest. He wanted to know more: why had the Iranians got a drone over Iraq?

General O speculated that the UAV might have been filming the Mujahideen al-Khalq, an Iranian exile group, at Camp Ashraf in Diyala province. It had come eighty miles into Iraq and had been flying around for about three hours.

Maliki looked at him incredulously. "Surely, General," he said, "your forces would have noticed it flying around?"

General O admitted that we had indeed noticed the UAV and had in fact shot it in the wing. "That is what caused the mechanical failure," he explained, beginning to look a little uncomfortable.

"So," Maliki continued, "it was not a mechanical failure. It was shot down by you!" Maliki was beginning to smile.

"It was a mechanical failure," General O insisted, relaxing now that Maliki was taking the news so well. "But it was caused by us shooting it!"

They were both laughing now. Maliki asked for more details so he could present the information to the Iranians and protest at their violation of Iraqi airspace.

AT THE END OF MARCH, an article appeared in the London *Guardian* and in the Iraqi media claiming that a Shia militia, Asaib Ahl al-Haqq, had struck a deal with the Iraqi government to trade the five British hostages they were holding for several detainees in detention camps in Iraq. The five Brits had been seized on 29 May 2007 in a raid on the Ministry of Finance. The attackers, who had been dressed in police uniforms, had kidnapped them in order to secure the release of their leader, Qais Khazali, who US special forces had detained earlier in 2007 and held responsible for the killing of the US soldiers in Karbala.

General O sent me over with the article to see Maliki. I drove over with Mike Juaidi, General O's interpreter. Maliki was upstairs in his small office. I explained to Maliki what was in the article. He responded, "They are evil, evil, evil." We were pressuring the group to stop fighting and to give up its weapons, but no deal had been reached. Maliki was visibly shaken and angry at the group's blatant attempt to claim the way to get detainees released was to kidnap foreigners and force an exchange. He felt Asaib were attempting to manipulate and shame the government. We discussed what to do. He proposed the government issue a statement denying the claims. He also wanted Asaib to put out a denial.

Maliki delayed his lunch guest, Larijani, the Speaker of the Iranian parliament, so he could finish his discussion with me. As I was leaving, I said to him, "It's a terribly difficult job being prime minister." He responded, "It's okay being prime minister in other countries, but it is terribly difficult in Iraq."

IN APRIL 2009, Obama made his first visit as president to Iraq. He was riding high on a wave of popularity, feted around the world. The presidential secret service were in-country making the arrangements for the visit. It was planned that Obama would arrive at Baghdad airport, then hop on a helicopter for the ten-minute flight to the Green Zone. At President Talabani's palace, the band was busy practising and the food was being prepared. But an hour before he was due to land, the weather changed and the helicopters were grounded. The secret service refused to contemplate Obama driving from Camp Victory to the Green Zone, and the US embassy thought it would be impossible to get Maliki to go meet Obama at Camp Victory. They reasoned that as he refused to set foot in the US embassy, he was hardly likely to agree to visit the headquarters of the US military. And if Maliki was not going to meet Obama, the embassy said it was not appropriate that other Iraqi leaders meet him.

General O was furious. What message did it send if the president of the United States made his first trip to Iraq and only met American soldiers? "Go see Maliki," he instructed me, "and see if you can persuade him to come to Camp Victory." I drove over to the White House with Mike. Maliki was having his afternoon siesta. I explained the situation to one of his aides. I asked him to wake up Maliki and tell him we were extremely sorry, Obama could not visit the Green Zone due to the weather.

General O asked if there was any chance Maliki could visit Obama at the airport. He knew this was a huge request to ask of the prime minister of a sovereign country, but please would he consider it?

I waited anxiously for the response. After ten minutes, I received a message that Maliki had agreed to go to Camp Victory to meet Obama. He would be ready in half an hour.

There was not a minute to spare! I contacted General O immediately to let him know. The main challenge was to ensure that Maliki's convoy would not be stopped at any of the checkpoints on the way to the airport and that he would be allowed onto Camp Victory. From my BlackBerry, I sent out a message to the key generals requesting their help in ensuring the safe passage of Maliki's convoy. I also e-mailed Robert Ford and Rebecca Fong at the embassy to let them know the meetings were on. I would get Maliki to Camp Victory. Please could they arrange for the other Iraqi leaders to get to Camp Victory, and sort out in which order they should meet Obama. Given how sensitive Iraqis were to protocol, this would not be an easy matter. In the original plan, Obama was to have met Talabani first. In the new plan, which I was making up on the hoof, everything depended on Maliki meeting Obama at Camp Victory— it now had to be the first meeting. If it did not happen, all other Iraqi meetings with Obama would be cancelled.

The pressure was huge. So much could go wrong. I knew if Maliki was stopped at any of the checkpoints, he would immediately take umbrage and turn around. I rode in the first car of Maliki's convoy, prepared to respond to whatever obstacles might appear. We drove at high speed for twenty minutes and reached the entrance to Camp Victory without incident. I began to say my prayers. This was the last and most difficult checkpoint to get through. I jumped out the vehicle, flashing my badge and shouting, "Prime minister of Iraq!" Fortunately, the checkpoint had received the order from headquarters. They let the convoy through without delay.

I began to feel a sense of relief, and now focused on directing the lead vehicle through Camp Victory to General O's villa, which had at short notice been selected as the location for Obama to meet the Iraqi leaders. We arrived at General O's and I steered Maliki into the living area, where I had to entertain him for half an hour or so before General O arrived

President Obama, General Odierno and Sky. *Photo by the author*

with Obama, accompanied by his chief of staff Rahm Emanuel and national security adviser Jim Jones.

I sat in on Obama's meeting with Maliki; and remained in the room for all his discussions with the Iraqi leaders. There I was, in the presence of Barack Obama, the president of the United States of America and the living embodiment of the American dream! After the crazy era of the neoconservatives, the US was now led by a man whose worldview I believed I shared.

Afterwards, General O introduced me to Obama, telling him that I was a big fan of his and had been sending the General material Obama had written ages before he became president. I had read Obama's memoir, *Dreams from My Father*, and had related so much to his life story: growing up in a single-parent family, poor, going to a school with children much wealthier and always feeling an outsider. Obama looked at me quizzically. I tried to explain: "Mr. President, I was trying to turn the General into a liberal." Obama looked at General O and laughed. General O shrugged his shoulders.

The day had gone well, or so I thought. Afterwards Rebecca Fong, the political officer at the embassy who had choreographed the arrival of other senior Iraqis and lined them up to meet Obama, told me there had been no waiting room at General O's to put the guests in. And if they stood in the reception, they would have bumped into Maliki on his way out—and none of them wanted that. The Kurdish leaders, some of whom had flown in from Erbil, had ended up being squashed in the bedroom of General O's bodyguard, whose laundry was strewn all over the bed. It was certainly not the treatment we received when we visited them.

It was Maliki's first visit to Camp Victory. He told me he thought it would make a good site for the Arab Summit in 2010. I passed this comment on to General O. The next day, General O asked his chief of staff to come up with a feasibility study to get all US soldiers out of Camp Victory in 2010, just in case the prime minister asked about it again. The chief of staff almost had a heart attack. Where on earth would he put all the US soldiers and contractors who currently lived on the base?

TOWARDS THE END of April 2009, US special forces carried out an early-morning raid in Kut in southern Iraq. It went wrong. The wife of a local sheikh was shot dead in the crossfire that ensued. There was a public outcry, with protestors gathering at the offices of the Provincial Council chanting the standard slogan: "No, No to America . . . No, No to Occupation . . . No, No to Israel."

Maliki issued a statement which was read on state television. He criticized the raid as a violation of the Security Agreement and called for the US military "to hand over those responsible for this crime to the courts."

The US military initially put out a statement saying the operation was aimed at suspected Shia militants and had been coordinated with and approved by the Iraqi government. The US forces detained six people during the raid but released them the same day. The sheikh whose wife had been killed was one of those released. In a media interview he explained that when people burst into their house in the middle of the night, his wife had picked up a rifle. "If only the Americans had knocked," he said, "we would have cooperated. Instead they came from four corners." The US colonel responsible for the area went with his Iraqi counterpart to the house and then to the Provincial Council to express condolences.

General O went to see Maliki. It was perhaps the tensest meeting they ever had. He promised the US would conduct an investigation into the al-Kut operation. "We have a partnership," he assured Maliki. But he censured Maliki for publicly criticizing the US forces. General O pointed out he could claim in the media that the Iraqi Army was sectarian and could condemn the Iraqi government because members of the Iraqi Army had recently killed three American soldiers in Mosul. But he had never done so, because of the partnership between the US and the Iraqi government.

Maliki hit back: General O could not claim that all Iraqi soldiers were out to kill American soldiers. "There are infiltrators!" he asserted. Maliki said he would hold anyone accountable who tried to kill US soldiers. Maliki said he had asked Iraqi commanders if they knew about the al-Kut operation. They had all said no. "So who conducted this operation?" Maliki asked. "Was it mercenaries?" He said he had heard that it was US special forces and demanded that those involved be brought to justice.

General O misunderstood what Maliki had said and grew irate. Red in the face and raising his voice, he angrily retorted that he was responsible for holding US soldiers to account. I put my hand on his arm and said to him quietly, "Sir, the prime minister said that the US should hold the soldiers to account. He did not say that they should be brought before the Iraqi judiciary." Mike, who had skilfully and accurately kept up with the translation of the heated discussion, clarified with Maliki that he was referring to the US holding its own soldiers accountable. This was different from what Maliki had announced in public. General O calmed down a little.

It was important, Maliki said, that they both agreed that all operations should be based on an Iraqi judicial warrant and should be approved by the Iraqi government, and that those detained should be handed over to the Iraqi authorities within twenty-four hours. If General O had the impression that the Iraqi government was not going after Asaib Ahl al-Haqq he was mistaken. "These people are our enemies before they are yours," Maliki declared. "They claim to be against the occupation, but there is no longer an occupation." He went on, "You embarrassed me in front of the Iraqi public." He had not given approval for this operation. "This incident may topple me. It is dangerous when the prime minister gets blamed. The killing of innocent people stirs emotions."

The next day, General O and I left Iraq on leave. This time, General O did not drop me off in Europe on his way back to the US. Instead, I flew out with Maliki on his private plane, a gift from Iran, as he was going to the UK for an investment conference. It was an eye-opening experience. I discovered that Baghdad airport was a real airport, with travellers everywhere, bag searches and immigration. It was another reminder of our bizarre existence and how we did not get to see so many of the things that Iraqis saw. The airport authorities were very kind and polite and took me to the VIP waiting room, before leading me out to Maliki's plane, where the Iranian pilots greeted us warmly.

Then with a screeching of tires and a whirling of dust, the prime minister's convoy arrived. Along with Maliki came his staff, Abu Mujahid, Abu Rihab and Tariq Najim; the minister of interior, Jawad Boulani; the foreign minister, Hoshyar Zebari; the deputy prime minister, Barham Salih; the spokesman Ali al-Dabbagh, and Dr. Amal, another of Maliki's female advisers.

The in-flight movie was *Mr. Bean*, a British comedy starring Rowan Atkinson as the hapless Mr Bean, which seemed to go down well with all cultures. I turned around to see Maliki giggling away. As the flight progressed, we all swapped seats on the plane, chatted and exchanged gossip. I was invited into the cockpit to meet the pilots, who were very charming and spoke excellent English. We talked about life locked up in the Green Zone, and they told me about their home towns of Isfahan and Tehran. I asked Maliki how he felt his meeting with General O had gone. He said these were difficult issues that both of them got upset over. "But the General is a good man—and I trust him," he said.

As the plane touched down at RAF Brize Norton—it did not have the right landing permits for London—I pointed out the window and said, "*Biladi*" (my country), holding up my British passport. "*Biladi*," chimed in a number of the Iraqis, pulling out *their* British passports and waving them back at me. I smiled. It was good to have some leave.

A fortnight later, I reconnected with General O in Bahrain where he was attending a CENTCOM conference. A plain-clothed American solider met me at the airport and took me to the residence of US ambassador, Adam Ereli, who I knew from when he served in Baghdad. There were gathered at his house were America's top generals. I had enjoyed my break in the UK. But as ever it was good to be back among my military friends.

30 JUNE 2009 marked an important landmark for the government of Iraq. It was the day Iraqi security forces assumed responsibility for security in their cities. The transition had for the most part been seamless. Key to the success was the spirit of partnership between the US and the Iraqis. A constant media drumbeat highlighted the release of detainees, the transfer of US military bases to the Iraqi security forces and successful Iraqi military operations. The Iraqis had shelved the referendum on the Security Agreement.

In the weeks approaching the deadline, General O took the minister of defence, Abdul Qadir al-Obeidi, and the minister of interior, Jawad Boulani, around the country to assess the security situation and the capacity of the Iraqi security forces. It was clear that security was improving, and that partnered operations were speeding up the development of the Iraqi forces. Mosul was the only city not ready for the Iraqis to take the lead, but the strategic gain of being seen to comply with the Security Agreement outweighed the tactical risks of ISF failure.

Maliki declared 30 June "national sovereignty day." In the preceding days, state television ran a "countdown to sovereignty" clock. In his address to the nation, Maliki praised the Iraqi security forces and described how his national unity government had quashed the sectarian violence that had threatened to destroy the country. No mention was made of the role played by US forces. That was left to President Talabani.

To celebrate the day, the Iraqis put on a military parade. We turned up at the parade ground which had been constructed in the 1980s to commemorate the Iran-Iraq war. We drove past the "Victory Arch," where two massive crossed swords were held aloft by giant forearms, modelled from real casts of the arms of Saddam Hussein, with the helmets of Iranian soldiers scattered at the bottom. Near the grandiose Tomb of the Unknown Soldier, General O took his seat in the front row alongside the Iraqi leadership to view the parade.

Army, police, traffic police, navy, special forces—all paraded past, decked out in their finest uniforms. Some marched, others drove their tanks, fire trucks and patrol cars. "Remember the military parade where Sadat was assassinated, sir?" I whispered in General O's ear from my seat behind him. The same thought had been running through his mind. But the parade passed without a hitch. It was a day of great pride for Iraqis.

17

TROUBLE ALONG THE GREEN LINE

We're just one checkpoint incident away from a civil war here.
—BRIGADIER GENERAL BOB BROWN

WITH THE WITHDRAWAL of US forces from the cities, the Kurds sought to expand the area under their control—and Maliki sought to prevent them. Maliki had ordered tanks up into the disputed territories, and Barzani had sent down peshmerga with artillery. Barzani warned that Maliki was becoming a new dictator, centralizing power and using his military rather than negotiations to resolve disputes. He had lost all trust in the prime minister. He complained that the US was helping to build up a large Arab army which would be used in the future against the Kurds. He claimed that Kurdish officers within the Iraqi Army were being replaced by Arab ones. But Maliki's moves against the Kurds proved popular with the Arab street—both Sunni and Shia—who felt that the Kurds had taken advantage of Iraq's weakness since 2003 to expand their territory and to take control of northern oilfields.

While Iraqi security forces and peshmerga were busy facing off against each other, al-Qaeda launched attacks against Christians and also against the Yezidi community, whom they considered "devil worshippers." Sunni nationalists from the group Jaysh Rijal al-Tariq al-Naqshabandi attacked peshmerga and the US Army, regarding both as occupying forces.

The provincial elections of 2009 had brought to power Atheel Nujaifi as governor of Nineveh. The agenda of his political party, al-Hadba Gathering, was to roll back the gains the Kurds had made in the province. In protest at being denied a share in local government, Kurds withdrew

from the Nineveh Provincial Council and mayors of Kurdish towns declared their secession from Nineveh. When Nujaifi decided to attend a
kite-flying festival in the Kurdish-majority town of Bashiqa, the peshmerga received orders to shoot him on sight. Fearing the situation might
deteriorate further in the run-up to the national elections in 2010, Maliki and Barzani both turned to General O for help.

I was familiar with the dynamics in the north, so in July 2009 General
O dispatched me to consult his commanders up there and to make recommendations. And he assigned Lieutenant Colonel D. J. Jones to assist me.

DJ had seen his fair share of fighting on previous tours in Iraq and had
the scars to prove it. He was delighted to be getting out of Camp Victory,
and believed we were on a mission to solve Arab-Kurd tensions. I had
to temper his enthusiasm somewhat by explaining that these issues had
been around for a hundred years, that we could help diffuse the tensions
but we couldn't solve these problems—that required political compromise between the leaders. DJ soon proved to have the intellect and the
temperament for the role.

On arrival in Mosul, we were met by Major General Bob Caslen, commanding the 25th Infantry Division, and his deputy, Brigadier General
Bob Brown. After a few pleasantries, iced tea and cigars, General Brown
leaned towards us and said, "We're just one checkpoint incident away
from a civil war here."

We explored practical steps that could be taken to manage tensions.
Based on our recommendations, General O set up a ministerial committee, comprising himself as chair, the minister of defence Abdul Qadir
al-Obeidi, the minister of interior Jawad Boulani, the chief of staff of the
army Babakir Zebari (who was a Kurd), KRG minister of interior Karim
Sinjari and the minister of peshmerga Sheikh Jaafar. The first meeting
took place in his office at Camp Victory on 16 August 2009.

I had recommended to General O that he use the initial meeting to
get everyone to agree to a set of principles that would guide the work of
the group. If we went straight into the tactical arrangements, they would
contest every detail. General O set the tone for the event. He allowed
everyone to speak, and by the end of the session had got them to agree
on six guiding principles.

In the next meeting, General O set out a two-phased approach for the way ahead. Phase I involved getting the different forces in the disputed territories to work together within a Joint Security Architecture, which included US forces, and which needed to be in place prior to the elections. Phase II involved the integration of forces locally recruited in Phase I into the provincial forces and national intelligence, allowing the withdrawal of both the Iraqi Army and the peshmerga from internal security.

The challenge of getting both sides to agree to this was that the Kurds liked Phase I—and hoped to keep the US forces involved permanently—while the Arabs feared that Phase I legitimized the presence of peshmerga below the "Green Line," the contested border between Kurdistan and the rest of Iraq. To move forward, we had to convince the Arabs that we were serious about Phase II, and would use our leverage on the Kurds to pressure them.

The US was able to offer assistance to train and develop Kurdish forces that came under the Kurdistan Regional Government (KRG) and were part of the recognized defence organization of Iraq. This proved to be a big incentive for the Kurds to merge their peshmerga into one force under the KRG, rather than maintaining them separately under the Patriotic Union of Kurdistan and the Kurdistan Democratic Party. Maliki signed a memorandum to integrate the two Kurdish brigades into the Joint Security Architecture in the disputed territories, thus giving the US the legal basis to train and equip them as federal forces.

GENERAL O HAD BUILT UP his relationship with Barzani over the years. In many ways, they were similar characters: straightforward, honest, loyal and stubborn. Earlier in the year, Barzani had invited General O to visit him in his village. We had flown north to Erbil on a C-12 turboprop plane and then boarded helos. The scenery was stunning. We went from dusty desert landscapes to menacing mountains topped with snow, separated by lush valleys. Saddam's forces had once passed through this land, forcing villagers to flee and razing houses to the ground. Since 1991, Kurds had come down from the mountains and returned from overseas to rebuild their communities. By the time we reached Barzani's village retreat, it was cold and pouring with rain.

Barzani was traditionally dressed as always in baggy trousers, jacket and cummerbund. He wore a red turban, donned only by those from the Barzan region. His home was very modest. And as we sat on couches in the living room, he spoke at length about the history of the Kurds, so much of which was about war and survival.

I told Barzani that in Jerusalem I had met Jews who the Barzanis had helped escape from Iraq. He nodded and mentioned that Yitzhak Mordechai, the Israeli former minister of defence, came from the next village of Acra. He went on to describe the visit of a US congressman and his chief of staff to Erbil. The chief of staff told Barzani they had met many years ago when he had been a little boy, fleeing from Saddam's persecution of the Jews. Barzani said the chief of staff had been in floods of tears as he told the story, his own interpreter was also in tears and he himself had struggled to maintain his composure.

As we sat eating lunch, Barzani spoke about the horrors of war. He once had found a woman and her baby, both dead. The woman had been breastfeeding the baby who had been shot through the head but was still attached to her breast. The image had never left him. He described finding a dead Iraqi soldier in whose pocket was a letter from his wife informing him of the birth of their son and asking what his name should be. The man had written a response, which he had not had time to post, recommending a name for the boy but saying that if he himself were killed his son should be named after him. Barzani ensured the letter was posted. "Everyone is loved by someone," he remarked.

On the flight back to Baghdad, I reflected on Barzani's words and his humanity. In our war the "enemy" had been so dehumanized. It had all been about stopping evil, killing terrorists, preventing these people from coming to the US. It had been a war of choice, not a war of necessity on home territory for one's survival.

DR. JABER AL-JABERI introduced himself to me as the political adviser to Dr. Rafi Issawi, the deputy prime minister of Iraq. Jaber was from Ramadi and Rafi from Falluja, but they had met at medical school in Baghdad in the mid eighties. Jaber had escaped from Iraq, lived in Paris for years and was secular. Rafi, in contrast, had lived in Iraq all his life and was very religious. But their friendship had stood the test of time—and the trials of Anbar. Both had tribesmen involved in the insurgency. And both had had a rocky relationship with US forces. Jaber never received compensation for his house which had been destroyed by US forces. Rafi's seventy-year-old father had been arrested and put in Bucca camp for six months until released without charge. Rafi had been the director of Falluja hospital in 2004 when the marines stormed the city. In the hospital he treated the casualties of the battles, innocent civilians among the insurgents. Back then, he would not even shake hands with an American. But he was now regarded as one of Iraq's rising stars, a highly talented and capable technocrat and politician.

At a meeting of the National Security Council in July 2009, Maliki directed Rafi to investigate the problems in Nineveh and work out a solution. I met Rafi and Jaber to discuss what could be done. Rafi had consulted a wide range of stakeholders from Nineveh and had identified the outstanding issues and the steps needed to resolve them. Rafi was pushing the governor, Nujaifi, to do a deal to get the Kurds back onto the Provincial Council.

The proposed Joint Security Architecture was contested in Nineveh. Rafi agreed to come to Mosul with General O for a joint session with the governor and the Provincial Council. They argued that eight thousand more police and six thousand more soldiers were needed in Nineveh, and that the peshmerga could only be withdrawn once these extra forces had been locally recruited. After much debate, Rafi got the agreement of the Council to move forward with the Joint Security Architecture. Jaber smiled at me across the room. We had prepared our bosses well—and they had delivered.

A NEW ELECTION LAW was needed for the 2010 national elections but the Iraqis couldn't agree on it. Rafi Issawi and Hadi al-Ameri, the leader of the Badr corps, were cooperating closely and had reached an understanding. But the hold-up appeared to be over Kirkuk, where the issue of the final status of the province had become wrapped up in the question of who was eligible to vote there. Arabs and Turkmen complained that the Kurdistan Regional Government had moved Kurds to Kirkuk in order to create a majority to win a referendum on whether Kirkuk should join the KRG. The KRG disputed this, claiming the Kurds who had recently moved to Kirkuk were those forcibly expelled by Saddam years earlier.

The United Nations Assistance Mission for Iraq (UNAMI) asked General O for support to help negotiate a text amenable to all the different parties. It was the closest military-UN relationship anyone had ever witnessed. Andrew Gilmour, the deputy special representative at the UN, said the UN felt much closer to the US military than to the US embassy. General O assigned me to participate in the UNAMI meetings so I could help the Iraqis reach consensus. Kemal Kirkuki, the Speaker of the Kurdistan parliament, came down to Baghdad to push a more hard-line Kurdish position. I knew Kemal well from my time in Kirkuk and went to see him in the al-Rashid Hotel to persuade him to moderate his view.

Finally, agreement was reached and parliament passed the election law on 8 November. General O choked when he heard the Speaker of the Iranian parliament, Ali Larijani, address the Iraqi parliament without any apparent irony: "Iran strongly supports the democratic process and congratulates the Iraqi people for having found the way to democracy." General O was pleased to note that many parliamentarians refused to meet the Iranian Speaker, and that members of the public spoke out against malign Iranian interference.

However, we were not out of the woods yet. According to the Constitution, the election law had to be approved by the Presidency Council. Vice President Hashimi decided to veto it. I went over to Hashimi's office and met Krikor Derhagopian, his adviser. Krikor was an articulate, well-educated Armenian Iraqi, who had recently completed his master's degree in the US as a Fulbright scholar. He spoke with a British accent, as he had attended a British boarding school in Cyprus. Krikor explained that Hashimi had vetoed the election law because of issues concerning "out of country" voting. Many Sunnis believed the majority of Iraqis who had fled the country were Sunnis and argued that they should be allowed to vote in the elections.

Sky with Aram Yarwaessi and his relatives in Darbandikhan. *Photo by Allan Yarwaessi*

General O went back to Washington, so I headed up to Kurdistan for a few days' rest. President Talabani had kindly given me use of one of his guest houses in Sulaymaniyah; and his adviser, Aram Yarwaessi, was looking after me.

Aram took me to his cousin's house for dinner. His aunt, Dilshad, was an amazing woman. A peshmerga in her time, she was famous for killing wild boar with an RPG and a Kalashnikov. Her husband was still a peshmerga and was stationed out near Khanaqin, and her eldest son was also a "pesh." We sat cross-legged on the floor with an abundance of food spread out before us: Kurdish burger, Kurdish chicken, rice with pomegranate, pomegranate sauce, dolma. After the meal, they took me through their family albums: pictures of peshmerga in the mountains; the tree under which the PUK had held its first meeting. Many of the men in the photos had been killed, including Aram's father.

Aram told me about his life. He had spent a year as a toddler in jail in Nasiriyah. Saddam had taken the family hostage in order to get their father to turn himself in. The third son had actually been born in jail, and so was named Asir (prisoner). After their release from jail, the family had gone back to Kurdistan, but had moved to Iran after Saddam's genocidal chemical-weapons attack on the city of Halabja in 1988.

The next day, we were blessed with fine weather. Aram, the pesh-merga and I piled into our two cars, and headed off towards Lake Dukan via the back roads.

We stopped in a village where Aram had once lived. It reminded me of Afghanistan: mud huts clinging to a precarious mountainside. It was hard to imagine Aram living like this. I asked him how he found the UK when he first got there. He told me of the family arriving in Heathrow airport, with blankets and one change of clothes. Everything else had been left behind. They had been taken to a council estate in Brixton. He woke up and saw black people everywhere. He could not believe his eyes. "Are we in England?" he asked his family. The family moved to Harrow on the Hill. A few days later, the house next door caught fire, and his father rushed in to put it out. And that was how they came under the wing of their neighbour, an elderly Scottish woman, Miss Kay, who took it upon herself to introduce them to British life and guide them through British bureaucracy.

We were still up in the mountains when I received a call from Molly Phee at the White House in Washington. The Kurds were taking advan-tage of Hashimi's veto to try to gain more seat allocations for themselves in the election law. Kemal Kirkuki had dug his heels in again. How could he be persuaded to support the election law? I explained Kemal's passion for protecting Kurdish rights, how the only person who could get him to budge was Barzani himself and that this would require assurances from President Obama.

The next day, the White House issued a statement saying Obama had spoken with Barzani and had expressed his support for implement-ing Article 140 of the Constitution which referred to "normalizing" the situation in the disputed territories—and for the constitutional review which the Sunni Arab nationalists were demanding. The law finally went through. Obama's involvement had made the difference.

As I was in the north, I thought I would call Sheikh Ghassan. "How are you?" I asked. "Fifty-fifty," he responded. This was good by Sheikh Ghas-san's standards. He was concerned at the lack of rain down near Hawija, not far from Kirkuk. At least that was not something he could blame on the Kurds. He told me he was thinking of running for election. He had been an independent member of parliament during Saddam's time.

"This is great news, Sheikh Ghassan, you must go out campaigning."

"Miss Emma, I do not campaign. I get votes based on my name and reputation."

"You must go round kissing babies, so that their mothers vote for you."

"Miss Emma, I will do no such thing!"

"But this is democracy, Sheikh Ghassan. You are supposed to go round kissing babies!"

"Ah, democracy . . ."

For so many Iraqis democracy had become synonymous with chaos and violence. I had now added kissing babies to further mar its reputation. In the end, Sheikh Ghassan decided not to run.

ARAM AND I DROVE OFF towards Halabja. On arrival, we headed straight to the memorial to those killed in the chemical attack. In the first section were pictures of Halabja before the attack, life in an ordinary Kurdish town. In the next chamber, there were dummies of women, children and animals in various postures of agonizing death. Photos taken by an Iranian journalist showed young and old killed by chemical bombardment: blood pouring out of their noses; distorted positions; three different types of chemicals, the guide told us. It was truly appalling. In the central hall, the names of the five thousand people killed in Halabja by chemical shelling were recorded on the walls. We visited the graveyard amid well-kept gardens. Two mass graves. Tombstone after tombstone, each with three names, undated. Everyone knew the date by heart: 16 March 1988.

In recent days, a gripping story had been reported on Kurdish television. A young man had been reunited with his mother who thought he had been killed in Halabja. He had been taken as a baby to Iran and brought up there by an Iranian family. Thanks to DNA, his natural mother had just been identified.

We drove through the lush fields, and then started to head up into the mountains to the area known as Ahmed Awa. The road became a narrow track as we continued to climb up and up, with pomegranate trees and the running river below us. We parked the cars, walked up to the water-fall and then climbed further up the mountain. It was a beautiful day and the scenery was stunning. When we turned around to go back, we saw a man with a stick silhouetted on the edge of the hill. We raised our arms above our heads, as if cheering. He did the same. We laughed. Our hearts were filled with the joy of nature, the happiness of being alive.

The next day, we went to Karadagh. Aram explained that the Kurds had taken refuge in villages very close to the mountains as they were difficult to bomb from the air. He pointed out the places that used to be so familiar to him. Here was his house. Here was the bunker which they used to hide in. Here was his bedroom. Over there was the bakery. Saddam's forces had razed everything to the ground, but the bunker and trees still remained.

Aram and his brother Allan used to keep dogs there. The German shepherd they had got from Baghdad had had puppies. One day they had been busy shampooing the puppies in the bathroom, when two Iranian guests walked in, to wash before prayers. They still laughed as they re-membered the horror on the faces of the Iranians, who considered dogs to be unclean! The Iranian guests happened to be Mahmoud Ahmadine-jad and Mohamad Ali Jafari (who would later become, respectively, pres-ident of Iran and commander of Iran's Revolutionary Guards). They had come to provide support for the PUK in their fight against Saddam and had lived with them for a month or so. Qasim Suleimani, the commander of the al-Quds Force of the Iranian Revolutionary Guard Corps, had been in a neighbouring village.

We drove back to Sulaymaniyah to watch the sunset from the top of Mount Goyzha. We drank wine and listened to Kurdish music. And I joined eight Kurdish men dancing under the stars. I was witnessing the resurrection of the Kurdish people.

As WE SAT in the embassy having lunch in mid December, General O lamented that it was his fifth Christmas in Iraq. He loved spending Christmas with his family. He had never thought he would spend even one Christmas here—in 2003, the military had expected to be home within months.

He recalled the other Christmases he had spent in Iraq. In 2006 he had just returned as commander of the Corps. The country was in its darkest days and the violence was horrific. Every morning he awoke to dreadful news. He thought Christmas 2007, the year of the Surge, was going to his last in Iraq. But he was back in Iraq for Christmas 2008, this time as the force commander. Christmas 2009 *would* be his last Christmas in Iraq. Of that, he was sure. Now, when he flew over Baghdad at night, he looked down on the bright lights, the busy traffic, the parks full of people. Iraq was so alive. Iraqis were safer than they had ever been since the fall of the previous regime. And they refused to be intimidated by terrorists. The spirit of the Iraqi people inspired him. Iraq still had a long way to go. But this Christmas—our last Christmas in Iraq—General O felt that all the lives lost and the sacrifices made had really been for something.

As for me and Christmas . . . my overwhelming desire was to decapitate Santa and all his elves. My nerves had started to fray at Santa's carols in the dining room, three times a day, every day, for the last couple of weeks.

As we reflected on our years in Iraq, I said to General O, "It is a great privilege working for you, even if it is leaving me slightly brain-damaged and emotionally traumatized." He turned to me and said, "You are my secret weapon!"

THE JOINT SECURITY ARCHITECTURE was established according to plan, with Phase I coming into effect before the 2010 elections. Through US-organized joint training, the Arab and Kurdish security officials had got to know each other, had had fun training together and had established working relationships. However, progress on resolving the political issues in Nineveh was held up by tense negotiations over the election law, where there were differences on how Kirkuk should be handled and the number of seats to be allocated to the three Kurdish provinces. Recruitment of the additional forces to Nineveh was also delayed.

A key part of the plan was to ensure freedom of movement for Nineveh's governor. Determined to test the new Joint Security Architecture at the earliest, Governor Nujaifi decided to make a trip to the town of Tel Kaif, within the disputed territories, in early February 2010.

Ignoring Kurdish objections, the US forces decided the visit should go ahead. In response, the Kurds brought down reinforcements and tried to prevent the trip from taking place. Crowds of Kurds gathered to block the governor's convoy and in the resulting melee shots were fired. The US commander on the ground, fearing his soldiers were under threat, moved in tanks to protect them and ordered F-16 fighter jets overhead to buzz the crowd. The Iraqi police detained eleven Kurds for incitement and on suspicion of attempting to assassinate Governor Nujaifi.

We were in Ankara at the time for discussions with the Turkish government on how to deal with the PKK, the Kurdish guerrilla group based in Iraqi Kurdistan. A few Turkish journalists had protested the visit, highlighting General O's role in the arrest of Turkish special forces back on 4 July 2003. (A Turkish action film had been made about the incident, *Valley of the Wolves*. It was extremely anti-American and had been hugely popular in Turkey.) I had got very drunk celebrating my birthday with General O and his staff and was nursing a terrible hangover. It was only when we returned to Iraq that we understood how serious the situation in Nineveh was.

Back in Baghdad, I was woken up at two in the morning by a phone call from Murat Ozcelik, the Turkish ambassador. He had received a report from Ankara that the Kurds had invaded Mosul. I had no idea what he was talking about. We had heard that some Kurds had been detained for shooting at the governor, but nothing since then. I promised to investigate and get back to him.

Once dawn broke, I received more information. There had not been an invasion, but Kurdish forces had kidnapped a number of Arabs in Nineveh in retaliation for the arrest of the Kurds.

President Barzani was furious. Every time he turned on his television there was video footage showing American tanks in a Kurdish village and F-16s flying overhead. The Kurds had been highly supportive of the US; not one single US soldier had been killed by a Kurd; so why, he asked, had the US behaved this way towards Kurds? When fighting broke out between Kurds and Arabs, whose side would the US be on, he demanded to know. He had never forgotten how America had let down his father in his moment of need in 1975, after the shah had suddenly cut support to the Kurds in return for Saddam's recognition of Iran's territorial demands. Mullah Mustafa Barzani had turned to America for aid, but Henry Kissinger had refused and Kurdish resistance had collapsed.

General O was irate at President Barzani's over-reaction. Neither Barzani nor General O would talk to each other. General O headed back to Washington, cancelling my leave as he went. Barzani's chief of staff, Fuad Hussein, and I were left to try to find a way through. "Dr. Fuad," I said to him on the phone, "we are both in the same boat. We either sink or swim."

The US embassy insisted the men accused of attempting to assassinate the governor should be put on trial, in accordance with the rule of law. I passed this message to Fuad, who yelled back at me, "*This is Iraq! There is no rule of law!*" Fuad and I decided the only way to prevent this escalating was to swap the detained Kurds for the kidnapped Arabs. But to do this I first needed to get "proof of life" of the Arab detainees.

I flew up to Erbil on the General's tiny C-12 plane. The weather was appalling. There was thick fog, the airport was closed and the pilots could not see the runway. They told me they only had enough fuel to make one attempt at landing. They dipped the nose down towards the ground but then pulled it up again. The landing had failed and I assumed we would turn back. "Ma'am, we're going to try again. We saw the runway at the last moment. We think we can do it." They knew how important my mission was. On the second attempt they landed the plane.

I jumped into a car and turned up at Dr. Fuad's office. He could not believe I had arrived. He looked out of the window. The weather was still terrible. I told him I needed proof of life of the kidnapped Arabs in order to convince the Nineveh Provincial Council to release the Kurds. Dr. Fuad said we would talk later. With some time to kill, and with a young Kurdish woman assigned to look after me, I let myself be taken to a new Lebanese beautician that had just opened in Erbil. I whiled away a couple of hours having my hair cut and my legs waxed.

Still hearing nothing and wondering if the Kurds would negotiate, we were on our way to a new shopping mall when my Kurdish companion received a phone call. She gave urgent instructions to the driver, who rapidly turned around and drove us to the headquarters of the Asayish, Kurdish intelligence. After an initial discussion with a senior official, one of the kidnapped Arabs was brought in. He told me he had been randomly stopped while driving his car in Nineveh. He even claimed that his grandmother was Kurdish. Two others were brought in, one after the other. Neither had any idea of why they were being detained.

As soon as I left the Asayish headquarters, I phoned Rafi Issawi, Iraq's deputy prime minister. "Dr. Rafi, I have proof of life." I also called Murat Ozcelik. The Turkish ambassador's pressure on Governor Nujaifi had helped secure the release of eight of the original eleven Kurdish detainees. I asked him to urge the governor to do a deal on the three remaining Kurds. Rafi phoned me back to confirm that the governor and members of the Nineveh's Provincial Council had agreed to the release of the detained Kurds in exchange for the Arab hostages.

The next day, I flew back to Baghdad and met up with Rafi and Jaber to plan how to choreograph the next steps. We flew up to Mosul together on General O's plane. Patrick Murphy, one of the very best PRT team leaders, bundled us all into his car and drove us from the military side of the airport to the civilian side. We had decided this was the best location to organize the prisoner exchange. Governor Nujaifi turned up, along with a couple of members of the Provincial Council. And the three Kurdish detainees were brought in.

I coordinated with Brigadier General Cucolo for the US military to pick up the detained Arabs from two separate locations in Kurdistan by helicopter. But just as I thought things were progressing in the right direction, there was a further twist. The three Kurds suspected of attempting to assassinate the governor had to be taken before a court so an Iraqi judge could formally release them from custody. Karim Sinjari, the KRG minister of the interior, suspected a plot. He had informers all around the airport who kept him regularly updated. He feared the three Kurds might not be released.

In the end, Rafi agreed to give Jaber up as a hostage to the Kurds to guarantee the detainees would all be returned. Jaber was not at all happy! He went with the Kurdish detainees, as well as Arab and Kurdish security officials, to get the requisite document from the judges. Jaber later told me the judges thought it was a very good deal—three Kurds for fifteen Arabs—and were happy to issue the release papers!

The two American military helicopters returned with the fifteen kidnapped Arabs, but Karim Sinjari insisted they remained on the helicop-

Jaber al-Jaberi, Sheikh Abdullah al-Yawar, Rafi Issawi, Athil Nujaifi, General Riyadh in Ninewa. *Photo by the Office of Sheikh Abdullah*

ters until the three Kurds returned. I spoke constantly on the phone to Karim. Reception was poor and we kept being cut off. The deal was on again, off again. This went on for four or five hours. In the meantime, the airport was open as normal for business. Travellers landing at the airport came through the hall where we were seated, greeted the governor and Rafi, and went on their way, oblivious to the high-stakes negotiations going on around them.

Finally, the three Kurdish detainees were brought back—and with them Jaber. And Karim gave permission for the Arabs to be released. They got off the helicopters and came into the room where we were waiting. Rafi hugged them and gave each some money. They still had no idea why they had been detained. The three I had visited in detention saw me and grinned. I smiled back at them.

Rafi held a press conference in which he spoke of the importance of national reconciliation and coexistence among all Iraq's communities. Afterwards, Barzani called Rafi to thank him for his efforts in resolving this whole affair.

It had been a long day. It was with great relief that Rafi, Jaber and I got onto the General's plane for the flight back to Baghdad. "You know," Rafi said, "isn't it great to do something that makes everybody happy? This happens so rarely in Iraq." It was true. We had prevented war breaking out between Arabs and Kurds, had stopped Turkey from invading, and had put relations between the Kurds and the US military back on track. Just another day in Iraq!

18

ELECTION
SHENANIGANS

My greatest fear is that we stabilize Iraq, then hand it over to the Iranians in our rush to the exit.

—GENERAL ODIERNO, February 2010

GENERAL O HAD RECENTLY WATCHED the movie *Charlie Wilson's War*, which showed how US interest in Afghanistan had ceased once the mujahideen had defeated the Soviet Army and driven them out.

He had a premonition the same could occur in Iraq. "I've invested too much here," he said, "to simply walk away and let that happen." He wanted the US relationship with Iraq to continue for years to come, led by the embassy not by the military. He believed twenty thousand or so US troops were needed to stay in Iraq post-2011 to train Iraqi security forces and to provide the psychological support to maintain a level of stability. He envisaged a long-term strategic partnership between the two countries.

Every time a congressional delegation visited, General O put up a slide showing why Iraq was important and why the US should continue to invest in Iraq through the Strategic Framework Agreement the two countries had signed in 2008. I thought he was overly optimistic about the US role in Iraq and the region, but there was no alternative vision coming from anywhere else within the US government. General O knew that for the mission to succeed, there needed to be a political agreement among Iraqi leaders. Otherwise all the security gains the troops had fought so hard for would not be sustainable. He took every opportunity to communicate the complexities of Iraq to the new Obama administration.

311

Robert Ford talking to tribesmen in the Marshes in Dhi Qar province. *Photo by the US Embassy*

For months, General O had tried hard to work with the embassy and to support the leadership of Chris Hill, the new ambassador who had taken up his post in April 2009. But he had begun to despair. It was clear that Chris Hill was miscast in the role. With his lack of regional experience, Hill was the wrong choice for ambassador. He had not wanted the job, but Hillary Clinton had persuaded him. The secretary of state admitted this when General O met her in early 2010 in Washington to explain the level of dysfunction at the embassy. General O complained that Hill did not engage with Iraqis, or with others in the diplomatic community—his only focus appeared to be monitoring the activities of the US military.

It was frightening how a person could so poison a place. Hill brought with him a small cabal who were new to Iraq and marginalized all those with experience in the country. The highly knowledgeable and well-regarded Arabist, Robert Ford, had cut short his tour as ambassador to Algeria to return to Iraq for a third tour under Crocker and turned down another ambassadorship to stay on in Iraq and serve as Hill's deputy. But

Hill did not want his advice on political issues and pressured him to depart the post early in 2010. In his staff meetings Hill made clear how
much he disliked Iraq and Iraqis. He wanted the embassy to be "normal."
His definition of "normal" included the requirement of grass within the
embassy compound. The initial attempts to plant grass seed had failed
when birds ate it all. Eventually, great rolls of lawn turf were brought
in—I had no idea from where—and took root. There was now grass on
which the ambassador could play lacrosse.

"Normal" also meant no foreigners at the embassy. The Brits had
tried and failed to get a follow-on SOFA, so all UK military had withdrawn by the end of 2009. At first, I didn't notice any difference. I was
used to functioning in an all-American world. But that soon changed. As
a non-American, I now had to be escorted when I entered the embassy's
chancery, which was where my desk was located. The ambassador clearly
wanted me out. I sought refuge with the military tribe. General Barbero
gave me an office in his headquarters across the road from the embassy,
where he headed up Acquisitions and Training. So I started going there
most mornings for the BUA, although I still lived within the embassy
compound. For the military, the greatest threat to the mission had become the US embassy.

ONE EVENING IN FEBRUARY, I was round at Dr. Rafi's house meeting with
him and Jaber to discuss the ongoing tensions in Nineveh. Rafi got out
his computer to show me the jingle recorded by Iraqiya, the political coalition formed to contest the forthcoming March 2010 election. A handsome young man was singing a song of love and unity for Iraq. Iraqiya
was campaigning on a non-sectarian platform. Led by Ayad Allawi, who
had headed Iraq's government in 2004–5, Iraqiya brought together leaders of the Sunni community (including Rafi) as well as secular Shia like
Allawi.

Election fever was high in Iraq. In 2005 only 2 per cent of Anbar
had turned out for the elections. After years of exclusion and insurgency,
Anbaris had decided to give politics a chance. Rafi knew it wouldn't be
easy. The governor of Anbar had been blown up only weeks earlier. We
had visited him in the US military hospital hours after the attack; he

had survived but had lost a hand. But despite the challenges, Rafi was optimistic and excited about the elections and the prospect of building democracy in Iraq.

In the run-up to the election, de-Baathification reared its head once more. Pushed by Ahmed Chalabi and the Iranians, a committee headed by Ali Faisal Lami (who we had recently released from detention where he had been held due to his activities with Shia militia) and which had no legal standing, had started to disqualify candidates. Its arbitrary rulings were approved by Iraq's Independent High Electoral Commission and some judges due to pressure put on them. The "verdicts" hit Iraqiya the hardest, but also Maliki's State of Law Coalition, and seemed aimed at putting sectarianism back on the agenda. Iran viewed a strong, secular, non-sectarian Iraq as a threat. It spread images of Allawi as a Baathist, of Iraqiya and mass graves, generating fear of a return to the Saddam era.

General O watched what was happening very closely. "We've got to keep Iraqiya in the game," he directed. We had fought so hard to create the political space for all groups to participate. It would be disastrous if Iraqiya pulled out.

Among those barred from running by the spurious committee was Salah Mutlak, the joint head of Iraqiya. I visited him on a number occasions in the al-Rashid Hotel, where he rented a couple of rooms. He was very depressed and highly stressed. He was a member of parliament and had participated in previous elections. Only a couple of months previously, Maliki had tried to persuade him to join his State of Law Coalition. When he refused, Maliki turned against him. Mutlak was an Iraqi nationalist, a secular man, not in the slightest sectarian—a Sunni married to a Shia. He had been a member of the Baath party in his youth but had been expelled for protesting the execution of Shia from Najaf. He had a PhD in agriculture and had spent years in Scotland. There were reports that his nephew had been interrogated and forced to confess to his uncle's involvement in terrorism.

On General O's direction, I advised Mutlak to leave Iraq to avoid being arrested on bogus charges but to urge his followers to participate in the elections and not to withdraw. It was the only way to create a better balance in the country. In our last meeting, Mutlak walked me out of the hotel to my car. We shook hands, saying goodbye. Days later, I heard he had moved to Jordan.

Another person to be targeted was Abdul Qadir al-Obeidi, the minister of defence. He was a Sunni but was close to Maliki and on the State of Law list. He had been jailed by Saddam and all his property confiscated. At the end of a scheduled meeting with General O, Abdul Qadir asked for a private word. He was deeply upset that he was being accused of being a Baathist after all he had been through. He had proven himself loyal to the Shia regime over the last few years. If he were barred, it would show no hope for reconciliation in Iraq.

The next thunderbolt in February was the request from the Iraqi government for Sultan Hashim to be transferred from US to Iraqi custody. Sultan Hashim had served as the minister of defence under Saddam. He was regarded as one of the most respected generals of the former Iraqi Army. He had surrendered to the Coalition in 2003 in Mosul on the understanding he would be treated with respect and dealt with justly, and had been flown down to Baghdad on Petraeus's helicopter. There he had been tried and sentenced to death—not the just treatment that he had expected and we had led him to believe he would receive. We suspected that Shia parties were requesting his transfer to Iraqi custody in order to execute him ahead of the elections to boost their popularity. If this went ahead, then Iraqiya's leaders would feel forced to pull out of the elections. I contacted Rafi, who was in Erbil. He immediately returned to Baghdad to meet Talabani, who as president was required to endorse death sentences, and gained an assurance of a stay of execution.

Iraqiya froze its campaigning and pushed for greater international commitment to oversee the elections and the democratic process. Rafi led the development of a Code of Conduct for the elections, and managed to get buy-in from the other political parties. In an attempt to stop the arbitrary measures and keep Iraqiya in the game, European Union heads of mission in Baghdad, spearheaded by the British ambassador John Jenkins, worked hard to get a statement published at the United Nations, alongside the quarterly report provided by Ad Melkert, the UN special representative in Iraq.

Fortunately, the UN statement convinced Iraqiya that the international community would monitor the electoral process seriously, and they went back out on the campaign trail. As I drove around Baghdad on my nocturnal excursions with Safa, I could see the posters of the different parties everywhere. The competition was intense.

THE NATIONAL ELECTIONS took place on 7 March 2010 and went more smoothly than we had dared hope. After a month of really competitive campaigning across the country, and wide media coverage of different candidates and parties, 62 per cent of eligible Iraqis turned out to vote. An atmosphere of great excitement gripped the country. Old and infirm were escorted to the polling stations; parents brought along their children. General O and I flew around in his helicopter, watching events from the air. The European Union and others had fielded hundreds of international poll-watchers alongside thousands of trained Iraqi election observers, while the UN provided the Iraqis with advice on technical matters related to elections. All this helped to sustain the credibility of the process.

The insurgents sought to create a climate of fear by planting bombs in water bottles and blowing up a house, but the Iraqi security forces stood up to the test. In the run-up to the elections, they prevented numerous bombs from exploding. Previously the protectors of the regime, the ISF now proved to be the protectors of the political process and the Iraqi people. This marked a significant change in culture. General O believed it was largely due to the influence of the US military. The result of the elections was still too close to call, but the US military predicted that Maliki's State of Law Coalition would win the most seats.

"WE WON THE ELECTIONS!" Dr. Rafi shouted excitedly down the phone. I could hear celebratory gunfire in the background. It was unbelievable. We had not expected Iraqiya to do so well. They had won ninety-one seats, two more than Maliki. *"Alf mabruuk"* (A thousand congratulations), I told him. Their agenda had captured the imagination of many Iraqis who dreamt of a country where they would not be defined by sect or ruled by religion.

I accompanied General O and Hill to the meeting with Maliki the next day. When Hill asked Maliki about his retirement plans, it was immediately apparent that Maliki was not contemplating stepping down. He claimed there was massive election fraud and that the Mujahideen al-Khalq (an Iranian opposition group, locked away in Diyala province) had used satellites to change the results in the computer. He was convinced the data input had been tampered with despite the computers being stand-alone, not attached to the Internet, and with thousands of election observers. His advisers had told him he would win big with over a hundred seats. He demanded a recount. Maliki was becoming scary.

There was no evidence of fraud to justify a recount, but the Iraqi electoral commission and the international community agreed to one, fearful of a repeat of the election fiasco in 2009 in Afghanistan, which had tarnished the credibility of elections there. In the meantime, Maliki's advisers told us he needed two extra seats from the recount. Otherwise, he would be blamed for losing Iraq for the Shia. Rather than joining a united Shia list as had happened in 2005, he had insisted on going separately as State of Law, in large part because the Shia parties would not agree on him to lead the list.

In parliamentary systems, the winning bloc is defined as the one that wins the most seats in the election, as that represents the will of the electorate. This was certainly the intent of those who drafted the Iraqi Constitution. Maliki asked Judge Medhat, the chief justice, for his interpretation of the "winning bloc." Judge Medhat, continually under pressure from Maliki, returned an ambiguous ruling, saying it could be either the bloc that received the most seats in the election or the largest bloc formed within parliament. This would be Maliki's escape clause.

General O urged that we should protect the process. "They have to let Allawi at least attempt to form a government first. If they don't, the election looks like a sham." He said we should not pick winners. It never worked out well. "We need to put our arms around Iraqiya and keep them in the game," as they were the ones being intimidated. Maliki had the advantage of being the incumbent with use of the apparatus of the state. General O and I did not think Allawi would be able to put a government together with himself as prime minister. But we thought he had the right as the winner of the election to have first go—and that this could lead to a political compromise among the leaders, with either Allawi and Maliki agreeing to share power between them, or a third person chosen to be prime minister.

General O was incredulous that the embassy did not want to do anything to help the Iraqis form a government. He instructed me to try to broker a meeting between Iraqiya and State of Law. They were the two largest blocs and an agreement between them would also best serve US interests. He knew this was not the role of the US military, but he was not prepared to sit back and do nothing.

I went to meet Rafi. He was the chief of staff for Iraqiya, responsible for taking forward the government-formation negotiations. Plan A, he told me, was to form a government with Allawi as prime minister. Plan B was for Allawi to choose someone else as prime minister, such as Adel Abdul Mahdi. While most of Iraqiya's constituents were Sunnis, they had also won votes across the south among secular Shia and from minorities. Around 20 per cent of Iraqiya members of parliament were not Sunni Arabs. By pushing for Allawi, a Shia, as prime minister they accepted that no Sunni would have one of the top three jobs. This was their attempt to break the Lebanon model of cementing sectarianism within institutions.

I asked Dr. Rafi whether he would consider an agreement between Iraqiya and State of Law. Their vision for the country was closer than that of other parties. The main obstacle seemed to be the personalities of Maliki and Allawi, both of whom wanted to be prime minister. Rafi had gone through all the different permutations of how to form a government. He argued that if Maliki did a deal with Iraqiya, then he could have a prestigious position such as president. If he did not, then he would end up simply as an ordinary member of parliament. In Iraqiya's calculation, they were Maliki's best bet.

I then went to meet Sami al-Askari. Sami had spent his years in exile in the UK, after stints in Iran and India. His family had remained in London when he returned to Iraq in 2003. Although he had left Dawa, he remained close to Maliki. Sami was part of the wing of State of Law that leant towards the West rather than Iran. I had got to know him over the previous year when dealing with the Shia militia Asaib Ahl al-Haqq that had kidnapped five Brits back in 2007. It had been Sami who had picked up the bodies of the dead British bodyguards and brought them to the Green Zone so they could be returned to their families for burial. And it was Sami who had delivered Peter Moore to the British embassy alive, after over two years in captivity.

Sami asked me to explain to Iraqiya that they should not negotiate from the belief that State of Law and the Iraqi National Alliance, which represented the other major Shia political entities, could never come back together. They could, and the Iranians were working hard to "guarantee" precisely this. But this option, he said, would not be in the best interests of the country. He believed that an Iraqiya–State of Law alliance, with Maliki as prime minister, was the best solution. For days, I passed messages back and forth between Rafi and Sami, preparing the groundwork for them to meet. They did so, and were pleased with their initial discussions.

General O regularly dined with the British and Turkish ambassadors. He wanted the British and the Turks to keep Iraqiya at the negotiating table and to advise them on the way forward. John Jenkins, the British ambassador, was a superb Arabist who loved the region and had served in Abu Dhabi and Kuwait, as consul general in Jerusalem (where I had first met him), as ambassador in Damascus and as the FCO's director for the Middle East and North Africa. He had also been ambassador in Rangoon during some of the worst days of the military junta in Burma, where he had worked closely and effectively with his US counterpart. Jenkins disagreed with Chris Hill—and made little effort to hide it.

I had got to know the Turkish ambassador Murat Ozcelik well through the traumas of the Nineveh hostage crisis. Ozcelik did more than any other individual to change the nature of relations between Turkey and Iraq's Kurds. During his tenure as the point man on Iraq, Turkey had stopped fearing that Iraq's Kurds would encourage secessionism in Turkey and started viewing them as close allies with a shared vision for the future of the region. I had witnessed how Ozcelik had helped persuade key Iraqis to support the US SOFA in 2008. He was a skillful diplomat and charming with it. He was so admired by the junior diplomats at his embassy that they grew moustaches to mimic his!

Ozcelik had been instrumental in helping to form Iraqiya as a non-sectarian bloc under Allawi's leadership. Turkey was determined there should not be a second Maliki premiership.

But negotiations were put on hold while everyone awaited the results of the recount and the de-Baathification edict. Iraqiya feared a plot to change the election results. They were right to fear.

TOWARDS THE END OF APRIL, General O met with Lieutenant General Aydan, the election security supremo, and Faraj Haydari, the chief commissioner of the independent electoral commission. Both felt that Iraq had held the best elections it was capable of and so did not understand the need for a recount, nor its scope. They viewed the new de-Baathification decision taken by the courts to disqualify fifty-two candidates and discount all their votes as politically motivated. The minister of defence was even more blunt when we met him. He said if this latest ruse was successful it would mean "the end of the elections." He went on, "It is a joke. No one in the international community will accept it."

When General O met with Dr. Rafi in his office, Dr. Rafi explained that Iraqiya feared the whole democratic process was being undermined. Iraqiya leaders saw their election victory being taken away from them, and feared attempts to brand them as Baathists and exclude them from political life. Having succeeded in persuading Sunnis to participate in the political process, they were fearful of how their constituents would respond.

At this point, General O had had enough. He drove over to Judge Medhat's office and, towering over the judge, told him the de-Baathification committee was not legal and its rulings should be ignored. Judge Medhat promised not to implement its decisions.

Maliki certainly gave the impression that he would remain prime minister. He had found a "legal" way to delay the certification of the results of the elections. During this period, he would continue as prime minister without a parliament to provide any oversight. He had control of the finances and the Iraqi security forces. Many ministers were not unhappy with this arrangement, as they got to remain in their posts. Maliki was using the time to try to divide the opposition. The longer he was able to draw out the process, the greater he estimated his chances of remaining in power because it generated a sense of the inevitable. Iraqis believed the US was supporting Maliki, otherwise why would he be allowed to behave in this way?

General O had continued to pay regular visits out to the troops to ensure the drawdown was on schedule, and that all the kit accumulated over the years of the war was being packed up and shipped home. But on one visit, General O gave instructions to a brigade, which was into its final month, to prepare to extend its tour. He knew this was difficult news to break to the soldiers. But the whole drawdown had been premised on the Iraqis forming a government relatively quickly. He had built in some flexibility to delay departure of units if conditions on the ground warranted it. US and Iraqi forces had succeeded in killing the top two al-Qaeda leaders in Iraq, Abu Ayyub al-Masri and Abu Omar al-Baghdadi. US special forces had been hunting them for years and had finally caught up with them on 18 April, not far from where Saddam had been found. Over the last couple of months, three-quarters of the al-Qaeda leadership in Iraq had been captured or killed. But General O nevertheless feared that the political indecision could lead to instability.

I was back at my room in the embassy when I received a message that General O wanted me at Camp Victory right away. The weather was too dusty for the helicopters, so Sergeant Norton drove me over in an SUV, with a Humvee as protection.

General O wanted the latest feedback on my discussions with officials from the White House who were visiting Iraq. They had been receiving such different reports from the ambassador and General O, and they wanted to make their own assessment. General O paced back and forth like an angry bull. It had taken two months after Iraq had held such a good election for the US administration to even consider becoming involved. General O wanted to know when the US government would say to Maliki that enough was enough. Was the US prepared to threaten that it would not recognize the legitimacy and credibility of the elections? He feared the Obama administration would simply roll over and not take a stand. The administration did not seem to care about Iraq, and just wanted to get out.

IN MAY, MALIKI CHANGED TACK. Realizing that neither de-Baathification nor the recount was going to give him the extra seats he needed, he made an agreement with the Iraqi National Alliance (which included the Islamic Supreme Council of Iraq and the Sadrists) to form a government and to prevent Allawi from becoming prime minister. But they still could not agree a leader. Nobody wanted a second Maliki premiership. Well, almost nobody.

After meeting with Chris Hill, General O strode down the embassy corridor looking visibly upset. "He told me that Iraq is not ready for democracy, that Iraq needs a Shia strongman. And Maliki is our man." General O had objected that that was not what the Iraqis wanted. They were rid of one dictator, and did not want to create another. General O frequently told his soldiers they were fighting long and hard, year after year, and sacrificing so much to build democracy in Iraq.

GENERAL BABAKIR, a Kurd who was the chief of staff of the Iraqi Army, invited General O and me to dinner at his house in the Green Zone. As ever, he served excellent kebab and ice cream. We joked about Brits and Americans. How would the US be remembered in Iraq? "For Power-Points and T-walls," I said. "And signs which say, 'Stay back 50 metres or you will be shot,'" Babakir added with a smile.

The television was playing in the background. Salah Mutlak, who I had advised to leave the country, was giving a live interview in Amman on one of the satellite channels. "What is he saying?" General O asked. Mike translated the diatribe about how the US was responsible for all the problems in Iraq. "Oh, shut him up!" General O said, shaking his head. I pulled out my phone and called Mutlak. In the middle of his interview, Mutlak started feeling his pockets. I ended the call. Mutlak continued with the diatribe. I phoned him again, and this time let it ring and ring. Mutlak completely lost his train of thought as he searched for his phone to try to turn it off. General O and Babakir could not believe their eyes. This was on live television. They collapsed with laughter. Mutlak phoned me after the interview. Only a Brit, he said, would play such a trick. But he too saw the funny side of it.

GENERAL O HEADED BACK to Washington for more consultations and I took the opportunity to escape from the toxic embassy by flying up to Kurdistan, hitching a ride with General Babakir. I had a posse of presidential peshmerga at my disposal, all of whom wore cheap black suits, and a female guide wearing stilettos. We headed out to the Zagros Mountains and the Cave of Shanidar, where Neanderthal skeletons had been found in the 1950s, believed to be around sixty-five thousand years old. We climbed up the paved path to the hill, me in my sensible US Army combat boots, my guide in her high heels. The views over the valley were stunning.

We drove on to the village of Barzan, which I had visited the year before, and went to the cemetery. Simple white stones marked the graves. In 1983, Saddam had ordered the abduction of eight thousand men and boys of the Barzani tribe to punish the KDP for its alignment with Iran. Their bodies had never been recovered. A couple of women dressed in black and a little child walked among the graves. We went on to the shrine of Mullah Mustafa Barzani, the great Kurdish nationalist leader and the father of President Barzani.

Sheikh Abdullah Barzani, the nephew of President Barzani, came out to greet us. He was delighted to have guests. We sat and spoke in a mixture of English, Arabic and Kurdish. He sat in full Kurdish garb, proud of his heritage and history. He must have been in his seventies. We discussed Iraqi politics and he said he wanted Allawi to be prime minister. I told him it had recently taken five days to form a new government in the UK, a delay which had caused great concern and a drop in the value of the pound. He laughed. It had already been months in Iraq since the election, with no sign of a government being formed any time soon.

Sheikh Abdullah insisted we stay for lunch and then was most apologetic that he only had simple food—he was not expecting guests, so had not slaughtered an animal. We ate rice, beans and salad with local bread. Seated at the table were his son and a few other Barzanis. As we talked, I could not help but wonder at this culture and what we in the West had lost. Sheikh Abdullah was so happy to share his table with a guest, a foreigner, and in time-honoured fashion to discuss the ways of the world with travellers passing through. He had such a strong sense of who he was, where he belonged, his heritage, his people.

The next morning, while I was seated at breakfast at the KDP guest house, a man in his thirties dressed in a black suit and bright-pink tie turned up. Fuad Hussein had sent him. He told me his name was Barzad, he was Yezidi and would be my guide for Lalish, the Mecca of the Yezidis, which was two hours' drive west of Erbil, forty miles north of Mosul.

I knew little about the Yezidis other than they had overgrown moustaches, shunned lettuce and did not like the colour blue. As the road took us past the Kurdish towns of Shaqlawa and Acra, I had plenty of time to find out more. Barzad explained to me that there were around half a million Yezidis in Iraq. He described their ethnicity as Kurdish and their religion as Yezidi. I pointed out that some Yezidis claimed they were not Kurds. Barzad said those mostly lived in Sinjar, and were paid by the Arabs to claim they were not Kurds!

Barzad told me Yezidis prayed twice a day, at sunrise and sunset, in Kurdish, in the direction of Lalish and theirs was the oldest religion in the world. According to their religion, God created the world and entrusted it to seven archangels, including Melek Taus (the Peacock Angel). Melek Taus refused to submit to Adam, and was therefore often identified by Muslims and Christians as Lucifer, the fallen angel. Yezidis had been persecuted for centuries as "devil worshippers" and al-Qaeda used this as a pretext to target them.

The mountains gave way to the Nineveh Plains. Barzad pointed out the township where he was born. Saddam had moved his community from their villages to this settlement, and had given their homes and land to Arabs. We then drove through a wooded valley up to Lalish, the holiest site in the Yezidi religion. I was reminded of the Holy Land and the memory of churches and monasteries situated in secluded locations. We parked the car and took off our shoes and socks. The land was hallowed. I walked across the courtyard. There was a large snake engraved beside the door to protect against evil. Inside the first vault, the tombs were draped with bright scarves. I was told to untie one of the knots, then retie it. Apparently, in so doing I was seeking help in solving one of my issues; and fixing the problem of a pilgrim who came before me.

We walked through to the next vault, where I was told to walk three times anti-clockwise around the tomb of Sheikh Adi, a key Yezidi figure

Lalish, the holiest site of the Yezidis. The serpent to the right of the door protects against evil. *Photo by the author*

who died in 1162. In the next vault there were jugs of oil to burn at night. In the final vault, I was told to walk up to the tomb, kiss it then walk backwards. Returning back the way I came, I was handed a scarf. I was told to close my eyes and then throw it into the air. Three times I did this, not knowing where exactly I was supposed to aim. After the third attempt, Barzad announced that I would never get married. I then climbed down a level below the ground to where the River Zimzim ran beneath the shrine. Yezidis believed this was the Spring of Life and brought their babies here for baptism.

On emerging, I was led up the hill, my bare feet burning on the sun-scorched earth, to where there was a tree covered in rags, for me again to unknot and knot three times. The tree was beside Mount Arafat. Legend had it that Sheikh Adi transferred Mecca's landmarks, including the famous mountain, to Lalish.

BACK IN BAGHDAD, with still no progress on government formation, I decided to make another journey, this time to the south. As arranged, Safa phoned me around eight in the morning. I headed out of the US embassy and then returned to put sunscreen on my face. Who knew how much time I would spend in the scorching sun today? I jumped into the car beside Safa. I was excited. I had been in Iraq all this time and had yet to visit the holiest shrines of the Shia religion. Safa was excited too.

On the outskirts of Baghdad, we linked up with the rest of our party. We were a convoy of four cars. Safa got out and sat in the front seat. Safa's wife—wife number one—got in beside me. I looked around to see who else was travelling with us. I recognized a number of individuals who had driven me around Baghdad over the last two years. They grinned. Everyone was animated.

We drove out of Baghdad, under the arch that proclaimed BAGHDAD, CITY OF PEACE. We followed the route the pilgrims took when they walked the sixty miles south from Baghdad to Karbala. There were stalls beside the road selling drinks. Old shacks. There was little sign of black-market activity these days—there was enough petrol in the gas stations. Then we passed through palm groves, set back from the road. (After the uprising of 1991, Saddam had ordered the groves to be cleared back three hundred

Sky visits Shia shrines in Karbala. *Photo by Safa al-Sheikh*

yards from the roads to prevent ambushes.) Soon we were in Mahmoud-iyah; and then in Musaib on the Euphrates. I looked down alleyways. Kids were playing. Shops were open. Poor, run-down towns and villages, which were similar to so many others in the Middle East.

Within an hour and a half, we were at the gates of Karbala. Safa's wife helped me put a *hijab* on over my head. I then put stockings on my feet. And finally the black *abaya*. I cursed men for forcing a black tent on women. Safa laughed. The magic wand at the entrance to the shrine "detected" explosives in the first car in our convoy, so that car had to wait. The rest of us parked beside the gates of the shrine.

Safa's wife took me to the counter to leave our shoes, and then to "security" to leave camera and phones and be searched. I tried not to trip on my *abaya* or to slip on the stones, as I headed down the entrance towards the Shrine of Hussein. There were thousands of people. Some were sitting on the ground praying, others were walking with great purpose. Every woman dressed like me in black. Men wore different outfits, revealing whether they were Iraqi or from Pakistan, Indonesia or Iran. The walls were covered with beautiful mosaics. Previously, this area had been open to the sky, but a roof had been added, also covered in mosaics. Rugs were on the floors.

We headed into the women's section to get up close to the Shrine of Hussein. The area was bright with lights, glass, silver and flourescent green. There was a swarm of women, determination on their faces, some with tears in their eyes. They pushed and nudged each other out of the way as they tried to get as near as possible to the shrine itself, to touch the outer screen. The Iranian women seemed to be the most pushy. Safa's wife told me that the influence of Iran was much stronger since 2003. She pointed to posters and to screens which beamed out messages. No one paid any attention to me; I might as well have been just another Shia woman coming to pray. We sat for a while and read in Arabic the prayer for a visit to the Shrine of Hussein.

We went outside to recover our belongings and then walked the few hundred yards down to the Shrine of Abbas. We heard the call to prayer, and everyone gathered inside. The women's section was small and already crammed full. We went to the outer section and sat on the ground with the faithful, as the imam led us in prayer. Old and young stood up, adjusted their *abayas*, bent down, knelt and touched the ground with their foreheads.

All over the world, in time-honoured tradition, Muslims answered the call to prayer. And that day, I felt privileged to join in prayer with the faithful in Karbala.

19

LOSING IRAQ

Why is the US picking the prime minister? This is Iraq. This is our country. We have to live here. And we care passionately about build-ing a future for our children.

—RAFI ISSAWI

FINALLY IN JUNE 2010, three months after the elections, State of Law and Iraqiya headed into negotiations. But there was little trust between the two. State of Law continued to insist on Maliki as prime minister, and Iraqiya on Allawi.

I met up with Sami. He explained why Maliki insisted on remaining prime minister. Allawi was a secular, non-sectarian Shia and the post of prime minister had to be held by a Shia from a religious Shia party. The formation of the government was perceived as a battle between Iran and the US. Everyone realized this, except for the Americans. The Iranians were active, while the US did nothing. Qasim Suleimani, commander of the al-Quds Force, continued to summon Iraqis to Iran. The Iranians, he said, intended to drag out government formation until after 31 August (the end of US combat missions) in order to score a "victory" over the US.

The Iranians had indeed not been idle. For years, the Baathist regime in Syria had sought to undermine the new Iraqi government by allow-ing foreign fighters to use their country as a launching pad for horrific attacks in Iraq. In August 2009, coordinated attacks targeted the foreign ministry and the finance ministry in Baghdad, killing around a hundred Iraqis. Maliki had blamed the Syrian president, Bashar al-Assad, for the murders. Now the Iranians were pressuring Assad to drop his support for Allawi and to agree to another Maliki term. They had put huge pressure on the Supreme Council to agree to a second Maliki premiership. With the Sadrists, they sought to persuade them, through intermediaries from Lebanese Hezbollah, that Maliki would ensure there was no US military presence of any sort in Iraq after 2011, and that the Sadrists would get key posts in government. Qasim Suleimani's major objective was to ensure Iraq was not integrated into the Arab world—and that it became a close ally of Iran. Maliki would be able to achieve this because all the neighbouring Sunni Arab countries hated him. As for Talabani, he desperately wanted to remain as president, and Qasim Suleimani was determined to keep him there. Their relationship went back decades.

I went to see Rafi and Jaber and showed them the photograph of myself in an *abaya* at the Shrine of Hussein. "You are now *Hajiyya*," Jaber said, using the Arabic term for a female pilgrim. He told me that as a child he had regularly accompanied his mother from Ramadi with three sheep to sacrifice at the shrines of Abbas, Hussein and Ali. Would Sunnis from Anbar ever do this again in the future, I wondered?

The discussion quickly moved on to government formation. "Where is the US?" Rafi asked. He referred to previous US ambassadors, describing how they had helped to bring Iraqis together. "Does the US have no interest in protecting the democratic process? If the US acknowledged that Iraqiya won the elections and had the right to go first, the others would not have challenged it. Does the US not care what sort of government is put together? Qasim Suleimani is very active putting together the Shia coalition. Does the US not understand what impact this will have on the region—and on internal stability in Iraq? Is the US not worried about Iranian influence in Iraq?" "The US only seems to listen to Maliki and Dawa," he continued. When he spoke to people in the embassy it was clear they favoured Maliki above Allawi.

On 14 June 2010 the parliament was finally seated. We understood that the thirty-day period for selecting the Speaker had now begun. However, Maliki insisted it did not begin until the end of the first session, which was currently adjourned and on which there was no constitutional time limit.

ONE EVENING in late June, Maysoon Damluji collected me outside the embassy and we drove out of the Green Zone towards the Mansour district of Baghdad. Maysoon was a member of parliament and a spokeswoman for Iraqiya. She had invited me over to her house on a couple of occasions for dinner and a glass of wine. Elegant and good looking, staunchly secular and from a distinguished, well-to-to Sunni family of doctors and politicians, she had worked as an architect for years in London and had exquisite taste in art. She also kept a pet dog, *Mishmish*.

Mansour looked great. Cafes were doing business. Shops were open. Maysoon pointed out the place where Uday Hussein was nearly assassinated years back. We got stuck in traffic and the car came to a standstill. "Just like government formation," Maysoon joked.

It was my first visit to the Hunting Club. Maysoon told me her father had never let her go there. It had once been a favourite haunt of Baathists who had lowered the tone of the place with their rough tribal culture which the elite families of Baghdad looked down upon. That evening, there were lots of families. Some men were drinking whisky, others drinking coke. Some women had their hair flowing, others wore headscarves, a visible sign of Iraq's growing conservatism.

We found Abu Taha, one of the regulars at General Abadi's Thursday evening parties. Abu Taha took us to a table near the stage. An Iraqi band was playing traditional Arabic music: Iraqi songs, Egyptian songs, oldies that everyone knew and clapped along to. The only interruption was caused by the electricity giving out, plunging us into darkness and silence. Everyone complained that they still only received between two and eight hours of electricity a day.

Maysoon suggested that evening that I go with her on a trip to the city of Samarra, eighty miles north of Baghdad. A week or so later, we set off in the morning. "I would rather be killed than kidnapped, wouldn't you?" Maysoon said to me. I had to agree. So we decided to take a three-car convoy, ourselves in the armoured car along with her two bodyguards. Ayad Allawi called Maysoon just before we set out and warned us to be careful. There were still bad people around. But Samarra was "Iraqiya territory," so we should be okay, he said.

We drove through Mansour, and met up with Abu Taha. After about thirty minutes, we reached the edge of Baghdad and headed north on the highway to Samarra. On the outskirts of Samarra, we were stopped at a checkpoint. Following the bombing of the city's al-Askari Mosque by al-Qaeda in 2006, people from out of town required special permission to enter Samarra. We did not have that permission. But by good luck a federal policeman appeared who recognized Maysoon as a member of parliament. He gave us a warm welcome and escorted us through.

So into Samarra we went. On all previous visits, I had arrived by helicopter and been escorted by the US military. Now for the first time I was seeing Samarra as a normal visitor would. We drove over the Tigris and circled around the town, until we reached the ninth-century Great Mosque, which had been commissioned by the Abbasid caliph al-Mutawakkil. We climbed up the vast, spiralling, snail-shaped cone of the Malwiya minaret, which stands 170 feet high. We sat at the top, which had been damaged in 2005 by insurgents, and looked out over the town.

Once we had descended, we bade farewell to the federal police, who had escorted us on the visit. Back in the car, Maysoon told me one of the policeman had informed her that he was an Iraqiya supporter, as were the others. He claimed he had been denied promotion because of this. He was from Duluwiya, and Saddam had killed his father and brother.

Abu Taha took us to have lunch at the house of his friend, Abu Omar. Abu Taha and Abu Omar had been in the Communist party together. All the family were there and were delighted to have guests. "There is nothing more wonderful than having visitors," Abu Omar exclaimed. They recognized Maysoon, and proclaimed their support for Iraqiya and for Allawi as the next prime minister. "We want a prime minister who does not see Sunni or Shia. Iraqis are not a sectarian people. Maliki will put us through a hundred years of solitude," Abu Omar proclaimed, complaining that Maliki was isolating Iraq from its neighbours. His son Omar had been accepted at Basra University, but they had decided not to send him there because his name was so "Sunni-sounding" and instead were sending him to Damascus. Their second son was called Hussein, a typically Shia name, so he would have no problems in Basra. As we talked, we tucked into the Samarra *masgouf*, grilled carp. It was delicious. Abu Omar tried to convince us to stay the night with his family, but we needed to go home.

THROUGH MAYSOON, I met a charming seventy-year-old man from Haditha. Sa'di al-Hadithi was an expert on Iraqi folk music. Maysoon had invited us both to lunch at her place, and as the beer and wine flowed, he told me his story. He did not leave Iraq until he was thirty-seven, when he moved to the UK; but now he had returned to the country of his birth. While a student of English literature in Baghdad, he had associated with the Communist party. He had been detained and brought before a judge. The judge asked him, "What do you think of Mullah Mustafa Barzani? Was he a traitor?" Sa'di replied that he did not know him, so he could not say. The judge asked, "What do you think of Abd al-Karim Qasim? Was he a traitor?" Sa'di again replied that he did not know him, so could not say. The judge was furious, and sentenced him to fifteen years in jail for not denouncing them as traitors.

Sa'di was beaten up by "fifty people" before he arrived at his jail. He spent his years in prison reading a hundred pages a day. If he wasn't able to meet his target one day, he would wake up early the next day. In jail they organized themselves into different committees, as most were "political prisoners." And so this became his life. Then suddenly, after five years, they told him he could go, which came as a shock. He did not know why they detained him in the first place or why, five years later, he should be released.

IN JULY, Maliki's fortunes appeared to take a decisive turn for the worse: the Iraqi National Alliance sent him a letter requesting he withdraw his candidature for prime minister; Iraqiya made it clear they would offer him the speakership of the parliament or the presidency, but not the premiership; and the Kurds explained they really did not want to see him as prime minister for another four years.

General O and Hill met Maliki and told him frankly that he had little support from other groups, so it would be very hard for him to remain as prime minister. Maliki continued to insist that only he could do the job, only he could save Iraq. "I dream I am on a boat," he said. "I keep trying to pull Iraqis out of the water to save them."

The embassy informed UNAMI, Allawi and other Iraqi leaders that Maliki had no chance of remaining prime minister for a second term.

GENERAL O WENT BACK to Washington in mid July for more meetings. He phoned to tell me that Vice President Biden had agreed to give Maliki and Allawi a deadline. If they could not reach agreement within two weeks on how to form the government, they should both step aside and let others have a shot at it.

However, when Biden phoned up the two leaders, he did not stick to the agreed line. Instead, he told Maliki that the US would support him remaining as prime minister, and he told Allawi that he should accept Maliki as prime minister. The US administration wanted to see an Iraqi government in place before the US mid-term elections in November. Maintaining the status quo seemed the quickest path.

The Arabic media provided wide coverage of what was described as the "US proposal" to keep Maliki as prime minister, and Allawi as president—or secretary general of a yet-to-be-created new security council. There was confusion as to why the US and Iran should both choose Maliki as prime minister, and this was fuelling conspiracy theories about a secret deal between those two countries.

After receiving the phone call from Biden, Allawi had called for a meeting of Iraqiya's leaders. When I met Rafi, he was incredulous: "How come one week the US was telling everyone that Maliki should step down and the next week telling Maliki he should be PM?" He went on, "Why is the US picking the prime minister? This is Iraq. This is our country. We have to live here. And we care passionately about building a future for our children." He was deeply upset. If Iraqiya was going to lose, it would rather lose to the Supreme Council, with Adel Abdul Mahdi as prime minister. There was no way that Iraqiya would accept Maliki as prime minister again. Jaber pressed me: "Either the Americans are stupid," he said, "or there is a secret deal with Iran."

Maliki dug in, and launched another attack. This time, he accused Rafi of being the leader of a Sunni militia, Hamas al-Iraq. He presented a file of evidence to General O. General O instructed his intelligence officers to go through the accusations. They were baseless. Breaking with normal practice, General O wrote a letter to Maliki stating there was no connection between Rafi and al-Qaeda or Hamas al-Iraq. When General O met Maliki, Maliki showed him a large file of "confessions" and "intelligence" from secret informants. He said he wanted Rafi to step down from his role as chief negotiator for Iraqiya. In a matter of weeks, Iraqiya leaders had moved from celebrating their election victory, to struggling for their own political survival.

Over a drink one evening, Clarisse Pásztory, a long-serving political adviser to the European Union in Iraq, told me why she thought the US analysis and approach had been so wrong. The US had engaged too late, and then had been in too much of a hurry to see a government in place. The US claimed the State of Law Coalition was less influenced by Iran than the other Shia parties, when in fact it was actually Ammar al-Hakim, the leader of the Supreme Council, and Muqtada al-Sadr who were standing up to Iran, not least in their refusal to support Maliki. The US argued that Iraq needed a strong prime minister and there was no one but Maliki. The political leaders, in contrast, did not want a strongman—they wanted anyone but Maliki.

The US, Clarisse continued, had ignored Iraqiya and did not believe it was significant. But they underestimated the support for Iraqiya and the popularity of Allawi far beyond his bloc; he was seen as the man who won the elections. She showed me an opinion poll conducted by the National Democratic Institute: 59 per cent believed Iraqiya should have first opportunity to form the government. Since the elections, support for Maliki had continued to drop. He was seen to be clinging on to power; only 14 per cent believed that he should be the next prime minister. Support for Allawi continued to rise, with 42 per cent now supporting him as the next prime minister. Finally, she said, the US was insisting the Sadrists be excluded from government formation. But the Sadrists were not Iranian agents. They were anti-occupation, not anti-West.

Christopher Hill left at the beginning of August and a few weeks later Jim Jeffrey took over as ambassador. Overnight the atmosphere improved and the feuding between the military and the embassy ceased. But it was too late. The damage had been done. By coming out in support of Maliki, the US had lost its ability to broker an agreement among Iraq's leaders.

And Iraqi elites were further apart than ever. I observed a meeting of the Iraqiya and State of Law negotiating teams. In the meeting, Hassan Sneid of Dawa, removed his shoes and bared the soles of his feet, revealing the scars of torture from decades ago. It was an extremely provocative gesture, implying that the Iraqiya team, which included the religious

Shia member Mohamad Allawi, were all Baathists responsible for what had happened to him. The room erupted. Mohamad Tamim, the Iraqiya member from Kirkuk, jumped to his feet shouting, "We did not do this to you!" It was awful. The meeting broke down in disarray.

VICE PRESIDENT BIDEN visited at the end of August 2010. Jim Jeffrey and General O met Biden before his meetings with the Iraqi leaders. In the internal meetings, a US official argued that Maliki was "our man," he would give us a follow-on SOFA, he was a nationalist and he would fight the Sadrists. Furthermore, he claimed Maliki had promised him that he would not seek a third term. "Maliki is not our friend," exhorted Jeff Feltman, the assistant secretary of state for Near Eastern Affairs, exasperated at the delusional nature of the discussion. But Biden had been persuaded by the arguments that there was no one but Maliki who could be prime minister and that he would sign a new security agreement with the US to keep a small contingent of US forces in Iraq after 2011. Biden believed the quickest way to form a government was to keep Maliki as prime minister, and to cajole other Iraqis into accepting this.

"Iraqiya genuinely fear Maliki," General O explained. They were scared he would accuse them of being terrorists or bring charges of corruption against them, and would arrest them. "We have seen him go after Rafi." General O described how Maliki had changed so much over the past six months. He had become more sectarian and authoritarian. Iraqis had reason to fear him.

Biden's adviser, Herro Mustafa, who had worked closely with General Petraeus in Nineveh back in 2003, brought me into the conversation. I tried to explain the struggle between secularists and Islamists, and how many Iraqis wanted to move beyond sectarianism. But Biden could not fathom this. For him, Iraq was simply about Sunnis, Shia and Kurds.

I tried another tack: "It is important to build belief in the democratic process by showing people that change can come about through elections, rather than violence. The peaceful transfer of power is key—it has never happened in the Arab world." At the very least, either Maliki or Talabani needed to give up their seat, otherwise they would think they owned them. However, Biden did not agree. He responded that there

Vice President Biden talks to Prime Minister Maliki, with Mike Juaidi translating. *Photo by the Office of the Iraqi Prime Minister*

were often elections in the US that did not bring about any change. Here I was, sitting in on the high-level policy discussion that would perhaps determine the outcome of the Iraq war, but none of my arguments made the vice president reconsider his decision.

Biden's easy smile had evaporated. He was clearly irritated by me. "Look, I know these people," he went on. "My grandfather was Irish and hated the British. It's like in the Balkans. They all grow up hating each other."

The conversation ended as we had to head over to the meeting with Iraqiya at Rafi's house. Allawi had gathered a dozen or so Iraqiya members. Some were in suits, others were wearing their finest traditional robes. There were Sunni Arabs, Shia Arabs, Turkmen Shia, Kurds and a Christian. The full tapestry of Iraqi society was sitting facing us, distinguishable only by their dress, clearly showing us the sort of Iraq they wanted to live in.

Biden started off smiling: "I know you people, my grandfather was Irish and hated the British." Everyone turned towards me. The Iraqis were grinning, expecting there was going to be a good spat between Brits and Americans. How could I stop Biden making a totally inappropriate comment about them all being Shia-hating Sunnis? Thinking on my feet, I said, "Don't look at me, Mr. Vice President, I am not the only Brit in the room." One of the Iraqis piped up, "I have a British passport."

Biden lost his train of thought and moved on. He said Al Gore had technically won more votes in 2000, but for the good of America had stepped back rather than keep the country in limbo while contesting the disputed vote-count. I couldn't help but wonder how different the world might be if the Florida votes had been counted and Al Gore had become president. For starters, we would not be in Iraq.

Allawi pretended not to understand that Biden was suggesting he give up his claim to have first go at trying to form the government, letting Maliki remain as prime minister. The meeting finished. After we left, I was sure the Iraqis would be wondering why on earth Biden had mentioned his Irish grandfather and Al Gore. Biden was a nice man, but he simply had the wrong instincts on Iraq. If only Obama had paid attention to Iraq. He, more than anyone, would understand the complexity of identities, and how people can change. But his only interest in Iraq was in ending the war.

GENERAL O AND I PREPARED to leave Iraq. I had left the country euphoric after the Surge. But this time I felt sad, angry and very afraid for Iraq's future. Washington had reneged on the promises it had made to Iraqis to protect the political process and it had betrayed the very principles the US military believed it was fighting to uphold. Instead, it had reverted to supporting the status quo rather than reform. But this was a status quo which was not tenable.

With the end of combat operations on 31 August 2010, General Austin would take over command of the remaining fifty thousand troops. There were many farewells to say and we did the rounds of all the Iraqi leaders. They all thanked General O for his efforts and wished him the best for the future.

I went to see Dr. Basima, who was a newly elected member of parliament. She was as blunt as ever: "The British are remembered for building roads and bridges which are still in operation today over a century later. But the Americans will be remembered for blowing things up and creating orphans and widows." She paused, before shaking her head and saying sadly, "The Americans missed all the opportunities." As she kissed me goodbye, her parting words were, "Promise me you will stay in touch—and let me know if you find a husband."

I also went to see Sheikh Anwar al-Assi, the paramount sheikh of the Obeidi tribe, who was visiting his younger brother Sheikh Wasfi in Baghdad. We chatted for a while before he looked me directly in the eye and asked, "Do you leave Iraq with a clear conscience?" I held his gaze. Iraqis were always so quick to criticize us, but were rarely willing to take responsibility for their own actions. "Our intervention caused so much death and destruction, and we have to live with that knowledge for the rest of our lives." Sheikh Anwar nodded vigorously in agreement. I went on, "But I hope that Iraqis will have a better future."

"How on earth can that be possible," Sheikh Anwar responded, "with the people that America put in charge of this country?" He continued, "You know, when we first met you back in 2003, we wanted to kill you. Now we think of you as a relative!"

"Sheikh Anwar," I exclaimed, "I thought we had always been friends!" His whole body convulsed in giggles.

"You must write a book," Sheikh Anwar encouraged me. "Do not cover up what happened. Reveal the truth about Iraqis. Write about us as people, about our hopes and dreams. Do not let us be defined by violence." There were tears in both our eyes when we shook hands.

One farewell was particularly poignant. An Iraqi general, whom I did not know, turned up at General O's office to present him with a picture frame. In it were two photos: one of General O and the other of the Iraqi general's two teenage boys. The teenagers were smiling, wearing soccer shirts in the colours of their favourite European team. One of the boys had got into difficulty swimming in a lake and the other had swum out to rescue him. They had both drowned. Tears poured down my face as the Iraqi general recounted the story. I had witnessed so much violence and horror in Iraq, yet this tragedy of two soccer-loving brothers drowning in an accident got underneath the defences I had developed to protect myself. There was no one to be angry at, no one to blame, no one to seek revenge against. The Iraqi general simply wanted to thank General O for showing him compassion and providing him with housing after the incident.

General Nasier Abadi threw a farewell party for General O and me in his garden, inviting many Iraqi friends and members of the diplomatic community. He was a wonderful host, as ever. I had recently travelled to Musaib to spend a weekend with him at his farm on the Euphrates. General Abadi called me to stand up at the front. He gave me a beautiful necklace and then read out a poem he had written:

> The ray of the sun gives us light
> The ray of the moon gives us charm,
> but when the Ray of Odierno relocates
> so will the ray of Emma from the Iraqi Sky . . .

WE WERE SEATED on his porch overlooking the lake at Camp Victory. General O was smoking a cigar. He had asked me to comment on his draft change-of-command speech. I noted that he may have worked with 2 corps, 24 divisions, 211 brigades, 1,000 battalions, but he had only had one POLAD. General O responded that that was why he suffered from post traumatic stress disorder. "Sir, you suffered from PTSD long before you ever went to war!"

We sat for a while in silence. "You made me a better general," he said. It was the greatest compliment he had ever paid me.

"You changed my life, sir. I can never thank you enough for the opportunities you gave me."

"What are you going to do when it is all over? I've never asked you this but are you going to get married? Have kids?"

"I think I've left it a bit late, sir," I replied, somewhat uncomfortable to be having this conversation with him. "I don't think that will happen for me." I went on, "When guys come back from war, they can sit in bars and impress girls with their stories. It's a bit different for women. No guy is going to want to hear my war stories about jumping on and off helicopters, being shot at."

"That might make any man feel inadequate," General O agreed.

General O was off to be commander of Joint Forces Command, where his task would be to close down the headquarters. He was getting a reputation as a "closer"! He had been told it would just be for a year, a holding job, until one of the big jobs came up. He asked me what I was going to do next.

"I honestly don't know, sir." He was being all paternal. "But don't worry about me, I'll find something to do. Something will turn up." I continued, "But first I need to find myself again, who I am, away from Iraq, away from being defined as your POLAD . . ."

We reminisced about our time together. Many Iraqis had told me how much they liked and trusted General O because he genuinely cared.

General O presented me with another photo album of our time together in Iraq, inscribed to his "consigliere" and "great friend," and thanking me for my dedication to him over the years.

"One day, I will write the story of this war," I told him. "It is an Iraqi story. It is an American story. It is my story." We had tried so hard. There was nothing I had done before—nor would ever do again—that would make me feel more proud. I had walked with a giant.

It was hard to let go. Robert E. Lee once said, "It is well that war is so terrible, otherwise we should grow too fond of it." But I was running on empty. It was as if everything I had ever learned, every experience of my life, had been in preparation for serving in Iraq during this tumultuous period. But by the end there was nothing left. I was exhausted. After years of trying to make the world a better place, I needed to understand it better.

General O had gone as far as he could to try to get the US administration to engage more, to uphold the election results, and to try to broker the formation of the Iraqi government through an agreement among the leaders. He had warned of the authoritarian tendencies of Maliki. He had campaigned at the highest level in person, and written countless reports. "I gave my best military advice," he said. But he had been ignored.

THE CHANGE-OF-COMMAND ceremony took place at al-Faw Palace on 31 August. Senior military commanders gathered for the occasion, along with members of the diplomatic community and Iraqi officials. The band played the military tunes which were now so familiar. And I sang along to the army song "The Army Goes Rolling Along" for the final time. General O stood and delivered his farewell speech with great passion. He spoke of the selfless service of the men and women in uniform, who worked so long and hard, through such adversity, to help a foreign people in a foreign land build a better future for themselves. He ended his speech with "Lion 6 out."

A long line had gathered to shake General O's hand and say goodbye. I hung around saying my farewells to the military men who had made me feel so much one of their band of brothers. Many thanked me for my service—and for looking after General O.

When I was done, I caught General O's eye, saluted him and walked out of al-Faw Palace for the last time.

PART IV

AFTERMATH

JANUARY 2012–JULY 2014

20

THINGS FALL APART

It's harder to end a war than begin one. Indeed, everything that American troops have done in Iraq—all the fighting and all the dying, the bleeding and the building, and the training and the part-nering—all of it has led to this moment of success. . . . we're leaving behind a sovereign, stable and self-reliant Iraq, with a representative government that was elected by its people.

—PRESIDENT OBAMA, Fort Bragg, 14 December 2011

I FLEW INTO Erbil's new international airport on 1 January 2012 and did not recognize where I was. For years, Kurdish friends had described their plans for the airport and taken me to see the site. Now they had done it! A new sixteen-gate facility, with one of the world's longest runways and a capacity of up to three million passengers a year. The service was superb. My details were registered in the computer. "Welcome to Iraq," the passport controller said to me. "We see from our records that this is your first visit to Iraq." I smiled.

Sitting in my luxury suite at the five-star Rotana Hotel in Erbil, which the KRG had booked for me, I sent out text messages to Iraqi friends wishing them a happy new year. Nuri al-Maliki, still the prime minister, was also sending out texts marking the withdrawal of all US forces from Iraq, saying, "All of us support the glory of Iraq and pride in our nation. I congratulate you and the Iraqi people on this historic day." CNN reported that the Iraqi government was calling it "Fulfillment Day," while certain armed groups were referring to it as "Victory Over America Day."

In a number of conversations, Kurds told me Iran had succeeded in driving US forces out of Iraq, and that even before the last soldier had departed, Maliki had launched a political coup aimed at crushing Iraqiya.

345

In the wake of the withdrawal of all US forces at the end of 2011, and on the plane back from his meeting with Obama in the White House, Maliki had instigated a warrant against Vice President Tareq al-Hashimi on charges of terrorism. Hashimi had fled to Kurdistan, then to Turkey. His bodyguards had given televised "confessions" and at least one had died in custody.

After General O and I left Iraq at the end of August 2010, Iran had succeeded in pressuring Muqtada al-Sadr to accept a second Maliki term as prime minister and hence ensured there would be no follow-on security agreement for a post-2011 US troop presence. The US helped hammer out a power-sharing agreement of sorts in Erbil but it was never implemented. In addition to being commander-in-chief of the armed forces, Maliki was now acting minister of interior, minister of defence, minister of national state security and national security adviser. Maliki had also reached a deal with Qais Khazali, head of the Iranian-backed militia, Asaib Ahl al-Haqq, which had kidnapped and murdered the US soldiers in Karbala and the British hostages.

A Kurdish official asked me, "Why does the United States keep calling Iraq a democracy, when it is heading back to dictatorship? Why does the United States pressure politicians to support Maliki and blame Iraqiya for the crisis? Why does America supply Maliki with F-16s that he may one day use against the Kurdish people?" The US appeared to be strengthening Maliki's regime rather than the Iraqi state. The Kurds had openly called for US forces to remain in Iraq. At every possible occasion, Kurds thanked Americans for their freedom and even invited American military families who lost children while serving in Iraq to visit, so that they could thank them for their sacrifices. But Kurds now viewed the United States as in decline, and regional powers as on the rise. They nervously watched the battle for influence between Turkey and Iran, the successors of the old Ottoman and Safavid (Persian) empires, and debated whether to remain neutral or take sides.

I flew to Baghdad where I linked up with Safa al-Sheikh and some of his friends and we headed south. Our destination was the Marshes, which Saddam had drained after his brutal crushing of the 1991 uprising to prevent rebels taking refuge there. Since 2003, there had been efforts to restore the Marshes, and we wanted to take a look. We spent a wonderful week boating on the Euphrates and the Tigris, visiting the location of the Garden of Eden, and the birthplace of Abraham.

In the car on the journey back to Baghdad, I discussed the political crisis facing the country with my companions, all of whom were Shia. They were pleased with Maliki's crackdown on "Baathists" and "terrorists," but were concerned at rising sectarianism. While Kurds and Sunnis claimed it was Iran that had pushed the Americans out of Iraq, the Shia took credit for it themselves.

Maliki, they said, was viewed as a strong and capable prime minister who would bring stability to the country, not dictatorship. They said that Sunnis would never accept Shia rule in Iraq and were constantly scheming how to overthrow the Shia and grab power. First they had tried insurgency. Then they tried elections in 2010. And now they were trying federalism. Even though the Shia were the majority in Iraq, the Sunnis had the support of all the Sunni countries and even the Western media. The Shia feared Saudi Arabia and Turkey were plotting to overthrow the Shia regimes in Syria and Iraq. Saudi Arabia was blamed for propagating vitriolic propaganda against Shia and supporting jihadi fighters.

It was gone midnight by the time we reached Baghdad and I was tired. As we entered the Green Zone, I noted the Shia religious symbols displayed at the checkpoint. I had wanted to stay with General Nasier Abadi but he had been forced to retire from the military, suspected of being too close to the Americans and had left the country. Instead Rafi Issawi, now the minister of finance, had invited me to stay with him. But when we reached Rafi's road we found a tank was blocking it, with the gun turret pointing at Rafi's house. It would not let us pass. I was furious, and got out of the car and paced around in front of the tank. "Safa, what does this tank think its mission is?" I said through the car door. Safa looked embarrassed. "Please get back in the car," he begged. I climbed back in the vehicle. "I can understand why the Iraqiya leaders have been complaining," Safa acknowledged.

There was also a tank, Safa told me, outside Salah Mutlak's house. Mutlak, as part of the deal finally brokered at the end of 2010 to form the government, had been given the post of deputy prime minister. Although he had been barred from participating in the elections through de-Baathification, he had returned to Iraq to take up his new post. But at the end of last year, Mutlak, tired of Obama's glowing praise of Iraq's democracy, had accused Maliki in the media of being a dictator. Maliki had sacked him.

"Why don't you come and stay at my house?" Safa offered. "Thank you, Safa. But Rafi invited me. They have prepared dinner for me, and are waiting for me inside." I had been texting back and forth with Rafi. "There must be something you can do," I urged Safa. He was the acting national security adviser. Safa climbed out the car and phoned General Farouq al-Araji, Dr. Basima's nemesis and the head of the OCINC, and explained the situation. He then passed his phone to the tank commander so that Farouq could give him the order to let us pass. Safa deposited me at Rafi's door before driving back to his own home. Rafi and Jaber welcomed me warmly. They calmed me down, as we sat in the kitchen eating the stone-cold kebab. Rafi's brother was there too. He was an Iraqi general but had just been forced to retire.

We stayed up late chatting around the kitchen table. Rafi and Jaber told me Maliki was pushing the Sunnis to the breaking point with his threats against their leaders, arrests of "Baathists," use of force against those calling for federalism and dismissal or "retirement" of army officers. They warned that Iraqiya politicians would not be able to control the street for much longer. They feared Maliki's policies were pushing Iraq toward civil war again. Jaber asked me, "Why did America give Iraq to Iran? Everything in Iraq is now controlled by Iran." Rafi shook his head. "How could America leave Iraq in such a state?"

I FLEW BACK to Iraq six months later to visit Kirkuk. I gazed out of the taxi window at the houses that had sprung up on either side of the road from Sulaymaniyah to Kirkuk. Concrete blocks had been planted willy-nilly, some painted in outrageous pinks and purples. Kurds had come down from the mountains, and were busy building in the valleys. The road itself was newly paved with white lines marking a double carriageway. "Is this Qaranjir?" I asked the Kurdish taxi driver, who was able to speak Arabic. He confirmed the thriving town we drove through was indeed the village that Saddam had razed to the ground in the eighties.

At the gates of the city, I bid farewell to my taxi driver, and transferred to the car of the three Kurdish peshmerga who had been sent to collect me. We drove into the city, passing the burning flares of gas that illuminated the desert landscape. Once more I smelt Kirkuk, and felt the tingling sensation on my lips from the petrochemicals. We skirted the airfield, where the US military had been based, passing the Quria police station. And then we turned left towards the government building, where I had set up my office back in 2003. It was nine years to the day that I had survived a rocket attack.

We pulled up at the house of Ismail Hadidi, parked the car and then walked over to his office. Ismail, a Sunni Arab, had served as the deputy governor of the province and now headed a local political party, Kirkuk Is Our Home. Someone had run ahead to let him know I was on my way, so he was standing at the entrance of his office laughing and shouting out, "*Salaam aleikum, ya Emmasky.*" (Peace be upon you). "*Aleikum salaam, ya Ismail,*" I responded (Upon you be peace). We shook hands and kissed on both cheeks. Ismail had not changed. His well-worn face and friendly demeanour were as I remembered. Ismail kept repeating, "*Ahlan wa sahlan, Emmasky,*" the familiar Arab greeting of welcome—"You have found family and flat land"—as he led me inside, pointing to the guest of honour's seat at the head of the room.

I sat down to Ismail's right and declared out loud, "*Allah bil kheir.*" "*Allah bil kheir,*" responded the other guests seated along both sides of the room. While I drank a cup of sweet tea and a small carton of mineral water, Ismail introduced me in the most exalted terms as an old friend, who had worked hard with the Coalition forces to try to resolve the problems of the province following the fall of the former regime, during a period which was "difficult" and "not natural." I nodded, thinking back to the many times Ismail had braved flying bullets to calm down tensions in the province—a natural mediator and moderator during a period of intense friction. I thanked Ismail for the warm reception, and said I was very happy to be visiting Kirkuk as a tourist and seeing old friends.

Ismail went around the room, allowing each of his visitors to introduce themselves. They did so, taking the opportunity to lay out the concerns that had brought them to his office. One had no money for his NGO and was looking for funds. Another represented the interests of citizens who had lost their 1957 identity cards, which were needed as proof of family roots in Kirkuk. Another represented the *wafideen*, Arabs who had given up their homes in the south and moved to Kirkuk for 10,000 dinars as part of the Baath party's Arabization programme.

"In Europe, you can become a citizen after four years," one sheikh announced. "I have lived in Kirkuk for thirty years. I know no other home. Why should I be forced to leave?" I responded, "So you are the new Sheikh Agar!" referring to the Provincial Council member who had been assassinated back in 2004 for standing up for the rights of the *wafideen*. Ismail clapped his hands with glee. "You see, she knows everything about us," he remarked to the group. "Yes, this man is the new Sheikh Agar!" I politely listened and wished them all well but offered no advice. I was no longer responsible for helping them find solutions to their problems.

At my request, Ismail gave me a tour of Kirkuk. We walked through the market, passing stalls selling caged birds. There were pigeons and hawks, as well as exotic birds apparently imported from Germany. Bird-keeping was a popular hobby for Iraqi men. I pointed out the pink, green and blue chicks, chuckling to myself, remembering how I had first come across multi-coloured chickens at Barham Salih's house back in 2003. We climbed up to Kirkuk's citadel. It had been beautified since my last visit, with green spaces set aside for adults to sit and children to play. We entered the double-domed shrine that housed the tomb of the Prophet Daniel. Kirkuk, like many parts of Iraq, had once had a flourishing Jewish community. As we left, Ismail handed a wad of money to the caretaker. "Tell everyone it is from Emmasky," he instructed. Back in 2003, we had handed out money, telling people it was from the Iraqi government.

After the meeting, Ismail Hadidi drove me over to the house of Sheikh Ghassan al-Assi in Hawija, south-west of Kirkuk city. We pulled up outside the house. Hearing our car, Sheikh Ghassan came to the door dressed as always in his long white *dishdasha* and black-chequered head-dress. He was trying to hold back his grin. "Hello, Miss Emma, welcome, Miss Emma!" We were now both smiling broadly at each other as we shook hands. His younger brother Sheikh Burhan appeared, giggling and shaking his head from side to side. We entered the house and Sheikh Ghassan gestured at a place for me to sit on the green couch. I looked around at the high ceilings and chandeliers, and the familiar photo of his father who had been the paramount sheikh of the Obeidi tribe. Once everyone was seated and drinks brought in, Ghassan sat down on my left. Soon, he and I were in deep conversation. He looked well and relaxed.

Ghassan complained that the government could not deliver anything. "They are useless people," he said. "They are stealing Iraq's money. They don't do anything for the people. Iraq has bad leaders. Iraq needs a strong leader to unite the country and to hold it together. There are many good Iraqis outside the country." He explained further, "I do not mean Baathists, but good, talented, skilled Iraqis."

Sheikh Burhan wanted to join in the conversation so we switched from English to Arabic. Ghassan told me he stayed out of politics and left it all to Burhan, who had replaced him as a member of the Kirkuk Provincial Council. Burhan asked me if I still worked with the US Army. "No," I told him, "I am now a university lecturer." "Wow wow wow, a professor!" he exclaimed, impressed like all Iraqis by educational achievement. I told him I remained in contact with American soldiers, and that they missed Iraq. *"They miss Iraq?"* He asked incredulously, his eyes widening. "Yes, they miss the country and the people," I responded. "They want to come back and see you." *"No, no, no, no!"* He laughed, wagging his finger at me. "We do not want them back here. It is much better without them!"

It was not the time or place to try to explain the influence Iraq had had on the lives of so many American soldiers who served there. A few weeks earlier, I had been invited to Fort Leavenworth in Kansas to help with the review of the counter-insurgency manual. "Should we not examine why we did not win?" I suggested. "Was it due to lack of overall strategy, or wrong tactics, or poor leadership?" But they were not ready to consider these questions. I noticed that a number of officers, after shaking my hand, crossed their hand over their heart, a mannerism they had picked up from Iraqis. Several asked me if I had news about specific Iraqis they had grown close to. One young officer had taken me to his house to show me the family tree of the Zobai tribe, and had proceeded to talk about the different members as if they were his own relatives. Some acknowledged how much they missed the sense of purpose and mission they had felt in Iraq and guiltily confessed that nothing about life back in the US could match it. They had come to Iraq to transform it; and yet departed having themselves been permanently changed by the encounter.

Ghassan asked for news of Colonel Mayville. "He was the best of them all," he said. The others muttered their agreement. I explained that he was now Major General Mayville and was in Afghanistan, commanding a division. "And how is General Odierno?" asked Ghassan. I responded, "He is now chief of staff of the US Army and is based in Washington. I saw him recently; he is doing very well." I teased Ghassan, "So you do like Americans." Ghassan explained that he liked them as individuals, but he did not like what they had done to Iraq nor the foreign policy America pursued.

"Nothing good came from America. They are an uncivilized people. They disrespect Arabs, not only in Iraq but across the whole region. And, furthermore," Sheikh Ghassan went on, "they have a secret deal with Iran, an under-the-table deal." He put his hand under the table to emphasize his point. "They handed Iraq to Iran on a silver platter."

Warming to his theme, Sheikh Ghassan told me, "The Arab Spring is all part of a Western plot to humiliate the Arabs, divide the region and keep it weak. It is shameful. Now look at the problems the US is trying to stir up in Syria." I picked up a cushion and hit him around the shoulders and head. The others roared with laughter as he fended off my attacks. Sheikh Ghassan made some more sarcastic comments about Western conspiracies and this time I punched his arm. Everyone cackled. They were enjoying themselves.

Media brought the "Arab Spring" into everyone's houses and there was much confusion about what was happening in the region. The failure of Arab states to open up political systems, to develop inclusive institutions and to generate employment opportunities was only too apparent as increasing numbers of young people took to the streets to voice their complaints. The protests in Syria, as elsewhere, had initially been about dignity and jobs. But Bashar al-Assad proved unwilling or incapable of dealing with the grievances and had instead declared war on his people. The peaceful protests had turned violent.

While we chatted, two of Ghassan's sons brought in the food and laid it on a plastic sheet on the ground. We moved across the room and sat cross-legged on the floor in front of large circular plates laden with rice and sheep. On smaller plates there was salad. Sheikh Ghassan tore off the tastiest portions of meat with his fingers and laid them before me. I happily broke off pieces of bread, parceling up meat and rice and scooping it into my mouth. The sheikhs looked on approvingly as I tucked into the food. I was very hungry.

Eventually Sheikh Ghassan and I took a stroll outside. "You must come back and visit us again, Miss Emma," Sheikh Ghassan said as I departed.

In the car, I reflected back to when I had seen General Odierno at a conference in London the previous month. We had chatted for hours over gin and tonics at the Royal Horseguards Hotel, slipping back quickly into the familiar banter that had developed between us after years together at war. He looked so different dressed in civilian clothes. "Have you started writing about us yet?" General O asked. "You know, when I was appointed Corps commander for the Surge in 2006, you were the first person I wanted on my team." I responded, "Sir, you were the only person I would have gone back to Iraq for." And then to lighten the moment, I continued, "I was worried you would raze the country to the ground like Genghis Khan!" We both laughed.

I had described my experience of testifying before the Iraq Inquiry. "My association with you, sir, has me branded a war criminal. It is you who should be in the dock testifying at the Nuremberg trials, not me!" I joked. Always quick to respond to my jibes, General O said, "Emma, I will tell them I was merely following the advice of my political adviser!" Later that evening, I had taken him on a stroll up Whitehall, and down the Mall to Buckingham Palace. It was just days after the celebrations of the Queen's Diamond Jubilee. I described to him how Brits had slept out in the streets in order to glimpse the Queen as she passed by in her carriage the next day. I had thought that flag-waving jingoism was so American. I had been surprised at the outpouring of nationalist fervour in the UK.

We arrived at the home of Abdul-Rahman Mustafa in Kirkuk city. I entered his house and immediately noted that it was old, modest and full of books. He appeared from a different room, smiling warmly as he shook my hand. "You look so well," I told him, "so much younger!" He chuckled. He had served as Kirkuk's governor for eight years but had been relaxing ever since his retirement two years ago. We caught up on each other's news, and then reflected on the time we had worked together in Kirkuk after the toppling of Saddam. We both laughed as we recalled what a crazy period it had been.

I noted that back in 2003 there had been fear that civil war in Iraq would begin in Kirkuk. I asked Abdul-Rahman for his explanation as to why, when the civil war did break out, Kirkuk had remained unaffected. "Social relations between Kirkukis of different backgrounds were very strong," he said. "It was not like Baghdad where people did not know each other so well. The political parties in Kirkuk were not as irresponsible as the Shia ones in Baghdad. And although there are Sunni and Shia in Kirkuk, there had never been any Sunni-Shia issues."

"Unfortunately, the Americans made so many mistakes in Iraq," he said, shaking his head. "They should never have deployed their forces across the country—they took over the running of everything, the day-to-day lives of Iraqis. They should have withdrawn to bases immediately, leaving Iraqis to run their own affairs. Then they should not have tried to transplant Western democracy to Iraq. It is not possible. Iraq is not a democracy. Change takes time. There are no democrats in Iraq. The new Shia leaders are very weak and inexperienced."

I asked Abdul-Rahman how he saw the prospects for Iraq's future. "The curse of Iraq," he replied, "is its oil money. Iraq has too much money. And this makes people lazy and increases unemployment. Despite all the resources, nothing gets done. Iraq is still going backwards. It is hard to see how the country will remain unified with such politicians in power. Iraq has good people but bad politicians."

IN JULY 2014, I was back once more at the Rotana Hotel in Erbil. It was packed with Iraqis. I observed politicians sitting together in small huddles late into the night, lamenting how Maliki was destroying the country and how the Iranians controlled the government. Many were familiar faces, and wanted to talk to me about the current situation and to introduce me to spokesmen of insurgent groups.

"This is a popular uprising," a man with a big, black Baathist moustache declared to me. He explained how the Sunnis had protested peacefully for a year, demanding an end to discrimination and the release of detainees. "But the government refused to listen to our demands and responded with violence against the peaceful demonstrators, first in Hawija, then in Falluja. We had no choice. We were forced to take up arms against the government." The others sat around nodding, looking at the man from Salah al-Din province with respect. "Maliki wants to carry out genocide against the Sunnis," he claimed. "He calls all Sunnis terrorists."

The conflict in Syria seemed to be re-enforcing sectarian narratives in Iraq. I asked him about the Islamic State—the Islamic State of Iraq and al-Sham (ISIS) or Da'ash, as it was called in Arabic—the successor to al-Qaeda in Iraq, which had taken control of a third of Iraq. "Da'ash is only around eight per cent of the insurgency," he said, as if quoting some scientific research. "But they have a big media image. For now, we allow them to be out at the front. We don't want to show our faces." He went on, "We will fight alongside Da'ash until we have overthrown Maliki— and then we will get rid of Da'ash."

I told them they were deluding themselves if they thought they could use the fanatical Islamic State against Maliki and then defeat it afterwards. The Baathists were fighting for power within Iraq whereas the Islamic State disputed the very legitimacy of Iraq as a state. Had they not seen what had happened in Syria? Among the Syrian rebels, it was the most extreme Salafi (fundamentalist) groups which had attracted funding and recruits and were wiping out others.

"Iraqis," I responded, "are good at coming together against someone they don't like. The 'moustaches' and the 'beards' have come together against Maliki," I noted, referring to the Baathists and the Islamists. "But what is your vision for the future, once Maliki is gone? What is the vision that you have for Iraq?" The Baathist could not answer. The man next to him interrupted with complaints about the Iranians and the Shia militia. I looked around at the group, but no one could articulate a strategy for creating a better future. I made my excuses and withdrew.

A former senior Iraqi government official came up to speak to me. He gave me a book of photos he had compiled during his time in the Ministry of Education. I flicked through it: images of him addressing the needs of ordinary Iraqis, working with American soldiers and civilians. It covered what now appeared to be the "golden era" of 2007–09, that brief period when we, and they, dared hope that Iraq was on the path to a brighter future.

I MET KEMAL KIRKUKI in his modest office in Erbil. He was no longer Speaker of the Kurdistan parliament, but remained part of the KDP polit-buro and close to President Barzani. "Hello, Emmasky!" he said warmly, shaking my hand. He steered me to a seat and provided me with a bottle of water, even though he himself was fasting as it was Ramadan.

Kemal sat down. I had never seen him look so happy or relaxed in the decade I had known him. "Kemal, you are grinning from ear to ear!"

"Yes," he replied. "We have Kirkuk!" I smiled back without respond-ing. Did he really believe the borders of Kurdistan were now fixed? For years, we had mediated between the different parties in these disputed territories. Now a new reality had been imposed. But how long would it last?

The Iraqi security forces had quickly disintegrated in June in Mosul in the face of the advance of the Islamic State. Although they far outnum-bered the Islamic State and had been better equipped, they were poorly led. There was no official chain of command through the Ministry of Defence. Instead, Maliki and his Office of the Commander-in-Chief gave instructions by phone call and text. Maliki had replaced competent of-ficers with people loyal to himself. Corruption was rife. Some had taken the funds meant to buy food for their soldiers. None gave orders to their forces to fight. The Islamic State had taken possession of all the equip-ment the US had supplied the Iraqi Army.

And the Kurds had taken advantage of the situation, deploying their peshmerga forces into the disputed territories. President Barzani an-nounced that Article 140 had now been implemented, and that the Kurds would never give up Kirkuk.

"Barzani did not want Maliki to remain prime minister in 2010. You knew that," Kemal recounted. He did not need to remind me. I remem-bered only too well the discussions. "Barzani told the Americans that Maliki is a very dangerous man who would destroy the country."

"Maliki is a very bad man," Kemal stressed. "He has brought about the destruction of Iraq." Kemal paused for a moment as he pondered how to phrase his next sentence. "But in my heart I am happy with Maliki because it is thanks to him that we Kurds will get our independence." Barzani had called for a referendum on Kurdish independence. There was no doubt about what the outcome would be. But how they would achieve it was another matter. The US had long argued that the Kurds would be economically better off remaining in Iraq and gaining their fair share of all Iraq's oil wealth. But in direct opposition to Baghdad, the KRG had signed agreements with international oil companies including Exxon and had opened a pipeline to Turkey. And now they had control of Kirkuk's oilfields. Independence was in their sights.

"Everyone is happy with the peshmerga," he assured me. Again I smiled back. The Kurdistan Regional Government now had a six-hundred-mile border with the Islamic State to control.

"Iraq has to be divided into three regions: Kurdistan, Sunnistan and Shiastan," Kemal declared. "It is the only way. We cannot live together." He reflected for a moment, then added, "Perhaps in the future, it might be possible for the three separate regions to create a federal arrangement."

After my meeting with Kemal Kirkuki, I returned to the Rotana Hotel and phoned Sheikh Ghassan. It was two years since I had visited him in Hawija. And now Hawija, he told me, was under the control of the Islamic State. The houses of his relatives, Sheikh Anwar and Sheikh Wasfi, had been blown up because of their cooperation with Maliki. Sheikh Ghassan had moved to Jordan with his family.

"Miss Emma, there is talk of dividing the country into Sunnistan, Shiastan, Kurdistan. This will create war. Where will the borders be? How will the water and oil be divided? . . . You know, Miss Emma, who controls this country? Iran, Iran, Iran . . . Our goal is just to keep our dignity, our heritage."

KRIKOR DERHAGOPIAN, my Armenian friend, flew up to Erbil from Baghdad to meet me at the hotel. His world had been turned upside down since the allegations made against his former boss, Vice President Tareq al-Hashimi. His office had been closed, his colleagues had been arrested and fled, and he had remained at home without a job for the last few years. It was only because he was a Christian that he was above suspicion.

Now, because he was Christian, his very existence in Iraq was under threat. Da'ash had given Christians the choice to convert, pay tax or flee. Krikor, like most of Iraq's Christians, was looking for refuge outside the country. He had applied for a visa to the US but had been rejected as a "security" risk.

I thought back to June 2011 when Krikor had invited me to his home in what was once a Jewish quarter of Baghdad. I had looked at the tapestries, rifles and photos on the walls, mementos of a bygone era of the monarchy. Krikor had told me that his great-grandfather had been such a supporter of the royal family that when he heard they had all been brutally murdered in 1958, he had fallen down the stairs to his death. Over lunch, Krikor's mother had told how the Armenians escaped to Iraq as refugees from the genocide in Turkey. "Many Armenians were taken in by Arab tribes around Mosul," she told me. "The Arabs were so kind and generous to us, bringing up orphans as their own children. We will always remember how good they were to us."

Christians had lived in Mosul for two millennia. Now they were leaving. Christianity in Iraq appeared to be coming to an end. Yezidis also were fleeing. Iraq's minorities no longer felt wanted.

THAT EVENING, just before ten o'clock, as I sat on the chair I had claimed for myself in the Rotana, I suddenly noticed Hoshyar Zebari, the Iraqi foreign minister, walking towards me. He was a little more rotund since I had last seen him but otherwise looked the same. "I can't believe my eyes," he said, "what are you doing here?" I stood up to greet him. He grasped me in a huge bear hug, lifting me off the ground. We were both laughing, so delighted to see each other.

Maliki had recently referred to Erbil as a "base for terrorists," accusing the Kurds of collaborating with the Islamic State. In response to the criticism, Kurdish ministers, including Hoshyar, had taken the decision to boycott the cabinet in Baghdad. In retaliation, Maliki had removed Hoshyar days ago from his post as foreign minister, a position he had held since 2003. "It is a total mess," Hoshyar said, as he sat down next to me. As in Saddam's time, Kurdistan had once again become a base for opposition to central government.

Minutes later I spotted Rafi, exactly on time for our appointment. As ever, he was well dressed in a dark suit and tie. I went over to meet him and brought him over to where Hoshyar was seated. They had not seen each other in a while and were quickly exchanging the latest gossip on Maliki and government formation. The elections had been held over two months ago and this time Maliki had won the most seats. But there was much scheming and plotting among Shia politicians to block Maliki from remaining in power. Sistani had written a letter to the Dawa party asking that they present a new candidate to be prime minister. The parliament had met that day and voted in a moderate Sunni Islamist, Salim al-Jabouri, as the new Speaker. The clock was now running for the selection of the president and prime minister.

Hoshyar left and within minutes Rafi and I were deep in conversation. He told me all his family was now living outside Iraq, some in Jordan and others in the Gulf. Having lived his whole life in Iraq, he was now an exile. I could tell how much that hurt him.

So much had happened to Rafi since I had last seen him in Baghdad in January 2012, when a tank had been parked outside his house. Towards the end of that year, days after President Talabani had been incapacitated by a stroke, Maliki had again accused Rafi of terrorism, arresting his bodyguards using exactly the same strategy he had deployed a year earlier against the vice president. It was the trumped-up charges against Rafi which had sparked the widespread Sunni protests. One Sunni had said to me, "Issawi is the best of the Sunnis. If Maliki regards him as a terrorist, then there is no hope for the rest of us." Rafi had been forced to resign as minister of finance and leave Baghdad. It was only thanks to the protection of the tribes in Anbar that he had escaped arrest by the special forces Maliki had sent to detain him.

"Was it inevitable that Iraq would unravel?" I asked Rafi. No, it was not, he assured me. Iraq had been moving in a positive direction. This downward trajectory began in 2010 when Iraqiya was not given the first chance to try to form the government. "We might not have succeeded," he admitted, "but the process itself would have been important in building trust in Iraq's young institutions." Bad decisions taken by Americans in 2010 destroyed the country, he believed. Since then, President Obama had regularly cited ending the war in Iraq as one of his greatest foreign policy successes. On 1 November 2013, with Maliki by his side in the White House, Obama stated, "We honor the lives that were lost, both American and Iraqi, to bring about a functioning democracy in a country that previously had been ruled by a vicious dictator. And we appreciate Prime Minister Maliki's commitment to honoring that sacrifice by ensuring a strong, prosperous, inclusive and democratic Iraq." He appeared to be paying scant attention to Maliki's growing authoritarianism and the deteriorating situation in the country.

Rafi listed the Sunni grievances that had steadily simmered until they had finally boiled over. Maliki had detained thousands of Sunnis without trial, pushed leading Sunnis out of the political process by accusing them of terrorism, and reneged on payments and pledges to the Awakening members who had bravely fought al-Qaeda in Iraq—sahwa leaders were dead, fled or in jail. The request by provincial councils in Salah al-Din, Diyala and Mosul to hold a vote on the formation of regions, in accordance with the Constitution, was prevented by force. Peaceful, year-long Sunni protests demanding an end to discrimination were met by violence, with dozens of unarmed protesters killed by Iraqi security forces. Maliki had completely subverted the judiciary to his will, so that Sunnis felt unable to achieve justice.

The Islamic State, Rafi explained to me, was able to take advantage of this situation, publicly claiming to be the defenders of the Sunnis against the Iranian-backed government of Maliki. In previous years, the Sunni tribes, supported by the US military, had contained and defeated al-Qaeda in Iraq, the forerunner of the Islamic State. Today, those same tribes were cooperating with the Islamic State in a popular uprising against the central government. Despite its perverted interpretation of Islam, they viewed the Islamic State as the lesser of two evils when compared with Maliki.

Faced with the advance of the Islamic State and the collapse of the Iraqi Army, Ayatollah Sistani had called on Iraqis to join the security forces to defend the state. The last time the Shia clerical establishment had issued such a call to arms was a century ago against the British. Shia militias used the announcement as an opportunity to remobilize. Already the Iranian general Qasim Suleimani was in Iraq personally directing operations, providing support to Shia militias, and embedding Iranian military advisers with the Iraqi Army. Fearful of the consequences, Sistani spoke out, asserting, "Sunnis are ourselves, not just our brothers."

We continued our discussion the next evening when Rafi took me to a restaurant for *iftar*. The place was packed with families breaking the fast. We walked towards our table and all heads turned to look at him, the celebrity on the premises. He returned the greetings. Most of these people, he explained to me, were Arabs from Anbar. President Barzani had shown great compassion, providing refuge to many fleeing the violence.

We broke the fast with dates, followed by lentil soup, and rice and salad. Then the meat arrived. One of the bodyguards piled heaps of kebab, chicken and lamb chops onto my plate despite my protestations over the quantities.

Rafi reflected back on his life as a doctor before the US-led invasion, and the weekends spent with his family in the land he loved so much. He described life as a student at Baghdad medical college and his career. He had always been religious and came from a religious family. But he had never been interested in or involved in politics. It was only after the US invasion that he was persuaded to step forward to represent his community. To me, he embodied the potential of Iraq for a better future, the hope for pragmatism to defeat extremism.

"How is General Odierno?" he asked me.

"He is very sad about what is happening in Iraq," I told him. He nodded understandingly. I tried to explain how the US military I had spoken with felt angry and betrayed. They had tried so hard, and now wondered what all the sacrifice had been for when they saw the terrible news out of Iraq. They had trusted that their civilian masters would not put them in harm's way without due reason. They had lost limbs, killed, and seen their friends die. They had felt at the time that their sacrifice was for something greater than themselves. It was hard to explain the contradictions. There was pride in service and strong memories of what they had achieved together and the bonds formed. After all the initial mistakes, the US military felt they had turned the war around during the Surge. They had done everything asked of them to the best of their ability. But all the gains had since evaporated. There was nothing to be seen from all the blood and treasure we had invested. Iran was resurgent, a proxy war was raging in the region and the US appeared to be in global retreat. No

US official had been held accountable for the decision to invade Iraq; nor for what happened after the overthrow of the regime; nor for the way in which the US departed. And few showed any signs of remorse. I felt tears welling up in my eyes. I looked away from Rafi, and focused on eating some mouthfuls of chicken.

"Will you come back and work in Iraq?" Rafi asked. "No," I responded.

"I'm one year younger than you," I told him. "I've got to get on with my life." I sometimes wondered if anything would seem interesting or important again. I had felt so alive in Iraq, with such a strong sense of purpose. The best times of my life—and the hardest times—were in Iraq. I now lived like an Iraqi exile, starting each day reading the news about Iraq. I still cared so much.

"You must keep visiting your friends," he said. "I will," I promised. I kept going back to Iraq once or twice a year because I loved the place and the people. But I was trying to build a life away from war, finding purpose teaching at Yale, inspiring a new generation to strive to make a difference in the world, passing on the baton.

"You worked so hard," he reassured me, like a big brother. Over my years in Iraq, I had seen where and how we could be effective in nudging people closer to each other, in mediating between factions and in brokering deals. I had learnt that violence was an extension of politics, that hatreds in this land were new, not ancient, that alliances could be forged and fractured, and that friendships counted for more than flags.

We had shared many good times together. It was only a couple of years ago, I reminded him, that he had gone to Lebanon to attend the funeral of Ayatollah Fadlallah, an influential Shia cleric. He showed me a photo of himself when he was minister of finance, praying alongside Muqtada al-Sadr in Najaf. But sadly the Salafism of the Islamic State was displacing the Sufism of Rafi. The once interwoven rich tapestry of Iraqi society was coming apart as groups became increasingly segregated and sectarian identity more prominent.

"Things will change again one day," I told him. "*Inshallah.*"

Despite the severity of the crisis, Rafi could still see a way to turn around the situation. If Maliki was replaced, if a new agreement was reached among Iraq's elites on how to govern the country and decentralize power, and if Sunni grievances were addressed, he was sure that

Iraq could hold together. The Iraqi security forces, which Maliki had so heavily politicized, needed to be reformed, with Sunnis recruited locally to fight the Islamic State. And the Shia militias, which had re-emerged in response to Sistani's fatwa to stop the advance of the Islamic State, needed to be demobilized.

By the time we left the restaurant, we were quite alone.

GLOSSARY

POLITICAL PARTIES
AND MILITIAS

AL-QAEDA IN IRAQ   Founded by Abu Musab al-Zarqawi, al-Qaeda in Iraq conducted incessant attacks against the Iraqi government, Shia civilians, and Shia holy places, seeking to provoke a civil war and the collapse of the state. It was also responsible for the deaths of Coalition Forces and UN officials.

ASAIB AHL AL-HAQQ   Shia militia, headed by Qais Khazali and supported by Iran. Its aim was to drive Coalition forces out of Iraq. It was credited with a number of successful attacks against the Coalition, notably the January 2007 attack in Karbala, which left five US soldiers dead, and the kidnapping and murder of British hostages.

BAATH PARTY   The Baath party in Iraq was founded in 1951 as part of a broader Arab nationalist movement. It ruled Iraq from 1968 until 2003, with Saddam Hussein serving as President from 1979 until his overthrow. The Baath party brutally crushed opposition, killed hundreds of thousands, and caused many Iraqis to flee the country. Membership of the Baath party was outlawed following the fall of the regime.

BADR CORPS   Shia militia of the Islamic Supreme Council of Iraq, headed by Hadi al-Ameri. Established in Iran, its initial recruits were Iraqi prisoners of war and deportees, under the leadership of Iranian officers. It was trained and controlled by the Iranian Revolutionary Guard Corps' al-Quds Force. After 2003, significant numbers of its members were incorporated into the Iraqi security forces.

DA'ASH   The successor to al-Qaeda in Iraq, Da'ash, also known as the Islamic State, took control of large swathes of territory in Iraq in 2014, and targeted Iraq's minorities. Abu Bakr al-Baghdadi proclaimed the establishment of a Caliphate in parts of Syria and Iraq.

DAWA   Shia Islamist group, established in Iraq in the late 1950s to defend Islam in the face of secularization and communism. Its ideological founder was Mohamad Baqir al-Sadr, who was executed in 1980. The Baath party issued a decree that membership of Dawa was punishable by death. Many of its members were killed; others fled. From 2005 onwards, the prime ministers of Iraq have all been members of the Dawa party.

HAMAS AL-IRAQ   A Sunni militia associated with the Iraqi Islamic Party.

IRAQI ISLAMIC PARTY   A Sunni Islamist party that was established in 1960 as the Iraqi branch of the Muslim Brotherhood. It was banned by the Baath party. It participated in the political process in Iraq from 2003 onwards.

IRAQIYA   Headed by Ayad Allawi, a secularist of Shia background, the Iraqiya party was formed to contest the 2010 elections on a non-sectarian, nationalist agenda.

ISLAMIC SUPREME COUNCIL OF IRAQ   The Supreme Council for the Islamic Revolution in Iraq was formed in Iran in 1982 under the leadership of Mohamad Baqir al-Hakim, who was assassinated in Najaf in 2003. It changed its name in 2007 to the Islamic Supreme Council of Iraq. It is currently headed by his nephew Ammar al-Hakim.

JAYSH AL-MAHDI (JAM)   Shia militia of Muqtada al-Sadr.

JAYSH RIJAL AL-TARIQ AL-NAQSHABANDI   A Sunni insurgent group associated with the Baath party.

KURDISTAN DEMOCRATIC PARTY (KDP) Kurdish political party founded in 1946 by Mullah Mustafa Barzani and currently headed by his son Masoud Barzani.

PATRIOTIC UNION OF KURDISTAN (PUK) Kurdish political party that split from the Kurdistan Democratic Party in 1975. Headed by Jalal Talabani.

PESHMERGA Security forces of the Kurdish political parties. Literally, "those who face death."

SADRIST TREND A Shia political party headed by Muqtada al-Sadr. His father, Mohamad Sadiq al-Sadr (Sadr II), the cousin of Mohamad Baqir al-Sadr (Sadr I), built up a mass movement among the urban poor as well as the neglected rural and tribal population. On 19 February 1999, Sadr and his two eldest sons were murdered.

SAHWA Literally "awakening," describes a revolt that began in 2006 by Sunni tribes in Anbar province against al-Qaeda in Iraq. Also called the Sunni Awakening, the Anbar Awakening, Concerned Local Citizens and the Sons of Iraq.

STATE OF LAW COALITION A political coalition formed by Nuri al-Maliki in 2009, incorporating the Dawa party.

ACKNOWLEDGMENTS

In writing this memoir, I relied on notes, diaries and emails that I kept during my time in Iraq. It has not been possible to mention all the people I met, nor to cover all the events that happened; deciding what to leave out was very hard. Some of the Iraqis mentioned are referred to by pseudonyms.

Thanks go to Ray Odierno and his staff for going through the manuscript in its entirety, and to the teams at the Pentagon and the UK's Department for International Development who also reviewed it.

For their comments on parts of the manuscript, I thank Neil Ciotola, Krikor Derhagopian, Pat Frank, D. J. Jones, Mark Landes, Reuben Loewy, Alysoun Owen, Graeme and Melanie Lamb, Bill Mayville, Hamish McNinch, Clarisse Pásztory, Harith al-Qarawee and Safa al-Sheikh. Special thanks go to my friend Laura Ziv, who gave me constructive feedback on every chapter. I could not have asked for a better reader.

A number of people have helped guide me through the process of writing this book. I am grateful to Clive Priddle and his staff at Public Affairs, Margaret Stead at Atlantic Books, Ben Buchan for his meticulous editing, and my agents Clare Alexander (UK) and Kathy Robbins (US).

The Jackson Institute for Global Affairs at Yale has provided me with a home to contemplate life after war and the mental space to write. I am indebted to my students for inspiring me and giving me hope for the future.

Finally, I wish to thank my friends who are always there for me, in particular Danielle Greenberg and Carl Bracey and their families.

INDEX

ABOUT THE AUTHOR

EMMA SKY is a Senior Fellow at Yale University's Jackson Institute. She worked in the Middle East for twenty years and was made an Officer of the Order of the British Empire for services in Iraq. She lives in New Haven, Connecticut.